The Information Superhighw
and Private Households

Walter Brenner · Lutz Kolbe (Eds.)

The Information Superhighway and Private Households

Case Studies of Business Impacts

With 110 Figures

Physica-Verlag

A Springer-Verlag Company

Prof. Dr. Walter Brenner
Lutz Kolbe

Technical University of Freiberg
Faculty of Economics
and Business Administration
Gustav-Zeuner-Str. 10
D-09596 Freiberg
Germany

brenner@bwl.tu-freiberg.de

kolbe@bwl.tu-freiberg.de

Cataloging-in-Publication Data applied for

Die Deutsche Bibliothek - CIP-Einheitsaufnahme

The information superhighway and private households : case
studies of business impacts / Walter Brenner ; Lutz Kolbe. -
Heidelberg : Physica-Verl., 1996

NE: Brenner, Walter [Hrsg.]

ISBN-13: 978-3-7908-0907-7   e-ISBN-13: 978-3-642-48423-0
DOI: 10.1007/978-3-642-48423-0

SPIN: 10527062   88/2202 - 5 4 3 2 1 0 – Printed on acid-free paper

Preface

Wolfgang Glatthaar
International Business Machines (IBM), Germany

The rapid developments in information technology (IT) will continue through the coming years. New application areas will be added. Whereas the use of information technology in the past decade has been concentrated primarily on business and public administration, in future the suppliers of information technology will develop an increasing number of applications for the *private household* (see fig. 1).

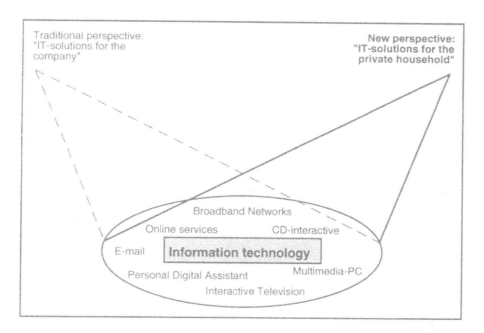

Fig. 1.   New perspective on information technology

This development has already generated considerable market dynamics. Latest forecasts for the USA suggest that by 1996 at the latest the private household will present greater sales potential for home computers than business and public administration.

Up to now the use of information technology in the private household has not been regarded as highly significant by either business or science, even though PCs have become widespread in the private sphere. In the ESPRIT framework there have been individual projects dealing with home networks, and in a number of Asian and European countries, as well as America, experiments with interactive television are taking place. Internet and commercial online services are experiencing rapid growth. This application area for information technology in the private household, which is generating increasing business attention, must also be the subject of appropriate research activities. And this research must be embedded from the start in a wide public dialogue, to provide signposts in the resulting information society.

This volume represents a very attractive and important step in this direction. It highlights important aspects of the information technology infrastructure, and describes potential applications, as well as pilot projects centring around the private household, thus undertaking pioneering work. It is the first holistic approach to deal with this new research area and its manifold implications.

Society, research and business in the tertiary markets need to become intensively involved with these developments, so that the new market potential can be realised and the nascent information society can develop into an open, democratic society characterised by justice and equality of opportunity.

Acknowledgments

The editors express their thanks to Mr. Volker Hamm, Miss Christine Fuchs, Miss Claudia Schubert and Miss Éva Tamáskovics for their assistance in the process of editing the book. Without their help and cooperation this volume would have been impossible.

Freiberg/Germany, October 1995

Walter Brenner and Lutz Kolbe

Preface

Wolfgang Glatthaar
International Business Machines (IBM), Germany

The rapid developments in information technology (IT) will continue through the coming years. New application areas will be added. Whereas the use of information technology in the past decade has been concentrated primarily on business and public administration, in future the suppliers of information technology will develop an increasing number of applications for the *private household* (see fig. 1).

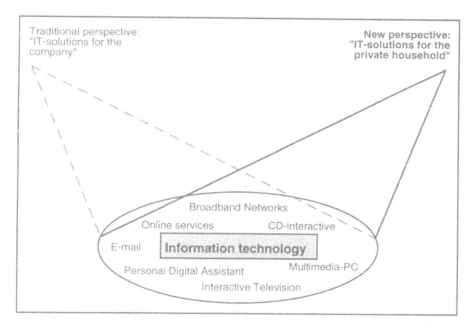

Fig. 1.   New perspective on information technology

This development has already generated considerable market dynamics. Latest forecasts for the USA suggest that by 1996 at the latest the private household will present greater sales potential for home computers than business and public administration.

Up to now the use of information technology in the private household has not been regarded as highly significant by either business or science, even though PCs have become widespread in the private sphere. In the ESPRIT framework there have been individual projects dealing with home networks, and in a number of Asian and European countries, as well as America, experiments with interactive television are taking place. Internet and commercial online services are experiencing rapid growth. This application area for information technology in the private household, which is generating increasing business attention, must also be the subject of appropriate research activities. And this research must be embedded from the start in a wide public dialogue, to provide signposts in the resulting information society.

This volume represents a very attractive and important step in this direction. It highlights important aspects of the information technology infrastructure, and describes potential applications, as well as pilot projects centring around the private household, thus undertaking pioneering work. It is the first holistic approach to deal with this new research area and its manifold implications.

Society, research and business in the tertiary markets need to become intensively involved with these developments, so that the new market potential can be realised and the nascent information society can develop into an open, democratic society characterised by justice and equality of opportunity.

Acknowledgments

The editors express their thanks to Mr. Volker Hamm, Miss Christine Fuchs, Miss Claudia Schubert and Miss Éva Tamáskovics for their assistance in the process of editing the book. Without their help and cooperation this volume would have been impossible.

Freiberg/Germany, October 1995

Walter Brenner and Lutz Kolbe

Contents

Part One: Introduction 1

Computerized Information Processing of the Private Household:
A Framework 3
  Walter Brenner and Lutz Kolbe, Technical University of Freiberg

Part Two: Infrastructures 23

In-home Infrastructures

Microsoft Brings Personal Computing Home 25
  Michaela Jaritz, Microsoft

Digital Devices and Advanced Technology for the Consumer Market................35
  Terry R. Hurley, Sony

Bang & Olufsen's Integrated Home-Networking with Beolink.........................47
  Peter Petersen, Bang & Olufsen

Out-of-home Infrastructures

Oracle Media - Enabling the Information Age 57
  Mary Callaghan, Oracle Corporation

SmartCards as Carrier of Personal Data and Documents 65
  *Bruno Struif, German National Research Center for
  Computer Science (GMD)*

Deutsche Telekom's Network Platform for Interactive Video Services...............75
  Norbert Maassen, Deutsche Telekom

Part Three: Applications 85

The Citizen's Information System "Dresden and the Frauenkirche
(Church of Our Lady)" - Realization, Experiences, Prospects 89
  Manuela Rost-Hein, IBM

Books of the Next Generation - Reading on the Electronic Frontier 99
  Florian Brody, New Media Consulting and Art Center College of Design

Electronic Agents and the Market Place: New Generations of Electronic
Services for Consumers 109
  Rob de Vogel, Philips Advanced Communication Enterprise (PACE)

Home Systems - The Vision 125
  David G. J. Fanshawe, Philips Consumer Electronics

Teleshopping: Today's Solutions and Future Trends 139
  Heiner Drathen, Daimler-Benz Interservices (debis) Systemhaus

Private Household Shopping Behavior 149
  Heribert Popp, Stephan Thesmann, and Peter Mertens,
  Bavarian Research Center for Knowledge-Based Systems (FORWISS)

Interactive Multimedia and In-Home Marketing 161
  Jonne R. M. van der Drift and Luc Stakenborg, CD-Matics

New Media: A Growth Market in Erotica and Pornography for Beate Uhse 173
  Petra Höper, Beate Uhse Group

SEGA Game Applications: Consoles, Games and Development
Possibilities 183
  Winnie Forster, Cybermedia,
  and Torsten Oppermann, SEGA

TV of the Future - The Future of TV 195
  Friedrich-Carl Wachs, Heinrich Bauer Verlag,
  and Johann-Reinhardt Wachs, Saatchi & Saatchi

Interactive Video-Services for the Residential Customer 201
  Claus Sattler and Niels Klußmann, Eutelis Consult

Information Technology and Applications for Elderly and
Disabled People 215
  J. A. van Woerden, TNO Institute

Part Four: Current Projects

Part Four: Current Projects 229

The Information Society - Developments in the Triad of Europe,
North America and Japan 233
   Roger Longhorn, Consultant to the European Commisson's
   DG III and DG XIII

Home Automation - Recent Developments in the Genesis and Diffusion
of Intelligent Home Technology in Europe, Japan, and the USA 251
   Thomas Heimer, Johann Wolfgang Goethe-University

Multimedia Application Services... 263
   Sadami Kurihara, Nippon Telephone and Telegraph

Time Warner Cable Full Service Network - Silicon Graphics Technology
and Architecture Overview.. 271
   Gary Sager, Silicon Graphics

Burda New Media's Multimedia Activities for Private Customers.................. 289
   Hubertus Hoffmann, Burda New Media and Europe Online

Agent Based Communication in Traffic Telematics...................................... 297
   Christoph Mayser, Martin Römer, and Georg Zimmermann,
   Berner & Mattner Systemtechnik

Part Five: Impacts and Implications

Part Five: Impacts and Implications....................... 303

Business Impacts

New Products and Services for Private Households on the Information
Highway: Facts and Obstacles... 307
   Joachim Niemeier, Multimedia Software GmbH Dresden

New Visions of Information Technology and Postmodernism: Implications
for Advertising and Marketing Communications.. 319
   Alladi Venkatesh, University of California, and
   Ruby Roy Dholakia and Nikhilesh Dholakia, University of Rhode Island

Seven Theses on Successful Market Development for Home
Management Systems 339
   Kai Howaldt and Mirko-Stefan Jeck, Roland Berger & Partner

Stand-alone Multimedia in the Private Household...................................... 351
    Felix Goedhart and Thomas Künstner, Booz, Allen & Hamilton

Strategic Management and Transformation in Converging Industries -
Towards the Information Society... 363
    Thomas Baubin and Bernd W. Wirtz, Andersen Consulting

The Multimedia Marketplace in the Private Household -
Some Observations and Comments.. 379
    Georg Rainer Hofmann, KPMG

Information Technologies in the Home: Policies and Markets...................... 385
    Norbert Mundorf, University of Rhode Island

Social Implications

Computer Use at Home - A Cultural Challenge to Technology
Development... 399
    Werner Rammert, Free University of Berlin

The Home in Transition: Social Implications of Home Information
Technologies... 409
    Felix van Rijn, Hogeschool van Amsterdam, and IFIP WG 9.3

Author Profiles... 419

Part One

Introduction

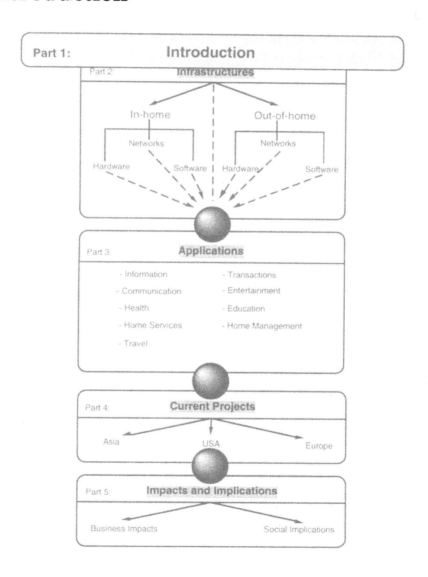

Computerized Information Processing of the Private Household: A Framework

Walter Brenner and Lutz Kolbe
Technical University of Freiberg, Faculty of Economics and Business
Administration, Germany

1   Introduction

Traditional business informatics and information management deals with information processing in business contexts. In the last decade information technology focused on electronic data processing in service, industry companies and administrative authorities.

But the use of information technology in the *private* household gains in importance: The market potentials of information technology for the future will arise from the situation that the computerized information processing influences almost every part of private life. Under these circumstances, first an discussion of modified requirements for infrastructures is indicated. In addition, new categories for applications in the private sphere have to be examined, especially in former usually "non-computerized" contexts (Jacobs 1994), such as health or travelling (see fig. 1).

Organizations like the IFIP (International Federation of Information Processing) with its working group 9.3 "Home-oriented informatics and telematics" (Brenner/Kolbe 1994), the European Union (European Commission 1994) and national initiatives like the US Information Task Force (Press Secretary 1993) are concentrating more and more on the private sphere.

The intensive world-wide discussion about "Information Superhighways to the consumer" or "multimedia in the home" reveals the high relevance and necessity for a scientific and comprehensive approach to this emerging field.

Given a structure for the contents, the authors from science and mainly business introduce infrastructures and typical applications. The convergence of both is pointed out by the description of authentic projects and important market impacts.

1.1   Structure of the book and definitions

We characterize *computerized information processing of the private household* (or *home-IT* for short) as all the infrastructures and applications the private user can take advantage of for private uses.

The book follows - so does this paper - a plan of five chapters (see fig. 1) which seems to be appropriate for describing and examing this emerging field:

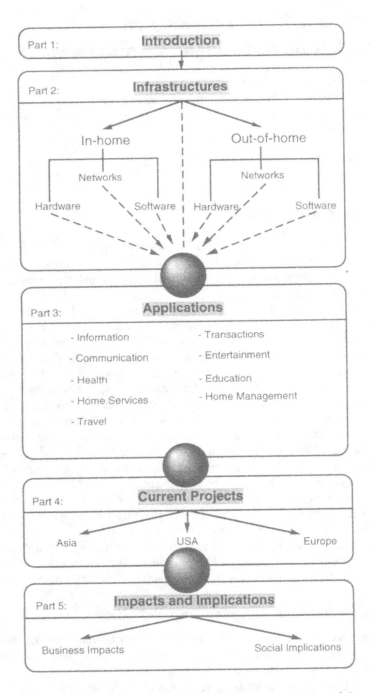

Fig. 1. Framework of computerized information processing of the private household and book structure

This *Part 1* as the introduction gives an overview about the relevance of this new research field. Basic concepts of infrastructures, applications and implications are introduced. Part 1 provides the structure of the whole book as your guide through the chapters.

Part 2 then describes the underlying infrastructures for the private household. It differentiates between the in-home and out-of-home sector. In both sectors networks, software and hardware resources are highlighted according to examples of several international companies.

This leads in *Part 3* to a comprehensive description of applications and IT-related functions of the private household. The main application types supporting the household's functions draw a picture of IT in the private household that goes far beyond "classic" types like tele-shopping.

However, infrastructures (Part 2) and applications (Part 3) must not be seen isolated. In *Part 4* current projects out of three different cultural contexts show how infrastructures and applications are combined to provide the consumer with services of a new kind.

Finally, *Part 5* deals with the main implications and future directions for the development towards the Information Society. Possibilities for exploitation of market potentials for businesses and the changing use of media through digitalization and interactivity are stated as well as the social issues inside the private household.

1.2   The way to the Information Society

More and more aspects of daily life are being affected by the creation of new information and communication technologies (ICT) or the upgrading of existing domestic applications (Tietz 1987). The American government's *Data Highway Initiative* (Press Secretary 1993) indicates that creating the infrastructure to extend the scope of information processing into the private home is a global challenge (Venkatesh/Vitalari 1986, Tietz 1987). In Europe, the "Bangemann Report" presented on the Corfu summit of the European premier ministers aims at a strategic *European Information Infrastructure* (European Commission 1994). The question of regulation or deregulation of markets is only a single aspect in our "information society".

To understand the implications of this quite unknown research field we have to clear up the underlying trends. At least five main streams can be identified:

Information Superhighway: The discussion about the computerized information processing in the private household gains in importance by the emergence of the Information Superhighway. Sometimes it is labelled with other terms like "infobahn", "data highway" or "communication highway". It means the linkage of all information users with all information providers through some form of market mechanism (Benjamin/Wigand 1995). One of the main objectives is the construction of access ramps to new sources of information using fibre technology or hybrid fibre-coax approaches to the home or neighborhood. Another goal is a plethora of new telematic services offered to private users such as interactive games or customized news (Reinhardt 1994).

Converging markets and strategic alliances: The concept of the Information Superhighway is supported by an obvious tendency in the development of markets, namely the consumer electronics, the computer and the telecommunication markets (OECD 1992) (see fig. 2). New challenges cannot be provided only by one of the market players. Know-how from various types of businesses is needed to implement such services. In order to face this problem there are two current paths: Companies are trying to diversify making mergers and aquisitions such as the Viacom-Paramount deal in the US. Thereby they want to ensure their competence in telecommunication, content and service. The other way is to build strategic alliances. This path is often used where each player is strong enough to compete alone but is willing to participate from the synergy. An example is the alliance of Time Warner and Silicon Graphics in the field of interactive TV.

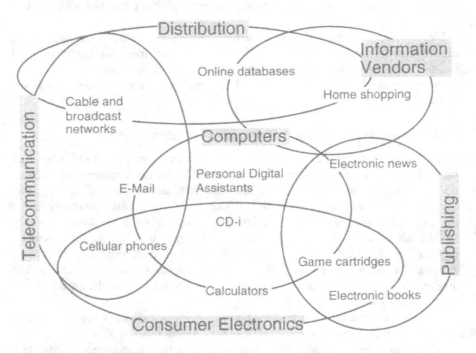

Fig. 2.   Converging markets and relation to products and services

Interactivity and individualization: Along with enhanced multimedia presentation and manipulation features (Graf 1994) comes the increasing wish for interactivity. The private user no longer wants to consume from the TV screen or being isolated with his home-PC. He wants to get in touch with the environment. According to this, the services have to provide a certain extent of individualization to the user. They can reach from local news from the neighborhood to completely individual ones compiled on given patterns (Brand 1990). The future aim of the *Information Superhighway* is to have one personal channel to every home and a back channel enabling interaction with the head-end.

This trend is supported by the specialization of information content. The target groups are highly segmented to personal, socio-economic or local criteria. For example there is an increasing number of special interest TV channels, e.g. exclusively for weather or travel.

Communication instead of pure information: In the last ten years the processing of pure information was of main interest to the market players. Now the view has changed: The central questions are now where the required information is located, how to obtain it and how to get it to the point of request. In other words the communication era is on (Philips 1994). This explains why the telecommunication sector gets more and more important. The high penetration rates of telephone and cable TV connections are a welcome installed base for home-oriented services.

Standard home devices and "killer applications": They are two main areas of concern in the field of computerized information processing of the private home: The first one deals with the infrastructures (Mundorf/Zoche 1994) and the second one with the services. Concerning the infrastructure the providers try to evaluate whether the PC or the TV will be the standard home device for the future. Both devices have their pros and cons. May be that the today's computer with TV expansion and the TV set with computer enhancements (set-top box) will lead to one hybrid device for all purposes like the modern copier-phone-fax-answering-devices (Reinhardt 1994). All providers of content are hesitating to invest feeling a strong uncertainty about the type of application which first is widely accepted by the households, the so-called "killer application". Short-term profits are expected from the games sector, but the potentials for the long term, e.g. by interactive TV, have not been assessed so far.

2 Information technology infrastructure for the private household

In future the private household will be linked via networks to an environment from which it obtains services. For instances, if the consumer does home-shopping he uses the in-home TV set and cable TV to view the products and then the out-of-home telephone network to communicate with the trader. This infrastructure can be subdivided into two significant areas: the *in-home* and *out-of-home* infrastructures (Brenner/Kolbe 1994).

The household is always located at a position interfacing with two different shaped worlds of information technology (IT) infrastructures: The in-home and out-of-home infrastructures (see fig. 3).

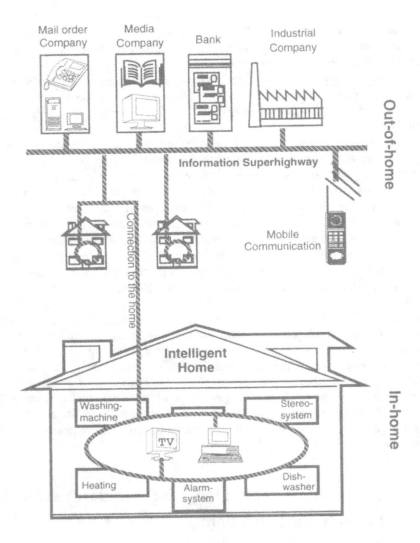

Fig. 3.   IT-infrastructures for the private household given by
the Information Superhighway

2.1   In-home infrastructure

The in-home infrastructure consists of all the software, hardware and networks that
are installed within the private household (see fig. 3), e.g. private branch
exchanges, home-computers or high fidelity electronics. The scope of private IT-
infrastructure is broader than that of businesses due to the included special
installation equipment for the residential home, e.g. heating and cooking.

2.1.1 Software

Software currently available for the private household is based, with the exception of computer games, on a commercial foundation. Developments in this area in the future will lead to a set of "standard software for the private household" which is characterized by its multi-media nature and intuitive user interfaces.

Advances in user interfaces: The most critical success factor to the penetration of a product into the consumer market will be the ease of use. It has to be "plug-in and play" otherwise it will fail. The control interfaces for multiple function devices like the integrated audio and video telephone with faksimile, answering machine and copier functions are fraught with coordination problems. Research reveals that the unskilled and occasional user needs intuitive graphical interfaces with a low complexity such as the new Microsoft look and feel environment "Bob".

Integration of various media: The software targeting the in-home area consists of a variety of media: sound, video, images, text and data are mixed together and can be treated interactively as one may prefer. A clear distinction into topics like information, entertainment and productivity is no longer valid. New terms like "infotainment", e.g. Microsoft-Encyclopedia "Encarta", or "edutainment", e.g. Intercomputer's "Chemistry world", characterize the convergence of former separated software types. Well known companies, for example Microsoft or Word Perfect, are forming new business units for the home market like the Microsoft "Home" product line.

For further details see the following contributions in this volume:

M. Jaritz from Microsoft, see pp. 25-34
F. Goedhart, T. Künstner from Booz, Allen & Hamilton, see pp. 351-361
G. R. Hofmann from KPMG, see pp. 379-384

2.1.2 Hardware

Hardware that is relevant to "information processing of the private household" is characterized by a high degree of specialization: the CD player is used to listen to music and the TV for viewing. As well as innovative product ideas and improvements to products, a tendency towards a combination of existing and new functionalities can be observed (IEEE 1992).

Integration of different functionalities: Especially in the consumer electronic market new products are positioned as multi-functional. The CDi-player (Philips), the Amiga CD32 player (Commodore) and Panasonic's 300 Real Multiplayer provide all the functionality as a video game device, audio- and photo-CD-player. In addition, each of them has the option for full motion video by adding a video decompression cartridge.

Mounting a "Tele-CDi adapter" to the Philips CDi player and connected to remote data bases it then can be used for tele-shopping, electronic banking or point of information (POI) in stores with an immediate update of data, for example if the prices change (Graf 1994).

Improvement of existing products: The best example for the development of devices already in place is the evolution of TV. German Telekom currently undertakes a trial under the code "VIDINET" (Video in Digital Nets). Instead of analog transmission the increasing capacity of channels enables digital TV in a high resolution quality (HDTV) and a changed format (16:9) with advanced functions like zoom or screen in screen (Ziemer 1994).

Product innovation: The electronic book player "Data Discman" with the content on a 8 cm disc by Sony provides a new random access to former sequential available information. With loudspeakers, LCD-display and TV- and PC-interfaces it can enrich reading with innovative functions.

For further details see the following contributions in this volume:

T. R. Hurley from Sony, see pp. 35-46

J. R. M. van der Drift, L. Stakenborg from CD-Matics, see pp. 161-172

F. Goedhart, T. Künstner from Booz, Allen & Hamilton, see pp. 351-361

2.1.3 Networks

Networks provide the basic framework for the entire future, "smart" in-home infrastructure by linking of various components via powerful, standardized "household networks" labelled Small Area Networks (SAN).

Integration of different networks: All current in-home networks are focused on specific fields of application: The "Beolink" network by Bang & Olufsen covers the audio and lighting sector as well as "Scenario" by Moulinex deals with the remote control of kitchen devices. Screening the market reveals that it tends towards integration. For example, the TeleVisionManager by IC Isenbügel Computer-technik uses the TV as an central control unit for all kinds of house actors via different interfaces, even those that are normally not programmable, e.g. blinds or lawn sprinklers.

Standardization: The aim has to be the unification of these networks using a common interface for all purposes combining audio, video and process data. Best known efforts are those of the ESPRIT-Home System conducted by EHSA (European Home Systems Association) or the European Installation Bus (EIBus) in Europe, the Smart House concept in the US and the TRON approach in Japan. The central questions are the topology, the adequate transport medium and the distribution of intelligence in such a network (EHSA 1992, Jeck 1993, Greichen 1992).

For further details see the following contributions in this volume:

P. Petersen from Bang & Olufsen, see pp. 47-55

D. G. J. Fanshawe from Philips Consumer Electronics, see pp. 125-137

T. Heimer from Johann Wolfgang Goethe-University, see pp. 251-262

K. Howaldt, M.-S. Jeck from Roland Berger & Partner, see pp. 339-350

2.2   Out-of-home infrastructure

The out-of-home infrastructure consists of all the software, hardware and networks that are installed outside the private household (see fig. 3) but which the private household can take advantage of in order to use components of the in-home infrastructure effectively, and thereby gaining access to new services. Examples are the CATV networks, central video server or wireless communication devices.

2.2.1 Software

Software in the out-of-home infrastructure can be sub-divided into two important areas: communication systems for network services, and database systems as storage locations for the growing mass of increasingly multi-media data.

Communication and information protocols: The software running on products like Motorola's "Envoy" (see 2.2.2) is provided by a joint venture, General Magic, with contributions of nearly all important market players like Matsushita, Philips, Apple, AT&T, Sony, Toshiba and Motorola.

It comprises "Telescript" and "MagicCap" (General Magic 1994). The first has the objective to serve as a standardized protocol for data transmission and information and the latter is a object-oriented development tool for a new generation of user interfaces. Initial services, e.g. "PersonaLink" by AT&T, are already installed or underway.

Multi-media databases/development tools: Besides the hardware the software requirements for multi-media data are looking for a respective solution: Oracle's "MediaServer" consists of four basic components: the relational data base management system, the cooperative server for parallel processing, a parallel text server and finally a video stream server for compressed videos. The multi-media authoring language "ScriptX" provided by Kaleida Labs, a joint venture by Apple and IBM, is incorporated as well in order to ensure the implementation of applications (Jupiter 1994).

For further details see the following contribution in this volume:

M. Callaghan from Oracle, see pp. 57-63
R. de Vogel from Philips Advanced Communication Enterprise, see pp. 109-123

2.2.2 Hardware

Hardware from the out-of-home infrastructure creates the platform for the provision of services that can be accessed by the private household. It includes central architecture hardware such as multi-media servers for video-on-demand systems, or mobile communication equipment.

Multimedia-server: Huge server installation are necessary to deliver a continuous stream of information to each household. In difference to former pure text data transmission, the new multi-media data requires complex and vast resources for storage and delivery of information. Different suppliers pursue completely different approaches:

While Silicon Graphics constructed a massively-parallel supercomputer called "Challenge-Digital-Video-Server" which pumps video streams to the household with an immense consumption of resources, Microsoft's "Tiger" is based on PC-hardware and scalable for central or local load (Silicon Graphics 1994; The Wall Street Journal Europe 1994).

New hardware for wireless communication: In March 1994 Motorola presented the first commercial Personal Intelligent Communicator (PIC) called "Envoy". It features enhanced methods for gathering and transfering data using the concept of information agents in intelligent networks. The "Envoy" is an advanced successor of Apple's "Newton Notepad", focusing on communication rather than on pure information processing and thereby making available a vast amount of data resources.

For further details see the following contributions in this volume:

B. Struif from GMD, see pp. 65-73
R. de Vogel from Philips Advanced Communication Enterprise, see pp. 109-123

2.2.3 Networks

Networks belonging to the out-of-home infrastructure constitute the link between the private household and the environment by means of which data can be transported to and from the household. As well as improvements in the transmission media broadband communication offers new dimensions for the private household.

Evolution of transport medium: The question central to the erection of a "data highway to the home" is the capacity and performance of the network. Future high speed broadband applications are supposed to use fibre optic lines. The German Telekom's project "OPAL" (Optical Access Line) concentrates on connecting 1.2 million households with fibre directly by the end of 1995. This FTTH (fibre-to-the-home) architecture or the hybrid fibre-copper FTTC (fibre-to-the-curb) type will even provide the possibility for advanced interactive video services (Ricke/Kanzow 1991).

Broadband communication/high speed networking: The broadband communication (B-ISDN) of multi-media information requires new methods and protocols of networking. The most discussed concept named ATM (Asynchronous Transfer Modus) combines the advantages of a packet and a relay switched network. It provides flexible bandwidth on demand and priority handling. A current prototype of the German Telekom connecting the cities of Hamburg, Berlin and Cologne works under a maximum transmission rate of 155 MBit/s (Armbrüster 1993).

Wireless communication: One of the most booming IT-markets is the wireless communication. Having the D1- and D2-net working under the GSM (Global System for Mobile Communication) standard already in place the third digital mobile network, the E plus-net, has been launched 1994 in Germany - at the moment covering only a few areas. This new network aims directly at the private user's mass market. Building a Personal Communication Network (PCN) the vision is that each citizen owns his or her own E plus-telephone.

For further details see the following contributions in this volume:

N. *Maassen* from Deutsche Telekom, see pp. 75-83
C. *Sattler, N. Klußmann* from Eutelis Consult, see pp. 201-213
G. *Sager* from Silicon Graphics, see pp. 271-287

3   Applications

In science and business of information management there are three traditional approaches to describe information systems: The *data-* (Scheer 1990), the *function-* (Mertens 1991) and the *organization-/process-* (Scheer 1994) orientated ones.

We have decided to choose the functional approach in order to highlight comprehensibly the influence of IT to private households' activities. The available applications intuitively recommend the functional approach as the first one to deliver tangible research results.

According to our state of research (Brenner/Kolbe 1994, Liesenfeld 1989) we identify nine main functions of the private household which can be supported by IT (see fig. 4).

Support functions:
- Information
- Communication

Application functions:
- Health
- Home services
- Travel
- Transactions
- Entertainment
- Education
- Home Management

Fig. 4.   IT-influenced functions of the private household

The basic functions "information" and "communication" are inherent in each other function. They will be referred to as *support functions* while the other ones are looked upon as primarily *application functions* ones because they make use of information and communication im- and explicitly.

3.1   Support functions

3.1.1   Information

Information is offered by all services in which the dissemination of information to the private household is central.

Electronic books on portable e-book players are one of the most notable examples for pure information. Encyclopedia, magazines, dictionaries or special topics like a collection of laws are available on different formats for proprietary players like Sony's "Data-Discman". "Bookware for Windows" for a PC environment provides hyperlink functionality, connectivity to video printers, find and select algorithms. Advantages that ordinary books haven't to show.

Electronic newspapers that can be read on the TV or PC screen are just in the experimental phasis and offered by some publisher's like the "Der Spiegel" on the World Wide Web (WWW) or the "Focus" magazine in Germany via ISDN lines. Interactive TV and multimedia broadband networks (AT&T 1993, Time Warner Cable 1993) are pre-requisites for customized individual news services that compile your own newspaper on personal preferences and interests like sports or stock exchange news as examined by MIT's Media Lab.

For further details see the following contributions in this volume:

M. Rost-Hein from IBM, see pp. 89-98
F. Brody from New Media Consulting and Art Center College of Design, see pp. 99-107
H. Popp, S. Thesmann, P. Mertens from FORWISS, see pp. 149-160

3.1.2 Communication

Communication enables the private household to establish bi- or multi-lateral contact to the immediate or wider environment.

In today's household home-faxes, intelligent private branch exchanges (PBX) and mobile digital cellular phones are of increasing use. The Motorola led "Iridium" project aims at the world-wide usage of mobile communication using 66 satellites. The next step of evolution is the penetration of e-mail to every household. In the more distant future, intelligent agents are gathering and compiling required information world-wide. New products like General Magic's potential network-standard "Telescript" will open the world of mobile, intelligent communication to everybody. A first service for this environment, PersonaLink, is provided by AT&T and offers mobile, smart electronic mail functionality (General Magic 1994, Philips 1994).

For further details see the following contributions in this volume:

R. de Vogel from Philips Advanced Communication Enterprise, see pp. 109-123
G. Sager from Silicon Graphics, see pp. 271-287

3.2   Application functions

3.2.1   Health

Health means all applications concerned with making provision for, maintaining and monitoring people's health.

The health applications for today's household are very limited in its range. In some countries we have smart cards carrying patients' data for billing and insurance companies or health consultancy software for private diagnosis and information about certain deseases. The next years will make this field more interactive as tested in some trials like the German BERKOM experiment in Berlin with multimedia remote diagnosis from specialists via picture phone (Ricke/Kanzow 1991). In future, expert systems will enable medical advice from each home without leaving the private house.

For further details see the following contribution in this volume:

B. *Struif* from GMD, see pp. 65-73
J. A. *van Woerden* from TNO Institute, see pp. 215-228

3.2.2 Home Services

Home services consist of systems that support home security, safety, cooking, heating, cooling, lighting and washing.

At the status quo home services comprise only special devices like networked kitchen devices controlled by the Moulinex "Scenario" system. This will extend to a comprehensive home automation with interconnected kitchen appliances, audio and video electronics and other systems like heating or washing. Some prototypes by the German company Miele prove that the TV can control the washing maschine (Jeck 1993). Beyond the year 2000 all home devices will have a built-in standard interface. The interconnection to out-of-home networks like the cable TV leads to the remote control functions for the private household, e.g. security mechanisms.

For further details see the following contributions in this volume:

P. *Petersen* from Bang & Olufsen, see pp. 47-55
D. G. J. *Fanshawe* from Philips Consumer Electronics, see pp. 125-137
T. *Heimer* from Johann Wolfgang Goethe-University, see pp. 251-262
K. *Howaldt, M.-S. Jeck* from Roland Berger & Partner, see pp. 339-350

3.2.3 Travel

Travel comprises all applications that support the selection, preparation and undertaking of journeys.

Today applications for travel are limited to central booking information systems for hotel or flight reservation like the START system. Some projects are now testing electronic travel catalogues where the customer needs not to screen thick paper files for the right destination and a description of the desired location (Ricke/Kanzow 1991, Graf 1994). Individual preferences will provide a search pattern finding the places of interest. But in the first stage these catalogues are mainly accessible from the travel agency. The future scenario includes interactive, multimedia booking from the TV chair via broadband network with immediate acknowledgements.

For further details see the following contributions in this volume:

C. *Mayser, M. Römer, G. Zimmermann* from Berner & Mattner
Systemtechnik, see pp. 297-302

3.2.4 Transactions

Transactions combines all the transactional functions like shopping and banking of the private household.

The functions "tele-banking" and "tele-shopping" are applications with some kind of tradition in the private household (Smith Shi/Salesky 1994, Jupiter 1994). Using the PC and ISDN or ordinary telephone lines the private user can do his bank business or order certain goods. Multimedia assistance, interactive and personalized offers complied out of compact discs or remote servers will be the next features. Today's limited services will extend to broader range, e.g. additionally investment and mortgage affairs. The evolution path for the 21th century provides electronic shopping malls with virtual sales-clerks, virtual shelves offering customized products even before you know yourself you would like to have them (eShop 1994).

> For further details see the following contribution in this volume:
>
> *H. Drathen* from debis Systemhaus, see pp. 139-147
> *H. Popp, S. Thesmann, P. Mertens* from FORWISS, see pp. 149-160
> *J. R. M. van der Drift, L. Stakenborg* from CD-Matics, see pp. 161-172

3.2.5 Entertainment

Entertainment includes those applications that can be used for leisure activities or for the purpose of entertaining members of the household.

The most notable example is the television (Ziemer 1994). At the moment it is a passive consumer electronics product. All interactivity requires a back-channel via telephone or cable TV lines. So-called set-top-boxes upgrade the TV-set with computer functionality and handle the processing and presentation of the down- and uploaded data (Hightext 1993).

At first networks-to-the-home will be ready to offer near-video-on-demand with special fixed time slots for a movie, pay-per-view and a limited number of services like interactive gaming with other participants of the network (Sattler 1994). The objective of the Time Warner/Silicon Graphics led Orlando project (Silicon Graphics 1994, Time Warner Cable 1993) is going far beyond: Fully communicative TV allows video communication via the TV-screen and full video-on-demand, i.e. digital videos whenever you want without time restrictions. Interactive videos with influence on the story itself are also on top of the future agenda.

> For further details see the following contributions in this volume:
>
> *P. Höper* from Beate Uhse Group, see pp. 173-182
> *W. Forster* from Cybermedia and *T. Oppermann* from SEGA, see pp. 183-194
> *F.-C. Wachs* from Heinrich Bauer Verlag and *J.-R. Wachs* from Saatchi & Saatchi, see pp. 195-200
> *C. Sattler, N. Klußmann* from Eutelis Consult, see pp. 201-213

3.2.6 Education

Education refers to all applications that train and educate members of the household in special skills or knowledge. In an increasingly dynamic private environment, this function will gain in importance.

The private household uses the type "education" for the training of special skills it is interested in. These computer-based training (CBT) or computer-aided instruction (CAI) software, e.g. language proficiency for the next holiday abroad or traffic rules in order to get the driving licence, is nothing extraordinary. The next stage will be distant learning environments where teacher and students are far away from each other connected via ISDN networks (van Rijn/Williams 1988). In addition, electronic, free accessible libraries open the field for self-education processes. The usage of artificial intelligence will substitute human teachers as far as possible and make them more efficient for special tasks. Virtual reality will help by visualization and demonstration of complex issues.

For further details see the following contribution in this volume:

M. *Rost-Hein* from IBM, see pp. 89-98
F. *Brody* from New Media Consulting, see pp. 99-107

3.2.7 Home Management

Home Management is the field of all the administrative functions the private household can perform. The private tax declaration via an interactive television network, the personal inventory on a consumer-PC-application or the financial management of real estate applying a personal spread sheet are examples of everyday life.

But also much more trivial functions, often labelled as productivity, like the personal word processing for private matters, the EDP-supported drawing of invitation letters for a family celebration or the management of the private audio-CD collection using a database application can be assigned to this topic.

Most of those products are initially built for the business sector and now adapted for private users. However, a lot of such applications are developed with respect to the deviating wants and needs of the private user (Miles 1988).

For further details see the following contribution in this volume:

M. *Jaritz* from Microsoft, see pp. 25-34
D. G. J. *Fanshawe* from Philips Consumer Electronics, see pp. 125-137

4 Projects

Infrastructures (see chapter 2) and applications (see chapter 3) must not be seen as isolated entities that evolve and develop for themselves, but as interrelated issues. The most of today's discussion is only technology-driven and neglects the involvement of a broad platform of applications. In turn, the mere consideration of applications prevents the view on the required platforms.

A possibility to bypass this problem is the description and later the evaluation of authentic projects and pilot trials like the Orlando Full Service Network by Silicon Graphics. Projects are the combination of infrastructures and applications and allow to have a look on a real working environment. Future implications, chances and risks can be assessed and results be used for the post-pilot phase.

We examine projects in the Triad Markets of Asia, USA and Europe. The US is at least five or ten years ahead compared to "sleeping" Europe in the developement and use of interactive media for private spheres. Asia with its complete different cultural, technology-assimilating approach without prejudice against new technologies has made a lot of steps into the Information Age - mainly unnoticed by the world's public - as the examples of Japan or Singapore reveal.

This is highlighted by the three following contributions in this volume:

Asia:	S. Kurihara from Nippon Telephone and Telegraph, see pp. 263-270
USA:	G. Sager from Silicon Graphics, see pp. 271-287
Europe:	H. Hoffmann from Burda New Media and Europe Online, see pp. 289-295
	C. Mayser, M. Römer, G. Zimmermann from Berner & Mattner Systemtechnik, see pp. 297-302
Comparisons:	R. Longhorn as Consultant to the European Commission's DG III and DG XIII, see pp. 233-249
	T. Heimer from Johann Wolfgang Goethe-University, see pp. 251-262

5   Market Impacts and Implications

There are development areas for business in the implementation of both infrastructure and applications for the private household (European Commission 1994). The development of integrated services and products will be one of the success factors; the convergence of markets provides a fertile ground for this evolution and paves the way.

The wave of mega-mergers seen in 1993/94 between cable television companies, media concerns and businesses with experience in providing content gives some impression of the potential economic significance (Ellis 1994).

We need new understanding about the three main sectors being mostly affected by the emergence of the computerized information processing in the home.

5.1   Business Impacts

All reseachers predict that market potentials are arising from IT-infrastructures and applications for the private home (Griffis/Lipoff 1994, Hansen 1994, Tietz 1987). At the moment most efforts are only signs of a "hype" or marketing campaign.

The central concern must be the definition of strategic plans within the enterprise to realize two advantages arising from this area:

First, the private households as a target group for information technology open a completely new promising market and chances for product demand. *Second*, by providing infrastructure and applications to the household the company itself gains directly by improving its economic figures. For instances, if a provider of washing-machines connects the appliances to a network, that delivers usage and failure data, the costs for maintenance personnel and repair logistics will go down. Additional benefits are all the information about the customers' habits and needs. This is a prerequisite for modern database marketing and the triggering of product innovation processes.

Existing product lines, business units and strategic plans should be reviewed or redefined for home-IT (Venkatesh/Vitalari 1986). Businesses will realize that the provision of information technology for the home helps to solve the classic problems of streamlining the organization, bringing costs down, improving quality and transforming value chains (Smith Shi/Salesky 1994, Benjamin/Wigand 1995).

The most important issues that have to be discussed for business matters are:

- alliances and partnerships between infrastructure, content and service providers in a converging market scene
- setting of international standards, e.g. for home networks
- development of prototypes of applications and infrastructures as well as building data and functional models for the private household
- undertaking of real life pilot trials and evaluation of their results
- redefinition of strategies and market concepts due to the different needs and wants of the private customer compared to the business sphere
- deregulation and liberalization of all relevant markets, especially the telecommunication area
- implementation of political and legal set-up conditions that encourage the market evolution

For further details see the following contributions in this volume:

J. *Niemeier* from Multimedia Software GmbH Dresden, see pp. 307-318
A. *Venkatesh* from University of California and R. R. *Dholakia*, N. *Dholakia* from University of Rhode Island, see pp. 319-337
K. *Howaldt*, M.-S. *Jeck* from Roland Berger & Partner, see pp. 339-350
F. *Goedhart*, T. *Künstner* from Booz, Allen & Hamilton, see pp. 351-361
T. *Baubin*, B. W. *Wirtz* from Andersen Consulting, see pp. 363-377
G. R. *Hofmann* from KPMG, see pp. 379-384
N. *Mundorf* from University of Rhode Island, see pp. 385-397

5.2   Social Implications

We are now on the edge to the "Information Society". Not only the working place is changing, but the domestic sphere is affected as well and will change essentially the shape of society (Kellerhals 1994). Therefore politics must identify this topic as crucial and discuss whether financial or executive activities are necessary. The technology assessment and the socio-cultural challenge to the issue of information technology in the home are of high relevance for science and product acceptance. Main questions for the research of social implications are:

- What kind of infrastructure and application does the consumer really *need*?
- What kind of infrastructure and application does the consumer really *want*?
- Do pilot trials bring up valid data for verification? Are results transferable from the US to Europe?
- What are the factors that determine acceptance? How are we able to influence them? Does acceptance change after early enthusiasm?
- What is the role of culture to information technology in the home?
- How will the structure of households and family life change with IT? What are the short-, mid- and long-term implications?

For further details see the following contributions in this volume:

W. Rammert from Free University of Berlin, see pp. 399-408
F. van Rijn from Hogeschool van Amsterdam and IFIP WG 9.3, see pp. 409-417

6   Summary

The market potential of information technology for the future will arise from the situation that computerized information processing influences every part of our private life. Under these circumstances, a discussion about modified requirements for infrastructures, applications and markets themselves is indicated. New types of former "non-computerized" applications in the private sphere, e.g. health, have to be examined. The residential applications for the household can be sub-divided into several main types. All of them are based on a common technological infrastructure, the "Information Superhighway".

The description of the status quo reveals that information technology in the private household is already ubiquitous. The visions and underlying trends of the near and distant scenarios show clearly that information technology in the private home will be one of the main future issues for information management. To realize that is a critical success factor for all competitors involved in this market.

The strategic importance of the *Computerized Information Processing of the Private Household* for business administration and information technology must be realized by all parts of the future Information Society.

References

Armbrüster, H., Die Flexibilität von ATM: Unterstützung künftiger Netzdienste, Multimedia- und Mobilkommunikation, in: Nachrichtentechnik und Elektronik, 1993, Part 1: No. 4, 172 pp., Part 2: No. 5, 223 pp.

AT&T Corporation (ed.), VCTV: A Video-On-Demand Market Test, in: AT&T Technical Journal, January/February 1993, 7 pp.

Benjamin, R., Wigand, R., Electronic Markets and Virtual Value Chains on the Information Superhighway, in: Sloan Management Review, Winter 1995, pp. 62-72

Brand, S., Media Lab - Computer, Kommunikation und Medien, Hamburg, 1990

Brenner, W., Kolbe, L., Future Business Spheres Arising from Computerized Information Processing in the Private Household, in: Proceedings of HOIT - Home-oriented Informatics and Telematics, Copenhagen, 1994, pp. 104-116

Brenner, W., Kolbe, L., Computerized Information Processing of the Private Household: First Outlook on Business Impacts, in: International Journal of Telematics and Informatics, 12(1995)2, forthcoming

Ellis, B. S., The Information Superhighway, in: Prism, Second Quarter 1994, pp. 89-104

EHSA (European Home Systems Assoziation), Home Systems Specification, ESPRIT Projekt 5448, March 15, 1992

eShop Inc. (ed.), eShop offers first electronic shopping technology, Press Release, San Mateo, January 1994

European Commission (ed.), Recommendations to the European Council, Europe and the global information society, Brussels, May 26, 1994

General Magic - Apples Antwort auf den Newton, in: MACup, No. 2, 1994, 18 pp.

Graf, J. (ed.), multiMedia, Informationsdienst für Medienintegration, 4(1994)10, pp. 1-3

Greichen, J., Value Based Home Automation For Today's Market, in: IEEE Transaction on Consumer Electronics, 38(1992)3

Griffis, P. D., Lipoff, S. J., At the Crossroads of the Information Highway: New Technology Directions in Consumer Electronics, in: Proceedings of the IEEE 82(1994)4, pp. 459-463

Hansen, H. R., Marketing über den Information Superhighway, in: Werbeforschung & Praxis, No. 5, 1994

Hightext Verlag (ed.), TV interaktiv - Hintergrund-Informationsdienst über Interaktives Fernsehen, Munich, No. 9, 1993

IEEE Consumer Electronics Society, IEEE Transactions on Consumer Electronics, "Special Issue on Home Systems", 37(1992)2

Jacobs, D., Fetish, in: Wired Magazine, Vol. 2.08, 1994, pp. 39-42

Jeck, S., Technologie im Haushalt 2010, Working Paper at the Wissenschaftliche Hochschule für Unternehmensführung, Otto-Beisheim-Hochschule, Vallendar, Germany, 1993

Jupiter Communications Company (ed.), Consumer Information Appliance, New York, 5(1994)2, pp. 2-23

Kellerhals, R., Neue Medien und Gesellschaft, in: technologie & management 43(1994)3, pp. 123-128

Liesenfeld, J., Der Haushalt als Leitstand: Der Endverbraucher am Endgerät, in: Alemann, von U., Schatz, H., Gesellschaft-Technik-Politik, 1989, pp. 141-169

Mertens, P., Integrierte Informationsverarbeitung 1, Wiesbaden, 1991, 8th edition

Miles, I., Home Informatics, Information Technology and the Transformation of Everyday Life, London, 1988

Mundorf, N., Zoche, P., Nutzer, private Haushalte und Informationstechnik, in: Zoche, P. (ed.), Herausforderungen für die Informationstechnik, Heidelberg, 1994, pp. 61-69

OECD (ed.), Telecommunication and Broadcasting, Convergence or Collision, Paris, 1992

Philips (ed.), Whole-person communications: a new vision, 1994

Press Secretary of the White House (ed.), National Information Infrastructure. The Agenda for Action, Tab. A - Tab. G, Washington, 1993

Reinhardt, A., Building The Data Highway, in: Byte International Edition, March 1994, pp. 46-74

Ricke, H., Kanzow, J. (eds.), BERKOM - Breitbandkommunikation im Glasfasernetz, Heidelberg, 1991, pp. 82-118, pp. 156-231

Sattler, C., Von Fernsehverteildiensten zu interaktiven Videodiensten auf Abruf, in: Communication Highway, IIR-Conference, Frankfurt/Main, May 05/06, 1994

Scheer, A.-W., Wirtschaftsinformatik, Informationssysteme im Industriebetrieb, Berlin e. a., 1990, 3rd edition

Scheer, A.-W., Wirtschaftsinformatik, Referenzmodelle für industrielle Geschäftsprozesse, Berlin e. a., 1994, 4th edition

Silicon Graphics (ed.), Interaktive Digitale Netwerke: Die nächste große technologische Revolution, Press Release, March 1994

Smith Shi, C., Salesky, A. M., Building a strategy for electronic home shopping, in: The McKinsey Quarterly, No. 4, 1994, pp. 77-95

Tietz, B., Wege in die Informationsgesellschaft, Stuttgart, 1987

Time Warner Cable (ed.), The Full Service Network, Time Warner Cable's Vision of our Telecommunications Future, News Release, May 1993

Van Rijn, F., Williams, R., Concerning Home Telematics, Proceedings of the IFIP TC 9, Amsterdam et. al., 1988

Venkatesh, A., Vitalari, N. P., Computing Technology for the Home: Product Strategies for the Next Generation, in: Product Innovation Management, No. 3, 1986, pp. 171-186

The Wall Street Journal Europe, Computer & Telecommunications Bulletin, January/February 1994

Ziemer, A., Digitales Fernsehen: Eine neue Dimension der Medienvielfalt, Heidelberg, 1994

Part Two

Infrastructures

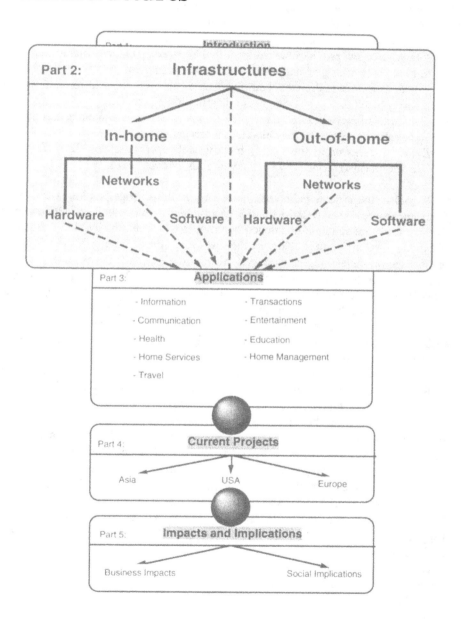

The introductory chapter provided a framework for this new area of research. The following cases are examples for their respective infrastructure business activities, i.e. manufacturers of software, hardware and networking products. This entails that they are describing their own - and sometimes egocentric - point of view to the home-IT world, their products and strategies. Market-leading companies of the IT business such as Microsoft for PC software, Oracle for database management systems and Sony or Bang & Olufsen for the cosumer electronics market set out the reasons for their engagement in the home-IT business.

- *Microsoft* shows the breadth of their products for the private users.
- *Sony* allows an in-depth view into their technology for digital home devices.
- *Bang & Olufsen* provides the reader with their strategy in the difficult market of in-home networking of audio, video and other appliances.
- *Oracle Corporation* decribes their approach to an open standard for multimedia services based on an enhancement of their traditional product.
- *German National Research Center for Computer Science* examines technology and application fields of the ubiquitous smart card.
- *Deutsche Telekom* as the world's biggest cable operator states their efforts to interactive video services by conducting trials all over Germany.

Of course, the articles presented offer a very heterogeneous picture. They range from a product oriented description of Microsoft and an in-depth technically paper of Sony to the more strategic positioned contribution of Deutsche Telekom. But that is exactly what the main problem of the market is about. People from technology are focused on developing nice gadgets whereas the people from marketing do not know to whom to sell the wonderful new devices. Moreoften, a long-term market strategy hasn't yet been established. Management is hesitating to concentrate on the increasing market share of residential users. The following papers are case studies of pioneers and should illustrate what can be done in this early stage. As a result, the residential market for the Information Superhighway bears huge potentials, but to the same extent risks and prospective losses.

The different depth of the articles reveals that the discussions within the companies are on completely different levels. So far there is no broadly accepted concept available that could give a more abstract approach like in systems engineering, e.g. data, function and process-oriented views. In this early stage of research we only can learn by assessing obviously successful testimonials. These home-IT pioneers may come from the mass market (Microsoft) or have outstanding competence as niche companies such as Bang & Olufsen. Either of which has met the specific requirements of its competitive market environment. Therefore, they may serve as case studies for successors or companies preparing for market entry. The current line of home-IT products and new services, its challenges for the suppliers and its benefits for the home users fixes the starting point for a further theoretical perspective in the chapters to follow.

The main concern of this section in the book is to provide insights in the area of infrastructure providers, their variety of products and to discuss about the quality of applied business concepts.

In-home Infrastructures

Microsoft Brings Personal Computing Home

Michaela Jaritz
Microsoft GmbH, Germany

1   Introduction

Software for home computers can offer virtually unlimited educational and entertainment capabilities - allowing arm hair sports fans to become experts at their favorite game; families to learn together using interactive instruction, simulation games and talking books; and empowering home-office workers to run their businesses with the finesse of a Fortune 500 corporation. Industry analysts agree that in North America as well as in other countries, the home market is the fastest-growing segment of the PC industry.

Microsoft's consumer division is one of the fastest-growing areas within Microsoft, with more than 600 people and more than 60 software titles. The number of products is expected to grow to more than 100 by June 1995. With some $500 million in revenue, the consumer division at Microsoft qualifies as one of the leading consumer-software companies worldwide and is the largest developer of compact disc, read-only memory (CD-ROM) software. Its mission is to produce high-quality, compelling and enduring software for everyone in the home.

Microsoft's consumer division develops and markets software in the broad categories of general reference, entertainment, children's software, and home and small-business management. The majority of titles produced in the consumer division are marketed under the Microsoft Home brand, which was officially launched in the fall of 1993. The consumer division also produces hardware, including the Microsoft Mouse pointing device, and the new Natural Keyboard peripheral and Microsoft Home Mouse. The consumer division products are sold throughout the world, and some titles are available in 27 different languages.

Microsoft Home software can turn the home computer into a reference library, a home office, a banking terminal, an entertainment center or a tutor. Microsoft's consumer-product portfolio includes market leaders such as Microsoft Encarta, the best-selling multimedia encyclopedia at retail; Microsoft Works, in the category of integrated productivity tools; and Microsoft Flight Simulator, a perennial favorite for game players and armchair pilots. Products launched this year include the first two titles resulting from Microsoft's collaboration with Scholastic, Inc., (Scholastic's "The Magic Schoolbus Explores the Human Body" and Scholastic's "The Magic Schoolbus Explores the Solar System"); the first two entries in

Microsoft's sports line (Microsoft Complete Baseball and Microsoft Complete Basketball); and the new exploration titles (Dangerous Creatures and Ancient Lands).

In this article, Microsoft discusses the following:

- recent marketplace changes
- who uses home software and why
- Microsoft's strategy for the home market
- the continually expanding range of Microsoft Home brand products
- alliances formed to help Microsoft produce high-quality Home brand products

2   At home with PCs

Personal computers have become an everyday part of the work landscape. PCs can be found in downtown headquarters and local lumberyards, branch banks and mom-and-pop shops.

During the past couple of years, PCs have also moved into the home. One-third of all U.S. households now have PCs. Home PC sales have soared, increasing by 40 percent between 1993 and 1994, and they're expected to double over the next four years, according to the market research firm Dataquest. And according to the Software Publishers Association, home-education and entertainment software are the fastest-growing application-software categories (SPA report 1994). This evolution also holds true for the European markets.

Several factors converged during the past year to fuel the growth in home PC purchases and usage. Those factors include dramatically lower hardware prices; compelling titles with terrific sound, video and graphics; and a fast-growing distribution network that includes not just traditional software outlets, but also superstores, bookstores and specialty shops.

3   Multimedia: PC powers that amaze and delight

A major factor in the growing home use of PCs is the acceptance of multimedia computing. Reading the enormous amounts of data that can be stored on CD-ROM optical discs (the same media used to play music in compact-disc stereo systems), multimedia PCs deliver digital sound and animated graphics and video, giving the personal-computing experience a dazzling impact that is orders of magnitude beyond anything that was possible just a few years ago.

How big is multimedia in home computing? The worldwide installed base of multimedia PCs skyrocketed from 2 million in 1992 to 12 million in 1994 (Multimedia PC Marketing 1994). The percentage of PCs with multimedia capability - now 20 percent - will nearly double in the next two years (Dataquest 1994). Microsoft believes that nearly 100 percent of PCs sold into homes during the 1994 holiday season will be equipped with CD-ROM drives, sound cards, speakers and other accessories that make for great multimedia computing.

And on the software side, sales of CD-ROM software titles are expected to more than double this year to $3.7 billion (Multimedia PC Marketing 1994). According to PC Data, Microsoft is the leading overall software publisher, capturing 22 percent of the total retail sales dollars. Microsoft commands 33 percent of the total dollar volume for business software, and accounts for 11 percent of total dollar volume for multimedia software (PC Data 1994).

4   Home computing is booming everywhere

Today, when consumers walk into mass-merchandising and warehouse outlets, discount stores, and bookstores, chances are they'll see a wide variety of computers and software at competitive prices. Dataquest estimates that the largest percentage of sales over the next two years will come from these types of outlets rather than from traditional computer hardware and software stores.

Microsoft is putting its Home brand software where consumers are. Home brand software is now sold in some consumer mass merchants, as well as warehouses, consumer electronics stores, major bookstores, and even some music and video retail channels. According to Patty Stonesifer, vice president of the consumer division at Microsoft, Microsoft's goal is to put Home titles within arms' reach of desire.

Microsoft is also using a variety of marketing techniques to broaden the appeal of home software. In the US the company recently kicked off a major consumer promotion in conjunction with Compaq Computer Corporation and Delta Airlines. This promotion, called Fly With Us, offers customers who acquire any two Microsoft Home software programs from any Microsoft reseller *one* free companion ticket on Delta Airlines. Other key include a new broad-reach advertising effort, the mailing of a special holiday catalog to more than 1 million registered users of Microsoft Home software, the distribution of a CD Sampler Disk that allows customers to sample more than 55 Microsoft Home titles before they buy, and an advertorial insert for daily newspapers and industry trade publications called The Consumer Guide To Multimedia Computing. The Microsoft subsidiaries in other countries around the world also have invested in new forms of communication with the home PS user: e.g. a PC-Adventskalender in Germany, partnerships with children's TV shows in France - just to name some examples.

5 Changes in how PCs are used at home and who is using them

What are those millions of people doing with their home PCs? In the past, most home computers were used to complete work brought from the office by a fairly sophisticated user, and to play complex games.

The situation is changing today. Adults are using their personal computers to be more productive at home for personal and household activities such as financial management, correspondence and record keeping. In addition, the role of the PC is rapidly expanding from a tool for adults to an easy-to-use appliance for the whole family. Many parents view a home computer as an essential tool in their children's education. Predictably, computer games remain very popular, and the introduction of PC-based multimedia capabilities, such as sound and full-motion video, has enabled developers to create products with greater depth and realism than ever before.

6 The Microsoft Home brand delivers high-quality software

More than a year ago, Microsoft introduced the Microsoft Home brand. In developing this brand, Microsoft's consumer division spent more than 5,000 hours talking with families to find out what they expect from their home PCs. This research included formal focus groups, testing in the Microsoft usability labs, working with kids and teachers in classrooms for an entire school year, and even working with families in their homes. Microsoft asked if these families believed a home PC would help them, what tasks they needed to accomplish, and how they liked to work.

Time and time again, the responses were the same. Many consumers feel the time is right for purchasing a computer for their homes. They want high-quality software that is compelling and enduring - software that's interesting and engaging and that will remain so after many hours of use. They want products that will make their computers a good long-term investment. They also feel that a computer is becoming increasingly important in helping their children learn more at school. Finally, families are always looking for new forms of entertainment.

The result of this extensive research is Microsoft Home, a broad line of software that includes home and small-business management products, kids creativity tools, and entertainment and reference products. These software products are tailored to suit the computing needs and habits of the wide variety of people in the home, while taking advantage of the advanced capabilities of today's easy-to-use, powerful and affordable PC systems.

Today, literally thousands of software titles are marketed to the home computer user. Consumers can count on products that carry the recognized Microsoft Home brand name to be of high quality. Microsoft defines a software product to be "high-quality" when it is both compelling (really engages the user) and enduring (offers lasting value and can be replayed). Other aspects of the high quality found in Microsoft Home products include the overall design, production value of multimedia elements, content that is timely and accurate, and superior performance and functionality (reliability).

7   Microsoft Home products

7.1   Helpful personal productivity tools for home and small-business management

To help manage household tasks, Microsoft Home includes products to help users track finances, manage mailing lists, create calendars and greeting cards, or even run a home-based business.

Microsoft Works, the world's best-selling integrated set of productivity software, is used by more than 11 million people. Microsoft Works includes a word processor, a spreadsheet program and a database. It allows the novice or occasional computer user to create letters, shopping lists, a database of business contacts, household budgets, and much more.

Microsoft Publisher, the easy-to-use desktop publishing program, is used for producing great-looking documents, such as brochures, newsletters and calendars.

Microsoft Money, the personal-finance package, is the first PC software package in the US to offer easy-to-use Bank On-Line capabilities to allow users to access their bank statements from home - essentially turning their PCs into ATMs. It also features Pay On-Line capabilities that let users pay their bills from home. New wizards - another first in Money - help automate tasks including retirement planning and tracking investments. Microsoft Money's online capabilities have first been introduced to the German and French versions of the product where they have become one of the most wanted features.

7.2   Children's software

In developing the company's first software designed specifically for children, Microsoft did its homework. Members of the software team at Microsoft spent 3,000 hours consulting with 500 teachers and academic experts, held more than 50 focus-group sessions with parents and kids, and spent another 1,600 hours over the course of an entire school year working with 300 kids in the classroom to get specific product feedback. This did not only happen in the US where the products where developed but also in European countries in order to make sure that the humor, characters and design of the products would work globally.

What did Microsoft learn? Children like the idea of their software embodying a special world, with built-in characters they can relate to. They want software to have personality, a sense of humor, and a sense of fun. Kids often want some initial help getting started with creative ideas and then the freedom to run with their projects independently. Kids like to emphasize words with elements such as color and shape rather than using boldface type or underlining. Most computer terminology is also irrelevant to children. For example, they have no idea what 8-point and 12-point type are. Terms such as "huge", "giant" and "small" mean much more to them. The Microsoft Home Kids' products put these findings to use in the following high-quality, compelling and engaging products for children:

Creative Writer is a creative-writing and publishing software title, and *Fine Artist* is a complete art and drawing program. Creative Writer and Fine Artist transport young computer users, ages 8 to 14, to the world of Imaginopolis. There, they are greeted by the wacky McZee character, who provides context-sensitive help and performs inspiring antics. Young users can relate to characters Max and Maggie, who share their specific expertise in writing and art.

Scholastic's *The Magic School Bus Series*, produced by Microsoft in cooperation with Scholastic Inc., series features exciting science adventures that transport young children on magical rides while introducing them to the wonders of science and technology. Inspired by Scholastic's best-selling book series and new PBS animated series, the software version starts with two titles: Scholastic's "The Magic School Bus Explores The Human Body" and Scholastic's "The Magic School Bus Explores the Solar System", both from Microsoft. Microsoft is also a major sponsor of "The Magic School Bus" series on PBS. Microsoft is currently working on getting this project established in other countries as well.

7.3   Sports and games - a world of entertainment

Microsoft Flight Simulator is one of the best-selling computer games, with more than 2 million units sold - 1 million of which were sold in fiscal year 1994. Flight Simulator and its New York and Paris scenery enhancement software allow users to experience hours of entertainment flying around the world, testing their skills in all types of aircraft - from a Lear Jet 35A to a Sopwith Camel. With Flight Simulator, users can circle the Eiffel Tower or land on an aircraft carrier. Also just released are two additional scenery add-on products, Microsoft Carribean and Microsoft Japan.

Microsoft Complete Basketball is the newest title from the Microsoft Complete Sports line. In association with the National Basketball Association (NBA), Microsoft Complete Basketball details the NBA's history, players, teams, season summaries and statistics. And, just like Microsoft Complete Baseball, the title will offer users an online feature to access current statistics.

Microsoft Golf 2.0 allows up to four players to experience the joys - and traps - of the renowned Torrey Pines golf course in San Diego, complete with sound and video tips.

Microsoft Golf Championship Course series of enhancements for Microsoft Golf includes realistic simulations of courses at Banff Springs, Mauna Kea and Pinehurst.

Microsoft Space Simulator offers the ultimate experience in space flight and exploration software. It provides an entertaining and educational means for exploring the universe and was developed in cooperation with NASA to help ensure realism.

7.4   Reference titles that make "looking it up" fun

Microsoft reference products take advantage of the latest PC multimedia capabilities and the huge storage and retrieval capacities of CD-ROMs, offering information and enrichment to both parents and children. These products are not just for research projects; they bring families together to learn and explore favorite topics and interests.

Microsoft Encarta '95 is an updated, enhanced version of the multimedia encyclopedia. Encarta is also Microsoft's top-selling home CD-ROM product. Encarta received a Codie award from the Software Publishers Association as the Best Home Learning Program for 1993. With hours of audio as well as film clips, animations and stunning graphics, Encarta offers children a multidimensional learning experience. A new feature called Interactivities helps users apply knowledge in a practical way and promotes more in-depth learning.

Microsoft Cinemania '95 is an interactive guide to the movies and the people who make them. It contains nearly 20,000 reviews of films from "Birth of a Nation" (1915) to "Four Weddings and a Funeral" (1994). Complete with video and audio clips and reviews from Leonard Maltin, Roger Ebert and Pauline Kael, Cinemania has a new Cinemania Suggests feature that helps users select movies to match their moods.

Microsoft Bookshelf '94, the popular multimedia CD-ROM reference library, is the new way to look it up. In the US version it includes new or updated versions of The American Heritage Dictionary, The Columbia Dictionary of Quotations, The Original Roget's Thesaurus, The Concise Columbia Encyclopedia, The People's Chronology, The World Almanac and Book of Facts 1994 and the Hammond Intermediate World Atlas. Bookshelf goes beyond printed reference works to offer video clips of scientific concepts and historic events, 80,000 spoken-word pronunciations, 60 animations, and powerful tools for interactive searching across all Bookshelf books at once. For the German version of Bookshelf, Microsoft has entered a joint venture with one of the major publishers (Bibliographisches Institut) in Germany and developed a product specifically for the German market, featuring such reknown reference titles as DUDEN, Meyers Lexikon and Langenscheidts Taschenwörterbuch Englisch.

Microsoft Dangerous Creatures invites exploration of more than 250 animals and their habitats. It includes more than 1,000 articles and hundreds of sounds and videos. Dangerous Creatures was produced in association with the World Wildlife Fund, which receives a portion of Dangerous Creatures revenue to support conservation efforts in the protection of species and their habitats.

Microsoft Ancient Lands brings ancient Egypt, Greece and Rome to life with nearly 1,000 illustrated interactive articles and hours of sounds and narration. With

Ancient Lands, users can explore these civilizations from the mystery of the Sphinx to the original Olympics and Roman cooking.

Microsoft Art Gallery is an interactive guide to the collection of the National Gallery of Art in London, including the works of Da Vinci, Raphael and Michelangelo.

Microsoft Multimedia Composer Series consists of Multimedia Schubert: "The Trout Quintet"; Multimedia Beethoven: "The Ninth Symphony"; Multimedia Mozart: "The Dissonant Quartet"; Multimedia Strauss: "Three Tone Poems"; and Multimedia Stravinsky: "The Rites of Spring". Each product provides an interactive look at the life, times and music each of these great composers, enabling users to explore CD-quality music in depth for the first time.

Microsoft's Isaac Asimov's *The Ultimate Robot* provides an interactive look at the world of robotics, featuring the work of the world's best-selling science-fiction author.

7.5   Hardware and accessories

Home computer users do not live by software alone: They also need hardware. While Microsoft isn't in the PC hardware systems business, it has long offered hardware products - such as the Microsoft Mouse - that enhance a user's computing experience. Microsoft Home brand products continue to expand on this tradition, offering products tailored especially to the distinctive needs of home users. In addition, PC accessories, such as screen savers, are available from this group.

Microsoft Home Mouse is the newest mouse from Microsoft and is designed for hands of all sizes, from children to adult. The Home Mouse also includes fun software that can turn the user's cursor into a skier or other whimsical shape.

Microsoft Mouse version 2.0 has a sophisticated new design to promote maximum comfort. Many computer users choose this mouse for its hardware design combined with its software features that support Windows-based computing.

Microsoft Natural Keyboard provides a comfortable, responsibly designed alternative to the standard 101-key keyboard. The result of more than 18 months of ergonomic research, the new keyboard provides a static, split-keypad design, three new keys, intelligent adjustability, built-in palm rests, and software features that make Windows-based computing easier and more enjoyable.

Microsoft Scenes version 2.0 includes seven new and updated collections of professional-quality, photographic-image screen savers for the Microsoft Windows operating system. They include a new edition of the popular Microsoft Sierra Club Collection, as well as Hollywood, Sports Extremes, Brain Twister, Flight and Undersea collections. The new collections also allow users to personalize their Windows-based PCs by adapting their own photos of family or friends for use as screen-saver images.

The above examples illustrate the variety and bandwidth of Microsoft Home software today.

8 Working with educators and administrators

Microsoft offers a range of programs and services to help parents, teachers and administrators discover the excitement and benefits of interactive multimedia as an aid to education in the following ways:

Help '94-'95: A free, one-day workshop, called Workshop for Educators Who Invest in Technology, Help'94-'95 is designed to empower K-12 superintendents and administrators to successfully create and implement school technology plans. Solutions are discussed for administrative automation, library automation, network design, teacher training, supplementary technology curricula, and school-to-work programs. During the initial year of the program, (which coincides with the 1994-1995 school year), the workshops will be conducted at 1,500 schools in more than 25 cities in the United States and Canada.

Teacher In-Service Training: Microsoft's in-service training program, scheduled to begin in 1995, will help school districts to increase classroom use of technology and decrease "technophobia". Training kits will include products and training materials. One individual per school district will attend a train-the-trainers session, where the person can learn the training material, becomes a local expert resource for the school's district, and executes the school's districtwide training.

Family Technology Nights: This program includes parents, as well as students and teachers, in the technology-education effort. Parents and children can take advantage of hands-on computer explorations with name-brand computers, and they can view the latest multimedia-software titles, such as Microsoft Encarta, Scholastic's "The Magic School Bus" series and Microsoft Creative Writer. Through this program, school districts, schools and individuals can become eligible to obtain software at no charge. Family Technology Nights are immensely popular with school districts. After conducting more than 300 programs across the country during the 1993-1994 school year, Microsoft received 3,500 requests for programs to be held during the 1994-1995 school year.

State partnership program: Microsoft works with more than 30 states and 20 colleges to bring technology solutions into local schools. Microsoft donates large quantities of software to state departments of education, enabling them to execute their teacher-training plans.

Education Software Summit: Microsoft sponsors this annual conference to educate education-software developers on the latest trends in educational computing. For example, the 1994 summit included sessions on moving to 32-bit applications and systems, using OLE technology to create integrated solutions, and leveraging multimedia CD-ROM course materials.

9   Alliances offer extra value to customers

Microsoft is not producing Microsoft Home software in isolation. It is working closely with established experts in many of its new markets to ensure that Microsoft Home brand products meet the real needs and interests of customers. Microsoft is teaming up with a wide variety of experts - including banks, publishers, and educational and nonprofit organizations worldwide in order to pursue the second aspect of Bill Gates' vision *A PC on every desk and in every home.*

References

Dataquest, cited in: The Wall Street Journal, Aug. 4, 1994

Multimedia PC Marketing Council and InfoTech, cited in: The Wall Street Journal, July 7, 1994

PC Data, September 1994

SPA report, "North American PC Software Sales", September 12, 1994

Digital Devices and Advanced Technology for the Consumer Market

Terry R. Hurley
Sony United Kingdom Ltd., United Kingdom

1   Introduction

The technology employed in today's consumer products has seen rapid advances in recent years. In the past, consumer technology was seen as the poor relation of technology in, for example, the professional, communications and aerospace markets. However this situation is changing, driven by the financial rewards of developing successful consumer products. In many areas such as displays, transmission techniques and video compression, the consumer market is providing the main drive for technological advancement.

Many consumer products are made possible by, not only innovative concepts and ideas, but also the best technical solutions at affordable cost. These solutions have been shaped by technological advancements, particular in areas such as storage devices where magnetic tape, magnetic and optical disks, and solid state memories have all developed at a tremendous pace, each one finding specific applications suited to their particular characteristics. Also in microprocessors and micro-controllers which can execute the equivalent processing power of 10's of MIPs. Tomorrow's processors will no doubt make these figures look pedestrian.

These trends have gone hand-in-hand with the development and establishment of standards and interchange formats, which not only help to ensure conformance to required parameters but have also encouraged widespread application and use of the technologies. Recently the development of new standards has been driven by the efforts of collaborative groups such as the Moving Pictures Expert Group (MPEG), European Digital Video Broadcast Group (DVB) and the ATM (Asynchronous Transfer Mode) Forum.

In products, these technical trends have encouraged the evolution from analogue to digital. But until recently we remained in a world of essentially passive black boxes in simple, hardware driven configurations. The TV, VCR and telephone being good examples. The future vision is one of interactive systems on global networks (the so called "Information Superhighway") which are software driven and remotely configured. Achieving this goal will need many technologies to be combined, developed and matured to provide the right solutions for the market.

These new technologies pose real cost problems to the manufacturers. The cost of new digital products is inevitably higher than the analogue products they are designed to replace. However this digital era is being driven by issues such as the new services that become possible, the lower bandwidths required to deliver digital services to the home and the belief that the cost of digital consumer equipment will steadily reduce as the scale of integration increases and the silicon technologies advance (i.e. smaller silicon geometries, higher speeds and lower powers).

The lower bandwidths have come about because of the breakthroughs made in compression technologies in the 80ies, enabling multiple digitally compressed signals to occupy the equivalent bandwidth of one analogue channel. This has been reflected in, for example, the complete direct to home (DTH) digital chain which has been established in the USA (Direct TV™ system) which started in April 1994 and new DVB digital systems which are planned for introduction in 1995 in Europe and Asia.

The next stage is the support of interactive services by using return channels to allow communication between the consumer set top unit and a server. Increasing bandwidths, real time response and symmetrical channels with full point to point connectivity will allow the migration to more demanding services such as networked games and virtual network worlds requiring the use of high performance 3D graphics in the set top box.

But are the technologies required to realise these new services so different from where we are today? More importantly what are the solutions that will be cost effective and successful in the market place? Today, broadcasters are committing themselves to real digital broadcast services on satellites. However interactive services are still being trialled and tested, with no major product roll-outs expected in the near future. So one of the key questions is will the new services come by revolution or by evolution of these first digitally broadcast TV services? The provision of interactive services may be limited using satellite delivery, but on cable networks the evolutionary approach from broadcast to video on demand is very attractive, when the investment costs and risks are considered.

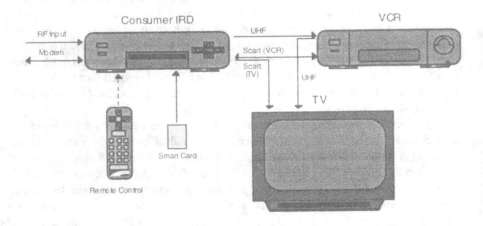

Fig. 1.   Connection of IRD, TV and VCR

This chapter explains some of the technologies which are being utilised in new consumer products by first describing the hardware being designed to receive the first all digitally broadcast services. A view is then given on how this technology will evolve to platforms which will support fully interactive services.

2   DVB Integrated Receiver Decoder

The Integrated Receiver Decoder (IRD) receives and decodes broadcast TV programmes, which may be delivered by satellite, cable or terrestrial means. It tunes to the required channel, extracts and decodes the selected data, checks the access rights of the user and outputs clear picture, sound or other services as needed to the user (normally via the user's analogue TV).

The input to the IRD can be fed from a satellite outdoor unit, from a cable network, or a terrestrial aerial. The satellite outdoor unit is required to receive the satellite transmissions convert them to a suitable intermediate frequency (IF) and feed them to the IRD, normally located close to the TV. The video and audio output of the IRD are fed to the TV directly at baseband through a Peritel (21 pin SCART) connection or at UHF with the re-modulated signal fed to the TV tuner, as shown in figure 1. A VCR can also be supplied with a composite signal. Picture aspect ratios of 4:3 or 16:9 can be indicated through the Scart connection (see fig. 1).

The appearance of a conventional IRD is shown in figure 2 with remote commander in figure 3.

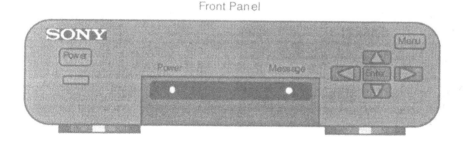

Fig. 2.   IRD appearance

The IRD front panel may have a set of minimal user controls and a display which are intended to enable basic operation without need for the remote commander.

Fig. 3.   Remote commander

User control is typically via a hand-held, infra-red remote commander, with on-screen display overlaid on the main video output. Together they provide comprehensive control of the IRD and support for sophisticated user interfaces. A minimal set of physical buttons for a remote commander is power on/standby, menu on/off, 10 buttons (0-9) for number entry, up-down channel select and five buttons for cursor control and select.

To meet the requirements of increased functionality alternative user input devices can be used by replacing the push button hand-held remote commander with roller/tracker balls, joysticks or keyboards.

2.1   Satellite outdoor unit

The satellite outdoor unit (ODU) receives the signals beamed from the satellite by a dish and converts them using a low noise block (LNB) (see fig. 4) to an IF of typically 950-2050 MHz. The LNB may handle signals which are polarised vertically or horizontally. The latest ODUs include monolithic microwave IC for miniaturisation and stabilised reception, orthomode transducer integrated LNB for cross-polarisation isolation (e.g. more than 35 dB) and dual linear polarisation input with dual output.

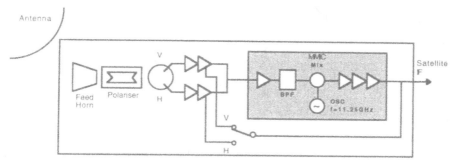

Fig. 4.   The low noise block (NLB)

2.2   Architecture of the IRD

The IRD essentially contains five main functional blocks. These are the channel or network interface, the conditional access sub-system (CASS), the MPEG decoder, output signal post processing and a control sub-system. Figure 5 shows these in more detail. The blocks are interconnected by the MPEG transport stream and a control bus.

The channel or network interface consists of a tuner, demodulator and channel decoder including error correction. The conditional access sub-system contains the hardware and software to access and descramble the received data. The MPEG decoder consists of the demultiplexer i.e. system layer decoding and the video and audio i.e. source decoding. Post processing provides output formatting, encoding of composite video, conversion to analogue and re-insertion of teletext. These functions are supported by a host processor which runs the software applications, operating system and the necessary drivers. A typical application on the host would be the program guide allowing the user to select a TV programme from information provided by the broadcaster in the form of service information (SI). The application may be either resident i.e. installed during manufacture and permanent or they may be upgradeable through a software download mechanism utilising the transmission path or a return channel e.g. PSTN modem.

2.3   Channel/network interface

The tuner isolates a single QPSK or QAM modulated signal from one received channel. This is demodulated, channel decoded and error corrected. The output is a MPEG-2 transport stream conforming with Draft International Standard ISO/IEC 13818-1 (ISO/IEC).

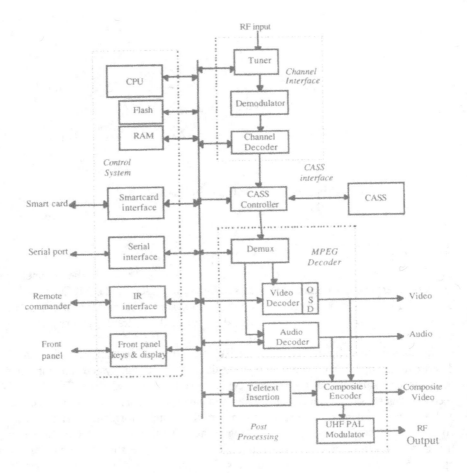

Fig. 5.   IRD System Architecture

A DVB IRD conforms to the DVB specifications as defined by the relevant ETSI standards and DVB documents. For example the DVB specification for channel coding and modulation with satellite transmission is ETS 300 421 (ETS a) which specifies QPSK Modulation, Viterbi channel coding, convolutional interleaving with depth I=12, Reed Solomon error correction (204,188) and PRBS ($1+X^{14}+X^{15}$) energy dispersal. The comparable document for cable systems is ETS 300 429 (ETS b) which specifies Modulation of 16, 32 or 64 QAM in 8 MHz channels, channel coding including an equaliser, differential decoder and symbol mapping, then convolutional interleaving, Reed Solomon error correction and energy dispersal which are in common with the satellite specification.

Using the DVB specification, satellite transponders of typically 33 or 36 MHz can enable bit rates of up to about 60 Mbits/s to be delivered to the IRD. After allowing for the overhead of channel coding and error correction, this provides capacity for up to about 50 Mbits/s of useful information. The IRD therefore needs to be able to process MPEG transport streams up to this rate.

The cable IRD receives digital television services via a CATV network with channel spacings of typically 8 MHz. The DVB specifications include the possibility of 256 QAM which again allows MPEG transport streams of up to about 50 Mbits/s to be delivered. In practice first cable systems are likely to use 16 or 64 QAM due to the availability and cost of the technology which reduces this maximum rate to about 38 Mbits/s.

2.4   Conditional access sub-system (CASS)

The digital data stream received from the Channel is passed to the CASS if present. The CASS contains all of the conditional access (CA) elements of the IRD. The CA system uses scrambling and encryption to control user access to the broadcast programmes. Transmitted information, which can be video, audio or data signals, is scrambled using a known secure algorithm. The DVB have specified a suitable scrambling system. The CASS performs descrambling of selected packets of the transport stream using control words or keys under the control of a security module.

The scrambling is initialised and synchronised using these keys which can be changed regularly, e.g. every 10 seconds. The keys are transmitted in an encrypted form using other public and personal user keys to encrypt them. The personal user keys are stored in the security module in the user's IRD. The most popular form of security module is a Smart Card, which has the advantage of being easily distributed to the user with the personal key programmed inside, and similarly it can be easily replaced if the card is lost or damaged or needs to be changed. The Smart Card is a vital component of pay-TV services because it ensures the user has paid for the services. However it is also the most common target for those who wish to use technical means to gain unauthorised access to the services, the most popular method being to clone valid cards.

The CASS can be embedded in the IRD or it may be contained in a plug-in module. For the plug-in case, the DVB have defined the 'conditional access common interface' for the module the first version of which has been defined using PCMCIA (DVB). The CASS contains the descrambler which implements the DVB specified de-scrambling algorithm and the decryption engine implemented on a security module which can be fixed inside the CASS or removable, as in the Smart Card.

The common interface allows the MPEG transport stream to be passed through the CASS so that selected transport stream packets can be de-scrambled. It also supports a processor interface so that the CASS has access to IRD functions where required. This could include the user interface for CA related messages and the use of a modem for communication with the CA subscriber authorisation system (SAS).

It is likely that in the future this interface will be used for functions other than the CASS. It could be used to add new functionality to the IRD when already in the user's home. For example it could be used to add memory, or to add additional processing to support more demanding services, thus allowing upgrade paths for the IRD.

2.5   Decoding

After descrambling the MPEG transport stream data is decoded. The transport stream consists of a number of programmes and other data multiplexed together. Each programme may be video, audio and data streams. Other data includes the PSI, SI, CA. The transport stream, at rates up to 50 Mbits/s, is first demultiplexed into the required elementary streams. Streams not required are ignored. The rate of each stream will depend on the requirements of the service, the actual rate being determined by the compression used or the amount of data needed to be sent. For example video is likely to be at rates between 1.5 and 10 Mbits/s dependant on the trade-off between picture quality and bit rate.

The elementary streams are then decoded. In the case of video and audio this requires decompression using the algorithms specified in the standards for MPEG2 video and audio (Draft International Standards ISO/IEC 13818-2 & 3 respectively) (ISO/IEC). Today the processing rates required for these functions mean that video decompression requires specific hardware and the audio decompression requires a DSP, however these functions are becoming available in single integrated devices with external memory for the compressed data and picture buffers. The complexity of these functions is high, which has led to some serious technical issues regarding their implementation. For example it takes some ingenuity on the part of the silicon designers to ensure that the total memory requirement to support MPEG2 video decoding can be squeezed into 16 Mbit of DRAM, particularly if space is to be made available in the same memory to store data for the generation of the on-screen display. Also although MPEG2 decoding technology has been available since 1993, new implementations are being developed to provide better 'designer friendly' system solutions and reduce the system cost.

In the future we would expect to see much more application specific solutions for the decoder engine of the IRD. This could include the integration of, for example, the decoding of data such as teletext and subtitling information which is then overlaid on the picture. We can also expect to see much more general solutions whereby audio and video decompression functions could be implemented in programmable code on a high power general purpose processor. Such functions could then be downloaded as an application by a remote server.

2.6   Post processing

After decompression, the video and audio signals are filtered and converted to the specified output formats. In the case of video, processing may be required to convert from the coded image format to the display format. The interpolation and aspect ratio conversion required is normally carried out in the MPEG video decoder. Re-encoding of the video components to a composite signal (PAL, NTSC or SECAM) and conversion to analogue are now available in a single silicon device, although it is likely that in the future all of this video post processing may be integrated into the MPEG decoder.

2.7 Digital VCR

As well as connection to analogue VCRs which record the PAL signal, future IRDs will connect to digital VCRs (DVC) allowing recording and playback of programs in compressed digital format. The interface between the IRD and the DVC carries MPEG transport stream and control data over a bus specified by IEEE P1394 (IEEE). This is a 3 pair shielded cable carrying time multiplexed data at up to approximately 100 Mbps. The DVC interconnection will carry a copy protection system to allow the broadcaster to prevent recording of the programmes.

2.8 Other interfaces

The IRD may support a number of other interfaces. For example it may have RS-232C to enable serial asynchronous data to be passed to external equipment e.g. a PC or games console. It may also have a PSTN or cable modem to allow the provision of a narrowband backchannel which may be used for services such as PPV or simple interaction in support of the broadcast services e.g. audience participation or simple home shopping.

2.9 Host processor

The host processor is likely to be a 16 or 32 bit device. Popular CISC processors are used in many applications due to familiarity, cost and the availability of development tools, but RISC processors are being used for performance reasons particularly where there is a requirement to process received data streams. The host requires memory to provide storage of the programme code, received data, working data and configuration data which may require a mix of DRAM (or possibly SRAM), FLASH (for applications) and EEPROM for configuration parameter storage.

3 The multi-media platform

The functional blocks required in other multimedia consumer devices are similar to those described for the IRD. For example in the latest generation of consumer games machines the general architecture may be like that shown in figure 6.

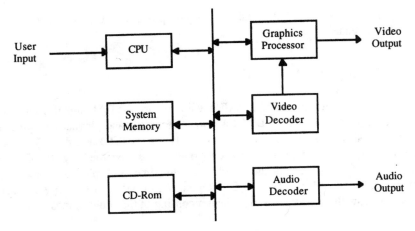

Fig. 6.   Architecture of a games machine

Unlike the IRD the architecture does not require a channel or network interface, but it does require a game or programme source such as CD-ROM. The information read from the disk has to be decoded, as does the channel data in the IRD. The main difference is that the information source in the games machine is under control of the local processor i.e. is a slave device. The processor can control both the rate at which data is read and the location from where data is read on the disk. In the IRD the channel data is delivered by a transmission system i.e. under the control of a remote process, and not the local processor.

In an interactive network environment the programme source (or TV channel) may come from either a local or remote source. Games may be played from local ROM or over the network using a remote ROM, or they may be downloaded to the local device and played from RAM. It would be possible for two or more such devices to interact using local and remote ROM in enhanced applications. In all these cases, however, the functional blocks remain essentially the same.

Any hardware platform is designed to support a number of services. It is obvious that the games machine must run any game developed for it, or an IRD must handle any expected TV service delivered to it. This is achieved by making the service or application independent of the hardware i.e. by providing hardware abstraction in the software layers.

By extending this concept to its logical conclusion, there are expectations that a universal multimedia platform can be developed that could be used as the hardware to support all interactive video services. The architecture or such a platform could look like that shown in the generic multi-media architecture of figure 7.

However when issues such as, the detail of specific market applications, the interfaces required to connect to existing technology, the pace of technology advancements, the problems of standardisation, and market competition are considered, it is clear that a single universal platforms is not realistic.

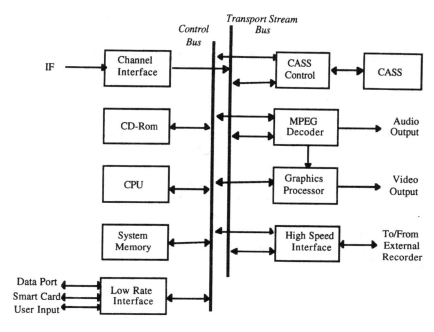

Fig. 7. Generic multi-media platform architecture

However it is necessary that open systems with specified interfaces are established for networked interactive services to ensure interoperable technologies leading to widespread use, competition and lower costs. This will drive the development of consumer devices with specific cost point targets and defined levels of functionality. Therefore a range of platforms could be envisaged which covers these required levels of functionality. At the lower end, the base platform could be the TV IRD possibly with a low rate return channel such as PSTN or cable modem. This would be capable of supporting essentially passive services such as pay per view (PPV) TV or near video on demand (NVOD). The first step up the range of functionality could be to utilise the return channel for basic interactive services such as game show responses, and audience voting or for simple home shopping. In this case the return channel is used to enhance the main broadcast service with additional unidirectional or bidirectional data.

At the high end the platform could be a fully interactive terminal device with a broadband symmetrical interface and a processing engine supporting 3D graphics and rendering. Maybe in that case there may be the possibility of realising the promise of many of the futuristic applications which are being discussed where virtual reality becomes a reality in our real world homes.

References

ISO/IEC, International Organisation For Standardisation, ISO/IEC 13818, Draft International Standard. Information Technology-Generic Coding Of moving Pictures And Associated Audio-Part 1 Systems, Part 2 Video, Part 3 Audio, Reccommendation H.222.0

ETS a, European Telecommunications Standards Institute, ETS 300 421, Digital broadcasting systems for television, sound and data services, framing structure, channel coding and modulation for 11/12 GHz satellite services

ETS b, European Telecommunications Standards Institute, ETS 300 429, Digital broadcasting systems for television, sound and data services, framing structure, channel coding and modulation cable systems

DVB, Draft Specification, Common Interface Specification for Conditional Access and other Digital Video Broadcasting Decoder Applications, DVB

IEEE, The Institute Of Electrical And Electronic Engineers, IEEE P1394, Draft Standard-High Performance Serial Bus, USA

Bang & Olufsen's Integrated Home-Networking with Beolink

Peter Petersen
Bang & Olufsen, Denmark

1   Introduction

This chapter describes the utilisation of computerised information processing in Bang & Olufsen products. First examples of consumer benefits in the products are given, then the present technical infrastructure is outlined, marketing experiences are summarised and at last future perspectives and strategies are stated.

Computerised information processing started with the introduction of the first microprocessor in a product in 1978. Since then the microprocessor has been an important component in almost every product, and it has paved the way for the Beolink concept.

The Beolink concept has four important elements: remote control, integrated systems, multiroom systems and control outside audio-video. The historic development has been as follows.

- 1973:   the first audio remote control
- 1974:   the first television remote control
- 1978:   the first integrated audio system
- 1981:   the first video remote control and integrated video system
- 1983:   the first audio multiroom system
- 1986:   the first audio-video remote control, integrated audio-video system and video multiroom system
- 1988:   the first light control
- 1991:   infra red remote control of audio-video from telephone

In fact the first remote controls were based on dedicated and not computerised information processing, but the concept was the same.

2   Consumer benefits

Adding true consumer benefits should always be a driver for innovations of consumer products. During the last decade we have seen technical developments fail, because they did not bring real customer values. Bang & Olufsen have used computerised information processing for consumer valued innovations for more than 15 years. We use Beolink as the common designation for these innovations.

2.1   Remote control

Remote control indeed adds consumer benefits. Simple and comprehensible control of your audio-video system from your favourite chair or wherever you want it, that makes sense.

We first introduced a dedicated remote control for one audio system. Later remote control became standard for all audio systems. These were then unified into one audio terminal.

In parallel we introduced the dedicated television remote control. This was updated to cover teletext control and further updated into a video (television, satellite and video-casette-recorder) terminal, when these sources were introduced.

The next step was the integration of the audio and the video terminals into one. We call it the Beolink terminal, which pioneered the one terminal philosophy. The number of terminals in the home is only determined by the number of places you need one. This made life simpler for users of both audio and video products from Bang & Olufsen. You only need to understand and use one remote control. You always get the right terminal, and you always get it right.

2.2   Integrated systems

Integrated systems adds consumer benefits like one touch control of the audio-video system and automated complex functions.

The first integrated system was a radio, tape-recorder and gramophone interconnected into an audio system. Consumer benefit were remote control of all components and one touch control: if you are playing radio and want to play tape, just press "tape" on the remote control or "play" on the tape-recorder. More advanced features was the real time tape counter and the record lock, which prevents unintentional change of a programme when recording a radio programme or a compact disc onto tape.

Next step was to do the same in a television-VCR (video-cassette-recorder) combination. Consumer benefit was remote control of the full video system from one terminal. The user interface for television, satellite and VCR was integrated. The same menu for all sources which included one timer programming menu to record a satellite programme onto tape, which is a quite complex function. More advanced features were also made possible like tuner dump, which means that you only have to tune programmes on the television; they are automatically downloaded into the VCR.

The last step so far, has been the interconnection of the audio and the video system into an integrated audio-video system. Added consumer benefit is to use the hi-fi speakers for both audio and video sound. In a split set-up with television in one room and audio in another room, you have access to audio in the television room and access to television sound in the audio room.

2.3   Multiroom systems

Multiroom systems meant another step in consumer benefits. The concept was first
introduced in audio and later in video.

Sound follows you all over the house, and so does the control of it. Sound and
picture from the central audio-video system can be enjoyed in every room. Just
press "satellite", and you are able to watch satellite programmes on the standard
television in the bedroom.

2.4   Control

The last element of Beolink is the control of functions outside the audio-video
system from the Beolink terminal and vice versa.

Light control has been included in the Beolink terminal, facilitating on/off,
dimming and pre-programmed light settings all over the house. Just press "Light"
"1", and light is lit from the bedroom, in the bathroom and the kitchen.

Remote control of audio-video has been included in a Bang & Olufsen telephone.
Turn down the sound of the audio-video system from the telephone when answering
a call.

2.5   Teletext

Teletext is also computerised information processing. The information is
transmitted as a part of the television programme, and it is processed in the
television. It means added value to the customer. News, television programme
guides and weather whenever you want it, are some simple examples. A more
advanced feature is Programme Delivery Control. It means cursor based
programming of a timer recording from the teletext programme guide and automatic
record start/stop at programme start/stop.

3   The infrastructure

The technical infrastructure of the Beolink has two essential elements: the internal
control structure of products including the on screen display of the television and
links between the products.

3.1   Internal control structure

Microprocessor control of audio-video products is the base for Beolink. Processor
architecture and computing power differs from product to product (see fig. 1). In the
most advanced product, we use a 16 bit processor from the 68000 family with
external ROM and RAM. The programmes are written in C. But we also have
simpler products with 4 bit single chip microcomputers programmed in Assembler.

The central microprocessor processes the information and commands to and from
the external links, it controls the on screen display and all functions inside the

products. Most integrated circuits (ICs) are delivered with a data-interface to control
their function. We use the IIC internal databus to control the different functions in
the set.

Processing is real time, based on a real time operating system. The programmes
are fixed and dedicated to perform the macro-control of the products. They are
always loaded, which means instant response - no loading time. A stand by mode
with very low power consumption, where only processing of links is active, means
instant response from the remote control 24 hours per day.

On screen display is used for menu guidance and very interesting for future
interactive services. In the present architecture the on screen display is generated in
the teletext display driver, controlled from the central processor. The display has so
far been character based like the teletext system itself. This is a limitation compared
to for instance Windows on personal computers, which is graphic based. New
teletext IC concepts and next generation (so-called level 3) teletext system have
graphic based display. Level 3 teletext is not in service yet, but the display driver
IC's are on the market and in use in products.

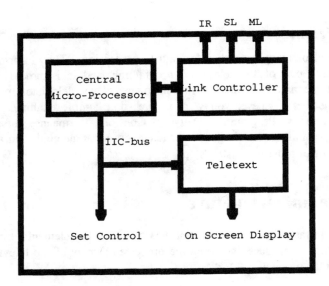

Fig. 1.   The internal control structure of a television

3.2   Links

Links are essential to system integration of products. They interconnect products
with signals and carry data-communication. In the Beolink concept we distinguish
between 3 types of products:

- *Master:* control a monitor (screen or speaker), send/receive signals to/from Sources and distribute signals to monitors in other rooms. There are two types of Masters: the Audio Master (radio/amplifier) and the Video Master (television). A Master can also include Sources, e.g. a satellite receiver in a television.
- *Source:* delivers signals to the Masters, e.g. a VCR.
- *Link-product:* receives signals from main room Masters for monitoring.

The most important Links are the wireless Infra Red (IR) Link from remote controls to Masters, the Source Link (SL) connecting audio and video Sources to a Master within one room and Master Link (ML) connecting products in different rooms.

3.2.1 Infra Red Link

The Infra Red Datalink from the remote control to the Master use a modulation frequency of 455 kHz. Data-speed is 160 bit/s, messages are 17 bit long, with 9 bit for synchronisation and address and 8 bit for the command.

3.2.2 Source Link

The Source Link interconnects audio or video Sources to the Master in a bus structure. The signals on the SL are stereo line signals, composite video signal and sync./red/blue/green video signals. Data-communication is the same as Master Link.

3.2.3 Master Link

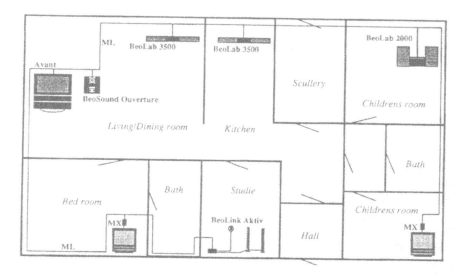

Fig. 2.   Illustration of the Master Link bus concept

The Master Link is the inter-room link, it interconnects Masters and Link-products from different rooms in a bus structure (see fig. 2). It uses three screened twisted pairs of wires: two pairs for left and right stereo signal, balanced line level and one pair for a balanced 1 Volt peak-peak data-signal. 16 products and 200 m wire can be connected without repeaters. The video signal is distributed on a coax, high-frequency modulated in the PAL standard.

Data-communication is two way at 19.2 kBit/s with collision detection. A RS 232 like protocol, adapted for the two-way bus structure, is used. The command protocol supports variable length data: simple commands, complex commands and status. The display protocol supports menu passing and client/server fill in fields. The protocol also have implemented algorithms for dynamic and automatic configuration of "newcomers" on the bus.

4 Market experiences

We have 15 years of experience from the market. These are product experiences being feed back to product development, marketing experiences and commercial experiences.

4.1 Commercial status

Beolink gives additional business for Bang & Olufsen, because we are able to sell more to customers. The synergetic combination of audio and video means sales of both audio and video to customers. We have evidence, that 25% of all Bang & Olufsen televisions being sold today are linked up to a Bang & Olufsen audio system at the customer. Multiroom systems means additional sales of loudspeakers. For every second audio master we sell also a linkroom, this accounts for 30% of the total loudspeaker sales. "Big ticket sales" of more than 25,000 DEM per ticket is estimated to account for 20% of total turnover.

4.2 Dealer experiences

This commercial reality did not come overnight. It is a result of an evolution where dealers played an important role, and where we learned from experience.

Making marketing and sales people understanding the consumer benefits of Beolink was the first hurdle. It is not self-evident, and in fact the best way to be convinced is to live with Beolink for a period. In our case a few dealers understood the consumer benefits and the concept from the beginning. They initiated the business. Today 20% of Bang & Olufsen dealers generate appreciable turnover from Beolink, so there is still room for improvements.

Selling Beolink is not a "cash and carry" and "plug and play" business. The sales person must demonstrate and advise the customer. Together they have to sit down and custom-design a Beolink system to the specific and individual needs of each customer. It takes time and it demands skills.

Installation at the customer is needed. To set up a multiroom Beolink-installation it is necessary to mount cables, plugs, connectors, infra red receivers and boxes around the house, and preferably hidden. Also this needs special skills. It is also necessary to make option set up of the products, in cases where it is not a main stream installation.

Compatibility is an issue. In many cases the customer already have Bang & Olufsen equipment, which should be used in the Beolink installation. If this equipment is not from the same season, compatibility has to be considered. Specifications change and are further developed. What is possible, and what is not possible must be sorted out, and maybe software has to be updated.

We offer a computerised configuration guide to dealers as a tool when designing and specifying a Beolink-installation. Documentation of products, options, accessories and compatibility is found in this guide.

Of the 20% of dealers selling Beolink, some have become very advanced. They do no limit themselves to audio-video installations. They combine the Beolink with control of other functions such as light, curtains, windows, doors, door cameras, heating, cooling, ventilation. They are pioneering home automation. Today Bang & Olufsen only supports sales of audio-video Beolink. The dealer is on his own regarding the other controls, and he solves this with tailor made gateways from the Beolink.

4.3 Marketing experiences

Beolink is only sold, if the sales people understand and value the benefits. In addition to that, they must have certain knowledge about technical matters, and they must have confidence about their own skills regarding this. If not, they are not likely to start explaining and selling. Training of sales persons is therefore an important parameter in making the Beolink business a success.

In the beginning we did not support Beolink in marketing at all. Dealers were on their own, and only a few found out. The next step, was to support Beolink by documenting all available specifications and accessories in booklets to dealers and by printing leaflets explaining Beolink to consumers. It became an accessory business.

Then we made sales packages with all accessories necessary for making for instance a linkroom with extra speakers. This made Beolink easier to understand and to handle for the dealer. Beolink became a product.

Today we have started producing integrated Beolink products. A linkroom speaker with built in infra red remote control receiver, a display and the switching relay. All you need is to connect the cable from the main room. It is a "plug and play" product.

5   Future directions and strategies

With the present Beolink infrastructure, we believe to be in a good position for future developments. We see several possibilities for expansion. The present Beolink business is not fully exploited, next there is evidence, that home automation finally is starting to take off commercially, and last but not least the multimedia convergence of computer, telecommunications and audio-video technologies creates new possibilities.

It is a fact that only 20% of Bang & Olufsen dealers actively sell Beolink. We want to make Beolink a core business for 75% of our dealers. The strategy to achieve this, is to simplify and to reduce complexity, by making Beolink "plug and play". The vehicles are the Master Link and new dedicated Beolink "plug and play" products.

The most advanced dealers are today making home automation installations with Beolink on their own. We want to expand Beolink to cover home automation installations. We do however not want to develop and produce these controllers, other companies are much better at that. The strategy is therefore to participate in partnerships, where different competencies are brought to the table of each partner. The vehicles are the Beolink terminal, on screen display of the television and gateways from the Master Link to other control links.

And finally the most debated subject in consumer electronics at the moment: multimedia. It is made possible by the convergence of computer, tele-communication and audio-video technologies. This convergence creates new possibilities. A significant growth in information processing in the home is foreseen. Information highways will bring: video on demand, home banking, home shopping, home working, interactive games, e-mail, e-magazines and so on to the home.

Many observers expect the computer and the television to converge. And for sure the technologies inside will converge. But we do not believe the way of using a computer and a television will overlap fully. There will always be two: a single user productivity oriented userconcept like the computer and a group user entertainment oriented userconcept like the television.

We have the intention to make the television an interactive device, that can access relevant programmes and multimedia services of the future.

The biggest challenge is to make the television infrastructure support interactive sessions. The personal computer already has the windows platform as an efficient tool for communication and interactivity. In the audio-video world there are several potential graphic based platforms, for this communication. Level 3 teletext which has already been mentioned is a candidate and the cd-interactive platform is another. This leads to the real important issue, that the audio-video industry agrees on a common interface platform for interactivity, and supports it.

The Beolink infrastructure is prepared for this. The processor architecture can be updated, the Master Link can be expanded to support client/server graphic based sessions and gateways to external communication networks can also be made. The strategy for Bang & Olufsen is partnerships in the converging business and international standardisation.

6 Conclusion

Bang & Olufsen has already made good business from the Beolink concept. The infrastructure can be further developed to connect to the information highway of the future. And we believe, that the television has a bright future as an interactive entertainment device.

Out-of-home Infrastructures

Oracle Media - Enabling the Information Age

Mary Callaghan
Oracle Corporation UK, United Kingdom

1   Industry overview

There will be major changes in the way businesses operate. Telephone, cable, hardware, and software companies are revamping the computing and communications infrastructure to create an Information Highway - a new popular network that will link the providers and consumers of information, entertainment, goods, and services.

New technologies, new business visions, and new financing are converging to form a backbone for this new electronic marketplace. Breakthroughs in network, data compression, video, computing, and software technologies, combined with appealing applications such as entertainment-on-demand, home shopping, education services, videoconferencing, and personalized publishing are driving this movement forward.

The Information Highway will provide a new distribution channel that will transform the nature of commerce. It will affect everyone: manufacturers, service providers, distributors, retailers, advertising media, and consumers. Manufacturers and service providers will be able to understand their markets better and produce more effective products because they will have more detailed customer requirements information. They will also be able to target the sales process more accurately and cut their distribution costs significantly by using electronic distribution methods. Distributors and retailers will also harness the power of information by providing electronic stores for the public. Consumers will benefit from the availability of highly personalized goods and services. They will pay less for these goods and services as retailers and service providers lower the overhead costs of operating physical stores. Consumers will also benefit from the convenience of instant access to a global set of merchants. They will be able to select from a multitude of novel entertainment, information, education, product, and communications offerings.

The construction of this electronic highway and marketplace is an immense challenge, both financially and technically. The sheer size of the investment required in laying down the fiber optic network is daunting. Telecommunications and cable companies will spend tens of billions of dollars improving the network and switches. Electronic service providers will spend billions of dollars creating their new "production" systems. An equal amount will be spent to outfit each home with a set-top (or other home electronics device) and to pay for the new services available on it.

Technically, this transformation of the business landscape depends on the smooth integration of the dozens of different hardware, software, and networking systems selected by these companies and the public. This integration is complicated by the rapid pace of technological progress that generates better solutions to each section of the Information Highway on a regular basis. The electronic marketplace is also moving into new technical areas by combining alphanumeric data with multimedia - pictures, freeform text, video, and audio - further increasing the complexity of the task.

For example, business applications like home shopping will pose complex challenges to the Information Highway. They will require a large volume of information - catalogs, photographs, fitting charts, promotional videos, inventories, and customer profiles. That information must be organized effectively to make it easy for consumers to browse through merchandise and purchase goods. Home shopping services will also handle inquiries, advertisements, purchases, credit checks, transfers, and other correspondence that will have to be routed accurately and securely. Customers from all over the world, using a variety of different home electronics, set-top, computer, and cellular devices will need easy access to the electronic stores. Links to the databases and operations of other businesses - suppliers, banks, shipping companies, and credit bureaus - will also need to be in place. Handling this diverse combination of requirements is a comlex task.

2   Oracle: The information management company

As a leading company in the management and distribution of complex information, Oracle is qualified to provide the software core for this new electronic marketplace. Its expertise in large-scale relational databases is crucial to the smooth functioning of the complicated services and transactions that will take place in the electronic marketplace. Oracle has a number of key strengths in its software architecture: portability, reliability, scalability, and open standards.

2.1   Portability equals hardware independence

As companies create new applications for the electronic marketplace, they need to confront the reality of a rapidly changing, heterogeneous technology landscape. Network providers will be using a variety of server hardware, communications networks, and application environments. Consumers will enjoy a multitude of new home electronics appliances. Electronic goods and services vendors will design their operations around a varied set of hardware and software.

Oracle technology deals with the challenges of solving business problems in a heterogeneous environment. Already running on more than 100 different hardware and operating systems around the world, the Oracle7 Server allows customers to develop applications that are fully portable among different hardware systems. Oracle's networking software, SQL*Net, links applications running at different platforms. Together, these products enable companies to develop mission-critical business applications that are stable, secure, and can run on any platform. Customers can move these applications as needed to take advantage of improvements in the price-performance of new hardware.

2.2 Reliability for continuous use

As usage of the Information Highway skyrockets, users will demand service 24 hours a day, 7 days a week. Oracle has traditionally supplied products for high-volume, transaction oriented applications. Using sophisticated techniques in redundancy, back-up, and security: This products set standards for high availability.

2.3 Scalability for smooth growth

Given the range and variety of interactive multimedia applications, companies need information management architectures that will scale to their requirements. Oracle designs its database management systems to adapt to different platforms with different processing capabilities. Developers can create an application for a dozen users and later deploy it to several hundred thousand customers - making the transition by merely upgrading their hardware.

Oracle is also a pioneer in porting its database management systems to massively parallel processing (MPP) architectures. The cost-efficient computing power of these machines will be extremely useful to many applications like entertainment-on-demand which will require hundreds of thousands of "information streams" that can carry movies, articles, music, or other products to individual homes.

2.4 Open standards for industry cooperation

Oracle realizes that it will not be able to solve all of its customers' problems alone, and actively seeks to collaborate with hardware and other software companies. In order to ensure that its customers receive the best applications possible, Oracle publishes its interfaces and data structures for use by third-party applications developers and has a strong Business Alliance Program to support these vendors.

3 Oracle and multimedia

Oracle has made critical breakthroughs in the management of "unstructured" datatypes - pictures, free-form text (memos, news articles, books), audio, and video - that will allow these datatypes to be easily incorporated into the electronic marketplace. Until recently, information management has focused on "structured" data which lends itself to organization in relational tables: invoices, financial ledgers, salas records, and other forms that have organization or structure embedded in them. Oracle7 allows users to search and manipulate this information quickly and efficiently.

With the rise of new applications such as entertainment-on-demand and personalized publishing, users now need to be able to manipulate information objects - movies and text articles - in the same way that they previously dealt with structured data. However, these new multimedia formats do not have a simple tabular structure. They are much larger than traditional data types and are more difficult to store. Audio and video data must also be delivered to the user in a continuous, real-time stream. Video cannot stop/start or slow down as system usage increases. These requirements pose a major challenge to traditional systems that break up data into small parcels and shuttle it through networks to be reassembled at the end-user site, or assume that "response times" of one second are acceptable.

3.1   Oracle Media

Oracle Media combines new technological advances that handle these requirements with the core design strengths of the Oracle Server. It dramatically expands the power of the Oracle7 Server by managing the storage, transport, and use of multimedia information. Home shopping applications will now be able to promote products by including photographs and advertising videos. Publishers will be able to create customizable magazines that allow individual readers to combine articles from all over the world. Schools will be able to create video classrooms to leverage teachers and scarce expertise and resources. Movie producers will be able to target special interest films to specific audiences.

Oracle Media presently consists of three products: Oracle Media Server - multimedia database management software; Oracle Media Net - client-server networking for interactive multimedia; and Oracle Media Objects - an application development and runtime environment. Together, these products create an open, virtual operating environment - a public platform - that gives companies independence from specific hardware and software environments. Companies can move forward into the new interactive multimedia marketplace using Oracle Media to construct their new businesses. Oracle Media can help companies grow smoothly and retain the freedom to transfer to ever-improving underlying technology.

Oracle Media Products - Oracle Media Server, Oracle Media Net, and Oracle Media Objects - form a layer between the hardware and the applications (see fig. 1). They provide translation services between the hardware platform (with its native operating system) and specific applications. They also provide needed services for organizing data, managing data traffic, protecting transaction integrity, ensuring system security, bridging to network protocols, and other system maintenance functions.

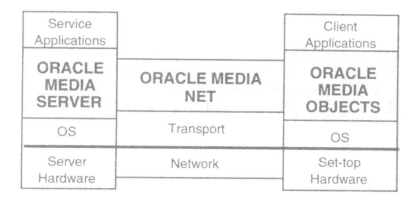

Fig. 1.   Oracle Media Architecture

3.2   Oracle Media Server

Oracle Media Server is a database management system that works with multimedia data types. It solves the major challenges of storing, manipulating, and distributing audio, video, image, and text information. Companies can now build interactive applications that incorporate both the core relational database features of Oracle7 as well as movies, music, memos, and other multimedia objects.

Because the Oracle environment is scalable, customers can build databases that serve from tens of users to hundreds of thousands of users. For example, a movie studio or cable company could easily build a movies-on-demand server that stores and manages the distribution of films. As the requirement or technology change, the company can upgrade its server, network, or client hardware and yet keep its application and business intact.

Oracle Media Server is also portable and will run on any server harware. One of the first implementations has been on an innovative and powerful architecture called massively parallel processing (MPP). This combination of the Oracle Media Server and MPP hardware delivers movies to tens of thousands of home consumers concurrently - at a fraction of the price of previous technology.

3.3   Oracle Media Net

Oracle Media Net enables applications to move all types of data across diverse network hardware. The interactive applications that will form the core of the initial electronic marketplace offerings pose many technical challenges for the network. For example, video and audio must be transported in real time with no interruptions or delays in order to be usable. Consumers will not de willing to wait, frozen midstream in a movie scene, while the rest of the data arrives.

Oracle Media Net solves the problem of managing the flow of data between the servers and clients. Oracle Media Net packages multimedia information, routes it through the networks with the appropriate priority and handling instructions, makes

sure it arrives at its destination, and than unpacks it for use at the other end.
Developers can create their applications without worrying about the constantly
changing complexity of the networks.

3.4   Oracle Media Objects

Oracle Media Objects is a complete authoring environment for creating compelling
interactive multimedia applications. Applications developed in Oracle Media
Objects can be deployed on the multitude of platforms and devices, ranging from
set-top boxes and game machines to personal digital assistants and desktop
computers. Developers who use Oracle Media Objects to create their applications to
other platforms without rewriting.

Oracle Media gives companies and developers the best of both worlds: an open
standard. Its architecture provides both investment security and technological
flexibility. Oracle publishes the application programming interfaces (APIs) for each
product so that they can be used by any hardware or software third party. It allows
developers to leverage the best features of each hardware and software system while
remaining independent of any closed environment. For example, a developer writing
a game application for a set-top box, computer, or other home electronics device
with unique features could use the machine's native authoring tools, along with
Oracle Media Net to manage network communication and Oracle Media Server to
store and run the core functions and data.

4   Oracle Media: driving the industry

Oracle has created the first multimedia engine and environment suitable for
deployment. Oracle Media is not just a trial system. Each element is designed to
meet the cost profile defined by the market. The cost per video stream, the cost per
set-top box, the scalability of server architecture, and the ability to work with
existing and new networks all attest to a clear understanding of the technical and
financial reality of the market. For example, Oracle Media Objects is explicitly
designed to run on a home electronics device with minimal computing and memory
capabilities. Oracle Media is designed to provide a seamless transition from
smallscale implementation to full public deployment.

Just as in any other infrastructure development, the first investors will be those
who most clearly see a rapid return. In the electronic marketplace, these investors
are likely to be telecommunication, cable, and entertainment companies. However,
the applications and demand for the Oracle Media do not end with these industries.
Corporate customers of Oracle7 are also pursuing a range of compelling applications such as videoconferencing, training, and document management. Oracle
envisions that providers of goods and services to the public as well as internal
corporate applications will soon expand the market for Oracle Media .

5   The Oracle solution

Leading multimedia server, set-top, and networking hardware manufacturers, as well as many telecommunication, cable, and entertainment companies have approached Oracle to collaborate in this effort. Oracle has explicit alliances to pursue specific market opportunities as well as a variety of joint technology development efforts to build links and portability with emgerging technologies.

In addition, the Oracle Consulting Group has teams experienced in finding solutions to companies' complex business goals. It is now working with several companies in creating this new interactive multimedia marketplace. Oracle Consulting Group will assist in creating applications with Oracle Media to run on a company's chosen server, network, and set-top hardware.

Oracle Media will help break through the financial and technical challenges to drive the industry forward quickly and profitably. In this coming year, the public will see full scale implementation of this new infrastructure several markets. Compelling services and applications will fuel the growth until a rich electronic marketplace becomes a reality accessible by all.

Oracle Corporation has created the software infrastructure for this emerging industry. Oracle Media Server, Oracle Media Net, and Oracle Media Objects together are the open standards vital to integrating each sector of the industry and allowing them to thrive.

6   Summary

Oracle Corporation is positioned to push forward the Information Highway and interactive multimedia revolution by solving some of the challanges of this emerging industry. Building on this broad experience in managing and moving complex information. Oracle has expanded its relational database management system (RDBMS) core to work with multimedia objects such as video, audio, graphics, images, and text. Oracle is also harnessing its open, flexible architecture - currently running on more than 100 platforms and operating systems - to facilitate the vital cooperation between the diverse, hardware and software components of the new industry. The new Oracle Media provides an open standard for the central infrastructure in this emerging electronic marketplace.   ·

References

Oracle, and SQL*Net are registered trademarks.
Oracle7 and Oracle Media Server are trademarks of Oracle Corporation.
Oracle Consulting Group is a Server.
All other company and product names mentioned are used for identification purposes only, and may be trademarks of their respective owners.

SmartCards as Carrier of Personal Data and Documents

Bruno Struif
German National Research Center for Computer Science (GMD), Germany

1 Technology

In 1968, two German inventors received the first patent for chipcards: Jürgen Dethloff and Helmut Gröttrup (see fig. 1). At that time nobody recognized which importance the chipcard technology would get later. The subject of the patent was an identificand, which could be represented by a card, a key or a token. The main feature of the identificand was an integrated circuit able to communicate with an identificator (i.e. a service device) by means of optical, capacitive, inductive or galvanic coupling. Contact-oriented cards as well as contactless cards have been anticipated, a fascinating and revolutionary invention.

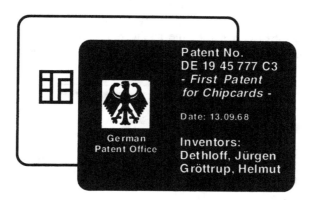

Fig. 1. Chipcard with first patent of chipcards

The roots of chipcard technology lie therefore in Germany, however, the first chipcard applications have been performed in France. A major role was taken by the French journalist Roland Moreno whose first chipcard patents are dated from 1976.

Already since many years, chipcard technology is applicable, and the enormous power and potential influence of this technology on every day processes becomes more and more evident. But until now only a few have understood, that there are cards in the market, where a real computer represented by a microprocessor chip is hidden in the plastic. Microprocessor cards, usually addressed as smartcards, belong therefore to the family of computers (see fig. 2), which starts with the most powerful supercomputer and ends up with the smartcard. Also memory cards have some intelligence and often security functions, but they are not programmable.

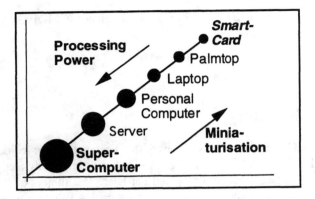

Fig. 2.   The smartcard as member of the computer family

A block diagram of a microprocessor chip shows the components of such a miniaturized computer (see fig. 3): there is the CPU, which executes more then 1 million instructions per second, and there are different types of storage: the RAM is the working memory, the ROM is the memory containing the smartcard operating system and the EEPROM carries the applications. So called crypto chips have additionaly a co-processor suitable for the calculation of complex cryptographic algorithms.

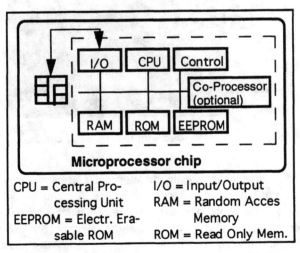

Fig. 3.   Simplified block diagram of a microprocessor chip in a smartcard with contacts

The smartcard operating system provides services for applications on the basis of commands. They offer usually a set of more or less powerful security functions and are suitable for the support of security sensitive applications. Fig. 4 shows an example for structuring access rights to an electronic document.

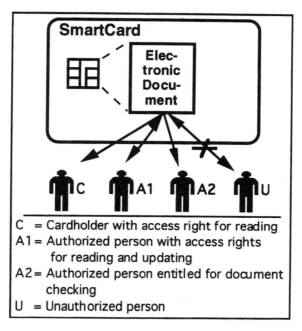

C = Cardholder with access right for reading
A1 = Authorized person with access rights
        for reading and updating
A2 = Authorized person entitled for document
        checking
U = Unauthorized person

Fig. 4. ·Electronic document and access rights (example)

SmartCards have usually a file organisation according to the ISO/IEC standard 7816-4 "Inter-industry commands for interchange". The files may have different data structures (see fig. 5):
- records with fixed length
- records with variable length
- records in a cyclic arrangement
- transparent structure

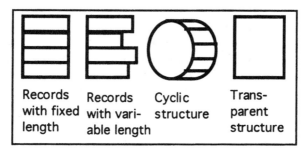

Records with fixed length   Records with variable length   Cyclic structure   Transparent structure

Fig. 5. File data structures

Records with fixed or *variable length* are designed for data sets with fixed or variable length. The *cyclic structure* is used for storing logging information e.g. information about performed transactions. Files with *transparent structure* contain data with a data structure not visable for the chip operating system, e.g. an electronic document.

The forthcoming technology will provide chips with more memory capacity thus enabling the storing of smartcard databases. In standardization process is the definition of an SCQL language (Structured Card Query Language), which will be a subset of the widespread used SQL. An SCQL data base contains data objects: tables, views and dictionaries. The security features allow to specify the access conditions and privileges, which describe actions performable on data objects: insertion, reading, updating and erasing.

A view is a logical sight on a table and is used to define further restrictions such as shown in fig. 6.

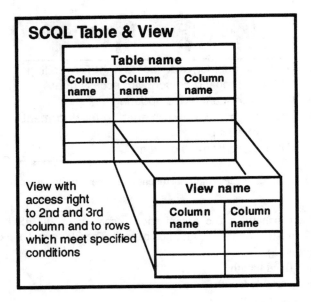

Fig. 6.   SCQL table & view

SmartCards allow also to perform special operations, e.g.
- mathematical functions such as incrementing and decrementing of values or change of currencies e.g. for the construction of a multinational electronic purse
- cryptographic functions such as encryption and decryption of data or computation and verification of digital signatures.

Digital signatures get more and more importance in a society which makes more and more use of information technology (IT) and electronic transmission of documents and messages. Digital signatures have the quality to allow trustworthy communications, since the authorship and the authenticity of a signed document is provable. Fig. 7 shows the production and verification of digital signatures applying the RSA algorithm defined by Rivest, Shamir and Adleman.

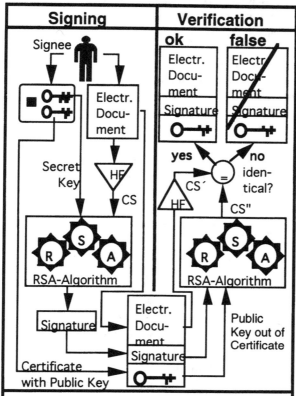

Each signee owns a keypair, consisting of a se-cret and a public key. The relationship signee/keypair is guaranteed by a certificate from a trustcenter. When signing, at first a checksum CS is calculated from the document to be sig-ned by applying a hash function HF. Then the checksum is transformed by the RSA signature algorithm using the signee's secret key. The transformation result is the digital signature. When verifying, the signature is retransformed by the signature algorithm using the signee´s public key out of the certificate. The result is a checksum which will be compared with that one derived from the actual document. If both are identical then the electronic document is au-thentic and has been signed by the signee.

Fig. 7.   Production/verification of a digital signature using the RSA algorithm

2   Applications

In the private domain a lot of IT systems and devices are in use, e.g.
- telephones with or without voice recorder
- mobile communication devices
- fax systems
- radio and television systems
- computers of all kind with or without network interface
- video recorders and CD-ROM systems
- videotex systems
- multimedia devices

Also chipcards have already entered the private sphere and will conquer further application areas. The use of chipcards started with telephone cards which work anonymously and which carry no personal data. Beside of this type, also chipcards for public phones are in use, which carry person oriented accounting information. Also the chipcards used for mobile communications ("GSM cards") carry personal information needed for billing.

Another application area relevant to private life is health care. In Germany, the health insurances launched a nationwide application in 1993 based on a federal law (first nationwide application in the world on the health care sector). 80 million cards are now issued. These cards are used in doctor's practices for delivering the insurance data in a machine-readable form. People interested to read the health insurance card in their private environment can buy e.g. a palmtop with a PCMCIA-card reader and software able to communicate with the health insurance card. Besides administrative applications in health care a lot of medical applications are under development or in field trials. Fig. 8 shows such applications.

Access to medical data shall not have only professionals in accordance to their qualification and privileges, but also the patient himself. His right of reading the data stored in his card shall not only be executable, e.g. in the doctor's practice, but also at home with appropppriate hard- and software equipment. To avoid un- authorized access, the data in a patient card have to be protected: the patient uses a Personal Identification No. (PIN) and a professional his professional card for proving his access rights.

Also banks and creditcard organisations use already or plan to introduce the chipcard as a new media for payment applications. The loading of an electronic purse shall not only be possible on special machines e.g. in the premises of a bank, but also from home using e.g. a phone with integrated chipcard reader and display. Further services to be performed at home using a PC with network interface are related e.g. to financial transactions which may be protected by a digital signature.

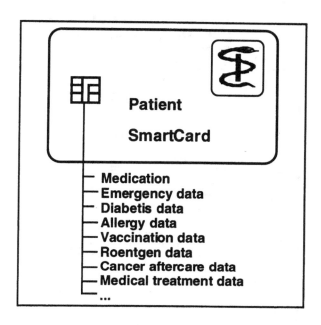

Fig. 8. Medical applications (examples)

Another type of application where chipcards are used at home, which carry personal data or data related to the personal environment or behaviour is video on demand or Pay-TV. With respect to access to information of all kind and not only to movies, new services will come up with the increasing usage and availability of Information Highways and concepts like "World Wide Web". The chipcard may be used in such a context for access purposes, electronic payment, and signing of orders.

Also car manufacturers have in mind to provide chipcards for different services. One of them is the "electronic car maintenance book". It is obvious that it is of interest for the car owner, to get displayed the maintenance data in his private environment.

Chipcards will also be used for carrying identification documents and official certificates such as a driver licence. From a technical point of view, these documents will be a structured data set using e.g. the encoding scheme of ASN.1 (Abstract Syntax Notation One). Since in such a document a photo and a handwritten signature of the in the document referred person may occur, so called inter-industry data elements have been already standardized for such a purpose. In order to be able to verify the authenticity of such an official document the digital signature mechanism will be applied. Fig. 9 shows a typical example of an electronic document.

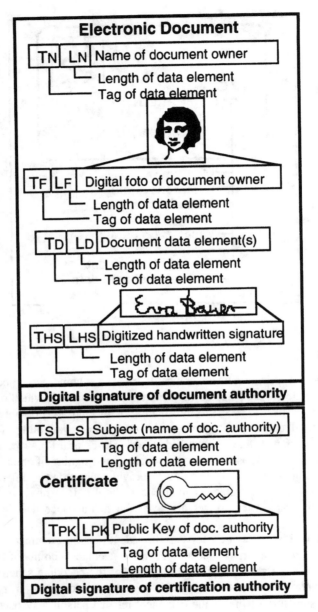

Fig. 9. General structure of an electronic document (example)

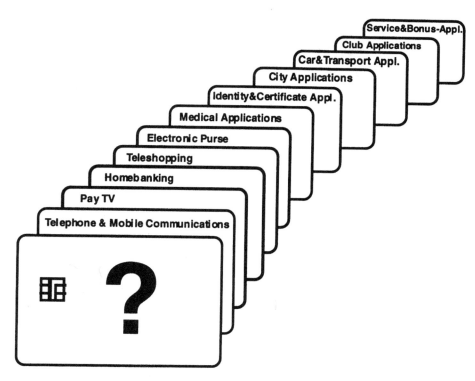

Fig. 10. Example of application areas of chipcards with personal data or personal environment related services

The phantasy cannot be rich enough to forsee all the forthcomming applications (see fig. 10). Also clubs, warehouses and enterprises of different types have or will introduce chipcard based applications. Chipcards have become a strong tool and a tremendous force for innovations. They will change and influence our behaviour as computers always do. It is therefore a great challenge, to develop and use chipcards in such a way, that we may benefit from this kind of technology and avoid technology induced consequences not wanted.

Deutsche Telekom's Network Platform for Interactive Video Services

Norbert Maassen
Deutsche Telekom AG, Section for Network-oriented Product and Service
Development, Germany

1   Dawn of a new media age

When pictures learned to walk.

The film business - or perhaps one should say the cinema - is one hundred years old this year. In October 1954, that is, some 40 years ago, TV entered the homes of our country with channel one's first news broadcast, the "ARD Tagesschau". The digital media age that is almost upon us will catapult the TV viewer into a new career: from a viewer to a programmer. The next few years will show how much use he makes of this opportunity.

A trend will get under way at the end of the 90s that will have an impact on our daily lives. Right now, only a blurred outline of this can be seen. Television and the computer are converging to form what is becoming widely known as the multimedia. The driving force behind this trend is coming from two directions and from two different markets:

- On the one hand, the traditional office communication applications, which are still separate (the transmission of text, data and moving images), will converge and also increasingly be used in private homes. Service experts speak here of PC-based and window-oriented interactive multimedia communication.
- On the other hand, the mass means of communication, television, will become "bidirectional" and open the market for interactive, multimedia mass communication.

Both markets can probably be served from a uniform technological platform in the medium term. Entirely new applications will then become possible as the costs for calls and terminal equipment drop - which will result in an enormous expansion of the entire market.

2   Evolution of services

If we take a look at the promising new range of multimedia services for residential customers, we see that these involve the so-called interactive video services. The term video services is a global term designating the entire field of video distribution and retrieval services as well as interactive services, as shown in the following diagram (see fig. 1).

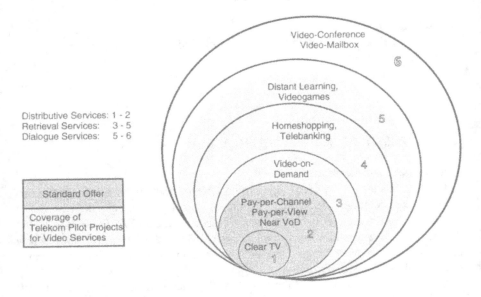

Distributive Services: 1 - 2
Retrieval Services: 3 - 5
Dialogue Services: 5 - 6

Standard Offer
Coverage of Telekom Pilot Projects for Video Services

Video-Conference
Video-Mailbox
6

Distant Learning,
Videogames
5

Homeshopping,
Telebanking
4

Video-on-
Demand
3

Pay-per-Channel
Pay-per-View
Near VoD
2

Clear TV
1

Fig. 1.   Evolution of video services

From a commercial point of view, the "pay TV" class of distribution services is an important starting point that paves the way for this new spectrum of products. The different forms include:

- Pay per Channel (PPC): well-known example in Germany: "Premiere"
- Pay per View (PPV): future advantage: you pay only for what you have seen
- Near Video on Demand (NVoD): the user can choose from a limited number of films offered - for example, top ten - with a reasonable waiting period - for example, 15 min. With regard to pay TV, it is noteworthy that not only will there be a transition from analog to digital signal processing in the near future but also, for the first time, there will be a backward or signalling channel. PPV and NVoD require a narrowband backward channel, if only sporadically, for the data needed to bill the customer for use made of the service. Home shopping should also be mentioned here, especially since this form of direct-response commercial has turned many a tired zapper into a spontaneous bargain hunter - a parallel evolutionary path in the direction of interactive video services, so to speak.
- In the future, interactive home shopping will involve not only giving a command to place an order, but also having an influence on the contents of what is shown, from a catalogue to a virtual showroom.
- Just like the armchair buying frenzy in front of the TV set, there will be two kinds of video games in the foreseeable future, first, the "simple" software

download onto the PC or console and second, the interactive adventure via the network-based server with "real" or "virtual" players. While the first version can already be implemented as a pay program, the second places considerable demands on the network's ability to respond (bottleneck signalling channel).

- Video on Demand (VoD), as a leading technological product, should also be mentioned. The user decides for himself when he wants to see what program, paying for what is requested. Video recorder functions are also provided, which are made possible with the interactive, digital broadband transmission channel together with the narrowband signalling channel.
- Video conferences and video mailbox are mentioned here as examples of future, enhanced multimedia services with a focus on business customers. The inclusion of online services via gateways is also being discussed.

3   Deutsche Telekom's role

The cards will be reshuffled in the future interactive video service business. New opportunities are also opening up for Deutsche Telekom AG (German Telecom) to position itself in an ever fiercer competitive environment:

- In the *transport business*: As the operator of the world's largest broadband distribution network (cable TV access) and owing to its leading role in the installation of fiber-optic accesses (OPAL), Deutsche Telekom already has created the prerequisites for the mass market of the future.
- In the *broker business*: A large potential demand can be opened up in a relatively short period of time through the network infrastructure - on the condition that the products offered can be properly brought to the customer. Deutsche Telekom will operate a server-based broker platform for this purpose.
- In the *program business*: Even though Deutsche Telekom does not provide the contents of programs, it plays a supporting role in editing and storing digital programs. Especially right now, at the beginning of the digital age, it is important to solve this "chicken or the egg problem". Suitable partners are being sought for this, for example, production studios or even VoD operators who have already gained initial experience.

3.1   Transport business

As already mentioned, Deutsche Telekom's broadband distribution networks, which have been installed on a large scale, provide favorable conditions for launching new video services. Right now, up to

- 31 PAL TV programs
- 36 UHF stereo sound broadcasting programs and
- 16 digital satellite radio programs

are being offered over a network that can serve 22 million households and to which 14 million households have already been connected (see fig. 2). Up to 15 other analog TV channels, each having a bandwidth of 8 MHz, are also available in the so-called hyperband, the frequency range between 300 and 450 MHz. The hyperband used to be reserved for the D2 MAC transmission standard.

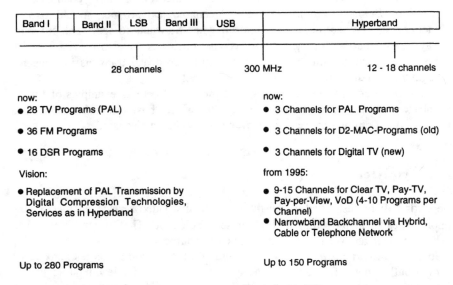

Fig. 2. Frequency range in cable TV networks

In quantitative terms, the existing digitization or related compression technology produces a tenfold increase in the number of available channels. In figures, it turns 15 channels into 150. This will clear up the channel shortage that frequently occurs.

In qualitative terms, digitization makes it possible to have better-quality image and sound tranmission up to high definition TV (HDTV). The focus here, however, will be on developing new, sophisticated services, from pay per view to home shopping, to fully interactive VoD and information services.

Deutsche Telekom has taken steps to install up to an additional 30 digital TV channels. 70 % of all the homes connected to cable TV will be able to profit from this in the short term. This means that at least the entire foreseeable demand can be met, which will primarily involve the distribution of foreign-language programs. These are very popular and will further enhance the attractiveness of cable TV. Additional channels can be provided as needed. Thus, Deutsche Telekom's product, the cable TV access, will in no way be inferior to direct reception via satellite. Deutsche Telekom is intensively preparing itself for the digital age in the media sector. This is clearly shown by its decision to stop investing in its own second-generation TV satellite system and instead, to take a stake in SES, the ASTRA operator. The main objectives of this cooperation are:

• to keep satellite and cable from developing in divergent directions

- to promote the development of uniform, simple and inexpensive terminal equipment for cable TV customers or subscribers to direct satellite broadcasting.

With its stake in SES, Deutsche Telekom has a business involvement in all satellite operating companies whose systems it uses for feeding programs into the cable network: in ASTRA, as a shareholder; in DFS Kopernikus, as the sole shareholder; and in EUTELSAT, as a signatory.

3.2 The broker business

In its role as a go-between, Deutsche Telekom sees it as its responsibility to ensure that all market partners have equal opportunities to gain access to the transport platform. What, from a strategic point of view, can be seen as an extention of the traditional transport business, will turn out to be a necessary and helpful link between supply and demand. I am talking here about a number of Deutsche Telekom support services, such as:

Buyer functions
- obtaining information
- ordering
- paying

Supplier functions
- providing customers with market information
- providing customer data
- sending out advertising
- processing orders
- encryption of contents
- billing and collection

Setting up and operating electronic markets
- providing server and storage capacity

These functions are offered by Deutsche Telekom in a competitive environment. In other words, if a service provider wants to have a direct link to his customers, the Deutsche Telekom menu, including the support services behind it, can be suppressed (level 1 gateway).

The broker platform needed for this looks, in principle, as shown in figure 3. Deutsche Telekom is developing the broker platform in several steps similar to the way described for the evolution of video services.

3.2.1 Pay TV market

The goals originally defined by the Media Service GmbH (MSG)
- creation of an open, uniform decoder infrastructure
- rapidly open up the market by offering an increased number of pay TV programs
- strengthen Germany as a location for the media

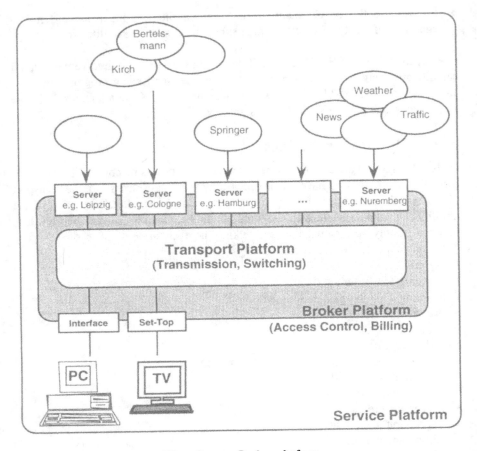

Fig. 3.   Broker platform

will be further pursued by Deutsche Telekom, taking into account the EU decision. The findings of the European DVB project (Digital Video Broadcasting) will be used in developing a suitable system platform. The products offered will range from "clear" TV, to (impulse) PPV, to NVoD. The modules that were identified as necessary are:

- encoder, scrambler, multiplexer
- transmission route studio-TV
- set-top box
- Subscriber Authorization System (SAS)
- Subscriber Management System (SMS)
- Card Issuing Center (CIC)

To ensure that the commercial launch will go smoothly and quickly for all concerned, Deutsche Telekom plans to call on both manufacturers and program providers to join corresponding working groups.

3.2.2 Interactive Video Services (IVS)

On the basis of experience gained with pay TV, Deutsche Telekom's broker platform will be expanded to include functions needed for interactive services. The main distinction between this platform and the pay TV structure is that multimedia servers will be installed in the network, which, in addition to having delivery and accounting mechanisms, will also reserve storage capacity for products. These products can be traditional programs (e.g. films) or complex "multimedia objects" for home shopping, telelearning, consisting of video, sound, graphic and text sequences.

Deutsche Telekom anticipates receiving major impetus for the development of IVS from its cooperation in DAVIC (Digital Audio Visual Council) and MHEG (Multimedia/Hypermedia Expert Group) as well as from its own research project IVES (Interactive Video Experimental System).

3.2.3 Legal aspects

In additional to the technical questions, the legal basis for this will also be investigated. With regard to Deutsche Telekom's broker platform, the following questions will be focused on:
- latitude Deutsche Telekom has for a directory service
- Deutsche Telekom as a service provider
- conditions of the Open Network Provision (level 1 gateway)
- data protection aspects:
    - making call data anonymous
    - limited storage time and guaranteed deletion
    - inaccessability for third parties

4 Pilot projects

Thanks to world-wide progress being made in the digitization, compression and transmission of video signals, such as Digital Video Broadcasting (DVB), Motion Picture Expert Group (MPEG) or Asynchronous Transfer Mode (ATM), and the capabilities of server systems, it is not only right to talk about interactive video services, but also to make them. This is, without a doubt, a risk investment, since there are currently more questions than answers about how much demand there will be for these services.

Thus, Deutsche Telekom is not only involved in planning a number of pilot projects initiated by various federal states or consortia, but has also introduced other pilot projects of its own with the aim of
- testing the interworking of conceptually different system solutions on the existing transport platforms (telephone network/ISDN, cable TV network, optical fiber) to determine which systems and possible combinations are preferable

- gaining experience for the further development of system components (servers, switches, transmission systems, set-top boxes)
- drawing conclusions for the expedient configuration of Deutsche Telekom access networks for offering new interactive video services economically

As plans now stand, there will be pilot projects in Hamburg, Cologne/Bonn, Leipzig, Stuttgart, Nuremberg and possibly Munich in the course of 1995. A demonstration project was launched in Berlin in February 1995 with some 50 "selected" cable TV customers.

4.1   Hamburg

The pilot project in downtown Hamburg will use the copper coaxial network as the transport platform. It was also possible to win the support of the Hamburg Chamber of Commerce for this project. A total of 1,000 people will be participating in this, 100 of whom will be testing specific interactive services.

4.2   Cologne/Bonn

One fiber-optic extension, also called a hybrid network, is being used in the Cologne/Bonn region to serve 100 test customers. The subscriber line is implemented via the passive coaxial network, i.e. the repeaterless part of the network.

4.3   Leipzig

The pilot project in Leipzig will take place on the transport platform of the fiber-optic network OPAL. In addition to video services with distribution and retrieval functions, interactive multimedia applications for business customers will also be possible with this network. 100 testers will have direct access here to the optical fiber highway.

4.4   Nuremberg

This pilot project was defined in an initiative taken by the city of Nuremberg and the Grundig company and supported by the State Government of Bavaria. 100 pilot project customers are to be served via the telephone network transport platform equipped with Asymmetric Digital Subscriber Line (ADSL) and another 900 via the traditional copper coaxial network on a trial basis. In this project, in particular, Deutsche Telekom intends to gain experience as a system integrator. It is the task of the system integrator to ensure the interworking of all necessary components, such as server, switches and settop boxes.

4.5   Stuttgart

Deutsche Telekom has, in principle, been given the go-ahead to participate with some 4,000 pilot project customers. The program, supported by the State

Government of Baden-Württemberg and the Alcatel SEL company and covering the Stuttgart area, is at the definition stage. Plans call for using a copper coaxial network as the transport platform with an optional fiber-optic extension.

Figure 4 shows the various projects (as of 12/94): The pilot projects, which are scheduled to run for 18 months, will provide insight into how ready the market is for the "daily use" of interactive video services. The programs offered will be crucial for the success of the new services. Since Deutsche Telekom does not offer programs itself, it will have to depend on the products of third parties. For this reason, it is already seeking to work out an extensive and attractive offer with suitable partners. An efficient broker platform will ensure that there is an alignment between supply and demand.

Place	Berlin	Stuttgart	Hamburg	Cologne/ Bonn	Nurem- berg	Munich	Leipzig
Number of Participants Distributive Services	50	max. 4000	1000	100	1000	1000*	100
Interactive Services	50	max. 4000	100	100	100	100*	100
Start	Feb. 95	II/95	II/95	II/95	II/95	still open	IV/95
Duration	1 year	1.5 years (in special cases up to 2 years)					
Offered Services	Pay per Channel, Pay per View, Pay-Radio, Near Video on Demand, Video on Demand, Service on Demand (Homeshopping, ...)						as in other pilots, additionally extended multimedia applications
Transport Platform	Hybrid**	Hybrid	CATV (Coaxial)	Hybrid	CATV/ ADSL	Hybrid	Optical Fiber (OPAL)
Back- channel Technology	Tele- phone	Hybrid	Tele- phone	Hybrid	Tele- phone/ ADSL	Hybrid	OPAL

*)   Current status of discussion
**)   Coaxial CATV Network and Optical Fiber

Fig. 4.   Comparison of pilot projects

Part Three

Applications

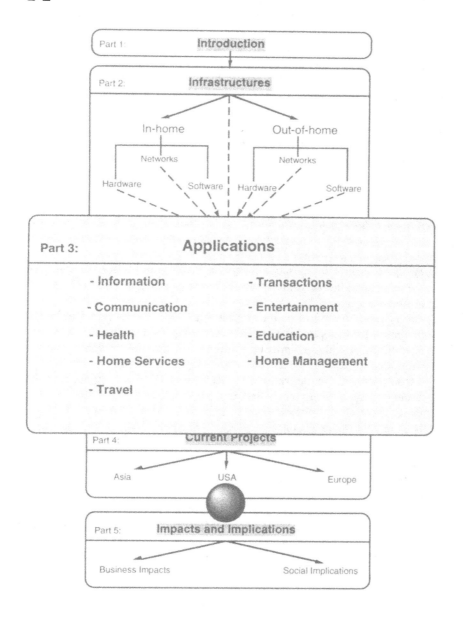

Part 1: Introduction

Part 2: Infrastructures

In-home   Out-of-home

Networks   Networks

Hardware   Software   Hardware   Software

Part 3: **Applications**

- Information   - Transactions

- Communication   - Entertainment

- Health   - Education

- Home Services   - Home Management

- Travel

Part 4: Current Projects

Asia   USA   Europe

Part 5: Impacts and Implications

Business Impacts   Social Implications

After the second chapter showed a couple of products which can be dubbed as "infrastructual components of the Information Superhighway" this section deals with the applications that - in order to meet the metaphor - make use of the highway infrastructure.

In general, all contributions of this section focus more on strategic and functional aspects of services rather than on an isolated product-oriented viewpoint. Hence, the status of reflection is one step ahead of those of the infrastructure chapter.

We can distinguish three different types of applications described in the articles to follow: *First* the group of applications which provides the private household with traditional services piggybacking the new, digital media, e.g. electronic reference information formerly presented in printed from (IBM, New Media Consulting). The *second* group brings completely new services exclusively enabled by the digital age, e.g. electronic agents (PACE). The *third* group adds a new value to a known services. This applies to home-shopping (debis, CD-matics) or the interactive forms of television (Eutelis Consult, Heinrich Bauer Verlag):

- *IBM* presents the development and the features of a citizen's information system.
- *New Media Consulting* shows how the world of reading will change under the influence of bits and bytes.
- *Philips Advanced Communication Enterprise (PACE)* describes an intelligent traffic application deploying smart agents and a new would-be networking standard.
- *Philips Consumer Electronics* covers the area of applications deriving from in-home networking of different devices which has not disclosed any fruitfull market up to now.
- *debis Sytemhaus* examines the process of a CD-ROM development as a system integrator for Europe's biggest mail order company 'Quelle'.
- *FORWISS* provides insights how information technology can support private shopping.
- *CD-Matics* uses the innovative CD-i and Tele-CD-i for electronic services; this could be a short-term success path to the new market.
- *Beate Uhse Group* pinpoints their activities to benefit from the Information Highway for their porn business. Though often neglected by analysts the market share is substantial and growing steadily.
- *Sega* reports about the most attractive application in the private sphere: interactive console gaming and future forms such as an interactive game channel on CATV.
- *Heinrich Bauer Verlag* reflect on the trends and evolution directions of the TV.
- *Eutelis Consult* analyses the often cited issue of interactive video services, its background and future scenario.
- *TNO Institute* presents an integrated environment for elderly and disabled people to manage their daily needs.

Central to the consideration of applications is the unexpected breadth and diversity of application types. It reaches from entertainment via transactional services (banking, shopping) to health services for elderly and disabled people. To keep this in mind is important because the residential applications of the Information Superhighway are wrongly equated with entertainment in all facettes like edutainment, infotainment or advertainment. However, to use the Information Highway for private uses means much more than having fun. Health or educational services are by far more essential for the economy as a whole, especially for the US which suffers from problems in its health (see the paper of the TNO Institute) or educational system. To overcome this is one of the reasons why the US National Information Infrastructure (NII) is so much supported by the Clinton/Gore government.

The objective of this chapter is to emphasize the diversity of the application types and the tension between seemingly wanted applications like entertainment and on the other hand more economically needed applications as health and education.

The Citizen's Information System "Dresden and the Frauenkirche (Church of Our Lady)" - Realization, Experiences, Prospects

Manuela Rost-Hein
International Business Machines (IBM), Germany

1   Introduction

The "Dresden and the Frauenkirche (Church of Our Lady)" citizen's information system informs residents and visitors about the 800 year history of the city, offers an overview of the most significant secular and religious architectural masterpieces and provides users with a detailed insight into the history of the Frauenkirche, built in 1726-43 by George Bähr. It is comprised of three chapters of equal length, each chapter equally important from a topical point of view. Some 350 pages of pictures and text shown on the screen are enhanced by historical and current documentary film sequences of about 40 minutes in length, 20 minutes of musical extracts from Dresden composers and singers, and quotations and poetry from leading literary figures and contemporary witnesses in Dresden. The multimedia application, that is provided in the form of a Point-of-Information (PoI) solution, is available on a daily basis and free of charge to those people visiting the pavilion on the Frauenkirche construction site. Furthermore, it is also available for purchase on a CD-ROM, whereby approximately 65% of the sales proceeds go towards the restoration. The technical equipment of the PoI system consists of an IBM pentium computer, a laser disc player and an IBM touch screen XT 21. It was decided not to compress the moving picture sequences in order to ensure maximum quality. The contents of the system have been transferred almost 1:1 to the CD-ROM, although the moving picture sequences have been compressed in MPEG standard.

1.1   How it all began

The archaeological reconstruction of Dresden's Frauenkirche (see fig. 1) is regarded as one of the greatest architectural challenges of this century. Never before has an attempt been made to rebuild an almost completely destroyed building with the original bricks which, upon completion of the church, will make up approximately one third of the entire construction.

Nevertheless, it is not only this fact that has lead to such an overwhelming amount of interest among the general public. The ruins of the church represented a peace memorial - even back in the days of the German Democratic Republic - and following a visit made by the Chancellor in autumn 1989, it became a symbol for the reconciliation of the East and West German states.

This interest is also reflected in the numerous amount of press releases and publications and is also the reason why the Frauenkirche construction site is one of the most well visited sites in the world. The Supporting Association for the Restoration of the Frauenkirche records no less than 2,000-3,000 visitors each day. A figure that naturally also reflects the increasing number of tourists visiting the city of Dresden. Since the fall of the Wall, Dresden has returned to being one of the most popular destinations in Germany.

Before it was destroyed during the war, Dresden was one of the most beautiful and lively cities in Europe. Even today, it still possesses valuable architectural masterpieces, formidable art collections and a great musical tradition. A number of reasons, therefore, for developing a citizen's information system - "Dresden and the Frauenkirche". Reasons that are indeed comprehensible for those looking in, yet they also followed an inner logic. IBM Germany has been supporting the restoration of the Frauenkirche since 1990 - a project that is primarily financed by private donations.

IBM's involvement and commitment is indeed complex. In addition to the transfer of funds and products, organization of charity concerts and support of general public relations work, an IBM employee, a so-called "secondee", has been especially released from his duties to work for three years on building up a marketing company with the aim of carefully, yet effectively marketing of the Frauenkirche.

In addition to its role as sponsor, IBM, as business partner to the consulting engineering firm, also provides solutions for the extremely complex task of archaeological reconstruction. IBM RS/6000 machines and the software tool CATIA enable architects to work with a 3-D model (see fig. 1). Without a function such as this, reconstruction projects of this kind would be almost inconceivable.

1.2   The virtual model

First of all a virtual reality simulation model was designed on the basis of this 3-D working model. This particular product unexpectedly attracted a great deal of attention when presented at the world's largest computer fair CeBIT in 1994 in Hanover. By putting on the data helmet, it was possible to take a walk through the virtual church (see fig. 1 and fig. 3).

The model was realized with the help of TDImage (Thomson Digital Image), the IBM Power Visualization System (PVS) - a RISC system working with 32 parallel processors - and the SP1 (8 x RS/6000) and several RS/6000 570 models. No less than 37 sources of light were used to create the interior of the church.

Fig. 1.   General view of the 3-D virtual reality model "Frauenkirche (Church of Our Lady)"

A remarkable computing performance was required in order to create the video of the photorealistic representation of the Frauenkirche (30 frames per second in HDTV television standard): up to eight megabytes memory for each picture, and for the entire video film, one million minutes of computing capacity on eleven IBM RS/6000 systems as well as a memory volume of about 45 gigabytes.

The outstanding attractiveness of the video, the overwhelming feedback following the CeBIT presentation and, last but not least, the obvious importance of the role of information technology in the case of this project provided further essential decision-making criteria for the development of the multimedia system. Furthermore, it became more and more evident just how an important role the restoration played for the public, the citizens of Dresden and in the media. There was a great need for information, the reconstruction of the church had always been a focal point of interest, time and time again.

1.3   Maximum target group optimization

Originally, the multimedia system was developed as a PoI system. Nevertheless, right from the start, the application was also planned to be additionally marketed as a CD-ROM product. That meant that the information system should address the interest of the largest possible target group. The PoI systems were designed for the visitor's pavilion on the Frauenkirche construction site and for other semi-public areas such as hotel lobbies, airports, and tourist information bureaus.

Following a successful start-up phase of the PoI systems in Dresden - an outstanding response in the media and among the general public, excellent feedback from users - the CD-ROM was then presented at CeBIT '95. Parallel to this, the disc went on sale in the visitor's pavilion. From the moment the CD-ROM was launched, a great demand was recorded both in the pavilion and at the CeBIT fair.

Back in the conception phase of the project, it was decided upon that the history of the church, its destruction and reconstruction must be embedded in the history and architecture of the city of Dresden (see fig. 2).

Fig. 2.   Example screen of the citizen's information screen showing aspects of the recovery operations

This, in our eyes, appeared to be a particularly good way of reaching as broad a target group as possible - Dresden fans, those people born in Dresden, those interested in history and architecture, educationalists, and multimedia freaks.

The wide range of persons within the target group, their age and interests, not only had an effect on the selection and depth of the topics involved, but was also reflected by a menu concept that was as simple as possible, comprehensible for even the most unversed user and quick to learn. Despite the considerable amount of data, after all there were 800 years of architecture, city and church history to convey, the system succeeded in offering the users an almost totally problem-free orientation. Observations that were made whilst the system was being introduced (in total six kiosks over a period of 2 weeks) confirm this statement.

A further indication of the fact that the information system fulfilled our expectations with regard to the target group was displayed by the presentation of the PoI system at the CeBIT. Throughout the fair, the author had the opportunity to hold a conversation with a number of visitors on the stand. This enabled him to find out where the interest in the application actually originated, which weaknesses were established and what was valued as particularly positive.

It was also interesting to observe the unfamiliar contact with such complex multimedia applications, even for the computer freaks visiting the CeBIT. Most of the reactions observed primarily showed the apparent undivided fascination for this new medium.

Visitors were most impressed by the ability of being able to "jump" within each of the chapters or from one topic to the next, taking a closer look at individual topics and, naturally, the virtual reconstruction in the form of video animation. The short film sequences that were blended into the system found some critic. However, this is a problem that relates to the current technological stand.

Menu management and the structure of specific themes were the two points most eagerly discussed. On the whole, however, it was agreed that the application adroitly "lead" the users through each of the topics. A great deal of attention was also paid to screen design. Because a lot of the material we had to work with was historical material from the archives, about 80% of the picture and film material is black and white. Besides the designer decided to use a gray background with only very few color elements. Early fears that the overall image would appear very colorless and boring were not confirmed. On the contrary: the design found great acceptance among all age categories and target groups.

The overall positive feedback was reflected once again in the great demand for the CD-ROM. Here, educationalists, multimedia freaks - surprisingly even the more "mature" freaks - Dresden and Frauenkirche fans showed particular interest in the product.

2　　The realization

A small team (designer, programmer and editor) worked intensively for about six months on realizing the system. The research work was a great deal less complicated than anticipated - with the help of the Sponsoring Association. The German photographic archive in Dresden was extremely helpful, with its remarkable amount of archive material of historical pictures, as was a Dresden cameraman, Ernst Hirsch, whose extensive film archive contributed considerably to the appealing qualities of the multimedia system.

Over and over again, users looked on in unbelievable astonishment when they realized it was possible to call up a parade of the Saxon king in 1911, the invasion of the Russians in 1945 or a film from Otto Dix's workshop. The filmed comparisons of the center of Dresden are also worth mentioning, documenting how the city looked before 1945, directly afterwards and then finally in the 1970s.

Nevertheless, it is the picture and photographic material that form the "foundations" of the application. The system informs the user in picture and text about all the significant buildings in Dresden, its architecture, sculptors and landscapers. Various photographs taken both inside and outside of these famous sights can be called up, and project in this way a complex image of the object in question.

The same applies to the history, visually prepared with historical engravings and wood carvings but also with more current material that takes the user into the most recent past. When designing the screen layout, it was thought to be particularly favorable to "ban" longer passages of narrative text onto a second page. The extract of the picture shown then is only the size of a postage stamp, the text, however, goes into more detail.

The texts were prepared by the editor according to the target group in question and were counterchecked by a Dresden historian and various "witnesses of time". The information system does not, however, claim to be a scientific documentation. Its purpose is to convey the most significant information in an entertaining manner and ideally to encourage users to take a closer look at one or two of the topics.

2.1   The multimedial Frauenkirche

The chapters "800 Years of City History" and "Architecture" are equal in length to the information on the "Frauenkirche". Yet it is inevitable that the latter subject is entered into in more detail. As an example, the system shows George Bähr's very first plans, more recent construction plans that were drawn up shortly before World War II, original quotations from official correspondence concerning the plans for the restoration immediately after the church had been destroyed, and naturally the reconstruction carried out on the computer.

The preparation of this particular topic had one aim: to convince and enthuse the users about the archaeological restoration and reconstruction of the church. Step by step we wanted to emphasize the role the church played in the history of Dresden, how it characterized the overall image of the city and just how much the people of Dresden had loved their church before it was destroyed.

For Dresden the Frauenkirche was far more than simply a house of prayer. It was the emblem of the city, the "stone dome", an architectural masterpiece of engineering; and it was a concert hall with remarkable acoustics where imposing performances of great musical work took place. An impressive indication of this characteristic is demonstrated by the excerpt of the final historical recording of the Silbermann organ.

A further important argument in favor of the project are the numerous plans and letters of correspondence that clearly show that shortly after the destruction of the church one was discussing the reconstruction using the old bricks. For ideological and financial reasons, however, these plans were not finally put forward in the 1960s.

The founding and the (successful) efforts made by the Sponsoring Association for the Restoration, not to mention the Frauenkirche Foundation, plus the fact that prominent politicians and personalities, above all the Federal Chancellor and the Dresden trumpet virtuoso Ludwig Güttler, engage themselves for the restoration, has meant that the discussions of the past have now become a part of the present.

The virtual reconstruction of the church can be described as the high point in the aim to provide a historical yet convincing argument. The 4-minute video is for the majority of the users without doubt the highlight of the application and often the most significant reason for them buying the CD-ROM. The perfect illusion of a church that already appears to exist, with every detail including the paintings in the dome and each of the sounds of the enormous Silbermann organ, takes even the most well versed multimedia experts by surprise (see fig. 3).

Fig. 3.   Inside part of the virtual church

If the user has been successfully convinced by what he has seen and heard, the system then provides him with all the necessary information on how he can contribute to the restoration fund or become a member in the Sponsoring Association, simply under the key word "Your Contribution".

2.2 The user guidance

When using the multimedia system and CD-ROM, the user should not be reminded of any other applications already available. For this reason, we decided not to use any symbols or icons, or windows that need to be opened or closed, and we made sure the terminology used could be easily understood by all potential users.

The hierarchy should be kept as simple and "flat" as possible to enable the user to enter and find his way around the system without any problems. Following an overview of the chapters, the user moves on to the second screen and already finds himself in the middle of the action!

With this second step he can choose one of the three chapters and now has the most important data on the screen (see fig. 2). Here he can either directly call up the topics he is most interested in or simply "browse" through the entire chapter for more detailed information on individual points of interest. In both cases, it is possible to call up additional information from up to 4 hierarchical levels - this includes further pictorial or textual information, music or film cuttings that are blended in. Naturally, with just one "click", the user can either continue to browse through the last level or return to the original menu.

Furthermore, the user can also click on a screen mask on the first screen (chapter overview) that contains a list of the most important film, music and text documents. Key words can be selected, guiding the user directly into the topic chosen.

A help function can also be accessed from the first screen. This provides the user with a one-page overview of how the system works. One particular feature that makes this PoI system in the Frauenkirche visitor's pavilion so special is the ability to link-up directly to the construction site itself: a camera that is permanently installed in a stationary crane provides the user with a bird's-eye view of the progress of the work and what is happening "live" on the site. This feature can be activated by a single touch on the first page of the screen.

A direct link like this was made via telephone line to the multimedia system presentation stand at the CeBIT '95 fair. Here, visitors were able to gain an impression of what was happening live on the construction site - with a moving camera. The video conference link was technically realized with hardware from the company PictureTel, an IBM business partner. The direct link, along with the virtual reality video, were just two of the most significant highlights of the CeBIT presentation.

It was our full intention that the capacity of a multimedia information system be exhausted by these numerous possibilities of selecting many different topics and media, and the vast range of historical film, music and photographic material scarcely published in the past.

It was our aim to provide a "tour", as intelligent and entertaining as possible, through an extremely complex topic. We wanted to make it clear from the start, even to the more skeptical users, what kind of advantages of information transmission are inherent in a system such as this.

In order to do so, it was indeed our intention not to venture into too much detail in some points. Although approximately 70% of the texts can be called up by the user, there are only two or three passages that take up more than one full screen page. The citizen's information system does not, therefore, compete with encyclopedic works on the topics covered in the system, it merely provides further information in an entertaining manner.

Contrary to what we had anticipated, the PoI system in the Frauenkirche visitor's pavilion is not only used as a kind of multimedia "fast food". To our surprise, the majority of users also made intensive use of the texts and detailed information. This resulted in an average usage time that was 50% higher than originally expected. This data is recorded by a statistical inquiry system integrated in the PoI system that, in addition to an exchange of personal experiences and opinions, also provides us with important criteria needed for the further development of the application.

The inquiry values for the blending in of moving picture sequences are also noticeably high. Beside the video animation of the virtual reality model of the church already mentioned, the historical pre-war pictures are also among the favorites.

3   Prospects

We have never regarded the citizen's information system "Dresden and the Frauenkirche" as an isolated application. On the contrary, we have always looked towards the prospects of extending the system to form an extensive city information guide, in particular with the characteristic of a PoI system.

Initial features reflecting this expansion have already been realized in the current version (May 1995). The user can call up general information about the opera, theaters, cinemas, and sightseeing tours. There is also a city map that pinpoints the most significant buildings and sights in the city.

A further possibility already considered by organizers and promoters in Dresden is an extension that, for example, includes a calendar of events - a feature that is optically distinguished from the unchanged standard chapters, and should be as easy to program as possible.

A similar update is also planned for the chapter on the Frauenkirche. New reports and film sequences on the progress of the reconstruction and restoration emphasize the role of the multimedia system as an information tool.

An extension also offers as well a whole range of additional areas of application: a number of hotels in Dresden have also expressed interest in setting up the PoI system in their lobbies, provided they are able to advertise their hotel in the system. A suggestion to which we are indeed favorably disposed.

In future, the PoI system is also to be equipped with a cheque card reading device, enabling those wishing to make a contribution towards the reconstruction to make a transfer, on the spot. This solution provides the first step into an additional service of potential city information guide systems: the user can print out tickets for a concert or for the cinema on a printer that is directly connected to the system. Payment is made via the cheque card. Ventures such as these have already been tested by IBM in other areas.

Technical data regarding the PoI system:
- IBM pentium computer
- 32 MB main memory

- 2 integrated hard disks, each with 540 MB
- 256 colors with a resolution of 1024x758 pixels
- developed under Authorware V2.01 for Windows

Technical requirements for CD-ROM:
- i486 or pentium processor
- DOS version 5.0 upwards and Microsoft Windows 3.1.
- 12 megabyte main memory (RAM)
- SGVA video board (1024 x 768), 256 colors
- sound board, mouse

The application has been developed under windows for commercial reasons. A version running under OS/2 is currently being programmed.

Books of the Next Generation - Reading on the Electronic Frontier

Florian Brody
New Media Consulting, Austria, and
Art Center College of Design, Pasadena, USA

1   Introduction

"By this art you may contemplate the variation of the 23 letters ..."
The Anatomy of Melancholy, part 2, sect. II, mem IV #1

Today reading has successfully made the transition from paper to the dynamic medium of the computer screen and is becoming a common experience in the world of electronic media. And while the computer industry does everything to convince us that *multi*media will be the glorious future of electronic communication we convey most of our concepts by writing and reading, be it on the computer, be it on paper. The electronic book as a platform to read on a dynamic medium is still in a very early stage both in software and hardware and may look dramatically different from what we expect it to be at this stage. Still the book is the primary source for text and thus a container of memory.

This paper looks into the quality of private memory and its impact on our dealing with electronic media.

2   The book

The fact that we see the book as a monolithic form tells us a lot about its qualities as a container of text. The written word guarantees continuity and truth. The latter is derived from the holy books and extend against better knowledge to much that we read.

Books have changed over the centuries and as we complain about today's screen resolution and the quality of text on the monitor we should compare this to any 16th century book that was equally hard to read. The quality of printed books showed a drastic decline in design and representational quality from the handmade manuscripts and it took a long time to get the technology and the design concepts of print under control. Books had different positions in society over the centuries and shared the fate of their owners in many ways. Books of Hours served in many ways as companions much like today the PowerBook (the laptop by Apple) and were highly personalized in its content, the 19th century saw a strong impact on personal libraries and books were sold without binding to allow the owner to have it bound to match the other volumes in his possession.

Our interest in books goes far beyond their actual value as containers of text. Books have a high value as fetish objects as much as extensions of our brain. By owning a book we extend our memory even without ever reading the book. The object of the book itself has an aesthetic quality not found in most computers and an electronic book will have to satisfy this need. Personal electronic devices such as electronic diaries and portable CD players have shown that this is possible. The separation of the container of the text and the book will lead to a total redefinition of the book but not to its extinction. We will get to a state when the concept of one book that holds any given information becomes acceptable. The information will be on a disc or online and probably more readily available than a book on paper one cannot find at a given moment.

Every electronic book concept will have to guarantee the stability of text as this is one of the main features of books vs. other media that we need not worry about the availability of text. Text on online systems is outside our control and by the time we revisit a given passage, it may have changed or disappeared. This makes us extremely insecure and the system hard to use. Text has to hold its promise as being uneraseable in order to convey the concept of a book.

3   The text

"Was man schwarz auf weiss besitzt, kann man getrost nach Hause tragen."
Goethe: Faust I.

In pre-literate societies, that which we now refer to as the "text" existed solely within the realm of the memory inside our heads. With the invention of writing, the text moved to the manu scriptum, the page written by hand, which like precious work of art, was a rare object and the act of copying manuscripts was a religious act. The technology of printing transformed the text into an exchangeable commodity, ever more plentiful over the centuries. The libraries have grown and are no longer working memories but became almost infinite storage spaces for printed paper.

When considering text we normally think about the written word printed with black ink on white paper. With the computer as a text processing machine the direct connection of text and its physical representation is broken up and text returns to its immaterial status it had in the age before printing. Electronic texts have no body, only mind - they close the circle to *the mnemotechne* of the classical ages.

The computer is less of a calculation machine (a computer) than a memory machine with a major disability compared to our memories, it cannot forget. We take advantage of this fact by using it as storage device for our texts and our thoughts. Many systems of artificial memory have been invented to store ideas and concepts that constitute our history.

In the 1980s the computer became a writing machine that memorized the text without an adaequate capability of representation. The Expanded Books project at Voyager looked into the task of a booklike representation of text on a screen in 1991 and with the arrival of the PowerBooks for the first time text could be made available for comfortable reading on a screen. The Expanded Books take the interface metaphor from the book as much as the book borrowed it from the manuscript. Although markup and search facilities are available, the interface is keept free from buttons and anything that distracts the eye from reading (see fig. 1).

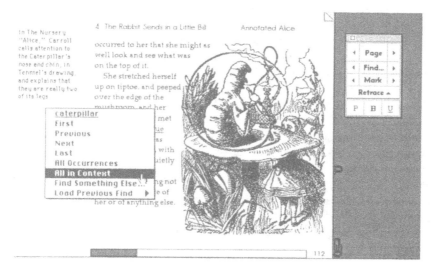

Fig. 1.   Voyager Expanded Book: The Complete Annotated Alice

As much as the impact of the printing press is not in the fact that the lead is pressed onto the paper, the calculations of the computer secondary to the representational qualities of text. The design of the hardware as well as the interface on the screen contribute to the readability of the text.

The computer spawns the electronic text, a volatile form that paradoxically returns the text to our heads while at the same time enmeshing it in an even more sophisticated apparatus. Through its digitalization it no longer rests in the universe of original and reproduction but transcends to a state where every reproduction is an original. Thus the user of the word processor becomes the third in the row of operators described by Benjamin (Benjamin 1973), the film camera operator and the operating surgeon. Both enter deep into the tissue of reality when doing the work, while the magical healer on one side and the painter on the other both keep a distance to their objects.

The image created by the camera operator is a virtual much in the sense the text created on the computer is virtual and needs to be projected onto a screen to be perceivable. And as we still have no screens that satisfy our reading needs we *print*

most of the texts onto paper, which remaps the dynamic and digital text back into
the world of print (Benjamin 1973).

4   The library

*"The universe (which others call the Library) is composed of an indefinite and
perhaps infinite number of hexagonal galleries, with vast air shafts between,
surrounded by very low railings."*
  Jorge Luis Borges, "The Library of Babel" (Borges 1962)

The library as a container of books and thus container of knowledge generates in
itself a strange quality of being alive. And this holds true for the big old libraries
like the Bodleyan or the British Library as much as for the private library at home.
It is a metaphor for the limits, or infinities, of the world and the knowledge it
encompasses. As much as the map is not the territory the library to a certain extent
is the knowledge, as it defines knowledge to the extent the recursive memory of the
book is in itself the source of this knowledge. With the computer as a container of
text, the situation has changed dramatically. Text is no longer directly related to the
page in a book but exists - somewhat "again" - independently for a physical representation as a memory unit. This puts libraries in a difficult situation. As much as
all libraries in the world suffer from a never ending search for new shelf space
which will be solved by electronic representation, the risk to become invisible as
the text need no longer be represented in a direct physical form (see fig. 2).

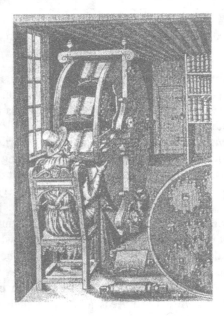

Fig. 2.   Early reading machine

While library catalogues in electronic form have fast become a desireable tool among librarians, electronic texts as primary texts and parts of a library collection are still rarely understood as books. Everything not printed and bound is considered "non-book material" and this negative definition makes it hard to overcome preoccupations. Due to the dichotomy of text on a storage medium and the need of a reading machine the collection process is unclear. Libraries may end up very soon with data they cannot access and museums with machines without proper data to run them. The disappearing knowledge about outdated machines, their configuration and the interdependency of hardware and software will make data faster obsolete than disintegration data storage.

The library as a refugium for text faces a conceptual crisis. The dream of total availability of text within the machine comes true and in the same time the text is no longer graspeable. Therefore the concept of the library as a memory place will have to adapt.

5   Reading

Reading has been for centuries and still is the prevalent activity that creates and defines the way we store and communicate abstract ideas. As much as the activity of reading has changed over the centuries, it constitutes one of the pillars western culture is based on. While writing and printing materials and technologies have changed, the printed word had always the character of permanence and stability. Looking at dynamic media one of the major questions is its transient quality which leads to the central question if the written word loses its primary quality by being transferred to this medium.

Today we use word processors and text processors and perceive them much in the way we got used to food processors. But while processing food is intended to make it more digestible (the first food processor was the open fire) word processors are memory generators. Winograd sees the word processor as a "medium for the creation and modification of linguistic structures that play a role in human communication" (Winograd 1986). His concern of the word processing computer is closely related to the visual representation of text and writing as a means of communication in a social network. The real virtues of the word processor, and in this way it relates to his relative, the food processor, are within its capability to build an artificial memory.

6   Hypertext

For Norbert Bolz, "the post-modern world is the world of the New Media" in which "the information processing system 'book' is clearly no longer up to the complexity of our social systems" (Bolz 1993). This is not the place to discuss if our society has become more complex but the book both in the conventional form as we know it and in its extended form as electronic book has proven to be exceptionally well adaptable to new forms of text. Early hypertext representations have been on paper, foremost the Talmud which is traditionally designed in a style where the main text is printed in the center of the page, surrounded by commentaries which in turn are surrounded by secondary commentaries. This complex system of references is laid out on a two-dimensional page and the remapping of the hypertextual links take place in our brain.

When in 1962 Ted Nelson first coined the term "hypertext" he planned it to be a universal computer program that would keep track of the divergent paths of texts and ideas (Wolf 1995, Nelson 1980). He planned it to be the underlying structure of Project Xanadu, the ultimate text database that would connect every text within itself and to all other relevant texts. Xanadu itself is described in "Literary Machines" a book on paper with "a chapter zero, several chapters one, one chapter two and several chapters three" (Nelson 1980). It is this polyvalent ability to enter, amend, and exit the text in a non-linear fashion that defines hypertextuality (Landow 1991). The representation of text on an electronic device adds a new form of dynamics which need not reflect hypertextuality. The dynamic medium offers to typography the temporal dimension and the chance for development. The design approach of "Liquid Typography" (Müller 1995) which maps the static graphemes onto the dynamic environment of the screen analyzes the adaequacy of text on a screen but makes no statement about the structure of the content represented within. While the Expanded Books keep the structure of the book on paper and add the power of the computer to make text more accessible, Liquid Typography redefines text as an evolving design process and hypertext concentrates on the multiple interdependencies of text (see fig. 3).

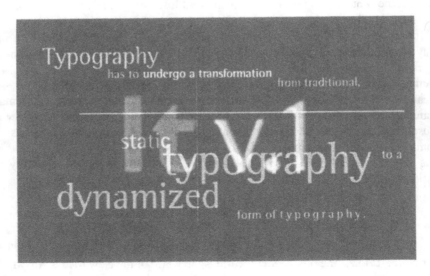

Fig. 3.   Müller: Liquid Typography

It is no coincidence that this universal Project Xanadu never even got near completion, by definition such a task cannot be achieved as it would create the universal library as described by Borges that nobody would be able to use. Hypertext is an attempt to codify all links to a given corpus by defining and classifying the connections on an intertextual and intratextual level. This generates a new level of textuality which in turn needs to be analyzed by the similar rules in order to function as text. Bolz points out that "true hypertext is a rhizome" which "requires a self-assertive user" (Bolz 1993) but it remains unclear if this true hypertext can come up to all the expectations.

7   Dynamic media

By using electronic technologies of representation we enforce the apparatus-free perception of reality even more than with film and the effect described by Benjamin in 1937 becomes a central position in the definition of new media:

"The equipment-free aspect of reality here has become the height of artifice; the sight of immediate reality has become and orchid (die blaue Blume) in the land of technology" (Benjamin 1969).

Bob Stein from Voyager often stresses the point not to pass up text when we think about new media. His experiment is to discuss the Gulf War with pictures only (Stein 1993). Being carried away by the marketing blurbs of the hardware companies we overlook the necessities of conceptual representation, often achieved only through text. We are at a very early stage in the development of new dynamic media, based on electronic representation. Our current status can be compared to film around 1903 when the attraction of the technology drew people into the movie theatres and the topics covered were of minor importance. The current interest in the WorldWideWeb has very similar sources and the fact that most of the information available on the Internet has little or no relevance has not stoped anybody from using it. Relevant to the topic of this paper a discussion on the future of reading is taking place on a New York based Web site between Bob Stein from Voyager, Sven Birkerts, the author of the Gutenberg Elegies and others and due to its transitory stage I am not even sure if it can be quoted (Feed 1995).

8   Conveyors of memory

The need to conserve i.e. stabilize text was apparent and different approaches to create an artificial memory were taken already more than 3000 years ago. The ars memorativa had an equal status to rhetoric both in roman and medieval times. Constat igitur artificiosa memoria ex locis et imaginibus (The artificial memory is established from places and images) (Yates 1978).

In western culture, books contain knowledge that can be shared, sold, or bought. Information becomes a commodity and as such, independent from man a radical shift from the antique model that posited memory as the primary container of knowledge, inseparable from the human mind. The ars memorativa were a major part of rhetorical training for any educated Roman, and the rules for the mnemotechne were of such importance that the later textual tradition still bears their imprint. Francis Yates points out the linkages between the two forms: "The art of memory is like an inner writing. Those who know the letters of the alphabet can write down what is indicated to them and read out what they have written" (Yates 1978). The rules for places and rules for images defined for the art of memory hold for books as well as for new media systems. Users of hypertext systems build imaginary houses in their minds to understand where they are in the story. When they become lost, it is because the system's designers have violated the traditional structures of the *mnemotechne*.

9   Text revisited

Text often exists in more than two dimensions. Scribes scratched hieroglyphs into papyrus, stonesmiths carved Latin inscriptions into stele, and printers from Gutenberg on have pressed type and ink, modifying the very surface of the paper. New printing and reproduction technologies abandon the third dimension. Laser printing lays two-dimensional text on the page, an effect closer to stenciling than engraving. Computer displays eliminate traditional notions of dimensionality entirely - leaving text to float in an electronic matrix. A linear text, with specified start and end points, is a stable text. The matrix in which electronic text floats is quite different - a flexible environment that allows multiple layers and n-dimensional reading variants. Nevertheless "we still read according to print technology, and we still direct almost all of what we write toward print modes of publication" (Landow 1991).

Just as the technologies of text production have changed, so have the functions of reading. Reading as a mental adventure is a relatively young concept. General access to the written word was until fairly recently restricted to the holy books. The special quality assigned to these books - the word of God - not only restricted their usage, but also assigned a quality beyond its primary semiotic character as a sign. In western civilization, the written word gained a truth value previously held by the spoken word. The arrival of electronic text forces a similar re-evaluation of the page-bound text. Although text in a computer is far less stable than the written or printed word we assign it a very high truth value. Early computer pioneer Joseph Weizenbaum of MIT remarked, "My father used to say, 'It is written in the holy books.' Today we say, 'The computer tells us'" (Weizenbaum 1978).

10   Live long and prosper

As much as generating a text not only allows us to express and communicate our ideas it contains also the pleasure of writing and the generation of an arte factum. The book as a conveyor of ideas as much as an artificial memory will be around for many years, both in the form we know it and in future iterations and generations to come. Books are ultimately memory objects not paper objects and as such play a role in our life.

References

Benjamin, W., The work of art in the age of mechanical reproduction, in: Illuminations, New York, Schocken, 1969 (first published in: Zeitschrift für Sozialforschung, V. 1, 1936)

Birkerts, S., The Gutenberg Elegies, Boston, Faber, 1994

Bolz, N., The deluge of sense, Speech at Doors of Perception, Amsterdam, 1993, transcribed on the Doors of Perception 1 CD-ROM, Amsterdam, Mediamatic, 1994

Borges, J. L., Labyrinths, Selected Stories, New York, New Directions, 1962

Brody, F., The Expanded Books Project - research report, Santa Monica, Voyager, 1992

Feed, Interactive journal on the World Wide Web at http://www.emedia.net/feed/, 1995

Gardener, M., The Complete Annotated Alice, Expanded Book, Santa Monica, Voyager, 1992

Landow, G., Hypertext, The Convergence of Contemporary Critical Theory and Technology, Baltimore, Johns Hopkins University Press, 1992

Landow, G. , Bolter, J. D., Writing Space: The Computer, Hypertext, and the History of Writing, Hillsdale, Lawrence Erlbaum, 1991

Müller, T., Liquid Typography - forthcoming CD-ROM, research project at Art Center College of Design, 1995

Nelson, T. H., Literary Machines - Edition 87.1, personal copy T. H. Nelson

Weizenbaum, J., Personal conversation with the author, 1978

Winograd, T., Flores, F., Understanding computers and cognition, a new foundation for design, Reading, Addison-Wesley, 1986

Wolf, G., The Curse of Xanadu, in: Wired 3(1995)6, 137 pp.

Yates, F., The Art of Memory, Hammondsworth, Penguin, 1978, p. 22

Electronic Agents and the Market Place: New Generations of Electronic Services for Consumers

Rob de Vogel
Philips Advanced Communication Enterprise (PACE), The Netherlands

1   Introduction

We witness the merging of the telecommunication, information processing and entertainment industries. Communication needs in this complex world can only be met by a more integrated approach in the design of communication devices, network and services.

The start up company General Magic has developed a set of technologies to address this: *Telescript*, a language to develop communication oriented applications and *Magic Cap*, an operating system and graphical user interface for communication devices.

An alliance, in which a large number of big companies cooperate, has been founded to develop the entire business around these core technologies. These new technologies and the electronic services that may be created with them are demonstrated by a number of applications, for both consumers and professional users.

2   Vision for communication

The process of communication is complex and this is reflected by the many different products we use in our homes and offices. We talk on the telephone, send messages by fax or e-mail; we create messages on lap-top PCs, voice messaging systems and answering machines. These products are effective and efficient, but they only handle a single task; in our information-driven lives they simply do not meet our communication needs.

To help define those needs we have developed a simple model which has three elements:

The first concerns the internal conversations that we conduct with ourselves. These private internal talks are hard to define, but our impulses and ideas have a way of resolving themselves into our busy business and personal agendas. They may also appear in a more structured form, for instance as "to do" lists, action list, directories, etc. Thus they reflect *our increasing need to remember*.

Many of the elements of these involve external contact: we need to maintain relationships with family, friends, business associates and institutions; so we have parties and meetings; we all call each other, leave messages, send faxes. This is the second element in our model. It reflects *our fundamental need to communicate.*

The third element concerns our appetite for information. We are happy to maintain a controlled "state of ignorance" about the world because we have ways of finding the information we need when we need it. Once we have found it, we use it; typically we then forget it. We also make use of information-related services: is there an early morning train to wherever? What movie can we see? Thus this third element reflects *our insatiable need to know.*

The model also indicates that its boundaries are seamless; we step forwards and backwards between random ideas, link them to information, turn them into communication, almost independent of whether this is related to business or private life. Thus we remember, communicate, know. This is the way people work and live and it is the way that telecommunication should be working. And it soon will be.

3 Turning vision into reality

3.1 Three areas need to be addressed

The model puts the individual at the center of events. It focuses on our pervasive need to communicate and the concept of reaching out to grab information whenever it is required. It says that this should be a simple, intuitive process. Because we are individuals, it recognizes the importance of customization; it's a model that enables every individual to define and manage his or her individual information and communication needs.

If the vision as described above is to become a reality, we need to satisfy the complex needs that are associated with this vision, and we must therefore address three basic areas:

- *Devices* that allow to manage internal and external communications. We have named them "personal intelligent communicators" and they will be a constant companion; they will reflect your personality, life-style as well as your needs and particular requirements.
- *Services* that give access to other people and to sources of information and the electronic market place. The telephone is now the service that performs some of this, but it must be enhanced to a service that enables and supports complementary and more complex communication acts.
- *Networks* that interlink the personal communicators with services.

3.2 Two closely interlinked technologies

Two core technologies have been developed by General Magic that form the basis for addressing the above:

Magic Cap (where Cap stands for communication application platform) forms both the operating system and graphical user interface for the personal intelligent communicators of the future. Embedded are a number of "local" applications (telephone and address directory, notebook, auto dialling function, games, encyclopedia, desk tools) and communication-oriented applications.

Telescript is an interpreted, object-oriented remote programming language for smart messaging, to develop communication-oriented applications and services. It forms the foundation for smart messaging. *Agents*, programs written in Telescript, can move around the network, meet and interact with other agents to perform certain task on behalf of their owner (Hanckmann 1994).

Both technologies are described in detail in the following chapters.

4   Magic Cap

4.1   Magic Cap for personal intelligent communicators

Magic Cap is the operating system and user interface for a new generation of communication devices: personal intelligent communicators (PICs). It has a built-in Telescript interpreter that takes care of the handling of the Telescript objects that are sent over the communication network to and from Information Providers as well as other users.

Magic Cap is designed for communication and it provides an easy, reliable way to stay connected to your co-workers, friends and family. It lets you send messages to people no matter what kind of communication tools they prefer: fax machines, phones, pagers or e-mail, or of course, other Magic Cap devices. Magic Cap technology veils the complexity of reaching those different communication methods by providing everything you need in a single, simple, personal intelligent communicator.

Magic Cap is supported by many hardware suppliers. The world's major consumer electronics manufacturers are part of the General Magic Alliance.

4.2   Magic Cap functionality

Magic Cap software offers the following functionality:

- Exchange electronic mail that has unprecedented rich content, including multiple typefaces and styles with text input by an on-screen keyboard, graphics, animation, sound effects and music, digital ink. Magic Cap comes with a rich collection of *stamps* to be used for ornamentation and to add specific functionality which is understood by the service to which Magic Cap devices are linked (such as "this message is urgent").
- Send messages to several addressees simultaneously via electronic mail networks, fax machines, pagers or messaging services.
- It incorporates an address book, which is referenced from many functions in the device: mail, faxing, controlling telephone functions, calendar, and third-party

applications. It keeps your address book automatically updated. Each time a message arrives, the attached "business card" of the sender can be automatically appended to the address book. It is one of the many ways that Magic Cap reduces manual data input.

- Datebook from which you can schedule appointments automatically. Notebook with structured formats including to do lists. World clock which keeps track of daylight savings time in different time zones. Calculator with basic and scientific functions built-in.
- Offers a telephone interface with various telephone tools (phone log, fast dialling, integrated address and phone directory).
- Filing capabilities which automatically files and discards correspondence.
- Built-in tutorials, hints, and help system, as well as construction tools for advanced users to customize Magic Cap, and in general customizations on many levels.

4.3   Three scenes: Desk, Hallway & Downtown

Users can get access to these tools and services by navigating through a number of scenes and selecting the representations of these tools and services. The three most relevant scenes are:

Fig. 1.   The Desk metaphor of Magic Cap

4.3.1 Desk

The Desk contains everything needed to communicate: In Box, Out Box, stationary, telephone, telephone directory as well as a number of generic office tools (archive, finder, calculator, spelling checker), all of which can be tailored to personal requirements (see fig. 1).

4.3.2 Hallway

From the Hallway there is access to a number of rooms where specific tools, support or services are offered: Game Room, Library (with tutorials and manuals), Store Room, Control Room and the Desk. Users can enhance the functionality of their devices by adding additional rooms to their Hallway, e.g. by acquiring a Language Course Room package (see fig. 2).

Fig. 2.   The Hallway metaphor of Magic Cap

4.3.3 Downtown

Downtown provides an easy way to access services, products and organizations. Electronic merchants are represented by shops in Downtown and as more and more organizations offer goods and services electronically, you will be able to assemble your own Downtown, composed of your favorite shops (see fig. 3).

Fig. 3.   The Downtown metaphor of Magic Cap

4.4   Magic Cap will come for many platforms

Magic Cap has originally been designed for small handheld devices, the size of
wallets, with a touch-sensitive screen in landscape format of 360 x 240 pixels.
Over time Magic Cap will become available for other platforms as well. A version
for Windows, to run on regular PCs and a version for the Apple Macintosh already
have been announced as products.

Later we will see Magic Cap (or variations of Magic Cap, optimized for different
circumstances and services) become available on other devices in the home and at
work: screenphones, television, fax machines, point-of-sales terminals, and pagers.

5   Telescript

5.1   Telescript concepts and characteristics

Telescript is an interpreted, object-oriented remote programming language for smart
messaging, to develop communication-oriented applications and services. It forms
the foundation for smart messaging. *Agents*, programs written in Telescript, can
move around the network, meet and interact with other agents to perform certain
task on behalf of their owner.

5.1.1 Basic technical concepts

Telescript is a language which allows software developers to create processes and let them communicate with one another, no matter on what computer these processes run. There are two kinds of process, *agent* and *place*. A place is a stationary process, while an agent can travel from place to place. Processes of both kind can be created on the fly.

An agent which is in a place can interact (or communicate) with that place by calling its operations. Agents can *meet* with other agents in the same place, which allows them to interact: they can call each other's operations. An agent can travel to other places by means of the *go* statement. It can *send* clones of itself to other places in parallel.

Next to these, there are other important concepts in the Telescript language which correspond with entities in the real world.

Each process (i.e. an agent or a place) in Telescript has an *authority* and *identity*. An authority corresponds with a specific person or organization in the real world, while an identity is used to distinguish processes which have the same authority. The fact that each agent has an authority implies that agents cannot be anonymous: the person or organization which they represent can always be determined.

A *region* is a set of Telescript places all operated by the same individual or organization. When an agent wants to enter a region, his authority is checked. Interaction of an agent with other agents and places can also be controlled.

The lives of both agents and places can be given an upper limit *(permit)* to avoid them from spending too much resources (e.g. time).

5.1.2 Properties

The Telescript language is *object-oriented*. It extends object orientation with features typically needed in a communication language: a Telescript program can define or discover, and then use new classes during execution, and agents can transport class definitions to remote engines and install them there.

The Telescript language is *interpreted*. Consequently, Telescript programs cannot directly access the computer on which they run. This is one way to decrease the risk of having viruses travel the network.

The Telescript language is *persistent*. If the computer on which a Telescript program runs crashes or is turned off, no data is lost. The Telescript interpreter secures all its data transparently, so the complete state of all Telescript computations is always recoverable.

5.1.3 Related technologies

The Telescript language is complemented with some other technologies, in order to be able to develop full-scale applications and services. The most obvious one of these is the *Telescript Engine*, which is the interpreter for the applications written in Telescript. The Engines form the places where travelling Telescript programs ("agents") can reside, and from where they are launched into and received from the communication network. So, one can say that agents hop from engine to engine through the communication network, and the engines take care that the agents perform the tasks for which they have come to that specific engine (for instance to extract information from a database to which the engine has access), or they make sure that the agents can continue their voyage.

Other related technologies deal with communication protocols and application development environments.

5.2   Telescript uniqueness

There are a number of reasons why Telescript is so well suited to become the standard for communication-oriented electronic services.

5.2.1 Faster development through powerful concepts

For application developers it is important to know that the Telescript language is designed for carrying out complex networking tasks like navigation, transportation, and authentication; it abstracts completely from the communication infrastructure (e.g. session management, intricate and heterogeneous addressing schemes, and intra-layer protocols). This means that it is easier to map concepts of a marketplace on the language. In other words, it reduces development time for communicating applications as well as their maintenance cost.

Agents and places: The concepts agent and place make it easy to implement communicating applications as interacting processes which are distributed over the network. As an illustration of the use of agents and places, one can look at the simple way user-friendly features can be implemented in a Telescript based messaging service:

- Easy addressing.
- One can send a message to someone else without having to know more than his or her name; complete addressing information will be brought by an agent to the originator, for use next time.
- Easy distribution. It is easy to send a message to several people at once, who may use different mail systems and different devices (like fax and pager). The class DistributionList (a place) resides in the outpost of its owner, maintains a list of address cards, and can do access control.
- Smart mailboxes. Mailboxes can filter incoming mail, and thus e.g. reject or archive mail, or, for instance if the message is urgent, send it to a pager.
- Interactive messages. Messages can be interactive, that is, upon display show buttons which trigger new actions, like making an appointment in an agenda, or sending a reply.
- Triggered messages. An agent may be in charge of monitoring events in a place, and send a message upon a specific event, e.g. at an airport in case a flight has been delayed.

These features can be implemented in other mail systems as well, but in the high level language Telescript it takes less development and maintenance cost.

Authentication: An information service can determine the customer represented by an incoming agent by means of its authority. It has to be emphasized that this allows the application service provider to collect data on who is accessing the service, how, and how often.

Value based billing: Telescript allows more refined billing than conventional technologies (e.g. videotex services). A bill can be based upon the actual value obtained by the user, and not on duration of the transaction.

5.2.2 Remote programming

A major implication of introducing Telescript is the possibility of remote programming: agents can be sent into the Telescripted networks and do tasks for the authority they represent. In this way, manufacturers of client software can extend, improve, and combine the functionality offered by manufacturers of server software:

- The decision to introduce a new communicating application can be made by a third party, independent of a network operator or application service provider .
- Communicating applications can be maintained easier by application developers, as parts of a service residing on different places in the network can be updated on the fly.
- For network operators it is important that network management can be done more flexible agents may autonomously monitor parts of the network and initiate actions where appropriate (comparable with a human operator who receives information at a central point from various sources, who has to combine these pieces of information and make changes manually).
- pieces of network management software can be easily replaced: a new agent is sent to the place and the old one is terminated.
- Extra functionality can be added by individual users. An agent may be in charge of monitoring events in a place, and send a message on a specific event, e.g. at an airport in case a flight has been delayed. Of course, the airline could offer this service, but as long as it does not, a user may customize the network himself.

In other words, Telescript turns the network into an open platform for communicating applications.

5.3 Network considerations

Public services based on the Telescript technology require a public communications infrastructure, that allows access from a variety of client devices to the service engines. Client devices can be mobile or desktop machines like PC and Apple Macintosh. Access can be wireline, using dial-up modems over PSTN e.g., or wireless.

The Telescript messages are network transparent. As access networks "any" channel can be used: analogue telephone lines ("POTS"), ISDN, GSM, DECT, Local Area Networks, cable television networks, provided that both the device/terminal and the server have the right interface to the transmission network.

Telescript messages are just bit streams between two Telescript engines that are connected via a network.

5.4   Telescript applications

Third party developers will, with the help of tools that have become available, be able to develop networked applications, written in Telescript. Like with all programming languages, there is no limit to what type of application developers may want to provide. There is one application however, that we expect to be offered to the public by any operator of Telescript platforms: *MagicMail*, a basic smart messaging service that guarantees that agents can travel the network and that thereby supplies the foundation for the electronic marketplace.

MagicMail is an application written in Telescript that brings smart messaging to the broad public. It offers smartness in messages, envelopes and in the mailboxes of users in the network. As it is by design a store-and-forward service, it requires that a service provider assigns a mailbox for each user, and each mailbox takes care of the intermediate storage of messages or agents that are exchanged between subscribers and suppliers of information and services.

Other Telescript applications will be developed for information service providers, and these can then make use of the underlying basic mesa. These applications can be accessed via the network by subscribers. Examples of services:

- Headline news services
- Hotel and travel information
- Home shopping services
- Banking applications
- Classified adds services

6   The Electronic Marketplace

Telescript technology integrates an electronic world of computers and the networks that connect them. This results in a world filled with Telescript places and occupied by intelligent agents. Such a place is permanently occupied by an agent associated with the place and can be temporarily visited by the agents of users or other authorities. For instance, a theatre ticket selling place might be occupied by a ticketing agent that provides information about theatre events and that sells tickets for those events. Such a ticketing place would be visited by the agents of interested parties in order to obtain information and purchase tickets. Examples of other places include news and information services and the mailboxes of intelligent messaging services.

Because of the nature of these electronic agents, being pieces of software that on behalf of their owners travel over communication networks and perform certain tasks, the services that can be realized with them are a full step beyond what can be witnessed in traditional services. It is possible to send out agents that monitor certain events and that take action once a certain condition occurs. It is possible for users to *orchestrate* services, meaning that depending on the results of earlier actions, the electronic agents adapt to the new circumstance they meet (Elixmann 1995, White a, White b).

This was demonstrated in a complex "live" route planning application, developed by Philips for CeBIT '95. It showed a person planning to travel from Munich to the CeBIT Fair.

An electronic agent accesses the database of the Munich public transformation services, to find the best connection from the point of departure to the Munich Hauptbahnhof (central railway station). After finding the arrival time at the Hauptbahnhof, the agent accesses the existing Bundesbahn train information service, finds the right train connection to Hannover and reserves a ticket (see fig. 4).

? Schedule	Tuesday, March 7	☞ Request

MUENCHEN	HANNOVER

Date of departure: WED. 3/8   at about: 09:30

Departure	Arrival	Train type / number
07:56	12:31	ICE
08:46	13:38	ICE
09:56	14:31	ICE
10:46	15:38	ICE

Fig 4.   Train time table information

Upon arriving in Hannover, the traveller's agent accesses via a public GSM cellular (data) network, an electronic routing service, that supplies detailed route directions. The traveller first selects the town for which he wants to receive information (see fig. 5).

After specifying in detail the required destination in that area (In this case the Hannover Fair area), a detailed map of the area is downloaded over the network and is displayed on the personal intelligent communicator of the traveller, together with a number of "pages" with route descriptions from point of departure to destination (see fig. 6).

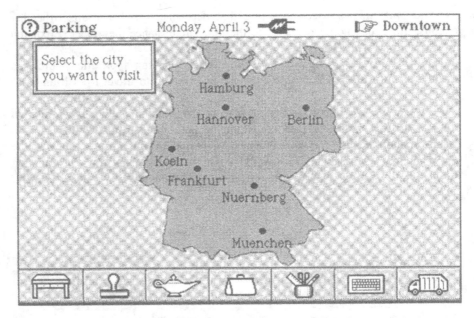

Fig. 5.   Selecting the area on which travel information is required

Figure 6 shows an example of a detailed road description.

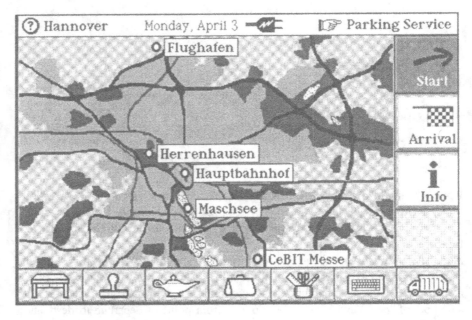

Fig. 6.   Detailed travel information supplied

The traveller then "posts" an agent on the network, to monitor the traffic conditions database. When a traffic jam is signalled on the route provided earlier, the monitoring agent informs the traveller via the public paging service and suggests an alternative road.

This was all done "live", with access to real world databases and making use of a myriad of networks: public analogue telephone networks, Datex-J, GSM and paging networks.

7   Development of a new industry

7.1   Cooperation required

The vision as described in the introduction is one with far reaching implications. The ambitious goals to develop simultaneously new communication devices, new electronic services and to ascertain that these new electronic services are enabled by the underlying network, can only be achieved by the joint efforts of a number of major companies in telecommunication, computing and consumer electronics. The General Magic Alliance was formed to make this happen. Telecommunication, more than any other modern industry, relies on the existence of standards to develop markets and business. None of the individual members could have been in a position to develop, promote and obtain support for a series of technologies that try to achieve this and set a de-facto industry standard. The General Magic Alliance is an effort to orchestrate such joint effort.

7.2   General Magic

General Magic was founded in 1990 as a spin-out from Apple, after Apple management concluded that the standard setting that was required for the realization of the original vision could not be carried out by one single company.

Over the following years a number of relevant companies were intrigued by the vision and convinced by the competence of the team at General Magic. These companies now form the General Magic Alliance, which at this moment consists of (in order of joining): Apple, Sony, Motorola, AT&T, Philips, Matsushita, NTT, Fujitsu, Toshiba, France Telecom, Mitsubishi, Cable & Wireless, Oki, Northern Telecom and Sanyo.

7.3   Worldwide developments

In September 1994, AT&T introduced the first commercial version of MagicMail, *PersonaLink*. This Telescript-based public messaging service provides a smart communication platform, and offers for each of its subscribers mailboxes to be used by the electronic agents, some first electronic services, gateways to X.400, Internet mail services and to fax services. PersonaLink very clearly addresses the individuals, the consumers and is *not* a corporation oriented service.

Experimental versions of a comparable services have been introduced in Japan. Philips has developed R&D versions of such services for a number of European network operators. First commercial services of this kind could be expected in Europe in late 1996.

In parallel to this, the General Magic Alliance is further developing the core technology, developing new families of devices and services, and will be bringing the technology to new communication platforms, such as in the CeBIT '95 demonstration by Philips, where Telescript agents where transported over the public GSM cellular network in Germany.

7.4   Strategies for Europe

Establishing Telescript as a public platform for smart messaging in Europe requires a great deal of detailed interaction with the public network operators, as the technology is complex and as the business implications of applying the technology can be far-reaching. The European arena is much more complicated than the American or Japanese, due to the rather high level of fragmentation and the existence of a diverse electronic service industry (Teletel in France, Bildschirmtext in Germany). A number of actions have started in order to stimulate the process of getting acceptance for Telescript as platform for electronic services, Europe-wide:

- Close cooperations with network operators, through the definition and execution of technical and commercial feasibility studies.
- A number of strategies are being worked out to secure investments in existing electronic services. Options are emulation, dual-headed services, Telescript applications on existing electronic services and toolkits for the development of new services.
- We recognize that Telescript has been positioned as a de-facto industry standard. This has been helped by the fact that Telescript is very high in the OSI layers. Together with the European network operators, the Alliance members are investigating the options to have Telescript accepted as a formal standard.

8   Conclusions

New emerging technologies will enable electronic services that will be steps beyond what is possible today. Standards are necessary, because of the very complex and diverse nature of these services and its constituent elements. Telescript and Magic Cap, two technologies developed by General Magic, are serious candidates to become these standard. The first experimental and commercial services based on these technologies have been launched. It will require enormous and well-orchestrated efforts by many players in the industry to have all elements in place: core technologies, networks, end-user devices and electronic services. A first step has to be made, but the roadmap foretells a journey of many years.

References

White, J., Telescript Technology: The Foundation for the Electronic Marketplace, General Magic White Paper, General Magic, 420 North Mary Avenue, Sunnyvale, CA 94086, USA, a

White, J., Telescript Technology: Scenes from the Electronic Marketplace, General Magic White Paper, b

Hanckmann, J., Intelligent Messaging, in: Mobile Communications International, Issue 17, Spring 1994

Elixmann, M., Mobility on Europe's Infobahn, in: Mobile Communications International, Issue 21, April 1995

Home Systems - The Vision

David G. J. Fanshawe
Philips Consumer Electronics APG, United Kingdom

1 Introduction

The 'home of the future' has been envisaged by many people over the years. Early writers saw an ideal society, with work minimised through the use of labour-saving machines, and the people able to use their increased leisure to pursue creative and enjoyable lifestyles. The 'pursuit of happiness' was written into the American Constitution as the principal benefit of a free society.

Following the industrial revolution, writers became much more restrained about technology's capacity to improve man's way of life: the social cost was all too apparent. But the dawn of the electrical age around 1900 brought a new optimism. Steam power had brought few direct benefits to the home, but electricity soon started to bring advantages in terms of greater convenience and labour-saving consumer products: light at the flick of a switch; heat without the labour of carrying heavy coal buckets, or sweeping out the ashes the next morning. Later, electricity brought in a whole new category of consumer product: home entertainment; which itself has had a major effect on our lifestyle.

Over the last century our homes have steadily filled up with electrical products. Most of these have little 'intelligence'. They may have a rudimentary form of automation - such as a thermostat to maintain temperature - but are essentially manually controlled, stand-alone units. Over the last decade or so we have seen more 'intelligent' products, based on the microprocessor. This makes the product much more useful. Benefits include self-alignment (to eliminate many of the tiresome adjustments which were necessary on older models), more flexible programming to customise the product to your particular needs, and higher reliability (because the product can compensate for deteriorating performance as it ages). Because of the added value, these 'second generation' products command higher prices.

We are now entering a new generation where products are not only intelligent, but can also co-operate with each other. This creates a 'Home System' (HS) of interconnected products which will support truly flexible automatic operations - and often without the need for professional installation of each new product added to the system. To be commercially successful, these products must give the consumer extra features and extra flexibility, and these must be clearly cost-effective. This means that it is vitally important for the manufacturer to get the underlying technology right, and follow a standard which all manufacturers can build to.

1.1   What do we want?

Emerging technologies are initially judged by how well they enhance our established lifestyle; then, as they become established, they begin to change our lifestyle. The Home System (HS) will surely follow this pattern. Initially HS products will be bought for very practical benefits: to save money, to protect property, to support and enhance our present lifestyle. At a later stage they will begin to change the way we live. Arguably, it is only then that we will really start to see the benefits.

Certainly we can identify some basic human needs which the home system should support. These are traditionally represented by 'Maslow's triangle' (Maslow 1954), where the most basic needs (protection, food, shelter) come at the bottom, and at the top comes 'self-fulfilment': the need which is never fully satisfied, however successful you become. Maslow's triangle tells us what the individual needs, but that is not the same as what he consciously wants; and it is these 'wants' which determine the products he will buy. Organisations concentrate on 'needs', individuals focus on 'wants'. This is an important difference between the consumer market and the professional one. The HS products will be consumer products, bought by individuals in response to their 'wants'.

As manufacturers and designers, we can maximise our commercial success by taking account of these 'wants', and ensuring that our products and systems offer clear benefits when judged by these criteria. They can be represented as a 6-level triangle (see Fig. 1). At each level there are two important personal questions to be considered:

- How important is this aspect?
- How much price premium would you pay for a product which offered it?

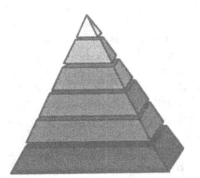

Pleasure

Convenience

Economy

Security

Safety

Environment

Fig. 1.   6-level triangle of wants

1.1.1 Level 1 - Environment

This is the most basic 'need': that the product should not harm the environment. Most consumers care about this, and prepared to do what they can to help. However, few of us are willing to pay a very high premium for 'environmentally friendly' products. It therefore rates low as a 'want'.

1.1.2 Level 2 - Safety

Clearly products must be safe, but we do not expect to pay a premium for this. We may, though, pay for 'extra' safety features. Car makers frequently highlight safety features in their adverts, but there is little evidence that this is seen as a selling point in other consumer products.

1.1.3 Level 3 - Security

Crime figures seem to be rising inexorably, and a recent UK newspaper survey showed 'fear of crime' rising even more rapidly than crime itself. Sales of security products are rising, but the proportion of disposable income spent on these remains rather low.

1.1.4 Level 4 - Economy

Saving money is a very powerful incentive to buy. For professional products it is probably the most important. Even for domestic purchases, the argument that the product will 'pay for itself' may be enough to clinch the sale - provided the message is understood, and believed!

1.1.5 Level 5 - Convenience

To the businessman 'time is money', and money spent on improving productivity is clearly a wise investment. In the home, saving time and effort may seem to be less important than saving money; however, most of the expensive products in our kitchens are bought purely for their convenience.

1.1.6 Level 6 - Pleasure

Clearly this is the most frivolous and least important reason for buying anything. Advertising a professional product as 'fun to use' must surely be the kiss of death - no corporation pays its employees to have fun, and this Calvinistic attitude is carried over into the home. We like to think that we buy things for sensible, practical reasons. Nevertheless, an impartial check on the bank account reveals that most of our purchases are strongly influenced by the 'fun' element. All our entertainment products (TV, video, hi-fi), and most of our hobby equipment (musical instruments, computers, craft tools and sports equipment) fall into this category; and if you add expenditure on holidays, entertainment and dining out you see how the 'fun' category dominates personal spending. Disposable income continues to increase, creating an expanding market for non-essential ('fun') products, and as the market increases, the prices tend to fall, making these goods even more affordable, and bringing them within the reach of yet more consumers.

This analysis is helpful for the definition of products, systems and services, and is a refinement of the technique which was used in the user requirements study for ESPRIT Project 2431 - Home Systems. History is littered with unsuccessful inventions which failed to find a market. We must ensure that the new products and services we propose are not just based on 'technology push', or even on 'social needs', but on a sound understanding of what the customer wants, and is therefore prepared to pay for.

1.2   Flexibility

One of the important differences between professional and domestic products is that professional ones can be more dedicated to a specific job. In the home we have a huge variety of tasks, and we expect our machines to be adaptable and general-purpose. Add the importance of low-cost, and we see why many domestic products fail to completely satisfy. Furthermore, each consumer is an individual with different 'wants'.

The key to solving this problem is modularity. Just as a small range of 'LEGO' bricks can be assembled into an infinite variety of models, so modular design enables a manufacturer to offer a wide variety of products with a small set of basic modules. This modular approach can also be extended to allow the consumer to 'mix-and-match' component products to produce a customised system. This concept is well-established in the hi-fi world, where the enthusiast will carefully select amplifier, CD player, FM tuner, tape deck, loud-speakers, etc. to create an ideal hi-fi system. Of course, no two consumers will agree on the ideal selection, but that does not matter because all have the satisfaction of knowing they got what was just right for them.

In essence, this same approach is used for the home system: modular products can be linked together into a personalised system. The user benefits are:
• Buy what you need now - add what you want later.
• Extend your system when you want to.
• Upgrade by replacing or adding individual products.

The concept is simple, but the technical problems are considerable. The consumer is not a technical expert, and will expect everything to work first time. Interconnection must be fool-proof, and compatibility between products must be assured - between products from different companies, and between old and new products. In addition, the added cost of the interconnection technology must be minimal, and well-justified by clear operational benefits.

1.3   Facilities

Linking the products together into a Home System provides facilities in three categories:
• Remote control - the concept of controlling your entertainment from the arm-chair is well established, but thanks to the link, you may be able to control any product from anywhere in the house - or even from beyond, through the

telephone system. Such free access may be a mixed blessing: it might be convenient to be able to unlock the front door from a distance, but annoying if another resident does it by mistake, and totally unacceptable if the 'hi-tech' burglar is able to do it. We will see later how these undesirable aspects can be avoided.

- Distribution of services - many services are brought to our homes via the telephone, cable TV, satellite, etc. Subject to legal restrictions, these services may be distributed around the home so that they can be accessed from any room. Services generated within the house can be distributed in the same way (e.g. music from a CD player, pictures from a surveillance camera).
- Automatic operation - products communicating and inter-operating without explicit human interaction has been the main focus for the Home Systems programme, and offers great scope for new business opportunities.

Remote control and flexible distribution of services are useful improvements, but Home Automation is the major benefit. However, it is a new concept for consumers, and the benefits will need to be clearly explained to induce the householder to invest in new equipment. Identifying the 'killer applications' is crucial. Smart energy management and security seem the most likely candidates in the short term.

1.4   Is it achievable?

Many researchers will be sharing their visions of the 'home of the future'. I will concentrate on the practical aspects - turning system concepts into the commercial reality of practical products. There is undoubtedly a potential market - and a very large one. So where is the business? Why are our houses not already fitted with these 'home automation' products?

To some extent we already have them - or at least, some of them. Central heating systems have been automatically controlling our environment for several decades, many homes have automatic intruder alarm systems (of varying sophistication), and some video entertainment systems have interlinked controls so that (for example) when you play a video tape the TV switches on automatically.

Of course, people's expectations for 'home automation' go way beyond this; but although existing systems are limited in scope, they do show the way ahead. Co-operation between products needs some intelligence within the products themselves, and a means of exchanging messages. The 'home bus' is that communication link. It may take the form of a thin wire, daisy-chained from one product to the next. Alternatively, the control signal can be carried on the mains cable ('power line signalling'), or an infra-red beam (like TV remote control) or even via a radio link (possibly using cordless telephone technology).

This was the starting point for ESPRIT Project 2431 - *Home Systems*, which brought together 10 major European companies (ESPRIT Project 2431 1989) in a 2-year co-operation to define a Home Systems Specification which could provide a practical and useful basis for products and sub-systems covering application areas as diverse as lighting, heating, security, domestic appliances, communications and audio/video entertainment.

The technical problems are very considerable. I will discuss the more important ones later. Although there have been many attempts to launch 'home bus' systems in the past, they have had little success. Some were too expensive, some were too restrictive (in terms of applications covered and choice of products). Most satisfied very few of the 'wants' identified above, and none offered a wide base of manufacturers making compatible products.

At the beginning of the ESPRIT Home Systems project in 1989 we surveyed the work done up to that point. As well as several single-manufacturer offerings, there were a few larger co-operative initiatives. In Japan a consortium of consumer electronic and telecommunications companies had completed their work and published the HBS standard (Electronic Industries 1986). In the USA there were two consortia: CEBus and Smart House. In Europe, the Eureka EU-84 project (IHS) was completing its initial phase. This work was the starting point for ESPRIT Home Systems.

From a study of previous work it was clear that:

- The communications aspect is not technically difficult (though selection of a good, cost effective solution for in-house use is by no means trivial).
- Compatibility between products from different manufacturers is very difficult to ensure.
- A fixed list of product types (e.g. 'light', 'TV', 'door-lock', ... as advocated by HBS) is not practical, because of new inventions and 'combination' products.
- An exclusive set of application categories (e.g. 'security', 'lighting', 'audio/video', ... as advocated by IHS) is not practical because of products (like 'PIR sensor' or 'camera') which can fit into several categories.
- A 'common command language' (advocated by CEBus) can never be complete (because manufacturers keep thinking of new features).
- Allowing each manufacturer to define his own command language (advocated by Smart House) is not practical because although products from different manufacturers can exchange messages, they do not understand them, so cannot co-operate.

It was clear that the major problems lay in the area of machine-to-machine dialogue (vital for automatic operation). It is not enough to receive the message; it must also be understood. In a competitive and fast-moving market like consumer electronics, product software may be modified every year to add new features. There is no way that a video recorder from Company A can be aware of all the features in a TV from Company B; and if products can only rely on basic functionality, any competitive advantage from a new feature is lost.

It is in this area of 'inter-working' that the real challenge lies, and this is where the ESPRIT Home Systems project made its major contribution.

2   Designing the system

Good architecture is just as important for the Home System (HS) as it is for the structure of a building. In the ESPRIT Home Systems project we started with a Requirements Survey to identify user requirements and key applications. We concentrated on the needs of a domestic residence (there are already Building Automation systems which address the needs of large industrial and institutional buildings). We identified the following key application areas:

- Lighting - introducing automation for energy efficiency and decor (e.g. 'mood' lighting).
- Heating - the main consumer of energy, so great scope for 'intelligent' control.
- Domestic Appliances - non-urgent processes like washing may be delayed until the next cheap energy period.
- Security - reliability can be improved with extra sensors and more intelligence.
- Communications - telephone and intercom services, with convenient access to external service providers.
- Audio/Video Entertainment - not just 'passive' entertainment, but hobbies and study material as well.

The Home System is essentially a distribution system to bring 'services' to the residents - wherever they happen to be. For example, the movie playing on the video may be watched in any room; your telephone calls should be automatically directed to the nearest phone, information should always be available on demand, and displayed on a nearby screen (or voiced through a convenient loud-speaker or telephone). In addition to these interactive services, the system is constantly monitoring the environment and taking action. Some of these may have been pre-programmed by the user, but many will be entirely automatic, and 'invisible'.

The householder may never know how many burglars were foiled by the security system, how many accidents were prevented by automatically turning off equipment which the user had left on, or how much money was saved through intelligent energy management. Of course, it is not mandatory for the products to be so modest about their actions, and a manufacturer may like to make a feature of status information - making the customer 'feel good' by indicating achievements, either on a built-in display panel, or by using a convenient TV as a display screen.

The system can also maximise the utilisation of shared resources. For example, when the video recorder is playing a tape, its tuner is not in use. This can be 'borrowed' by a TV set (possibly in another part of the house) to display a second TV programme as a small insert picture on top of the main one. Modular products are inevitably dearer than combination products (the 'music centre' with all the components built into one cabinet, and fed from one power supply is cheaper than an equivalent stack of hi-fi 'separates'); but the flexibility and freedom of choice is one justification; and, in the case of the distributed Home System, equipment sharing is another. Home System products are 'location independent'. If I buy one high quality player (located anywhere in the house) the high quality service can be brought to me wherever I am. There is the further benefit that bulky equipment can be located out of the way (e.g. in the attic or the cellar), but controlled and enjoyed throughout the house.

2.1   Decision making

The key to an effective system architecture is recognising the central role of decision making. For conventional products, the decision making element is the user. He/she sets a goal, and evolves a control strategy to achieve it. This is a command driven model, so in principle the messages are one-way.

e.g.:   "START RECORDING"

In practice this is unreliable without confirmatory feedback. A simple acknowledgement provides reassurance that the command is understood and will be acted upon.

e.g.:   "START RECORDING"
         "OK"   (or "ERROR")

A more comprehensive 'indication' is desirable when there is a problem. This allows the controller to cope with the unexpected.

e.g.:   "START RECORDING"
         "ERROR - NO TAPE PRESENT"

The controller now has some useful information which may help in formulating a strategy to solve the problem. This analysis is equally appropriate whether the 'controller' is a human operator, or a microprocessor. In the latter case, it clearly does not matter whether it is located inside the product being controlled, or in another product - provided we ensure that there is only one controller in charge. We will see later how to achieve this.

The main benefit of separating the 'decision-making' element from the 'activator' element is economic. Although microprocessors are cheap, and every HS product will have one, the amount of intelligence (i.e. the size of the memory chip and the amount of software it contains) does have a bearing on the cost of the product. It is therefore essential to minimise the software requirement in each product by optimising the partitioning of intelligence between products.

2.2   Home Systems architecture

In the Home Systems architecture we define two basic types of entity: the DEVICE and the FEATURE CONTROLLER. Many products contain several devices: the component devices in a TV might be: "Display"; "Sound System"; "Tuner"; "Teletext Decoder". Those in a washing machine might be: "Water Valve"; "Detergent Dispenser"; "Heater"; "Drum Motor"; "Pump"; "Door Lock". In both cases there will be a control panel linked to a "Feature Controller" which co-ordinates the actions of the devices in order to provide the 'service' ("Watch TV", or "Wash Clothes"), and any special features ("Auto Tune", "Economy").

'Devices' have minimal intelligence. They receive 'commands' from the Feature Controller, and 'do as they are told'. A complex product (such as the TV or washing machine) is conceptually modelled as a sub-system - a set of devices linked to a Feature Controller - but it is up to the product designer to decide whether each device will be connected to the Home Bus. The advantage of doing this is that individual devices can then be available to external controllers. This allows the sharing of their application resources (as explained above), and it also enables an external Feature Controller to add supplementary features. However, the cost of bus interface hardware for every device within the product will not always be acceptable. In this case the HS product appears as a 'black box', and the other products in the Home System will only be able to communicate with that product's Feature Controller.

Devices are rather simple, and in this way we minimise the incremental cost of HS. Some products may not need a Feature Controller at all, and an entire sub-system may only need one. A lighting system for the whole house might have just one Feature Controller (which might be built into a central switch panel, but could be remotely located). The heating system might have one for general control, but there may be another one in the boiler, dedicated to maximising the efficiency and safety of that product. Coming to the entertainment system, I would expect to find rather a lot of Feature Controllers. For a start, each product will have one containing its own inherent features. There may be one dedicated to managing the in-house video distribution (re-using spare channels for locally-generated signals), and others providing special features between entertainment products, or allowing the TV to be used as a display panel for other systems in the house (e.g. graphics to display energy usage, or indicate services in use and any charges being incurred).

2.3   Data transfer

A control bus allows us to remotely control the products, and also supports fully automatic operations. The control messages are short (typically a few bytes), so a relatively slow serial-data 'packet service' is perfectly adequate. The general-purpose wired bus defined for HS (called TP-1) can handle about 30 commands per second. If a product is already transmitting, another product will have to wait for a gap, but the delay is rarely more than a tenth of a second.

Some applications, however, need to exchange more data. A few kilobytes (for on-screen menus or product set-up tables) can be transmitted over TP-1 with little delay, but more data-intensive services require either a much faster packet service, or a wide-band real-time channel. This cannot be provided on TP-1, but TP-2 can offer ISDN-style data channels (it is designed to handle 14 digitised voice channels), and the CX medium (coaxial cable) provides a flexible wide-band (800 MHz) real-time service, which can be divided into several FDM channels - for example: 30-50 TV channels. The channel allocation can be intelligently controlled (by a special Feature Controller) to support any mix of audio, video and data channels, provided the overall bandwidth does not exceed the cable capacity.

A third network service is Power Feed. Many products will have their own power supply; but some units connected to one of the wired media, TP-1 or TP-2, may have modest power requirements, in which case it is useful to power them from the bus.

3   Managing the system

To meet its promise, the Home System must deliver pleasure, convenience, economy, security, safety and environmental protection - all at an affordable price, and with readily obtainable, fully compatible products which need no professional installation, and are easy to use. The key to achieving this is System Management, which can be categorised into Network Management (controlling the communications between products) and Application Management (controlling the way the products interact and work together).

3.1   Network management

Each message is transmitted in a data packet which contains 'header' data. This includes the destination and source addresses, and message priority. Network management acts like a postal service, ensuring that any 'undeliverable' messages are 'returned to sender', reporting and correcting problems, and maximising the efficiency of the messaging service - particularly under heavy traffic conditions.

Address management, whereby a new product on the bus obtains a unique address, is also part of Network Management. Under HS rules, this can be fully automatic (and normally will be for consumer products), though HS products can, alternatively, have locally set addresses (typically used for professionally-installed products such as lights and switches).

3.2   Application management

An application is a service which the Home System provides. That service (e.g. detecting intruders and taking action) will be a commercial product which the consumer buys. It will take the form of a product containing embedded software. It uses the 'application resources' of other products already connected (e.g. various sensors to detect human presence, alarms to deter intruders and warn the occupants, cameras and video recorder to provide evidence, telephone to call for assistance). It communicates with them via the bus. Because this new product (a 'Feature Controller') can use the existing (general purpose) HS products, instead of needing a full set of dedicated peripherals for each new application, this makes the application much more affordable.

The new product first finds out what products already exist on the network, and what they can do. This allows it to build up a list of devices it can use. Most of the devices fall within standardised categories, and respond to standard commands. Thus a Feature Controller can (for example) not only recognise the existence of a video recorder (irrespective of its make or model), but also tune it to the camera output channel and command it to start recording.

Strictly speaking, it is not a 'video recorder' which is recognised, but a 'tuner' and a 'deck' (i.e. the relevant sub-units of a video recorder). The distinction may sound pedantic, but is a very important one. Real products often contain several electro-mechanical and electronic sub-units, some of which are fundamental to its operation, while others add extra features (and may not be present in a low-cost product). For a video recorder, the tuner and deck are fundamental. It may (optionally) have extra units such as a stereo decoder, teletext receiver, a screen (so you can see what it is recording), and even a second deck to allow copying. In a competitive market where manufacturers may choose to put a screen on a video recorder, or build a tape deck into a TV, terms like 'video recorder' or 'TV' can become rather arbitrary: somewhat confusing for the human user; and totally baffling for a microprocessor!

In a home system, the functionality is determined by the sub-units, and their physical location is entirely arbitrary. This leaves the manufacturer free to select whatever components he wishes to include in his product, and also create new combination products. Furthermore, since all these competitive products are made from a small set of sub-units, with well-defined basic functions, they can easily be recognised and operated by an external Feature Controller.

With all sub-units controllable by any Feature Controller we need to ensure that no conflict occurs when two Feature Controllers want to control the same device. This is handled by a 'Token mechanism'. A Feature Controller can only control a device if it holds its Token. When a Feature Controller wants to operate a device, it first requests the Token. If the device reports that its Token is already held by another Feature Controller, the two Feature Controllers must negotiate for permission to control the device. There is also a 'bundle mechanism' which allows a Feature Controller to claim a complete set of Tokens from all the devices necessary to execute that particular application.

4   Creating home system (HS) products

For the manufacturer of consumer products, the main attraction of HS is probably the prospect of 'plug-&-play' products. This is a business he knows well - the customer buys the product, takes it home, plugs it in, and it immediately starts working. Not only are HS products just like familiar ones in this respect, they are able to work first time, even without the user setting them up, because they immediately start communicating on the bus, and then set themselves up.

HS products are also ideal for specialist (niche) markets, because of their modular structure. This means that standard units can be configured for special applications (e.g. systems to help the disabled or elderly live a more normal life).

4.1   Product design

To gain maximum benefit from a home system, the component products should be designed so that their resources can be shared - i.e. the products themselves should follow the rules of HS architecture, with their sub-units capable of being controlled by other (external) Feature Controllers, as well as any which may be built into that product. Although such 'well-behaved' products will be extremely useful, and result in the most cost-effective solution for the large home system, it is left to the manufacturer to decide just how 'transparent' his HS product shall be, with due regard to cost and purpose.

The door lock which secures your house is just one example of a product which should not be controllable by any Feature Controller that might be plugged into the system (we must guard against the 'high tech' burglar). This particular product should not be modelled as an HS 'Device' (which would lock and unlock whenever it received a valid command), but as an HS 'Feature Controller', directly operating the lock mechanism. The door lock then becomes an intelligent product which can provide a much higher level of security.

It is most important to ensure that manufacturers making compatible products still have the maximum possible freedom of choice in terms of unique selling points, and the facilities provided by their product - both in relation to their operational functionality, and their availability to co-operate with other products through the home network.

4.2   Components

Cost is always a crucial factor for consumer products, and the incremental cost of adding the bus connection must be kept as low as possible. Dedicated chips are already in development, but HS can also be implemented with commodity components, such as the popular (and low-cost) 8051 microprocessor. For a cost-sensitive product, the 8051 can look after the bus communications, system management, and application code (features). For more demanding applications the designer may prefer to partition these functions, either by using a second 8051, or a dedicated bus controller chip such as the MB86046B Home Bus Protocol Controller.

4.3   Software tools

Like most consumer products nowadays, HS products rely on software which is 'embedded' in a chip. This software includes the logic of the specific application, as well as the standard HS communications and management code. The simplest way to create this integrated piece of software is on the *HS-Tools Developer's Workstation*. This was developed by Philips APG in an extension of the ESPRIT Home Systems project. HS communications and system management software libraries are built into the Workstation, and the user only has to define the application code for the product (in 'C'). The Workstation then compiles this, including the HS libraries, to create two versions of the complete product software: a version which will run on a PC (for testing or simulation), and product code which will run on an 8051 microprocessor.

The Workstation can also be used to simulate a product, or even a complete system comprising several products. This is useful in the definition phase to enable the implementor to try out different strategies, features and configurations before committing to expensive engineering. Nor is the simulation time wasted, for the final version of the simulation 'C' code becomes the source code for its 8051 cross-compiler which creates embedded software to realise the first prototype. This prototype can then be connected to the Workstation, which becomes a test-bed on which your new product concept can be exercised within its envisaged system. The component products of this system, if they already exist, can be connected to the Workstation. It then acts as a 'bus monitor', logging all messages and enabling the test engineer to confirm correct operation (or revealing problems which can immediately be corrected). If any of the system components do not yet exist, the Workstation can simulate the missing products, and (at the same time) run the diagnostic tests. The development environment is optimised for rapid development and prototyping, minimising the time to market. This easy-to-use tool brings HS product development within the capabilities of the smallest company, and should lead to a rapid increase in the HS product base.

5   Conclusion

I sometimes ask people, "How many microprocessors do you own?" Some will look blank and uncomprehending, but most will confidently say, "None", while several will confess to one or two. Almost certainly they have at least 20, and probably a lot more. What most people do not realise is that the microprocessor is not restricted to the PC: it is at the heart of almost every TV, video recorder, washing machine, microwave oven, and telephone; and is already well established in vacuum cleaners, sewing machines, food mixers, radios - virtually every electrical product in the home. Yet this revolution has been so quiet that most people are unaware that the reason their new products offer so many attractive automatic features is due to a microprocessor inside.

I believe the Home Systems revolution will be almost as unobtrusive. Technology should not intrude. It should serve quietly and efficiently - like the perfect butler. Indeed, the Home System may be able to offer ordinary people many of the facilities which the rich get from a butler: automatically turning things on or off when you forget; learning your preferences and offering services which are likely to appeal to you; providing expert advice; taking care of the tiresome jobs; monitoring expenditure. Like all technological revolutions, it will probably change our life-style. It will certainly offer a great many business opportunities for manufacturers, installers and service providers.

References

Electronic Industries Association of Japan (EIAJ), Standardisation of Home Bus System, June 1986 (in Japanese)

ESPRIT Project 2431 - Home Systems. Members were Philips (co-ordinator), ABB, AEG/Daimler Benz, British Telecom, GEC, Legrand, Thomson CE, Thorn EMI, Siemens and Zeltron. The 2-year project began in January 1989, and was followed by a 14-month ESPRIT Project 5448 - Integrated Interactive Home, which validated the specification and demonstrated integrated applications.

Maslow, Abraham H., Motivation and Personality, Harper & Brothers, New York, 1954

Teleshopping:
Today's Solutions and Future Trends

Heiner Drathen
Daimler-Benz Interservices (debis) Systemhaus Dienstleistungen GmbH, Germany

1   Introduction

Currently companies present their goods and services using a wide range of different media. The aim is always the same: To raise the customers' desire. At last, one wants to sell.

Customer penetration and thus selling itself is restricted by federal law and rules. Mail-order companies have the best position in this context, as they bring their "warehouse" to the customers' living rooms. Orders can be submitted at any time (by mail, fax, phone or videotex). This flexibility nowadays is also desired by other trade companies. The slogan is "all goods, any time, anywhere".

As children are more familiar with personal computers (PCs) and the more or less convenient applications than today's typical customers, this technology is the evolving platform for retailers to prepare themselves for future customer "attacks".

Multimedia product presentation and multimedia products state a new way for exciting and convenient shopping. The path seems to be clear: Starting with conventional POI systems, it leads via CD-ROM to teleshopping and (still science-fiction!?) to "ALICE", the foreseen housefriend in future kitchens. This is still a long way to go, but the future has already begun, so electronic shopping should become a strategic target for retailers today. Entering this technology at an early stage enables and encourages managers and personnel to experiment with different approaches to find their best solution.

The most exciting challenge is to incorporate the "high touch", i.e. the direct and personal contact to the customers, into the "high tech" approach of today's and future solutions. This is to take advantage from the technical power of the electronic shopping assistants in creating sophisticated screens, adventure elements and a high level of user-friendliness. The intention is to make the customer feel comfortable on an exciting shopping-adventure tour to finally order the products (s)he has seen.

Each project in this area of "multimedia shopping" is best characterised by the following attributes:

- complex
- tough time scale
- limited budget and
- interdisciplinary (very different skills are required)

Such a project consists of diverse components which are (roughly spoken):
- artwork for screens, sounds, videos and texts
- user interaction: navigation, search, order
- online communication: videotex, online services, back-channel for interactive TV (I-TV)

Thus integration of these components as well as the very different kind of people is the real challenge within multimedia projects.

The following article describes aims and solutions for a multimedia application produced for one of the world's leading mail order companies, the Quelle Schickedanz AG in Fürth. It will cover benefits and restrictions of nowadays implementations (drawn from the Quelle project) for the companies as well as for the end user.

For this we will start with a brief description of the project history. We will show, which goals Quelle wanted to achieve with the CD and what debis System-haus did to meet these targets.

Based on this section we will discuss the limitations posed on such projects be it today's hardware or project timescale.

The closing section will deal with future scenarios and even with a long term vision of a "Virtual Warehouse".

2   Scope

Multimedia is one of the most used words in today's DP departments and even in the consumer market. No PC vendor will distribute advertising material without the magic word. Even if those machines are not even suited for very simple and poor animated applications (4 MB RAM) they are in the center of customers' interest.

No wonder that software vendors and DP personell all over the world are planning and already implementing multimedia applications and multimedia features even for classical business- and technical applications.

The following list gives some examples of where multimedia is used today:
- education and training
- point of information systems
- games
- visitor conducting systems
- travel consulting

All of this is right at the beginning. Only for Germany analysts expect a market growth of 1,000% by the year 2000 in the area of multimedia. These margins are related to an absolute amount of five billion DM today. So it is not surprising, that ever more vendors enter the scene.

This article will not cover the multimedia trends for application areas listed above. We will deal with the exciting area of article presentation and (of course) selling-support.

3   "Die Quelle CD-ROM - Hier werden Sie interaktiv"

This slogan has been used by Quelle to launch the first really professional and "media-adequate" article presentation on CD-ROM on the German market. The first edition of 50,000 CDs was sold out within four weeks. This illustrates how big the demand for shopping CDs and multimedia features is. But let's put it to the start.

3.1   Quelle's goals

To be honest, in the beginning our thoughts were like this: "Of course they want a CD as OTTO has one." But after the first talks it was obvious, that Quelle wanted much more than the biggest player in the mail-order scene. Investigating OTTO's first approach we all together found out, that it was a pretty poor solution just to digitalize a couple of catologue pages and put Cindy Crawford as eyecatcher onto the first page. This was not what we felt a multimedia approach should look like.

It was Quelle's major target to have a "media-adequate" product presentation (as they called it). That meant, a computer screen is not a catalogue page. Be it the horizontal format of the screen or the limited ability for true colour presentation. On the other hand a computer based product presentation allows for much more flexibility in the area of user guidance and of course for a lot of multimedia fun. So it was obvious that something completely different was to be designed. The following list comprises Quelle's requirements:

- state Quelle's leading position in the area of technical innovation
- provide a product for new customer acquisition (address the "game boy generation")
- don't drop the "classical" Quelle customer
- gain experience in electronic product presentation. This incorporated some "second-level" targets, which illustrated the benefits of electronic product presentation by incorporating functionality and features, a print catalogue cannot provide.
- don't try to copy the print catalogue
- transport a "shopping is fun" feeling to the end-user
- illustrate "true" benefits of the CD

3.2   The solutions

The first and maybe biggest challenge for such kind of projects is to map such high sophisticated requirements to a very limited budget and timescale. Furthermore, today's hardware in typical households is pretty poor. Most end-users own something like a 386 PC with about 33 MHz, 4-8 MB main memory and a more or less slow video adapter. Real multimedia animation can be boring if it is presented on such machines. Even today PC vendors don't hesitate to claim their 4 MB machines to support "multimedia", if they have only a CD-ROM drive and a sound card.

As really sophisticated multimedia effects such as videos, animations and good sound are very memory consuming, a bottomline had to be found. With Quelle we agreed on a 486 DX 2 PC with 66 MHz and 8 MB main memory. This seemed a reasonable compromise between quality and available platforms in the end-user market.

Other compromises were necessary due to a timescale of less than four months for the project. A couple of improvements and "gimmicks", as we called funny multimedia effects, had to be put on the requirement list for the second generation.

But enough of problems and limitations. What we delivered to Quelle in early February 1995 was nevertheless an impressive illustration of how product presentation can look like today. This could only be achieved by toughly monitoring the creative and technical approaches. For each idea the question "What does it contribute to the targets?" had to be answered. And here is what we did:

The most important task of a shopping CD is of course to help in selling goods. So the focus for this CD was put on an area we called *screen-design*. This is, how are the articles presented to the user. The approach chosen for this project was to have a full screen presentation for each major product. This product is supported and not disturbed by other screen elements. This is an individually created background for each product page and (sometimes) nice "gimmicks" to surprise and animate the user. Furthermore almost each screen builds up one layer after the other, so the feeling is much like viewing a film.

Nothing looks like a computer screen, a "window" or a scroll bar. No "technical look and feel" has been incorporated. Only the minimal amount of control elements are visible. Additional information is only displayed on user request so the product is not disturbed by anything else.

For a broad acceptance not only nice screens are neccessary. The system must be easy to use. So another focus was *user-friendliness*. Together with Quelle we designed a "cockpit" with four functions on each product page. Scroll forward, scroll backward, viewer, info. The scrolling functions are symbolised by icons known from consumer electronic devices such as CD-players or VCRs. To furthermore improve learnability of the system, a colour code and a sign code concept were used. The colour code is: "Wherever something is displayed white on blue you can click to control the system." The sign code is: "Whenever the cursor changes shape from arrow to hand, you can reveil something." That means, you have found some hidden gimmick and pressing will show what it is. That is all a user has to find out to completely manage through the system. Things cannot be much easier.

One thing a print catalogue never can provide is individuality. Each customer gets his copy of the 1389 pages with washing machines on pages 700 and following or so even if he is never interested in them. So mail-order companies are looking for solutions to this problem. Obviously a print catalogue cannot resolve the contradiction between cost efficiency and individuality. But electronic catalogues can. One approach (much more sophisticated solutions are possible with online services and I-TV, see below) has been incorporated on the CD. With very powerful search functions the user may compile his or her individual catalogue. Successive searches with different criteria may be used to assemble a product list over shop boundaries neglecting anything he is not interested in. Scrolling through the articles is then done on the basis of this product list and not longer through the whole catalogue. Of course the user may cancel this function whenever he wants.

What do you do if you want to order something from a catalogue? You take out the order form (Where the hell have I put it?) fill in the article name (How did they spell it?) and the order number (Was it -89 or -98 at the end?). You repeat this several times, then you post a stamp on it (Why do I have none?) and finally mail it to the mail order company. As this does not only read very complicated but prooves to be boring in practical life most mail-order companies have installed services to allow for ordering by phone or fax. But this does only resolve the problem with the stamp.

A real breakthrough can only be achieved by a combination of electronic product presentation and an online ordering facility. Today the commonly used online service is videotex, or as it is called in Germany: BTX (Bildschirmtext). This is why the Quelle CD provides functions and facilities to automatically order via videotex. No puzzling around with numbers, names and stamps. The only thing the user has to do is to select the article(s) during his shopping walk through the CD and later on "click" on the "order via BTX" button.

As an additional benefit, he gets immediate response about actual prices (which may be less than the catalogue price) and availability.

All these things sound very technical and theoretical. To not forget the shopping fun we have incorporated a couple of video and audio gimmicks. Among others, the "Lion King" spot from Walt Disney is on the CD as well as the TV-spots from Quelle itself. A roaring lion accompanies a "Lion King" towel and clicking on a lamp switches it "On" and "Off".

There is a lot more of functionality and fun on the CD but it is not our aim to tell an exhausting story of what we did. So if you are interested in more, just have a look at the product itself.

4   The benefits

Whenever somebody spends money for something, he expects to have some measurable or not measurable advantage from this. So what advantages takes a trade company from such a CD and which ones takes the end-user (by paying five to ten DM for the product)?

We will discuss this in two sections:
- benefits for retailers and end-users
- benefits from selecting the *debis Systemhaus* as solution provider

4.1   Benefits for retailers and end-users

The last section has shown how the targets of Quelle have been met by the project. So most of the advantages for mail order companies are already obvious. For this section we expand the scope to retailers as a whole.

Today opening hours for stores and warehouses are restricted by federal law. Even where these laws are not so restrictive as they are in Germany, long opening hours put a heavy load on retailers profit due to high costs for personell and energy. Furthermore big warehouses don't increase overview and convenience for the customer. Germany's biggest warehouse, the KaDeWe in Berlin states that almost every second customer leaves the store without having found the articles he came for.

Even if you take time for shopping, didn't you ever feel you could spend your time better than looking for a parking place, dazzling around in overful warehouses, carrying bags and packages through bulks of people, all in a hurry?

A lot of these problems can be overcome by amending physical product presentation in a warehouse by a "product CD" or online product presentation. The customer can pre-select the products at his PC. He gets the feeling to control the scene instead of being controlled by selling personell, other customers or restricted opening hours.

In the next step he may order the selected goods even from the warehouse in the city. This is similar to what he does today with pizza or spaghetti. No laws tell him when he has to buy.

Imagine the following scenario: You come home from work at 7 pm. Turning on the television results in a "Blob", the tube is broken. That means, the football match will take place without you. What a nice evening. What if you could turn on your PC, have a look at the TV sets of several warehouses and select a new one. Let's go further, you have found a suited set, click on the order button and 50 minutes later the technician delivers the new TV at your door. Just enough time to plug in the machine before the football match begins.

This is not science-fiction. Anything described here is possible with today's technology. The only thing missing is a warehouse that provides this service.

Thinking a bit further (still no *vision* required) lead to a lot of solutions, today's customers would gratefully accept. I guess, each of you, dear reader, could amend the list by three examples without long thinking.

4.2   debis Systemhaus

The Quelle-CD project has proven it and all investigations concerning future approaches lead to the same conclusion. Multimedia projects are more than the sum of their parts. These parts are among others:
- creative design work
- technical design work
- online communication
- business skills in the retail market

One of the most complex challenges is to make all these skills come together and, of course, work together.

Multimedia agencies are small, flexible, innovative and, in a good sense, a bit chaotic. So they are best prepared for executing creative work. Other units have a deep knowledge in the area of telecommunication. But there does not exist the one company with best skill in all areas.

This is why such multimedia projects require an experienced system integrator. It is his job to bring the different skills (always the best in the special area) together and make them work for one common goal. No one else than he can be responsible for project management, accordance to timescale, and fitting of interfaces. It is not up to him, how a screen is designed or how a communication line is established, but it is up to him that the product on the screen is properly ordered via the line.

This requires a special skill and well established procedures for project management and quality assurance not available in (most) small companies.

The debis Systemhaus as the biggest German Systemhaus is best prepared for this kind of work (as has been stated at least during the CD-ROM project). It has standardised procedures for project management, well tested lifecycle models for all kinds of project, even System Integration projects and, being ISO 9001 compliant, an independant quality management organisation, which ensures the high quality targets put on such projects.

Most of the jobs sketched above can be performed within other units of the debis Systemhaus or by associated companies.

5   The future

As we have seen, things are right at the beginning. Now that CD-ROM drives and narrowband communication lines and services become cheaper and cheaper, the market has come into motion. It is not easy to tell where things are going. Terms like "Online Services" and "I-TV" are only two examples of technologies that will become important for electronic product presentation in the near future.

5.1   Online services

Today information providers like CompuServe or good old Telekom make their information available on central database servers. The access for the end user at home or in his office is via telefone line and modem. These communication lines are called narrowband lines, because their transmission rate is much below 1 Mbyte/sec. Nevertheless they are fast enough for all kind of text and binary data. Even pictures and sound can be transmitted if they are properly compressed.

In autumn 1995 some very powerful companies will enter the online scene in Europe. Among others these are Microsoft (Microsoft Networks), Burda et al. (Europe Online) and Bertelsmann (America Online).

Along with these network providers their demand for information providers will rise. One fascinating application area is product presentation. It is obvious that extending the CD-ROM approach by online facilities opens a new field of applications. To give three examples:

One of the selected articles is sold out. Via online services, Quelle can suggest alternatives for which the screens are provided from the online server. Furthermore the sold out article can be logically deleted from the CD.

Mail-order companies know a lot about wishes and buying behaviour of their customers. So they can assemble an individually customised catalogue for the logged-in customer. For the first step, screens may still come from a CD, but the system may be controlled via an online server. In a later phase the CD may become obsolete; i.e. the screens and animations may come from the online server as well.

Prices and products on the CD can be updated whenever the user connects to the online service.

One of the major advantages for the upcoming online services is that they are cheap. As they use the current telephone network, no investment is required for cabling systems. The only costs for the customer comprise of a modem (about DM 150) and an initial software package (today about DM 50 for CompuServe). No additional hardware is required and you can subscribe immediately.

The drawback however is, that shopping still takes place in the home office rather than in the living room. As mail-order companies state, this is not the normal surrounding for relaxed shopping. Most mail-order customers scroll through their catalogue while lying on the sofa. Furthermore most mail-order customers don't even have a PC.

5.2   Interactive TV (I-TV)

The magic word for Germany's big mail-order companies. Quelle as well as OTTO and Neckermann have decided to bet on that horse. Unfortunately all will loose within the next few years.

But what is I-TV? What is the "I"? As this "I" stands for "interactive" it suggests that the end user is allowed to take some influence on what is going on on the screen (apart from zapping).

Applications are teleshopping, games, Video on Demand, education and others.

While Online Sevices communicate via the narrowband telephone network, I-TV uses wideband television lines. That means, first of all, I-TV is only possible within Cable-TV systems. Moreover, I-TV requires a lot of investments, as video-servers for wideband communications are needed and even today's cable TV networks do not provide the bandwidth required for Video On Demand.

To be "interactive", the customer needs a "back-channel", that is a line that leads from his living room to the video server. This back channel is required because TV-systems are not designed (different from telephone lines) for "backwards data traffic").

No standards have been defined for this today.

These tremendeous costs are the reason why I-TV comes very slowly over the land. Some pilots will start by the end of 1995 in Berlin, Hamburg, Stuttgart and some other German areas none with more than 4,000 households. I expect (and so does Bertelsmann's chairman Middelhoff) I-TV to be of importance by 2010.

Studies in the U.S. and Hong Kong have proven that customers' behaviour while watching TV is "passive". They don't want to act in any way. I am in doubt, that teleshopping applications will alter them.

Anyway mail-order companies state "to reach the customers where they want them: in their convenience area." Instead of struggling around with this big catalogue, the customer will scroll through the teleshopping programme of Quelle or Neckermann and order immediately.

The "virtual warehouse" might be in each retailer's dream. Imagine a customised warehouse for each end-user in his own living room. He walks around, inspects and selects products. Of course only those, he is interested in today. Later he walks to the cash zone and pays with his credit card, all without even raising from his chair.

But this really is still science-fiction. Although first approaches are known from Mercedes Benz where you can assemble and test your virtual Mercedes to order it after a test-drive.

Nevertheless for the moment we will not further investigate this approach. Maybe Quelle will be the first retailer to come up with this solution in ten years. Then debis Systemhaus might well be the solution provider again. And this will be reason enough to come up with a new article like this.

Private Household Shopping Behavior

Heribert Popp, Stephan Thesmann, and Peter Mertens
Bavarian Research Center for Knowledge-Based Systems (FORWISS), Germany

1   Introduction/Overview

In future, computer aided purchasing for households might turn the following scenario into reality (see fig. 1): In the privacy of her home, Andrea decides to buy a new shirt. Now she has several options to choose from: she can surf the World Wide Web (WWW) and look through the offers of national and international suppliers or she can hunt for bargains in her regional home shopping network. Another possibility is the use of CD-ROM catalogues of big mail order companies. For home shopping she employs a standard TV and a set-top box. An alternative would be a Multimedia PC. She chooses regional home shopping and can now select one of the electronic product catalogues (EPC) of various multistores. Some of these EPCs are already supported by an advisor system to simplify the selection of a suitable shirt. Electronic shopping centers (malls) represent an alternative way of searching for bargains without being limited to individual stores. Later, Andrea places her order via telephone or data connection.

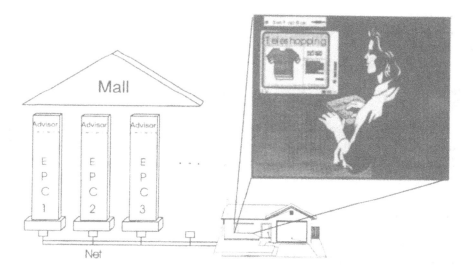

Fig. 1.   Teleshopping using Electronic Product Catalogues (EPC), advisor systems and a mall functionality

Home Shopping needs electronic sales assistants. Key features of successful salespeople include the ability to adapt to the customer's problem fast on the basis of having only limited information, to cope with fuzzy hints and to present a problem solution satisfying the customers' information needs.

Electronic salespeople are expected to have the same capabilities. A set of reference solutions that can be slightly modified reduces the length of the sales talk (Popp/Lödel 1995). The use of fuzzy terms (e.g. "A shirt which is cheap and good") could be facilitated by a fuzzy multicriteria analysis (Popp/Lödel 1995). A user-orientated presentation, in this case a user classification, means that the sales consultant takes the buyer's knowledge and preferences into account when defining the types as well as the quantity of information presented: detailed technical data about a product will lead to technical enthusiasm when presented to a technically experienced person, where exactly the same pieces of information would lead to a lack of interest, or even disappointment, when presented to a rushing inquiry. In these cases, user models are very helpful (Popp/Lödel 1995).

All different phases of a normal sales pitch have to be supported by computer for the household shopping:

- opening of the conversation with the modules contact, welcome and creation of a positive atmosphere
- requirements analysis
- meet the demand with help of electronic catalogues, product databases, videotex (e.g. BTX)
- presentation of the preselected products' attributes using multimedia or even virtual reality
- adaptation of the problem's solution to customer specific requirements (configuration, financing)
- order
- payment
- delivery

2   Opening a conversation

At teleshopping the sound speaker welcomes with friendly words or the program attracts the attention using eye catchers, e.g. animation or video sequences or a little game.

3   Requirements analysis

The electronic shopping process starts with the requirements analysis that is meant to be a suitable introduction for customers without expert knowledge about the product. In general, customers are not delighted if they have to answer many questions in order to purchase an everyday item. They expect the salesperson to put a precompiled offer on the table right away and to adapt it according to their needs.

There are some indications from marketing research that the performance of salespeople heavily depends on their ability to invoke the profile of the closest typical customer and adapt this profile to the individual. A customer typology offers a sensible compromise between regarding every customer as a completely unique case and viewing all of them as an average case. Three major steps are necessary to develop a consultation model which fits this idea (see Popp/Lödel 1995 for details):

- A customer typology and product classes have to be created.
- The model needs a classification rule which maps individual customers to a customer type.
- The links between products and customer types have to be defined.

Therefore, the interview by the advisor systems should be kept general and refer to the various application situations rather than to technical details. The first step's aim is to identify the customers' problems and wishes and to generate a requirements profile for suitable products from this analysis. To minimize the effort necessary to accomplish this first step and to present a basis solution fast, Lödel's concept of requirements analysis is based on user stereotypes, which are activated by basic pieces of information. The user attributes representing the types lead to a requirements profile including necessary product features. There is a possibility to modify and supplement all assumptions of the advisor system. Such a stereotype could be the classification of a high school-age son who wants to buy a PC as a mobile standard user without expansion needs.

As soon as the user has communicated his requirement type a suitable stereotype is activated. If the user is content with all preferences, the system selects all products which fit the internal requirements profile completely or in part and rates them with a grade of suitability. To derive suitable solutions resp. products from these profiles, methods of artificial intelligence, such as Fuzzy Logic and Case Based Reasoning, may be employed.

Now the customer selects one of these preselected items and switches to corresponding pages of the electronic catalogue for more detailed information.

4   Meeting the requirements

4.1   Types of teleshopping

The online system *BTX* that had been introduced in Germany ten years ago was found lacking in many respects. Shortcomings included the low speed (2400 Baud) that made the search for a product a trial of patience. Another reason was the graphic display which was by far not up to date. Nowadays, mail order companies achieve over 500 million DM sales revenue per year via BTX. Over the last two years, the success of Datex-J (14400 Baud), successor to BTX, has been increasing fast. According to the Deutsche Telekom AG, more than 1 million bank accounts are run via Datex-J today. This service is used by about 750,000 people and offers a graphical user interface called KIT (Windows-Based Kernel for Intelligent Communication Terminals), bringing high resolution graphics on the screen (Danke 1994). In the early 80ies, the *Minitel* service was introduced in France. Meanwhile 6.5 million Minitels (1200 Baud) are used in French households. Revenue of 2.3 billion DM was achieved by the various services (mainly information services). Since 1990, the photo-capable Télétel network (9600 Baud) runs where the new customer terminals allow immediate payment of orders via an integrated credit card reader (Cats-Baril/Jelassi 1994).

Actually, in the US 7.2 million private customers use online services like CompuServe, Prodigy and America Online. World-wide online services are e.g. *CompuServe* with 2.6 million users and Internet with more than 20 million people. Among the Internet services *WWW* offers virtual sales places which the customer can enter intuitively (e.g. an Internet Shopping Network with the entrance doors Guided tour, Members only and Membership office) (ISN 1994). In the WWW it is possible to see and compare suppliers' offers around the world. Very detailed information about the customer's needs may be sent by e-mail or saved onto the WWW server directly. Therefore, the selection becomes larger which means that resources could be bought cheaper or in better quality (Jaros-Sturhahn/Löffler 1995). All participants of a service can start an electronic shopping trip around the clock. To access and compare all relevant offers and to select the most attractive one, the help of a specialized database service supplier (online service provider) is necessary.

For *TV home shopping* is popular in the US, infomercials are broadcast continuously via special cable TV channels. These infomercials are shows of up to 25 minutes where the show's host explains the benefits of his product, usually mixed with the newest Hollywood gossip. The order lines' telephone numbers are faded in every five minutes as well as the conditions of payment. In larger US networks, electronic shopping centers have been established - the so called Video Malls - where every shop books time windows or even its own channels to present its products in infomercials. In Germany, infomercials have not been successful to the same extent. German broadcasting stations are allowed to broadcast only one hour of infomercials per day. Increasing acceptance is reached by Direct Response TV. Spots of 30 to 60 seconds in length and with faded in phone number have been broadcast within the normal block of commercials and are intended to promote impulse buying (Burkhardt 1995).

PC owners with *CD-ROM* drive may search for products systematically in catalogues on CD-ROM, as offered by Otto AG and Quelle AG, and watch video sequences presenting the product's features and usefulness. The company 2Market, USA, sent out free CD-ROMs in time before Christmas 1994 on which dozens of the most popular mail order catalogues with tens of thousands of products were stored. A large market exists for this type of service because 15 billion print catalogues are sent out per year in the United States. The technical conditions are fulfilled because private households in the United States will own about 15 million multimedia PCs in 1995 (n.a. 1994). An order could be placed using phones or modems.

Interactive shopping could be improved further by more multimedia capability and user comfort. American trials lead to a concept where a video server offers catalogue sortiments via predefined and fixed channels, from which a viewer can select individual products using a remote control. In this case, it is necessary to expand the TV with a special decoder. The normal telephone line serves as a back channel, fiber optic networks make direct two-way communication possible. Another alternative would be a connection of the PC to the TV cable.

4.2   Hardware

The existing hardware technology for electronic shopping applications is characterized by the fact that besides more text orientated online services (CompuServe, Datex-J) mostly isolated PC solutions are used, where the communication ability restricted to a modem or ISDN based transfer creates problems.

This situation causes several difficulties with the end user such as setting up all communication options of the PC. Most suppliers of the electronic shopping industry have so far only provided the possibility to print out an order form or fax which has to be sent to the service or product supplier in the traditional way.

Concerning the presentation of a product or a service, several other problems occur because audio-visually attractive presentations require PC equipment far exceeding common standards. Such equipment often causes compatibility problems with the supplier's equipment because of special configurations.

Defined standards of a Multimedia PC (MPC II) are a minimum consensus rather than a performance orientated future platform. Furthermore, attractive electronic shopping systems occupy large amounts of PC resources which casts some doubt on the continued use of these systems. In future, central high performance media servers with very large capacity, which are placed far away from the user's PC, high speed connections to these servers via public networks and a standard interface (set-top box, interface card) in the user's device (TV, PC) will play a more and more dominant role (see fig. 2). The impact of highly interactive software on net load and the availability as well as the application specific selection of suitable distribution and communication networks for a given transfer volume or a given transfer intensity are quite unclear. The system requirements are shown in figure 2.

5   Presentation of product features

Electronic catalogues are a special type of digital representation systems. They owe benefits compared to a conventional paper catalogue. EPC are capable of promoting corporate identity product in the presentation (for example by using striking sets of colors and the company logo). Advertising of this kind strengthens the customer's link to the supplier although nearly all contacts are realized via electronic shopping.

Server	Today	Client server architecture, PC and workstation based
	Tomorrow	Video server in an ATM network
Communication	Today	Modem, ISDN, Datex-J, video text, internet
	Tomorrow	B-ISDN, interactive digital TV via satellite, cable
End user devices	Today	Multimedia PC (800 x 600 pixel with 256 colors), Tele CD-I (500 x 300 pixel)
	Tomorrow	Digital set-top boxes, workstations

Fig. 2. System requirements - today and tomorrow

5.1 Functions of electronic catalogues

This section describes functions of electronic catalogues in the context of electronic shopping (Thesmann 1995).

Access: Basically, the access to a catalogue should be possible in three ways:

- Application orientated: the customer is able to describe the problem (see chapter 3).
- Attribute orientated: the customer knows all criteria which are relevant for the problem's solution.
- Product orientated: the opinion building process has progressed far enough to result in a search for clearly defined products or services.

Retrieval: In large conventional paper catalogues the user possibly has to leaf through many pages until he finds the desired piece of information. In EPC an active system of descriptors offers possible attributes and their values. An index search is already offered by many electronic catalogues.

Presentation: The electronic catalogue integrates text, graphics, animations, video (still and motion pictures) as well as sound. Examples of presentations are shown in figure 3 and figure 4. The use of virtual reality is not relevant at the present stage because of the enormous hardware resources as well as huge development efforts required.

Navigation: To avoid the well known "lost in hyperspace" problem, particularly for unexperienced users, electronic catalogues need a series of navigation and orientation aides: local, regional, global and temporal (Mertens et. al. 1994).

Help: Electronic catalogues are equipped with a context sensitive help function covering contents (glossary) as well as the system itself (system help).

User protocols: To act adaptively, user protocols are necessary, e.g. the FORWISS sales assistant (Mertens/Lödel 1993) recognizes user behavior at several different key points and formulates an internal hypothesis about the cognitive skills and the buyer type of the user. Some electronic catalogues create full process protocols to allow an analysis of consumer behavior.

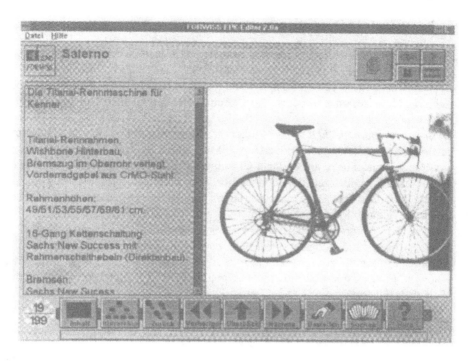

Fig. 3.   Page of an EPC (produced by FORWISS, Erlangen) for bicycles

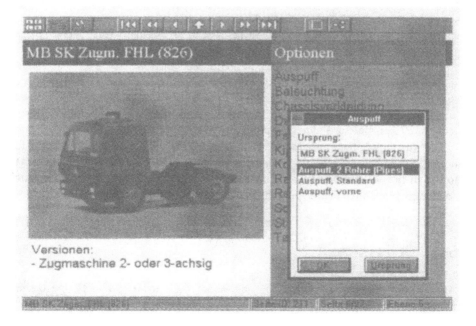

Fig. 4.   Page of an EPC (produced by roccas multimedia, Nuremberg) of miniature
models for collectors

5.2   Electronic mall

A basic innovation which has recently become possible in electronic shopping is a mall functionality. This mall functionality acts like a roof covering different electronic catalogues (see fig. 1), it could also be compared to a department store (with a wide selection of products). An electronic shopping mall should fulfill the following conditions:

Global orientation help: This function offers directories of all integrated catalogues, suppliers and products. A classification by retail category is also possible. A customer searches for a CD player. To avoid a search in catalogues without HiFi devices, a global orientation help could give an overview of all relevant suppliers. Then, the customer jumps only to pages of electronic catalogues which are relevant to his problem.

Thesaurus: A consistent use of expressions (for example for product names) is unlikely in several different electronic catalogues. A thesaurus supports the customer in case the product cannot be found because it is listed under a different synonym. For example a cassette recorder could be found in the Tape Deck chapter of an electronic catalogue.

Multi language capability: To ensure a user friendly handling, the possibility to choose between several languages should be available.

Comparing offers: A delicate subject with respect to competition laws is a comparison of products of different suppliers, for example regarding prices. From the customer's point of view, this option is absolutely desirable because it enables a fast overview over the cheapest offers. On the supplier's side, the differentiation attributes for identical products are reduced to the price.

Special offers: As common in print media, a company may rent several introduction pages to publish their best bargains.

Additional functions: With the help of additional functions like games or classes in cookery, the user acceptance of the system in general increases. Another idea is that customers should be able to access a kind of black board where classified ads could be placed implementing a fleamarket functionality. Additionally, different cultural events, cinema and theater programs could be published.

The functions mentioned above shall be realized in an electronic mall for households in Nuremberg by the competence centre in electronic shopping (CESH) to which the authors belong. The competence centre TeleCounter intends to build an electronic mall for the people living in the "Bodensee" area (Schmid 1995).

6   Advisor

After a customer becomes knowledgeable about the various products, the desired products have to be integrated into a concrete offer which often has to take technical restrictions into consideration. For more complex products, additional advisor modules are important facilitating:

- consistency testing (which additional component does apt to the system?)
- financial analysis (cash, credit or leasing considering effects on taxation)
- technical process comparisons (possible within the product lineup of one supplier)
- profitability calculation (possibly a simple break even analysis)

Prototypes for such consultation modules already exist for the FORWISS sales assistant (Mertens/Lödel 1993).

7   Order

The user selects the desired products from an article list structured in some way and combines them to systems if needed. The electronic catalogue system generates an offer including all prices and product codes.

8   Payment

In the future, electronic orders in networks will be paid for online as well. First Virtual Holding Inc, San Diego, processes the credit card number typed in by the buyer and arranges the transfer of the order price from the buyer's account to the seller's account. Another way of payment is used by the Dutch company Digicash, which issues virtual money, so called cyberbucks, that consists of a digital code and represents a certain value. These cyberbucks can be exchanged, but only Digicash can reconvert them into real currency (Hendricks 1995).

9   Delivery

Here, a new branch of the economy with a big logistical task develops. From an ecological point of view, this kind of centralized supply is superior because not every household uses a car to get to the shopping center and a delivery service finds the most economic way to reach individual households.

10   Usage potential

For the three most interesting regions Europe, USA and Japan, the following empirical statements might be made:

A research of the Handels-Trendletter emphasizes home shopping as a central element in trade. About 54% of managers assume that the amount of home shopping will increase enormously because it fits the customer's wish for more convenience (n.a. 1994a). In Europe, the PC more than the TV is the main control device for multimedia. The penetration of private households by multimedia equipment is highest in Germany. However, the utilization level is significantly higher in Great Britain.

An Arthur D. Little survey among US private households revealed in May 1994 that 26% of the survey participants would buy a product from an electronic catalogue service offering the same price. Among these, 28% would purchase significantly less products from print catalogues. 75% of those interviewed would decrease their shopping trips to local shops for the benefit of electronic home shopping (Burkhardt 1994). More TV shopping can be found in the USA.

In Japan, all necessary chinese characters have to be typed in using the japanese syllable fonts. This font problem heavily restricts private PC use. Therefore, only few PCs are found in japanese households in comparison to other industrialized nations.

A new type of mail order customer exists: The big mail order houses are reaching mostly women above 35 years of age, a group without any special interest in computers. Now, new market segments are targeted with digital offers. In 1993, the typical user of an American PC/modem shopping system matched the following profile: more than 70% are aged between 18 and 44 and mainly male. More than 50% have a gross income of DM 35,000 or more (von Ammon 1994). For this reason, offers for these affluent and technically interested consumers have to be put in electronic catalogues.

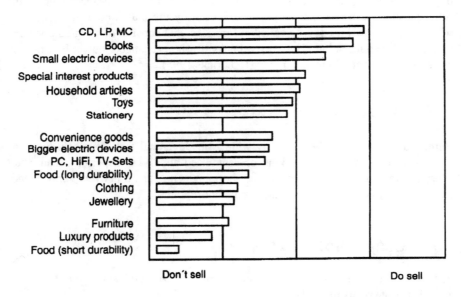

Fig. 5. Suitability of different products for home shopping

An empirical study carried out by Witte yields the potential for home shopping according figure 5 (Witte 1995): CD, books and small electric devices are fully suitable to be ordered via home shopping. Furniture, luxury products and foods of short durability are only less apt for home shopping. For an order of clothes, it is imaginable that customer data and photos of his face and figure are stored in his computer so that he could get a test view of himself wearing the selected clothes. About 70% of the trade managers are missing the emotional component of a shopping trip in the home shopping application. It is crucial for the acceptance of home shopping to incorporate strongly activating elements to this shopping alternative, particularly as far as low involvement products are concerned.

11   Conclusion

Diller sees the elements of home shopping's utility for consumers as follows (Diller 1995) :
- *Individuality of contact and of buying:* The customer decides about the time (when) of purchase without the restrictions imposed by business hours. He buys from home (where) and in the desired intensity (how long). Furthermore, he is supported in his buying decision by an IT-controlled select function which grants autonomity in the choice of information (what).
- *Cost reduction in contact:* electronic shopping reduces significantly the customer's time commitment as the trip to several shops becomes unnecessary. At the same time, costs for these trips are avoided. And perhaps products could be sold cheaper because cost intensive sales staff is not needed anymore.
- *Comfort:* a customer is not forced any longer to go to a shop in person, uncomfortable waiting times are avoided and products are delivered directly to home.
- *Positive image:* The user of an electronic shopping offer profits from a gain of prestige because he shows his open-mindedness to new technologies.
- *Exclusivity of product offers:* Via electronic shopping, access to a wider product assortment is possible which is impossible or difficult to obtain by traditional means.
- *Anonymity of contact:* For example in the field of purchasing health or beauty products, a customer surely intends to keep his anonymity to a maximum degree.

References

Brenner, W., Kolbe, L., Die computerunterstützte Informationsverarbeitung der privaten Haushalte als Herausforderung für Wissenschaft und Wirtschaft, in: Wirtschaftsinformatik 36(1994)4, pp. 369-378

Burkhardt, R., Macht kontra Markt, in: TopBusiness, 1994, No. 10, pp. 118-126

Cats-Baril, W., Jelassi, T., The French Videotex System Minitel: A Successful Implementation of a National Information Technology Infrastructure, in: MIS Quarterly, 1994, March, pp. 1-20

Danke, E., Aktueller Stand und Zukunftsperspektiven von Datex-J, in: Telematica Kongreßdokumentation, Nuremberg, 1994, pp. 280-284

Diller, H., Internal CESH-report, FORWISS Erlangen, 1995

Hendricks, B., Virtuelle Portokassen, in: Wirtschaftswoche, 49(1995)9, pp. 114-117

ISN, Internet Shopping Network, URL=http://www.internet.net:/, 1994

Jaros-Sturhahn, A., Löffler, P., Das Internet als Werkzeug zur Deckung des betrieblichen Informationsbedarfs, in: Information Management, 10(1995)1, pp. 6-13

Mertens, P., Breuker, J., Lödel, D., Ponader, M., Popp, H., and Thesmann, S., Angebotsunterstützungssysteme für Standardprodukte, in: Informatik-Spektrum, 17(1994)10, pp. 291-301

Mertens, P., Lödel, D., Ein wissensbasiertes hypermediales Angebotsunter-stützungssystem, in: Management & Computer, 1(1993)3, pp. 175-181

n.a., Shopping per CD-ROM, in: Wirtschaftswoche, 48(1994)51, p. 9

n.a., Electronic Shopping, in: GDI-Monitor, 1994a, No. II, p. 29

Popp, H., Lödel, D., Fuzzy Techniques and User Modelling in Sales Assistants, in: User Modelling and User-Adapted Interaction, 1995 (in press)

Schmid, B., Electronic Mall: Banking und Shopping in globalen Netzen, Stuttgart, Teubner, 1995

von Ammon, E., Katalogistik, in: Screen Multimedia, 1(1994)12, pp. 106-107

Thesmann, S., EPK-Editor - ein Werkzeug für Aufbau und Pflege Elektronischer Produktkataloge zum Einsatz in kleinen und mittelständischen Betrieben, PhD Thesis, FAU Erlangen-Nuremberg, 1995

Witte, E., Die Akzeptanz von Tele-Shopping, Kabel & Medien Service, München, 1995

Interactive Multimedia and In-Home Marketing

Jonne R. M. van der Drift and Luc Stakenborg
CD-Matics, The Netherlands

1   Introduction

Electronic Superhighway and multimedia have become the buzz-words that can be read about in almost every magazine, newspaper or trade-journal. A giant hype has been created, suggesting the upcoming of an equally giant new industry. How bitter is the truth: no multimedia platform has yet received a wide market acceptance, many new product launches remain just announcements, many proclaimed mergers are cancelled and even more start-ups never grow profitable. Big money is invested in what prove to be even bigger disappointments.

Before exploring the opportunities managers and entrepreneurs should also consider the risks and threats. What are the main forces restraining a large scale implementation of the Electronic Superhighway?

Investments

Building the Superhighway requires gigantic investments. For a small country as the Netherlands Mr. Ben Verwaayen, president of KPN, the Dutch post and telecom operator mentioned early 1995 an amount of 22 billion Dutch guilders. Even if this can be reduced to half we speak of investments almost twice the costs of the new Dutch freight railroad into Germany.

Consumer

The consumer of today is still unfamiliar with the electronic (interactive) services of tomorrow. What kind of services they are going to use is still uncertain. How much are they prepared to pay and in what form they prefer to use them are yet unanswered questions.

Tariffs

The need of reduced telecom tariffs is evident. Example: at the present telecom rates it is impossible to offer attractive prices for a video-on-demand service. For this would mean that the customer is paying more than double the amount of the price of a recent rental videotape (or video-CD in the near future). In the case of home-shopping marketers should realise that the costs of visiting and browsing in an electronic (virtual) store will be compared by the consumer with the costs of visiting the physical store.

Legislation

In many European countries present legislation and political issues prohibit common sense solutions such as the integration of cable-tv networks (broadband and video) and telecom networks (switched and suitable for interactive services).

The only way to find out how these restraints can be overcome is to develop interactive services based on existing infrastructures and multimedia systems and test them in the markets. Not waiting but learning now for tomorrow. In this article the authors invite you to share their practical experience of interactive multimedia projects for business-to-consumer marketing. After some useful tips on common pitfalls when taking up a multimedia project the article describes the components, features and application of TeleCD-i, a smart combination of CD technology and telecommunications. It finishes with a case description of a homeshopping pilot within the Netherlands.

2   Multimedia "from opportunity to action"

Given the content of the term "multimedia" the danger exists that companies focus on technological instead of business and marketing issues. Of course a sound understanding of technology is important but in their search for viable multimedia applications companies should rather take corporate goals and objectives as a starting-point, such as:
- How can multimedia improve the quality of our products and services?
- How can multimedia enlarge our competitive advantage?
- How can multimedia give us an entry to new markets?
- Do we want to enter these new markets?
- If yes, in which areas and how to create synergy with existing activities?

In our consulting practice we find a growing interest in multimedia because of the versatility of application opportunities in numerous business sectors and branches. For most companies, however, multimedia is a new area and sadly but true many initiatives often lead to a dead end for a variety of reasons, such as:
- There is no genuine commitment from top-management.
- Projects are technology driven.
- The choosen technology is still in its laboratory phase.
- The projects conflict with established interests.
- Marketing and automation departments do not cooperate well.
- No project goals are formulated by which success is not measurable leaving afterwards no justification for the initial investments.

We believe, however, that with the right approach the emerging multimedia and electronic services market offer outstanding business opportunities. But design and development of a multimedia project within a company is difficult. It requires experience, dedication and patience. But above all it requires a pragmatic approach and lots of common sense.

To prevent a multimedia project from the above mentioned pitfalls careful preparation and planning is needed. Planners should not hesitate to hire outside knowledge and expertise. Within the upcoming multimedia market there is a great variety of professional services already available ranging from highly specialised top video artists to turn-key multimedia production houses.

3   Compact Disc Interactive (CD-i)

Compact Disc Interactive (CD-i) is based on the CD technology that in a relatively short period found massive application in the Audio-Compact Disc. A Compact Disc (CD) is a handy carrier of digital information with the following characteristics:

- compact and light weight (low distribution costs)
- large storage capacity (one CD contains 650 MB similar to approx. 900 floppy discs)
- durable (permanent quality)
- cheap to reproduce (pressing costs)
- play back only (not recordable)
- environmental friendly (recyclable)

The well known Audio-CD contains (primarily) music in digital form. But music is not the only form of information that can be stored on a CD. Also photos, speech, graphics, text, video and programmes can be recorded digitally on a CD.

These possibilities gave the starting signal for the development of the Compact Disc Interactive standard. The standard describes how the various information formats should be stored on a Compact Disc and which functions a CD-i player should offer to play back a CD-i disc. The main objective of the CD-i standard (also called "green book") is to create a worldwide interchangeability of CD-i, like previous with the Audio-CD.

To play CD-i programmes (titles) the CD-i player, at present sold already for US$ 499, is connected to a television set in a similar fashion as the videorecorder. For optimal sound quality the audio channel of CD-i can also be reproduced via a Stereo HiFi set (see fig. 1). CD-i players by itself can perfectly play Audio-CD's thereby creating a gigantic replacement market.

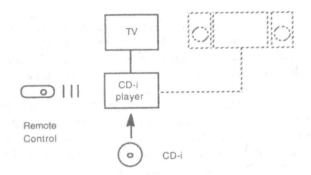

Fig. 1.   Connectivity of the CD-i player

Typical for CD-i is its interactivity: the user can control the sequence of CD-i programmes. Without this interaction playing CD-i would be comparable with watching a Videotape. The interaction between user and CD-i player is purposely kept easy and simple. With a remote control device the user can move a cursor across the television screen and make choices by pressing one of the buttons (marked • and ••).

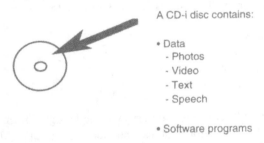

Fig. 2.   Contents of the CD-i disc

To enable interactivity a CD-i disc contains next to data (photos, graphics, speech, video, music, text etc.) software programs matching the operating system of the CD-i player which actually is a computer in disguise with advanced video and audio capacities (see fig. 2). The operating system controls the presentation of data and the processing of user (re)actions. Since a CD-i title developer is free to compile both data and software, CD-i offers an extremely flexible and powerful medium for numerous application areas.

The combination of powerful presentation and ease-of-use offer numerous application areas on consumer and professional markets. In the consumer markets for example in the area of (children)education, entertainment, music with video-clips, games, reference and (hobby)course ware. But also in the business market already thousands of applications have been produced throughout the world varying from training, point-of-information, product and company presentations, annual reports to service manuals.

4   TeleCD-i: CD-i and telecommunications

For companies that want to act now and start with their own multimedia pilot on the consumer market TeleCD-i is a fine illustration of a so-called "networked multimedia system" that can be applied today using existing infrastructures and proven technology.

TeleCD-i was developed by Amsterdam based CD-Matics together with Philips Media. It is a powerful medium merging CD-i and telecommunications (see fig. 3). It extends CD-i's versatile multimedia capabilities with up-to-date information and electronic transactions (orders, reservations, payments etc.). With TeleCD-i companies can finally offer electronic services which are both effective and easy to use.

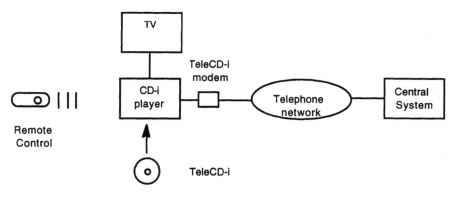

Fig. 3.   Components of the TeleCD-i system

To communicate with your ordering system, the CD-i player is connected to the telephone network using the Philips TeleCD-i Assistant, a "plug and play" modem especially designed for CD-i players. Your TeleCD-i can be used at home, in the office or on the shopfloor.

5   TeleCD-i production process

In this paragraph we clarify the TeleCD-i production process: the various stages before the consumer actually can start using a new TeleCD-i. We also include indications of the costrelations of the various stages of a TeleCD-i project (percentages between brackets).

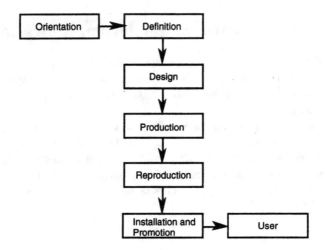

Fig. 4.   TeleCD-i production process

For the effective and efficient realisation of a TeleCD-i production a phased project approach is chosen (see fig. 4). The phases define clear milestones enabling the safeguarding of the project realisation in time and money. It also spreads the costs over a number of phases which are each preceded by a Go/No-go decision. Below we give a description of each phase with indicative cost relations (percentages between brackets). Obviously these are depending content and scope of the project. The definition study therefore will give a more accurate costindication.

Phase 1   Orientation (Acquisition)

During the orientation phase the companies can obtain already an impression of the possibilities and benefits of CD-i and TeleCD-i. There are a number of tools available such as the Philips TeleCD-i brochure and demonstrator, trade press clippings, seminars etc.

At CD-Matics we support companies during this phase with product presentations, demonstrations and discussing the general application possibilities of TeleCD-i. However, to receive a clear insight in the costs and benefits of the foreseen application and the consequenses on both strategic and operational level, the next step should be a definition study.

Phase 2   Definition study (5-15%)

The purpose of the definition study is to clarify the nature, magnitude and scope of a TeleCD-i project before the actual realisation phase. With a feasibility study the user needs and communication objectives are clearly defined. They form input for a global description of the content of the (Tele)CD-i. Thus creating insight in the magnitude and scope of the application and the costs for the next phases.

The results are delivered in a clear (English written) report that can serve as a basis for obtaining budgets and can be used as a tender document when calling for proposals among CD-i production companies. It also creates a better startingpoint when negotiating with later hardwaresuppliers such as Philips, Sony and Goldstar.

Part of the study is an inventarisation of existing assets and infrastructures that can be used for the design, production and actual use of the TeleCD-i. Finally the strategic and operational aspects of the TeleCD-i project will be described. Here the TeleCD-i solutions will be compared with those of other multimedia platforms.

Phase 3   Design (20-40%)

During the design phase the content of the TeleCD-i is worked out in detail and put in writing. This design will be the basis for all future production activities. Naturally the client is closely involved to bring in the necessary know-how on the content. During the design phase also the TeleCD-i connection with the central server and other remote systems is worked out in detail (architecture, capacity, data-exchange protocol).

The result of this phase is a design document describing the interaction-model. It also determines the requirements of text, audio, graphics, video and other media assets. After the approval of the design document the production phase can commence.

Phase 4   Production (40-60%)

At this stage CD-Matics will realise in co-operation with specialised CD-i production facilities (CD-i studios) the TeleCD-i production. The highly costintensive production of the media assets (audio, graphics, video, stills etc.) is done during this phase. Also the CD-i software will be developed to bring the total to an interactive presentation. During the production process CD-Matics will bring in the required TeleCD-i datacommunication software and connections with the newly installed central server. If desired existing remote systems will be expanded and/or adjusted.

It is possible to build in a test phase during which will be worked with a smaller platform that simulates the functions of the final central server before the actual connecting to existing systems. The result of the production phase is a working TeleCD-i production in the form of a special Write One compact disk. This disc will be extensively tested to eliminate possible errors in the application. After acceptance by the client the TeleCD-i can be pressed in the required number.

Phase 5   Reproduction (10-20%)

Reproduction is carried out by specialised CD pressing companies. The TeleCD-i can be packaged and completed with label and booklet explaining basic installation and user modes.

Phase 6   Installation, Promotion, and Distribution (5-15%)

After reproduction the disk will be installed together with the TeleCD-i hardware and the chosen display units. This should be accompanied by a promotional campaign aiming to stimulate use of the system. From this stage on usage (frequence, nature) and effectiveness can automatically be measured via the central system.

6   In-home marketing with TeleCD-i

There's a multitude of TeleCD-i application areas. Just to stir your imagination take a look at the following application examples:

- *Tele-catalogue:* With TeleCD-i, mailorder companies can finally put together a catalogue that will attract, and keep customers attention. Up-to-date information from the central databases is added to the high quality audio-visual presentation on the CD-i disc. And by clicking the button the customer can directly order. This way, special offer campaigns can reduce stock surplus. At the same time, ordering out of stock articles can be prevented, improving customer service. TeleCD-i combines the benefits of print and electronic media.

- *Homeshopping:* Shopping with TeleCD-i is fast and easy - the TeleCD-i contains an attractive product overview together with a cooking program, presented by a famous chef. Clicking the button suffices to order all the ingredients needed. On the same disc it is possible to walk through the shop. Through audio-visual presentations the customer will immediately recognize and order products and brands. Time of delivery can be negotiated. Consumers don't have to waste their time in queues any more. They can order at any moment: by day, at night and in the weekend.

- *Telebanking:* A growing number of banks and financial institutions provide electronic telebanking services to their customers, both in consumer and business markets. TeleCD-i is an ideal medium for expanding these services. For example: a customer consults the travel insurance module on TeleCD-i. An interactive dialogue with an advisory module will result in an insurance-policy, which can be "signed" by clicking the button.

- *Travel:* TeleCD-i is the travel agency at home or in the office. CD-i is a great medium to promote tourist attractions and travels. Futhermore, with TeleCD-i you can present last-minute offers. Or provide your frequent customers with an electronic reservation desk. Travel guides on TeleCD-i will give all kind of up-to-date information on the place of destination (such as: weather forecasts, snow heights, travel advice and a cultural events calendar). This way, TeleCD-i surpasses the possibilities of traditional media.

- *Telegames:* Many exciting CD-i game titles are already available. TeleCD-i games can be played by a group of persons in different locations (multiplayer). Being connected by a network all players simultaneously participate in the gameplay, providing an extra dimension. In the business market these techniques can be used in simulation training, for example in management games.

- *Advertisements:* Advertisement columns are very popular for selling goods, second hand cars, houses and even dating. Advertisement columns on TeleCD-i add value because they provide a search facility to make a personal selection from the current (possibly very large) database of advertisements. The search profile can be stored for re-use.

- *Teleeducation:* CD-i's powerful audio-visual presentation capabilities, in combination with user interaction, make it an outstanding medium for instructive and educational programmes. TeleCD-i enables the teacher to automatically monitor study progress, take in homework and provide feedback.
- *Ticket reservation:* TeleCD-i is also the "ticket booth" for cinema, theatre and (pop)concerts at home. The TeleCD-i will show a map of the concerthall, displaying the available seats. The user buys the tickets by selecting the seats and pays by creditcard. TeleCD-i ticket booths can be part of a theatre's seasonal program on CD-i. Next to text and photo's it contains music fragments and, for example personal invitations from artists to come and see their concert. Or they can be part of a cinema magazine, containing trailers of films and other cinema columns.
- *CD-i pay-per-play:* Using premium rate telephone numbers, you can automatically charge the user each time for playing a CD-i game or watching a digital video.

Thus TeleCD-i offers many *opportunities* for companies in the following lines of business: mailorder and teleshopping, market research, department stores and retail, publishing and broadcasting, banking and insurance, telecommunications, travel and tourism, (public) transport. TeleCD-i offers a number of important and distinctive *advantages* to other media for those companies that want to market their products and services to the customer at their home.

Benefits for the *customer* are:
- homeshopping from living-room via TV set (familiar)
- 24 hours, 7 days a week (convenience)
- easy-to-use for everyone (housewives are not PC wizards!)
- integrates house magazine, catalogue and shopping list (all in one)
- supports funshopping and browsing (e.g. cooking and buying tips)
- minimal telephone costs, no charges when browsing (combination on-line/off-line)
- visual information supports product/brand recognition (shop or advertising reference)
- customized information on assortment and articles (just-in-time, to-the-point)
- attractive nice-to-know information (full motion/full screen video and digital audio)
- extra usage of CD-i player (co-justification of purchase)

Opportunities for *companies* are:
- communicate directly with consumers in their living-room via TV
- not confined to the typical 30 second TV commercial slot
- presentation facilities far beyond those of many existing means
- create and maintain one-to-one relationship with customers

- electronic handling of orders (less mistakes and lower handling costs)
- fits easily into existing infrastructures
- easy migration towards future interactive television developments
- CD-i players are standardised as opposed to bewildering variety of PC types and generations
- low reproduction- and distribution costs in comparison with print (mass distribution)
- almost unlimited expansion of assortment (x,000 articles) and index structures (for maximum freedom of choice and optimal marketing flexibility)
- supports the high quality image of marketleaders.
- multi-applicable: at home, in-store, at work or elsewhere
- effectively influence the ever less predictable buying behaviour of the customer during an early stage of the buying process (at home when making choices)

7   Albert Heijn's homeshopping TeleCD-i pilot

Being part of Dutch multinational Ahold, Albert Heijn is Holland's largest foodretail supermarket chain with a marketshare of almost 30%. It has a high-quality/high-service profile and a sound reputation for innovation in marketing, service and distribution methods. Under the name James Telesuper, the company already runs a home-delivery service for almost 10 years. With help of a printed shopping catalogue customers can place their shopping orders in a number of ways:

- phone
- fax
- mail
- videotex
- PC-modem
- voice respons

Via these media a customer can make instant price comparisons. Given the expanding assortment growing from 3,000 to more than 14,000 articles these present media prove to be quite limited. Just the catalogue needs to be enlarged by a factor 400.

Therefore Albert Heijn searched for a new medium that is easy to use and can store and present lots of information. The choice of TeleCD-i was made because Albert Heijn recognised the following features to their benefit:

- aimed at mass consumer market
- multimedia presentation (music, speech, text, stills, video and graphics)
- easy-to-use, also for the elderly
- on-line connection for automatic order registration via telephone network
- to be used in "social friendly" environment, the living-room
- relatively low reproduction and distribution costs

Albert Heijn decided to start with a market pilot in the area of Haarlem, west of Amsterdam. The goals and *objectives* of the pilot were as follows:

* to experience the opportunities of this new medium
* to evaluate the role of CD-i in home-shopping
* to test its readiness, use and convenience among existing and new customers
* to estimate the consequences for large scale implementation

For the test, which runs since September 1994, a TeleCD-i has been produced that offers the user various shopping possibilities. "Runshoppers" can directly run to their personalized standard shopping list or simply select from the productlist. For the real "Funshopper" there is a complete Albert Heijn supermarket with 10 productgroup departments (vegetables, groceries, housecare, personal care, butcher, bakery, candyshop, wine and liquor etc.) that circle like a caroussel "around" the viewer.

The disk also contains nice-to-know information such as recipes, calories, additives, a wine encyclopedia, films (in Digital Video) about the production processes of well known products that are sold under the Albert Heijn private label like peanutbutter or chocolate. Albert Heijn foresees that brand-manufacturers will be involved in future editions with audiovisual product presentations.

To update the disk with information on prices and weekly promotions the user needs a special modem (the Philips TeleCD-i Assistant) which they receive free from Albert Heijn during the test. Browsing through the disk does not require on-line communication thereby saving enormously on telephone costs. At the end of the shopping round the modem is also used for placing orders.

8 Interim report on results of the Albert Heijn pilot

In January 1995 the first qualitative research was done through panel discussions with users. Indeed the distinction between runshoppers and funshoppers was clear. Runshoppers did not seem to care much about the extra information. Just handy ordering lists but with strong visuals of the articles since also runshoppers refer to color and package (brand recognition).

Funshoppers however prefer a more social environment, the livingroom and the familiar TV-set. The first research clearly indicated that CD-i shoppers often had multiple person shopping sessions. They loved the extra information like the recipes, the videos on the production and quality assurance processes, new products, nutritionvalue and ingredients and all this in the form of entertainment. Significant was the desire of participants to have "control" over the system. Indeed the person responsible for the daily shopping prefered to do so on the couch next to a cup of coffee and "certainly NOT in the little room where husband or partner usually plays with his PC".

Installation and controlling the hardware and making the connection via the telephone network in the background caused no problems or complaints at all. Even the many elderly persons among the participants could get around with the technology. With the release of a second edition in March 1995 (new products) the experiment will be continued to at least the autumn 1995. Albert Heijn will further study purchasing patterns since "the participants bought more goods on average than those ordering shopping by phone, fax or personal computer" as quoted by a company official.

9 Conclusions

Multimedia is a promising and exciting new area that can be explored by almost any company and institution to create better and intensified customer relations. Electronic distribution of multimedia is no real alternative leaving packaged media such as the CD the only practical way to reach the consumer at home. However smart combinations like TeleCD-i offer immediate opportunities to enter the areas of home-shopping and home-banking at relatively low cost.

Implementing and offering electronic services has both technical and commercial implications for organisations. This also holds for TeleCD-i. Thorough groundwork is necessary to clearly determine the why, what and how of your electronic service based on TeleCD-i.

Good preparation and project management is a must and can save lots of time and money during the realisation phase during which your own employees cooperate with outside suppliers. It is of vital importance that the complexity of the project is well calculated.

For the marketing and commercialisation phase it is often possible to cooperate with other parties already active on the multimedia market, not in the least with Philips Media. They operate in most countries a customer base with names and addresses of all consumers that own a CD-i player. Matching this with your own customer base can give a flying start of your pilot saving the costs of locating your prospects.

Given the diversity of disciplines that are involved within a multimedia project (marketing, sales, communication, logistics, customer service, automation) the manager and entrepreneur should safeguard the project from hobbyism and undesired effects of sub-optimalisation since anyone within the company should benefit from the newly obtained know how and experience. Do not hesitate to ask for existing expertise for example through the partner network of Philips Media where you'll find lots of specialisms and disciplines united.

New Media: A Growth Market in Erotica and Pornography for Beate Uhse

Petra Höper
Beate Uhse Group, Germany

1 Introduction

The spread of computers into the private household brings new opportunities for many enterprises. Within a brief period a new, rapidly growing market has emerged in which market shares are not yet firmly established. Given this, the Beate Uhse Group has responded relatively quickly to secure market potential.

In general, it can be said that new markets in the erotica sector are recognized and exploited very quickly. It is undoubtedly the case that the supply of erotica and pornography has contributed to the spread of the consumer hardware needed for the new media. This has certainly been observed in the past for the introduction of new technologies such as the video recorder.

The use of the new electronic media within Beate Uhse is aimed exclusively at the retail customer. To date consumers are offered a variety of soft-erotic and pornographic multimedia products on diskette, Photo-CD and CD-ROM. These products do not require online links. Online products from Beate Uhse can be accessed via Bildschirmtext (BTX - the German Teletex equivalent) and the Internet.

The emerging sales success should permit constant growth in online and offline services, rendering the new media business area increasingly important.

2 Multimedia in the Beate Uhse Group

2.1 The multimedia concept and its significance for the Beate Uhse Group

The multimedia concept is currently on everyone's tongue. But however widely it is used, everyone understands it to mean something different. In principle, multimedia simply refers to the linking of previously separate media in a single piece of equipment. Films, photos, graphics, music, and text can be combined with each other. Suitable storage media are diskettes and, given their large storage capacity, CDs.

In its multimedia business area Beate Uhse combines all the products that customers can obtain on CD or diskette. Beate Uhse's first diskette product appeared at the end of 1993. This involved the electronic implementation of an illustrated volume, which provided the customer with an erotic work of reference including film, photos, graphic animation, text and sound.

Within a year Beate Uhse had created over 60 products on diskette, CD-ROM and Photo-CD. The product range extends from simple PC games through video and graphic animation to an elaborate adventure game. And new products are being added all the time, whether in-house products, or external products being included in the Beate Uhse range.

2.2 The use of multimedia applications in the Beate Uhse Group

As with all its products, Beate Uhse differentiates between soft-erotic and pornographic merchandise. An exact definition of pornography is not simple. Legal pronouncements predominantly regard pornography as the depiction of individuals in a crude, titillating manner which reduces them to mere objects of sexual lust. Both what is shown and how it is shown are relevant. Both must tend to the extreme. In general, visual material can be regarded as pornographic if primary sexual characteristics crudely dominate the foreground, and if the limits of sexual decency based on generally accepted values are unequivocally broached.

Pornographic products may only be sold in places that cannot be either entered or seen by people under 18. Such products can only be advertised within severe limits. This limitation does not apply to soft-erotic products.

Consequently, the pornographic multimedia products are generally available only from in-shop retailers, such as the Beate Uhse stores or other retail premises to which young people have no access. The soft-erotic products are additionally available by mail order and sometimes from newsagents.

About 70% of Beate Uhse's multimedia products are soft-erotica. In order to offer the customer a balanced program of pornographic computer products additional products are bought in from external suppliers.

2.2.1 Content and function of multimedia products on diskette

The diskette products produced by Beate Uhse are almost exclusively soft-erotic in content. The most complex product is an electronically implemented illustrated volume which deals with more than ten areas of partnership issues verbally and visually. It allows information to be accessed quickly and simply using an integrated remote control. Graphics, video, sound and additional game sequences provide the user with an entertaining, erotic PC handbook which he can browse in an interactive fashion. Similarly, but not always so lavishly, other illustrated volumes have been implemented. Thus the customer can obtain erotic reference material on a variety of themes at various price levels.

In addition, Beate Uhse has also produced some low-price PC games on diskette. From erotic puzzles or slot machines, to brick-outs, labyrinths and erotic pairs the user is offered amusing entertainment. In these games erotic photos or film sequences are hidden which the use can see if the game is played successfully. Here, we are not really talking of interactivity since the process depends on the character of the game. Selection possibilities are largely restricted to choosing levels of difficulty.

To round off the range Beate Uhse also produces soft-erotic and pornographic screen savers and slide shows on diskette.

2.2.2 Content and function of multimedia products on Photo-CD and CD-ROM

In addition to the diskette products, Beate Uhse has also produced 17 Photo-CDs and 33 CD-ROMs to date. The Photo-CDs contain almost exclusively soft-erotica. They are all produced using Kodak's Portfolio Photo-CD format and each contain 100 photos. A limited degree of interactivity allows the viewer to select photos from different areas using a menu. Each photo also has background music.

The user is provided with a wide variety of themes within the Beate Uhse product range. Special themes, such as PVC and leather or bizarre erotic games are given their own Photo-CDs. But the customer who is looking for a variety of themes can also choose from a series of Photo-CDs with many interesting high-resolution photos.

Beate Uhse's CD-ROMs are compiled in a variety of ways. One segment is based on Beate Uhse's Blue Movies Cinema and contains pictures, graphics, text and a 60-minute film. Each screen is in colour.

From the start-up menu the user can choose between the film itself and an editorial section in which he can obtain information about the company, its products and services. When he selects the cinema the viewer is taken at the click of the mouse through an entrance into one or two foyers. From here he can enter various cinema screening rooms and watch his film. Typically, he can also use a menu to view the film either in speeded run-through, at normal speed, or in individual frames.

The user is continuously presented with new menu points from which he can quickly access his favourite sequences. As with the Photo-CDs the customer has the option of choosing between general and specialised areas from the world of erotica. The degree of interactivity is significantly higher than for the Photo-CDs. Direct intervention in the progress of the film is not possible with these CD-ROMs, however.

In addition, Beate Uhse has implemented its mail order catalogue on CD-ROM. This allows the user to browse through the merchandise on offer broken down by product group. If he wants to know more about a given product a click on the illustration in question will generate an enlargement with additional information and prices. If the product is wanted he can select the variant and size and enter them in an order form which can printed using a print option.

As well as the usual product information, the CD-ROM also contains text excerpts, film sequences, a slide show, computer game and other surprises. This represents a relatively high level of interaction, since the user can experience this CD-ROM via a wide variety of routes. Even if the basis for the CD-ROM is a catalogue, Beate Uhse regards this product principally as a sales product, given the multiplicity of additional benefits.

A further multimedia product from Beate Uhse is a lavish soft-erotic adventure game. The user experiences an adventure through Germany. He visits a variety of towns where he finds himself in bars, hotels, restaurants or the Reeperbahn, awaited by many surprises. The objective of the game is to use up the supply of condoms in his luggage. In many situations, however, he receives additional condoms. Experimentation, trial and error are required to change the scene. By clicking on objects actions are initiated, films are seen, sounds, music and speech are heard. This game has the highest level of interactivity of computer products produced by Beate Uhse. The user can take different routes and in this way determine the course of his journey.

2.3   Advantages and disadvantages in the use of multimedia products

The combination of film, sound, text, graphics and pictures creates an environment in which exciting new products can be developed which offer the customer great diversity. Speedy access possibilities render such products much less rigid than video films or books. Favourite erotic sequences can be found quickly. The user can also abandon his erotic program quickly, however, which can be advantageous in the case of unexpected disturbances. At the click of a switch he can immediately change to another program.

One disadvantage is the limited storage capacity of the storage media. A diskette quickly reaches its limits, and even CDs can only store a maximum of 74 minutes of film.

Although development costs are relatively high, producing copies of diskettes or CDs is much more economical than books and video cassettes, especially at low volumes. Multimedia products are also often much easier to implement, which is a particular advantage of the catalogue on CD-ROM. For example, pages can simply be exchanged or prices altered via databases.

One problem is the wide diversity of computers on the market. The constant stream of new systems and accessories make it difficult to create software that can be used by the vast majority of computer owners. With these new media one should also not assume that the user understands all the finer points of his computer. This sometimes gives rise to very complicated customer queries.

The rapid hardware developments also continuously raise new decisions for software manufacturers. If products are created at the frontiers of new technology, the limited availability of the user equipment renders the potential market very small. Furthermore, at this early stage it is often difficult to recognize which standards will dominate.

If products are designed with low system requirements in order to reach a wider potential market, then performance limitations are inevitable. For example, films can only be shown using a section of the picture and do not have the usual video quality.

You often hear the objection that the computer is an unsuitable medium for erotica, simply because it is seldom located in the bedroom. This neglects the fact that erotica is typically used to stimulate the observer to subsequent independent action. And that is not only possible in the bedroom.

2.4 Multimedia: A growing business area for the Beate Uhse Group

The interest in soft-erotic and pornographic multimedia products is considerable. The demands on quality and inventiveness are constantly increasing. Especially in the higher price range, the customer expects ever greater interactivity and polished programs. More is expected of the supplier now than even months ago, which makes the production more cost- and time-intensive.

If the customer is satisfied he often becomes a repeat purchaser. He is actively interested in the products and prepared to express his views on the product questionnaire cards that accompany the CDs. This provides the supplier with valuable tips for future production.

The spread of computer technology into the private household means that computers are no longer used primarily for business purposes. The customer is looking for entertainment, which he can also find in the erotic program. The spread of user equipment increases the demand for software. And good software widens the market for hardware.

Within a year Beate Uhse raised its turnover in the multimedia area from 0% to 5% of total group merchandise turnover. New products will extend this area further. Concrete preparations are underway for CD-I (Compact Disc Interactive), Video-CD and CD-ROM in MPEG 1 format. This will permit full screen films to be played in good video quality. Earlier exploitation of this potential seemed inappropriate given the limited availability of the user equipment.

New developments such as the MPEG 2 technique or increasing CD storage capacity are monitored continuously. Only when the user equipment required is available will planning become more concrete. Observations extend to the much discussed Cybersex. By using a computer, together with a hood and suit equipped with sensors, the body receives not only images but also sensations. This technology is still very immature and the necessary equipment very expensive.

Despite rapid developments, storage media such as diskettes will certainly be significant for some time and will continue to be used by Beate Uhse. The various storage media and systems do not replace each other serially, but are offered in parallel.

3   Beate Uhse's online services

3.1   The concept of online services and its significance for the Beate Uhse Group

The concept of online services contains a wide spectrum of information and entertainment, provided by a variety of companies over data networks either free of charge or at a price. The data is usually stored in mainframes, sometimes linked to external computers. It is accessed by the user from his terminal via his local network node.

With the introduction of BTX Beate Uhse offered its first online services in 1985 on the BTX network. At that time the service was extremely simple. It was limited essentially to a joke-of-the-day and an information service which allowed direct ordering of merchandise. In mid-1992 the entire program was overhauled and extended. Since then the consumer has been presented with a varied and well-maintained service incorporating a dialogue system and much more. Then, in 1994, there was entry to the Internet.

3.2   The use of online applications by Beate Uhse

All the extracts offered by Beate Uhse via the online service which can be freely seen by any user are exclusively soft-erotica. This is necessary to avoid contravening the relevant regulations, which were mentioned above in Section 2.2. The services available to everyone are continuously monitored by Beate Uhse. If necessary they are immediately censored.

This is not the case for live dialogues in which users can make contact and communicate with each other. These dialogues are accessible only to the two individuals involved in the contact, the wider public is excluded. Beate Uhse does not check these contents, as this is neither possible nor necessary for legal reasons, since these conversations are equivalent to normal private telephone conversations.

3.2.1   Content and function of online services via Bildschirmtext (BTX - Teletex)

BTX is an online service administered by Deutsche Telekom via a central control. All data are stored, monitored and controlled by the control centre. The information that can be called up via the Datex-J network is typically organised into pages. This allows the user to make his selection.

Beate Uhse offers a variety of erotic services via BTX on the Datex-J network, which the consumer can call up, sometimes free, sometimes at a charge. "Sextreff" offers the customer an interesting possibility in the form of a live dialogue in which he can make direct contact with other participants. Using a name chosen himself he enters his preferences into a visiting card. To select his dialogue partner he can query the visiting cards of other participants, and send or receive messages to or from them. Parallel communication with several participants is also possible.

To increase the attractions of the dialogue system, animators are used. Hence the user can find a dialogue partner at any time, even when no other private participants are using the system. These animators also fulfil the role of censor. Whenever more than two people have access to a service it is necessary to make continuous checks that no pornography is transmitted. This applies, for instance, to the contents of visiting cards and mailboxes.

In the dialogue system participants can also swap advertisements, make contact with other participants via mailboxes, or receive the latest erotic news.

Beate Uhse's range of services is not limited to live dialogue, however. Under the heading of "Small Ad Secrets" he can discover all the insider terms that are frequently used in contact ads. The erotic magazine offers soft-erotic stories from the best Beate Uhse novels. Furthermore, text extracts from the Beate Uhse magazine can be viewed or the daily updated "joke of the day" can be called up.

The information service provides the participant with the opportunity to make direct contact with the Beate Uhse Group. This is very convenient for the customer in the case of queries and can provide the supplier with important feedback about his products.

Of course, the customer can also browse Beate Uhse's erotic mail order product range and place direct orders. At the moment this program is available in text only. Very soon, however, it will be available with product photos as an enjoyable shopping experience.

Another interesting service is the Photo-BTX which allows users to obtain soft-erotic photos on his screen. The coarse-grained quality that was typical of the original BTX is past history. The photos can now be received in appealing quality, and the picture quality is improving all the time.

This development will be considerably furthered by the Datex-J decoder available from Beate Uhse from June 1995 in KIT standard (window-based Kernel for Intelligent communication Terminals). The KIT decoder can do anything that current multimedia applications can, namely, play film and sound and display high resolution graphics. In addition the KIT standard offers the same user comfort as a windows program. All functions can be controlled by mouse via a graphic user interface.

With the introduction of the KIT decoder the BTX program will also be extended, so that participants can exploit the multimedia potential of the new technology using interesting applications.

3.2.2 Content and function of online services via Internet

For a short time services have also been available from Beate Uhse over the Internet. Internet is a world-wide data network, which, in contrast to BTX, is self-administered. Each supplier is responsible for his program and structures and maintains his system himself. Transmission is effected by decentralized, external computers, whereby the user need have no knowledge of the physical structure of the data carried or of the computers involved.

At present Beate Uhse only offers its mail order catalogue on the Internet. Individual product pages allow the user to leaf through the program and view product information and illustrations. A separate order page allows the customer to place direct orders.

Although the Internet places no restrictions on the type of new services, Beate Uhse is not planning a comprehensive expansion of its services on the Internet. The reason for this is the absence of collection procedures. As long as their is no possibility of collecting charges Beate Uhse will only use the Internet for advertising purposes.

3.3   Advantages and disadvantages in the use of online services

The general advantage of online services is the direct contact with the customer. For the supplier this means that he can continuously provide the customer with up-to-date information about company news, the product range or special offers. Orders or information from the customer can be responded to quickly, and the customer can be addressed personally and effectively. The success is clearly measurable. For the customer, the online service is available at any time, and comfortably from the home too.

One advantage in using Datex-J is the low running cost to the supplier. The customer too is faced with attractive charges at only DM 3.60 per hour. If he makes use of expensive services he can monitor charges himself using the time display.

The user can learn about and operate BTX intuitively. Very simply he can access a wide range of products, services and information. This makes BTX equally interesting for both private and business users. Using direction pages, easily absorbed abbreviations, advertising headers and key word combinations the user can easily find the program he wants.

Although BTX started off relatively sluggishly in the early years, in the meantime there are more than 700,000 participants registered in Germany. The predominance of business benefits at the start has also altered. Currently, 63% of BTX access is from private users.

Arguments against BTX are that the system is at present still too slow and susceptible to breakdown, and as a result it is not suitable for quick data transfer. In addition the limitations on graphic possibilities will only be removed in the future.

BTX is centrally administered by the Telekom. This means that a supplier's BTX products must conform to specific Telekom guidelines. The fact that some of these rules are very narrowly defined can prove an obstacle, particularly for suppliers of erotica. On the other hand this provides the consumer with a certain degree of protection.

The decisive advantage of central administration by the Telekom is the procedure for collecting charges. The supplier can be linked up to this, allowing reimbursement for charged services to be transferred to him by the Telekom. Here, the Telekom offers a secure and relatively cheap service which guarantees the payment of supplier reimbursement.

Unfortunately, such a charging procedure is not provided by the network for Internet. As a result collecting charges is difficult for suppliers, especially since, in contrast to BTX, we are talking about a worldwide data network. For this reason, only those services are profitable in which the user can place direct orders from the range with the supplier. This applies to the mail-order catalogue, for instance.

The costs to the supplier depend on the structure of his services and the type of link. Each supplier bears the costs of his own link. The costs incurred by the participant vary greatly. He obtains access via his nearest Internet provider, to whom he pays access charges and for pages called up by volume. The billed costs vary from provider to provider.

Each supplier manages his own system via external computers himself. There are no guidelines laid down, as with BTX, for example. Consequently, he can make his system more attractive as he wishes, without substantial constraint. However, the absence of control means that legally questionable services have a certain latitude.

3.4 Online services: a new communication channel between the Beate Uhse Group and the consumer

Interest in online services is increasing. In 1994 BTX saw about 700,000 participants make contact with 2,500 suppliers and recorded a total of 129 million linkages. This corresponds to a growth of 43% on the previous year. The majority of users are between 25 and 45 years of age, which corresponds almost exactly with Beate Uhse's most significant customer segment.

The growing number of private users means that entertainment services, which includes Beate Uhse's services, are in growing demand. In addition 60% of BTX users make use of the possibility of mail order purchase. This way of placing orders is also increasingly important to Beate Uhse.

The user acceptance of individual services can be measured quickly. This provides important information about the attractive structuring of services. Customer contact via the information service also provides a useful opportunity to explore customer wishes in concrete terms, allowing the market position to be extended.

Beate Uhse's services on the Internet are still very new. Nevertheless, the customer response to this service is at present quite satisfactory. Order placements from the mail order service are also rising. Extension of the Internet service would therefore be desirable. However, this only makes sense when greater value creation opportunities are available.

In contrast, Beate Uhse is constantly extending its service via BTX and adapting to new technical conditions. Consequently, multimedia will play a large role there in future. The KIT decoder opens up excellent opportunities here. The combination of CD-ROM and BTX is also planned. The most important functions would be available offline on CD-ROM, up-to-date product information and similar data could be called up online by the user. The first step in this direction will be the mail order catalogue on CD-ROM with online links.

Involvement in other data networks is also subject to consideration. The barriers to entry for suppliers of erotica are typically very high, however. Networks such as Compuserve refuse services with erotic content altogether. As a result there is no immediate need for action.

4   Concluding observations

In the use of the new media two business areas have defined themselves for Beate Uhse. The multimedia business area covers all the existing soft-erotic and pornographic products from Beate Uhse that can be sold on diskette, Photo-CD and CD-ROM. Multimedia allows the products to be structured with greater flexibility and variety, but it also places greater demands on the producers. Rapid developments and the multiplicity of computer systems increase the difficulties in producing software for a wide market. Hardware and software standards are not yet clearly established, which increases insecurity for both producer and consumer.

The second business area covers the provision of online services, which at present is restricted, in Beate Uhse's case, to the BTX and Internet data networks. Online services via BTX are already well established. New possibilities for multimedia applications means that this BTX service will be extended further in future. Internet services have thus far been restricted to advertising for Beate Uhse's mail order merchandise. Extensions to this service will only follow if a charge collection system is created.

The development of new media is under constant observation. Beate Uhse has decided on the permanent expansion of these business areas, and regards the new media as an interesting long-term market offering the consumer a new variant in the world of sex and erotica. Of course, inter-personal relationships cannot be supplanted by even the best technique.

SEGA Game Applications: Consoles, Games and Development Possibilities

Winnie Forster
Cybermedia, Germany, and
Torsten Oppermann
SEGA, Germany

1 Introduction: video games as interactive entertainment

1.1 History and definition

At the end of the 1970s, only visionaries recognized that the first video game machines and home devices represented the birth of a new medium, namely that of video and computer games. By 1994, they had grown into a US$ 10 billion market, combining the characteristics of older media (sound, vision and animation) with interaction and thus opening up a whole new world of entertainment for consumers.

Originally, video games were considered primarily as a visual medium; their coarse, low-colour pictures stood in the shadow of the cinema, TV and video. Even after the improvement of the graphics quality (picture resolution, speed of movement and the number of colours that could be shown simultaneously) and the use of multi-channel sound from the mid-1980s, computer and video games remained a niche medium, apparently hardly able to offer intelligent entertainment and complex contents. However, compared with the first steps of the film at the end of the 19th century, the new medium developed in line with advances in computer technology at break-neck speed.

The spectacular, TV-like graphics and the acoustic background (CD music, speech output and sound-FX) - thanks to which video games have now shed their abstract exterior - are important for the commercial success on a global market. However, as regards the effect of the medium on the individual person, it is only of secondary importance - underneath the audio-visual luxury, interaction remains the outstanding feature of video games.

Just as the film developed into the most important medium of the 20th century through the characteristic of animation rather than sound or colour, it is interaction that makes video and computer games an independent form of representation.

Picture, sound and animation remain the secondary characteristics of video games, with which the young medium (until the early 1980s still monochrome and without sound and so not dissimilar to films at the turn of the century) is unable to challenge the established forms of expression. But through interaction this entertainment form sets itself apart from its "competitors": video game contents are not just portrayed (as for example by a comic or film) but can and must be controlled and changed by the consumer.

Technical progress has been as important for video games as it was for the film. From the very beginning, the outstanding feature of these two media (animation in the case of films, and interaction in video games) was present. Only the graphic and acoustic quality has been improved. As a result, both media lost their abstraction and conveyed and depicted increasingly complex contents and so reached a growing public. Films and, with a certain time lag, video games left the funfairs and backyards and reached many millions of households around the world.

1.2   The human-computer interface

The interface between machine and user has been in the foreground in the development of the computer and video games. Even before Apple presented the personal computer as an easy-to-use device, the first gaming machines were installed in public places. For many members of "generation X", Japanese and American gaming machines (from Atari, SEGA, Namco and others) represented the first contact with a computer. The machines simulated simple stories which the players could influence with a joystick or trackball. To guarantee the success of the early video games, players were intuitively able to understand how to control the figures (normally an abstractly drawn comic hero, vehicle or spaceship). Players did not have to go through a learning process before they could handle the machine, although it was only possible to really master the given tasks and problems with exercise. Players could only experience the entire story if they were successful. The simulation of physical principles such as centrifugal force was already included in the first video games ("Asteroids", "Space War", "Defender").

At the end of the 1970s, besides the action and real-time games, game genres were developed which did not demand reflexes and hand-eye coordination, but challenged the intellect of the players. Text-based adventure and strategy games were controlled via the keyboard rather than the joystick. The game programs reacted to the input of one or two words or commands. The main component of the software was a database, from which the suitable answer was selected by the so-called parser. By giving the correct command, a player opened up a new chapter in the story, which confronted him with new obstacles and puzzles. While these adventure and strategy games were more complicated to operate and established themselves on home and personal computers, action and skill-based games shaped the development of the arcade games and video game consoles. Computer games were for an academic group, while video games were for the mass market and so aimed at technical lay persons. With the high-performance second wave of video game consoles (from 1982: "Intellivision" from Mattel, "Colecovision" from CBS), video games became more attractive audio-visually and more complicated in terms of content. But they were not more successful. Complicated input units (e.g. joypads with integrated numeric keyboard) were unable to establish themselves and games which were too complicated for lay persons disappeared just as quickly. Only products that allowed players to play at once without having to study the rules had a chance on the market.

While American manufacturers tried to counter the collapse of the games market in the mid-1980s by extending their machines with keyboards, speech modules and new memory media, the Japanese machine maker, SEGA, took the opposite path. The SG 1000, SEGA's first home console, was an uncomplicated console for players in all age groups. Technically, it was able to play on television sets the SEGA software that had been proven in the arcades. To reach all age groups and levels of education, SEGA's game consoles and similar machines of their competitors were equipped with simple operating elements that could be understood at once. In the programming of the game software, the design of a suitable interface between player and program (human-computer interface) remained the principal problem. The games designers experimented with colours, symbols and semi-intelligent menu structures so that players could feel immediately at home and recognize intuitively the ability of their game figures in relation to the surroundings, even in a novel graphic environment (after the two-dimensional graphics, SEGA also represented game worlds in isometric perspective and 3D from 1980). The game procedures had to follow a comprehensible logic and the player's interaction had to have a clear, immediate effect on what was happening on the screen.

The lead which Japanese games makers have established in the development of user-friendly hardware and software, is reflected today in the unsure steps being taken by outside firms in the fields of "interactive entertainment". The combination of computer technology, entertainment and interaction which electronics, media and telecommunications groups are trying to achieve has already been a reality for 20 years in the form of the video game. And in the future too, there will be no other interactive entertainment medium besides the computer and video games.

1.3   Primary characteristics of video games

Video games
* are leading the way in defining the concept of interaction and are so far the only interactive entertainment medium
* can be intuitively learned and used and as a result reach all age groups and education levels
* can convey content with any degree of complexity.

In addition, the following video-game characteristics are important:
* They bring future technologies down to the consumer price level and into private households and the mass market.
* They are suitable for the secondary exploitation of content (films, comics, music).
* They are suitable as an advertising medium: advertising messages can be integrated into the game graphically, acoustically, in the form of animation and/or interactively.

2   The SEGA range of video game consoles

2.1   History of SEGA

1951   Founded as "Nippon Goraku Bussan Co."

1960   The company is renamed "SEGA Enterprise Ltd.", with SEGA standing for "Service Games".

1964   SEGA enters the arcade video gaming business, taking over the Tokyo-based "Japan Machine Manufacturing", a maker of jukeboxes and slot-machines.

1965   Founder David Rosen sells SEGA to Gulf & Western Technologies, continuing as CEO.

1979   Rosen acquires a distribution company founded by the Japanese entrepreneur Hayao Nakayama.

1983   SEGA introduces its first laser-disc game ("Astron Belt"), the first 3D-video game ("SubRoc") and its first consumer video game home console, the "SG 1000". All were marketed in Japan. Hayao Nakayma becomes Vice President of SEGA. The Japanese assets of SEGA are bought by Rosen, Nakayama and other Japanese investors for US$ 38 million.

1984   SEGA is bought by a partnership of the SEGA Enterprise Japan management and "Computer Service Co., Ltd." (CSK) forming SEGA Enterprise Ltd., a Japan-based company.

1985   SEGA of America is founded.

1986   SEGA products are distributed in Germany by "Ariola Soft", a wholly owned subsidiary of the Bertelsmann Group.

1987   SEGA Enterprise Ltd, purchases the company, "Linguaphone", making the first step into the education/edutainment market.

1988   The 16-bit game console "Mega Drive" is introduced in Japan. SEGA Enterprise Ltd. is listed on the 2nd Tokyo stock exchange. "Virgin Mastertronic" distributes SEGA products in Europe. "Virgin Games" takes over the distribution for Germany.

1990   EGA Enterprise Ltd. is listed on the 1st Tokyo stock exchange.

1991   SEGA Enterprise Ltd. acquires "Virgin Mastertronic" and "Virgin Games".

1994   SEGA SATURN, SEGA's first 32-bit game console, is launched in Japan.

2.2   Master System and Mega Drive

The hardware products of SEGA illustrate the technical development of the game consoles. After the monochrome, soundless gaming machines at the end of the 1970s, SEGA developed the first home machines at the beginning of the 1980s. This led to the launch of the SEGA Master System in 1986. Originally, these home consoles were used to exploit the successful arcade software. Later, games were specially developed for the home market.

An 8-bit Z80 3.6 MHz CPU worked inside the Master System. The 8-bit machine was able to portray a good 50 colours with a resolution of 240 x 226 pixels; the sound was still reproduced through a mono-channel. In 1989, the Master Drive was superseded by Mega Drive, the first video game console based on the 16-bit (the CPU was a 68000-related chip from Motorola) and one of the most successful to date. Worldwide, 25 million Mega Drive basic consoles were sold. As a 16-bit machine, the Mega Drive (marketed in the USA as "Genesis") had more computing power than the Master System. It also offered enhanced graphic and acoustic capabilities (see fig. 1).

In the case of hardware for interactive applications, the computing power of the CPU (or from 1990 the increasingly used special chip) is important in managing the increasing quantities of sound and graphics data. The amount of software also increased. Until the introduction of CD-ROM, video games were supplied on ROM modules, whose size grew by a factor of 2000 from 2 KByte (1980) to 4 MByte (1995) in the end. Thanks to the decline in ROM prices, the price of a game module both for manufacturers and consumers has remained steady in the last 15 years. In 1992, SEGA introduced a CD-ROM drive ("Mega CD") in Japan. This was introduced in Europe in 1993. The new memory medium (capacity: about 600 MBytes) is important economically for the video game medium. However, while the manufacturing costs of a CD-ROM drive are low, the access times are relatively poor compared to a ROM module, which delays the interaction of the player with the graphic game environment. CD-ROM - unrivalled as a cheap sound and vision carrier in the multimedia sector - is not yet fully accepted as a video game storage medium, since consumers expect immediate feedback from a game. The hardware manufacturers are currently trying to remedy this defect with faster CD drives and an integrated RAM memory, in which the CD data is stored temporarily.

2.3   SEGA SATURN: Hardware and primary field of application

The SEGA SATURN, which was launched in Japan at the end of 1994 and on the European market in the autumn of 1995, has a double-spin-CD drive and a 512 Kbyte RAM buffer. The data required in a given game situation is not loaded from the CD but from the faster RAM buffer.

The SEGA SATURN dispenses with ROM modules, which are expensive to produce. Instead, the games are supplied solely on CD with a storage capacity of about 600 MByte. Two 32-bit 28.6 and 20.0 MHz CPUs from Hitachi form the heart of the system. As a powerful RISC console, the SEGA SATURN is suited to manipulating 3D graphics. 3D models of rooms, vehicles and objects can be rendered, shaded and moved by the hardware in real time. With low storage space requirements, 3D animation produces more realistic movements than the traditional bitmap graphics, which produce the impression of movement similar to a cartoon film with the aid of given animation phases/frames. 3D animation is indispensable for driving and flight simulations. However, it will soon supersede all other animation techniques also in the field of mental and action games as well as graphic adventures and interactive movies.

SEGA SATURN is already being produced and marketed by other electronics manufacturers under licence. In Japan, SEGA SATURN variants from Victor (JVC) and Hitachi have been available since the beginning of 1995 (see fig. 1).

	Mega Drive	*SEGA SATURN*
year of release	1988	1994
European release	1991	1995
CPU		
main	Motorola 68000	Hitachi SH2 (x 2)
	16-Bit CISC	32-Bit RISC (x 2)
speed	7.6 MHz	28.6 MHz (x 2)
co-processors	Z80A	SH1, 68EC000
	16-Bit CISC	32-Bit RISC, 16-Bit CISC
speed	12.5 MHz	20 MHz, 11.3 MHz
memory (RAM)		
main	512 Kbit	16 Mbit
video	512 Kbit	12 Mbit
audio	64 Kbit	4 Mbit
cd block	—	4 Mbit
backup	—	256 Kbit
graphics		
resolution	320 x 224 to 320 x 448 pixels	320 x 224 to 704 x 480 pixels
colors	64 (512)	16.7 million
sound	10 channels stereo	32 channels stereo
storage media	ROM-cartridge	CD-ROM (doublespin)

Fig. 1.   Technical specifications: SEGA Mega Drive and SEGA SATURN

2.3.1 Secondary application: digital video

To coincide with the release of the SEGA SATURN consoles in the US and Europe, SEGA will be supplying an MPEG extension. The plug-in module makes it easier to play the 100 or so digital video (DV) films that are sold by BMG, Philips and other smaller firms. Through licensing agreements, Hollywood productions from all the major studios (MGM, United Artists, Paramount, Columbia Tristar) are available on digital video CD.

The DV films are coded in MPEG-2 format and have a picture quality almost equal to VHS. Acoustically, DV films with their DolbySurround or THX coded soundtracks are superior to their VHS counterparts. Since about 10 new digital video titles are appearing each month, this format will retain its significance until the introduction of a new video CD standard (announced both by a Time Warner/Toshiba alliance and also by Sony and Philips).

2.3.2 Audio CD

All normal music CDs can be played on the SEGA SATURN. The operating elements of an audio CD player are integrated into the operating system of the SEGA SATURN and displayed graphically on the screen. The SEGA SATURN can be connected to any normal amplifier, but its sound is reproduced via the television set (see fig. 2).

Fig. 2.   User-interface of the audio CD feature

2.3.3 Photo CD

With a special system CD, the SEGA SATURN can be used as a photo CD player and can reproduce digital pictures with a maximum resolution of 1536 x 1024 pixels and 16.7 million colours (32 bit depth of colour, "true colour"). The photo CD format defined by Kodak is primarily used in the semi-professional, professional - and also private - field for archiving pictures.

2.3.4 Other applications

The combination of a RISC hardware, the basic console, and the additional MPEG cartridge, also permits other applications such as edutainment software, interactive comics and interactive video clips, catalogues, point-of-sales and point-of-information software. Whether the manufacturers will use the many varied multimedia capabilities of the SEGA SATURN will ultimately depend on the dissemination of the hardware and the availability of the development systems provided by SEGA.

For the Japanese market, Hitachi has also supplied a karaoke adapter. However, since this Japanese leisure-time activity has few friends in Europe, this accessory will remain in the Far East.

2.4   Technology transfer: arcade games and "virtual reality" theme parks

The development, production and marketing of gaming machines is the main business of the SEGA group. The most advanced SEGA games are created in two special development departments of the Japanese parent company (AM 1 and AM 2). These are only converted years later for the home market. New hardware is also designed in the SEGA gaming machine department. As long as the technology is too expensive for the consumer market, modern SEGA gaming machines (e.g. the "Virtua" series) earn money in arcades and special SEGA amusement parks. There, the acceptance of the software is also tested and afterwards SEGA considers whether modifications are necessary.

In developing its gaming machines, SEGA cooperates with hardware makers from other fields. For example, "Desert Tank" was created in conjunction with Martin Marietta, a manufacturer of simulation devices and a supplier to the US Army, Navy and Air Force. Martin Marietta was pleased with its initial foray into the civil mass market through this cooperation and in exchange SEGA received 3D-special chips and customized simulation software.

Once they have been developed for the arcades, SEGA products such as the trail-blazing formula 1 simulation "Virtua Racing" are exploited several times. First, SEGA converts the successful software for the complete home hardware range. In the case of "Virtua Racing", versions appeared successively for Mega Drive, the 32X adapter and the SEGA SATURN. Compared to a new development, only minor alterations in the software were necessary. SEGA develops and markets the home versions itself or grants licences to a third party publisher - the SEGA SATURN version of "Virtua Racing" for example is published by Time Warner.

SEGA also profits from the above-mentioned hardware development. Both the Mega Drive and the SEGA SATURN are based on special chips that were tried and tested in arcades. The designers and engineers of the gaming machine department experimented with 3D graphics rendered in real time and network games long before the required hardware for the home market was affordable.

2.5   Games on demand - the SEGA Channel

In 1994, in conjunction with the American cable giant, TCI, and the media group, Time Warner, SEGA opened the "SEGA Channel". As an alternative advertising and sales channel, this online service supplies SEGA games on demand to households - initially in 12 test markets.

The software is received via satellite by an operator and hardware is provided by General Instruments and Scientific Atlanta (costs of the "headend" equipment: about US$ 5000) and passed on to the household in question. There, a special US$ 100 adapter (also produced by General Instruments and Scientific Atlanta) holds the software in its memory until the basic console is switched off. The cable customer decides how long he keeps a title once it has been paid. He also pays a monthly fee to SEGA Channel for the reception.

Besides Time Warner's Full Service Network, which had not yet left the experimental stage in the spring of 1995, the SEGA Channel is one of the first operating interactive TV projects. At present, the SEGA Channel offers the following services:

- game downloads
- previews: future SEGA products are presented to the customer as demos with limited playing capability.
- tips on SEGA games
- news
- competitions
- PR: all SEGA press releases can be called up.

The games and preview demos which can be downloaded are changed every month. At any one time, customers can choose between up to 50 titles. To draw the attention of the traditional SEGA customers to the novel service, SEGA1 will also develop some titles specially for the SEGA Channel and not supply them as ROM modules.

During 1995, SEGA is planning to reach 20 million households with its games channel and so gain one million customers. Technically, every American cable operator can offer the SEGA service and every cabled household in the US can receive the SEGA Channel. Many cable operators see games-on-demand as a "killer application", which is technically easier to implement than video-on-demand, the digital selling of video films at the press of a button.

The joint venture opens up new ways for SEGA and its developers, third party producers and licensors to reach a new group of customers (mainly but not exclusively young people) - whether it be for advertising purposes or for the secondary exploitation of the company's own games library. The SEGA Channel will mainly offer back catalogue titles which are no longer available in shops. Thus, SEGA does not consider its SEGA Channel to be a competitor to the traditional sales channels. Instead, it intends to use it to push the sales of module games. According to a SEGA survey, SEGA Channel subscribers spent 30% more money for Mega Drive games modules after one test month than players not tied to the Channel. The latter group's purchasing activity fell by 30% in the same period. Brand-new SEGA products can be tested via the Channel, but not played fully from beginning to end. Customers who like a demo version can purchase the complete game from the traditional outlets. These new products are only offered through the SEGA Channel after two months.

However, the SEGA Channel does not yet offer its customers "genuine" interactivity. Since SEGA is using the existing infrastructure for data transmission, it is not possible, for example, to arrange multi-player competitions between customers in various states. Interactive services will only be possible, in addition to the one-way downloads, when the high-performance two-way network - the much talked about "Information Superhighway" - has been established in the US or Europe. Yuzo Narimoti, President of SEGA Digital Communications, sees no problem in the limited capability of the existing telecoms infrastructure. "Automobiles have prevailed in the world without waiting for the completion of highways". Until such time, the manufacturers will use all available technologies: twisted-pair phone lines, co-axial CATV lines, fibre and satellites. Regardless of whether we experience the data highway in this or in the next century, SEGA has already gained important experiences with the SEGA Channel.

2.6   SEGA in the Internet

Via modem and conventional phone lines, the FTP server of SEGA and the related World Wide Web page offers customers a similar range of services such as those provided by SEGA Network. Only game downloads and previews are not available. Under the address *segaoa.com*, about 30 million Internet users can access information, news and tips as well as pictures and sound documents on SEGA games (see fig. 3).

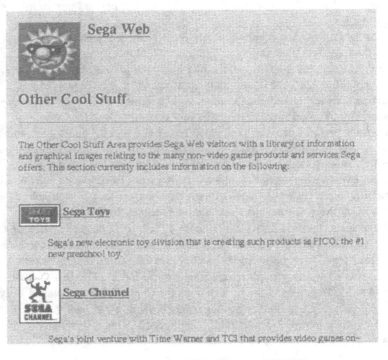

Fig. 3.   World Wide Web page of SEGA

3   Summary

Despite the broadly based SEGA hardware range, which also embraces the "Pico" learning computer and the portable video game "Game Gear", the group's main interest is focused on the SEGA SATURN. Although the SEGA SATURN is not compatible with the other consoles in the SEGA family or with the CD-ROM machines of Philips, Sony, Panasonic or multi-media PCs, its high-performance architecture permits conversions from any of these formats. PC games and numerous multi-media applications can be converted to run on the SEGA SATURN with no loss of quality, just like gaming machines or (in improved versions) the 16-bit products of the Mega Drive. Some parts of the software (3D animation, film sequences and music) can be transferred in their entirety without any changes from another CD-ROM format (e.g. PC).

Game consoles such as the SEGA SATURN are playback media for various kinds of "content": games, films, music and digital photos. Since the SEGA SATURN can play all normal audio CDs and a large part of the available digital video feature films and is also compatible with Kodak's photo CD format, it is a multi-media console in the narrower sense of the term. From the end of the century, SEGA SATURN-related products will also offer films in a quality that is superior to TV as well as all kinds of interactive services, games, data and speech transmission, trading and communications. Compared to producers of other consumer electronic machines which also work as multi-media playback devices, video game makers such as SEGA have a decisive edge with regard to interactive applications and entertainment. In addition, the hardware of SEGA and its competitors is already installed in households throughout the world. In 1993, 69% of all households in the US with children between 12 and 17 possessed a video game console from SEGA or Nintendo. This is why, twenty years after the original video game "Pong", electronics and chip manufacturers, content providers (film studios, publishers and record labels) as well as cable and telephone companies are interested in the market for video and computer games.

In the case of SEGA SATURN too, the hardware is easy to use. It can be connected to any normal TV and the stereo system and it makes use of CDs, an established storage medium and also one which technical lay people are familiar with. In comparison to a PC of similar power, the SEGA SATURN is less expensive and more user-friendly. The SEGA SATURN will reach a new target group, which for the first time will come into contact with computer technology through games consoles. In the medium term, video games will reduce the importance of "passive" TV as a leisure-time medium, just as the TV has largely superseded older media.

To ensure that the technical and content quality of video games keep up with its growing significance, industry-assisted gaming academies in Japan are training the creative and commercial people in the sector. Since the mid-1980s, technology, media and organization specialists have been working in the R&D development departments of the major manufacturers. SEGA has R&D operations in Japan and the States (SEGA Technical Institute, SEGA Interactive Los Angeles, SEGA

Midwest Development) and employs free studios and development companies in
Europe in France, the UK and also Hungary. As a location for video game
developers, programmers and producers of digital entertainment (see fig. 4),
Germany remains behind the US and Japan - and also the UK and France - even
though Germany as a market has a volume of US$ 1 billion. At the moment, fewer
than 1% of all video games are developed in Germany.

Fig. 4.   Example of a game screen

The activities of SEGA described above demonstrate the will and ability of a
successful game producer to leave the traditional toy market and market technology
of the future at an affordable price thanks to mass production.

TV of the Future - The Future of TV

Friedrich-Carl Wachs,
Heinrich Bauer Verlag, Germany, and
Johann-Reinhardt Wachs,
Saatchi & Saatchi, Germany

1   "Our TV sets are dinosaurs, fossils from an ancient world..."

It was a hot day in August 1969 and I - like probably many others - can recall it quite well: For the first time a man, Neil Armstrong, set foot on the moon and billions of "earthlings" left on their homeplanet witnessed those spectacular pictures from outer space via TV. Since we did not have one at home in those days everybody gathered at my aunt and uncle's who had recently bought one for the occasion. What it looked like? It was a ghastly monster in a very sixty - ish design, big and ugly. But it was highly effective: it filled one corner of the living room and everybody squeezed into seats and sofas in front of it in order not to miss those sensational black and white pictures and the crackling sound of Armstrongs legendary line: "It's a small step for man, but a big step for mankind..."

Thinking about the TV sets of today one can provocatively state the following simple fact: nothing much has changed! After sixty years of television, the TV sets are still comparatively simple. Ok, it's colour now instead of mere black and white and the remote control makes it unnecessary to get up in order to change channels. And the sizes vary: From the size of a watchman they reach to 2 x 2 meter home entertainment-centers. But apart from that? Can we communicate via TV, can we interact or participate in anything going on around us, can we download data for work or play? We cannot. Apart from teletext that adds written information about each station in the blanking interval no progress can be registered on the way to use the medium. It still is broadcast, i.e. one (or many) channels provide a linear 24 h program for an unspecified number of recipients who then have two choices:

- I want to watch TV, yes or no
- I want to watch this particular program now, yes or no

The appearance of VCRs has somewhat modified the second choice, since it enables its proprietor to "timeshift" his urge to watch a certain program at a point in time of his choice. But it did not change the fact that television sets were (and still are) dinosaurs, fossils from an ancient world.

They have remained fossils although the TV-landscape around them has changed considerably: For decades, German TV-households could only receive the limited choice of two (East-Germany) or three (West-Germany) public programs. The monopoly for the public stations in Germany ended in the mid-eighties when new technologies of program distribution were at hand: With the upcoming use of satellites and cable to transmit content the terrestrial frequencies started losing weight and more distribution capacities became available for competing stations. That was when commercial competition started tracing ARD, ZDF and the regional 'third' programs. Suddenly there was a wide variety of different channels. It took some time before RTL, Sat.1, Pro 7 and the others got off the ground, but they managed to become more and more successful and continuously lured viewers away from the public broadcasters. Today, the market share ratio between commercial stations and their public counterparts is already an impressive 60:40 (1994), with the latter constantly losing ground. So the choices increased a lot and one would think that subsequently the average TV-consumption would skyrocket accordingly. Surprisingly enough, this did not occur. The average number rose over the years, but only modestly so and not visibly connected to the growing choice of programs.

Did the good old TV set react in any way to those fundamental changes in TV landscape? It did not. And how could it? The mere fact that there was - as critics put it - "more of the same old thing", i.e. a greater variety of free TV channels, did not call for technical modifications. Ok, a split screen for simultaneous use of several programs and a freeze frame option would have been nice, but not even these innovations reached mass markets. "P.O.T." (= plain old television) endured and remained.

2   "Living on the edge (of a technical (r)evolution)..."

But things are about to change: With the appearance of digitalisation and videocompression a new level of technology has been reached and it will bring up a complete redefinition of what TV will mean in the future. Maybe it is bold, but this is more likely to become a revolution than a simple evolution.

What is it all about? The trick is that audiovisual signals, i.e. moving pictures and sound, are not distributed analogously any more, but are transformed into digital information data packages. These are then compressed by a complex technique that allows them to be transported much more easily via cable and satellite. In the near future, this will even be possible for terrestrial distribution. This diminution of data packages subsequently allows to crunch vastly greater quantities of digital information into the existing distribution channels - welcome to the 500 channel - scenario brought up in every Information Highway discussion these days!

There will - of course - not be 500 channels of the kind we know today: 24 h linear programming for masses is not what we are talking about here. It should simply be clear that the technological capacities will be there for hundreds of different "contents": where today one single program is distributed videocompression paves the way for up to 10 different programs instead. If an average Telekom-cable system in any given city in Germany contains 28 channels today there would be room for up to 250 additional forms of programming. And a satellite with 16 regular transponders could henceforth transport the data capacities necessary for 160 digital "contents"- be it movies, sports, games or whatever (see below).

The bottom line is: There is no longer a bottleneck in distribution - at least from a technical point of view. It will be possible to send every imaginable capacity and content from broadcaster to customer. But it will only be viable for broadcasters if enough people can receive these "data packages" in order to attract either advertising revenues or subscription fees from a sufficient number of subscribers.

Now this is an unknown factor in our scenario: The ordinary TV household cannot simply tune into these data packaged new contents. In order to receive the videocompressed signals you need to have an "Integrated Receiver Decoder" (= IRD) that does the decompression and decryption for your TV set. It is a small black settop device which will have to be connected with your TV set. It will have a modem built into it in order to pass on information via telephone lines. This will also facilitate a certain degree of interactivity for the customer. The price of the first generation of IRDs will be approximately DM 1,000 before it will sharply decrease because of economy of scales. At a later stage the functions of the IRDs will be integrated directly into a future generation of TV sets. But for the time being the main questions are: How many people will buy such a device over 1, 2, 5 years? Who will market them? And why would people want to buy them, i.e.: what will be offered?

Too many questions for now. There is lots of room for speculation. One thing, though, is sure: With this new technology we will live to see new forms of television. New offers of program, service and information will come up. The customer will be able to choose from a great variety of offers. He will be able to interact and actively create his individual entertainment. Once the technology is there, the market will begin to unfold. And the technology is already in place: Standards for digitalisation and compression are being set, the satellites with digital transponders are about to be launched (ASTRA 1 E is due for the fall of this year, Eutelsat's Hotbird 2 for 1996) and the German Telekom will have three digital cable channels ready (in the Hyperband) by the end of 1995. All the content providers are preparing new types of programming for the digital world.

3   "Twin worlds: analog ages and digital dreams..."

Let us come back to the analogous world again for a minute. After this outlook into the near future one might ask: And how is this scenario going to affect today's TV-landscape? What will be the imminent impact on existing stations and the dual system consisting of public and private networks in the German market?

I believe that changes will be slow and creeping instead of fast and radical. In the analogous world we will have more free TV special interest channels - for women, children and rockfans. Many of those are in the process of being planned and launched these days. We will also live to see the rise of local and regional TV-stations for the big cities and their suburban surroundings - such as "1A Berlin-Brandenburg", "TVMünchen" and "Hamburg 1". All business is and will remain local and this simple truth will push these stations through and implement another missing element of a complete TV market such as the American in Germany. The local/regional stations might even build their own network at the end of the day.

The public stations are going to stay as a part of a functioning market, too, although the pressure on them will increase: If they want to survive, they will have to change their structure and their spending because in a world of sliding market shares and rising fees they are running into a legitimation gap. Nobody will understand why they should receive even more money than today (approximately 8 billion DM of fees brought up by the 32 million German TV-households) if they keep losing ground to the unpaid for, advertising supported commercial competitors. They should rethink their strategy and concentrate on their core competences such as information, education and culture instead of copying pure entertainment where they can only lose.   ·

The analogous world will remain "intact" for some more years. We will live in a "simulcast" situation, where both the analogous system and the digital world will coexist. The digital community will steadily grow and more and more households will have the equipment to enter the new world. Still, the market shares of the key players (RTL, Sat.1, ARD/ZDF, Pro 7, RTL 2 and the others) will not slide dramatically. But with each new digital customer the scale will be tipped a little further and finally the analogous technology will share the fate of vinyl records (LPs) in their losing battle against the upcoming CD: Try to find your favourite piece of music on a record in a store today and you get the idea.

4   "The new variety: Into the great, white open..."

All this will only work if the range of new offerings is attractive enough to convince the customer to invest in the new technology. As I mentioned they will have to pay about DM 1,000 for the settop device at a first stage (later less) plus additional money for what they desire to see/get. Let us take a closer look at what might be offered:

- *Video on Demand (VoD) or Near Video on Demand (NVoD):* Digitalized movies or other video offerings available whenever they are requested. Viewers will be able to fast forward, pause, rewind and replay them - all without the use of a VCR.
- *News on Demand (NoD):* Video clips showing current headlines, but also update analyses and in-depth-reports - organized according to subject. Viewers can select

what interests them and skip over what does not interest them. They can also compare the coverage provided by different news sources, or simply defer to their favourite - but on their own schedule.

- *Games on Demand (GoD):* Video games can be called up on demand, and not just the high-tech games we associate with the video arcade. Instead, such prosaic adult games such as chess, solitaire, bridge, checkers etc. will be at hand.
- *Homeshopping:* Not the regular American cubic zirkonia-type of annoying show, but shopping in which the consumer has the control of what areas to explore. A virtual shopping mall invites the viewer to a variety of shops and brands, direct marketing activities are possible via video catalogs.
- *Teletravelling:* Instead of browsing through a dull catalog, the consumer watches a video of the city he wants to visit and takes a close look at his potential hotel.
- *Teleticketing:* No more standing in line for those rare opera seats - you do your reservation via TV and get a scene from the opera with it.
- *Telebanking/Financial Services:* Consumers can review their accounts, monitor investments, and keep track of their money. They can also seek advice and information.
- *Telemedicine:* Access to doctors and hospitals for routine or emergency advice will be possible.
- *Educational Services* and *Distance Learning*
- *Videoconferencing*

These are only examples. Much more can be imagined and is in the making. Field tests and pilot projects are currently launched in different German cities. They all aim at evaluating what the consumer really wants and how the pricing should be in order to make the new offerings economically viable. Telekom is trying their cable and telephone systems for the ideal distribution channels and the most efficient techniques, the content providers such as TV-stations, publishing houses, mail order companies, banks etc. work on the best possible way to present their products and hard- and software players are testing the new generation of equipment. My company, Heinrich Bauer Verlag, is actively engaged in several of those projects. Our aim is to find new outlets for our strongholds in the print business: Being the biggest European magazine publisher we believe in transforming resources and know-how from the print into the audiovisual sector. One example: With a market share of 50% in the TV guide segment (6 different titles with a total of 10.6 million copies sold each week) we want to implement program navigation-products that help the customer to find his way through the wide variety of new offers. We will use graphic interfaces in a user-friendly design in order to avoid elitist specialisation that prevents market success.

This leads me to a more general aspect of the future of TV in the digital world:

5   "What's it gonna be: TV or PC...?"

What will be the "center of attraction" in the future: Will the old TV set mutate into a multimedia PC with a manual as thick as the Manhattan Telephone Directory or will the PC take over and become the family entertainment mashine? There is lots of rumor about the convergence of the two towards a multimedia entertainment center. I do not believe so. I do think that the TV set of tomorrow will stop to be a fossil and will be upgraded to interactivity and a certain degree of computing. This will happen in two ways: First through a back channel via modem (first step: integrated in the IRDs, small bandwith, telephone line. Second step: integrated in the TV set, broader bandwith, cable system) which enables the customer to interact, and secondly through a "revamped" remote control that will have to be designed extremely user-friendly and easy to handle. In combination with touch screen techniques or user interfaces the untrained user must be lead to work his "entertainment center"- TV set and to like the choices he is offered there. If this effort fails, many digital dreams will not come true. But at the end of the day, the TV set will remain in its habitual place, that is the living room, the bedroom, the attic. It will be used mainly for entertainment purposes, not so much for bank transactions, services of any kind or working/learning. It is still and will remain a leisure instrument that will adapt to the new forms of leisure activities - but not more.

The PC, on the other hand, will integrate the functions of a common TV set. Even now you can watch TV with your PC and the CD-ROMs are only one step in that direction. Still, nobody in his right mind will watch a movie in a 2 x 2 cm rectangle on the low right side of his computer screen while sitting at his desk and filling in income tax forms on his PC. The clear distinction between work (PC) and play (TV) will remain - no matter what the digital wonderworld will come up with.

As with so many other technological innovations, thus, existing consumer benefits will be supplemented rather then supplanted by digital interactive television - we will pick the cherries from the new offerings and keep what we liked about plain old TV. Therefore it seems highly likely that future TV will be able to cater to a decisively increased number of consumer needs. So it's pleasant prospects for the medium.

Interactive Video-Services for the Residential Customer

Claus Sattler and Niels Klußmann
Eutelis Consult GmbH, Germany

1   A step towards the Information Highway

The Information Highway is the basic term for a wide range of services in different areas of telecommunications, computing and entertainment. These services include high-speed data transfer over ATM (Asynchronous Transfer Mode) networks or other data services, such as Switched Multimegabit Data Services (SMDS) via Distributed Queue Dual Bus (DQDB)-networks. Presently booming online-services are further examples for services attracting public interest now. The success of the Internet - especially since introduction of convenient user interfaces like the World Wide Web - shifts online-services also in the discussion of the Information Highway. Wide introduction of ISDN offers digital connections not only for business users and fiber in the loop as well as cable TV (CATV) networks enable private users to use broadband services. The PC offers multimedia today and a complete generation has been grown up with this technology.

This chapter focuses on a single section of all these services and applications: Video-services for the residential customer. Outgoing from a look upon the development of other value added services in the past, some basic technologies and market scenarios of possible players is outlined. The outlook presents a timescale of trials and the possible introduction of video-services on a large scale.

2   The development of value-added-services in the past

Value-added-services (VAS) did not develop as expected in the last years. In spite of all optimistic forecasts the turn-over laid far behind the expectations. For service-providers of VAS, for example database-provider or e-mail-provider, it was very difficult to establish the service, to find clients and to explore markets. This situation did not change very much over the years. Generally speaking, VAS are mostly treated as service-features, added to the more attractive network-services, and not as independent real (value-added) services.

A fundamental requirement for setting-up successfull VAS is a certain number of possible subscribers. Additionally, another key-factor is the availability of terminals, which are used by the subscribers to access VAS. In case, the terminals are not or not on high numbers available when the VAS starts, for example with a limited number in a field trial, it is essential to take care of a possible mass-production and decent costs from the consumers point of view, right after the test-phase, if the VAS starts its regular service.

Database-services and videotex mostly offer text-based informations, even if the CEPT-standard for videotex enables the service-provider to set-up pages with a limited number of graphical elements.

Database-services entered the market at a time, when PCs and modems even in the business-area were exotic tools. Videotex entered the market in Germany with the aim, to offer this service to the private consumer, who first had to buy an additional terminal, which had to be linked to the TV-set. This and the low speed were the main reasons, why videotex (in Germany called Bildschirmtext, BTX) did not reach the expected number of subscribers. For example, in 1980 a consulting company predicted a bright future for BTX, because it was expected to become the favorite service for data transfer for small and medium enterprises (SME). In 1982, the Institut der Deutschen Wirtschaft expected 50,000 computers linked to BTX, one million subscribers for the year 1986 and 1.5 million subscribers for 1987. The real number for 1987 then was 58,000.

The success came in 1991 after a change in the marketing strategy and a move from the TV as terminal to PCs with modems as terminals. Since then, the number of subscribers is constantly growing on an actual rate of 50,000 subscribers per month. Today, the now called Datex-J-Service (in 1995 the name will again change: Telekom-Online) serves about 800,000 subscribers.

In a slight better situation are the service providers of private information services over the telephone network. With the start of the field trial in 1992 a number of 7 million telephone main lines were the basis. In the meanwhile, these services are offered on a regular basis in whole Germany, but the expectations of the service-providers still remains unsatisfied.

These audiotex-services use voice-information for the selection of the informations by the user and the information, offered by the service-provider. Speech-recognition made respectable progress over the last years, but dialogues still are short, consist only of a small number of words and are therefore inconvenient and unnatural from the users point of view. The information output to the user is limited due to the limited ability of the users acoustic reception for pure acoustic informations. This fact strictly limits the form of the presented informations. Call-and-fax-back-services are one possibility to solve this problem and to present more information together with pictures, tables and structured text.

Another very important fact is, that the human being explores its environment by using all senses, not only the acoustic sense. Actual telecommunication services does not pay much attention to this perceptive faculty, as they are focused on audio- or text-information. The user of such a service notes this restriction by the above mentioned unnatural dialogues and an unsatisfactory information reception.

In contrast to the telephone-network and -terminal based services, television and video-tapes support the ability to deliver audio-visual information - today mostly referred to as multimedia-information. So far, both have some very restrictive limitations. In case of VAS, the time of accessing a service is not fixed. An individual user can access the service with all supported information at every time he wants to. Television as a broadcast service cannot be influenced in such a way by the user (therefore in this case he is referred to as a viewer - a passive consumer). Videorental is a kind of service, where a user can influence the time and the programme he wants to view, but choosing and renting a video and watching the video are two different actions which differ by time and place. Additionally, the time and place of renting a video is limited to certain shops and by the opening hours.

Up to this point, some important factors which influence the set-up of a new service have been pointed out: the number of terminals, multimedia and individual control by the user. These factors lead to new telecommunication services, which are determined by:

- private consumers, because there is a large number of households with an appropriate number of terminals (TV-sets)
- multimedia-ability
- interactivity

So far, there were some technical limitations. The above mentioned factors require a broadband channel to the consumers home. New technologies make this possible.

3   Broadband services to the homes

Today, there are different channels and networks, which can be accessed by the private consumer:
- telephone network
- cable TV broadband network
- satellite broadcasting
- terrestrial TV reception

Almost every home has a telephone. In the civilised parts of the world, 95% of the households are connected to the telephone-network. So far, due to technological attributes of the twisted-pair-copper line in the access networks, broadband services in decent quality were impossible.

CATV-networks, satellite and terrestrial broadcasting offer broadband services in high quality, but the total number of channels is limited without the ability to dedicate an individual channel to every single home. This means, it is not possible for a consumer, to select a programme and to receive this programme via satellite or terrestrial broadcasting individually.

Actually, there are some very interesting technical developments in all these areas, to use the available band-width more economically. In general, there are two different ways.

The first way is the area of videocompression. A digitalization of a PAL colour-TV signal requires a data rate of 140 MBit/s. With sophisticated compression algorithms it is possible to reduce the large amount of redundancy of the single pictures and to reduce the data rate to an average value of 2 MBit/s. With MPEG II (Motion Picture Experts Group, Standard II) the first powerful standard is available since the end of 1994. Further standards for applications in the field of telephone- and handheld-terminals with datarates of several hundred kBit/s are under consideration and are expected to come in 1996 and 1997 (MPEG III and IV).

The second way of using the existing band-width is to use more spectrum-efficient transmission codes in order to reduce the band-width assigned to one channel on the physical medium.

In case of the telephone network, there are two main developments. The first is a new transmission code for twisted pair cables, called Asymmetric Digital Subscriber Line (ADSL). This transmission code was invented in the USA by Bellcore and first tested in New Jersey at the end of 1992 for data- and video-communications between some schools. ADSL can be configured in different ways, but generally supports a broadband and narrowband channel to the subscriber, which enables the user to receive a simplex digital broadband data stream and a duplex analogue narrowband channel for telephony. Apart from that, a very narrowband digital backchannel (16 kBit/s) from the subscriber to the local switch is supported. This configuration leads to the attribute 'asymmetric'.

ADSL supports up to 8,192 MBit/s over 4 km. Longer distances are possible, but reduce the data rate. The European standard is under consideration by the ETSI and expected to come 1996. It probably will define different configurations of forward- and back-channels dependent on the service (ISDN vs. POTS) and the distance. Additionally, new technological developments will lead to ADSL 2 and ADSL 3. ADSL 2 is expected to be defined for fullduplex-channels with 384 kBit/s and distances of 3 km and ADSL 3 is expected to support fullduplex-channels of 6 MBit/s over very short distances of under 2 km.

The other development in the field of telephone-networks is to offer a broadband access network. This is achieved by introducing fiber in the access network. There are different strategies, general referred to fiber in the loop (FITL). All strategies summarized under FITL differ concerning the costs. A very old rule states, that 30% of a network costs are in the access network. For this reason, fiber in the loop is introduced in different ways, depending on the services expected to offer in the next years and the expected return on investment.

The strategy called fiber to the home (FTTH) offers a real broadband solution. There is a fiber link from the local switch to the terminal in the consumer's home. The disadvantage of this solution are the high costs, which are the highest of the here introduced strategies. For this reason, FTTH is a solution for the business-sector or for areas with short access lines, like high densely populated areas.

Fiber to the (last) amplifier (FTTA) introduces a fiber link from the local switch to the last amplifier layer of the CATV network, which results in a hybrid network. This strategy is also well known as fiber to the curb (FTTC), which means a fiber link from the local switch to the curb of a street and a TV cable serving the street.

The discussion under experts is presently taking all strategies under consideration for a cost-effective solution of FITL. The most advanced programme in this field is presently running in Germany, where till the end of 1995 a number of 1.2 million households in the new Eastern parts of the unified Germany will be connected to a fiber access network. All different strategies will be implemented here. There is a strong international interest in the experiences of this programme.

Another point of the discussion is the role of ADSL. Regarding the upgrade of the access networks with FITL, the question arise, if we really need ADSL. Most experts state that ADSL is only a temporary solution, because it enables a network provider today to introduce broadband services without introducing FITL, but in the long run, no service provider will refuse to introduce FITL. Another question is the number of subscribers, from which on the costs for a single ADSL-modem in the local switch for every subscriber will exceed the costs for a FITL-solution.

All these mentioned questions are under theoretical discussion and practical trials world-wide now.

Regarding CATV- and satellite-networks, these capacities can be exceeded by using digital transmission technology. Today, an analogue TV-channel requires a bandwidth of 8 MHz. Digital technology leads to a fourfold higher number of channels in CATV- and satellite-networks.

Additionally, CATV-networks use only a limited range of frequencies (today usually 47-326 MHz). There are plans, to use the range up to 450 MHz or up to 862 MHz, but this requires a complete technological change of amplifiers in the network. The benefit is space for hundreds of digital channels.

A so far unsolved problem is the back channel. The CATV network of today is designed for broadband services without any individual dedication of a channel to a subscriber and without any flow of data from the subscriber to a kind of control center. Until now, the telephone is the only way for a subscriber, to send data to, for example, a service provider or a network control center.

Satellite networks today already deliver a large number of channels to every home with a satellite dish. The number of satellites will still increase in the next years with digital transponders. So far, the request of the TV industry is high and it can be expected, that this will last the next years till the end of the decade.

A very important point, which influences the development of interactive broadband services may be the state of deregulation in a service area. Competition in the field of networks and services leads to a pressure to introduce new services. In areas, where CATV network and telephone network are owned and operated by different companies, the market pressure may force the one or the other to set up broadband services much faster than somewhere else, where a company holds a monopoly and owns both, the telephone network and the CATV network.

In some countries with two service providers, one operating a CATV network and the other operating the telephone network, CATV provider have started to enter the field of telecommunication services. They now offer telephone services, especially if they followed a long term strategy and laid twisted pair cables in the past together with the CATV cables. In theses service areas, telephone companies now start to offer video-services with ADSL, vice versa.

The following picture (see fig. 1) presents an overview about the basic structure of the customer, the access network, the video server and different providers involved in the process of delivering contents to the private household.

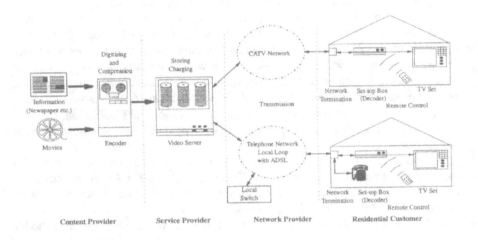

Fig. 1.   Overview: On-demand-services

4   Development of video-services

Video-services is the general term for a number of different services. They differ regarding the type of information presented and the degree of individual choice of the subscriber. Common for all is the ability to support broadband multimedia services with high quality moving pictures, still pictures, audio information and text (see fig. 2).

Note, that still the discussion is in progress and that many of the following terms are defined in different ways by different parties engaged in the discussion (service provider, network provider, media companies, film producers). There is much space for interpretation.

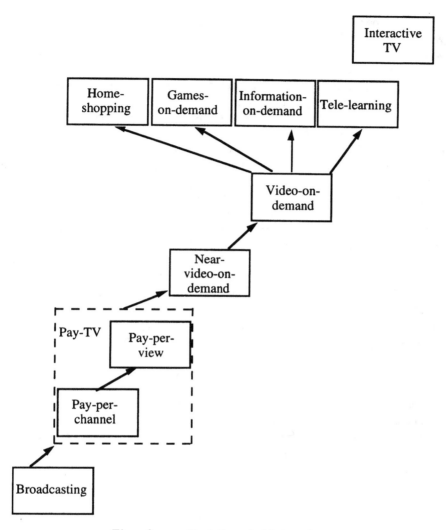

Fig. 2.   Evolution of video-services

The first development in this sense was pay-TV, which already is established today. Programmes are broadcasted in a coded way, but can only be decoded with a special receiver and a key. This key can be bought from the service-provider, to which an additionally monthly fee has to be paid. Because this fee has to be paid independently, which part of the programme is viewed, this form of Video-services is often and more precisely referred to as pay-per-channel (PPC). You pay and have the right to watch the programme of a complete channel for a whole month.

The next step ist to pay only for the really watched parts of the programme. This leads to a variation of pay-TV, called pay-per-view (PPV). In the case of PPV, the viewer only pays for the parts he really views. So far, it is unclear, if he pays for the minutes he watches a programme or a single part of the programme (if he starts watching a show, he might pay after a test-phase of five minutes en bloc for the whole show, independently from the fact, that he might switch off after twenty minutes). So far, no experiences with different charging strategies have been made, but charging for a whole show or programme is more probable than charging for a certain time independently from a programme.

Pay-TV does not enable the viewer to influence the selected programme, for example by choosing the time he watches a programme, by choosing the programme itself or finally to influence directly the action of the programme he watches. These different grades of influence are represented by different video-services.

The raise of the number of channels in CATV-networks to several hundred will as a first step lead to a broadcast service called near-video-on-demand (NVoD). In a NVoD system there are a number of channels with the same programme, but at different stages of the programme. This means, for example, a movie starts every 15 minutes on one of the channels. If a viewer of such a programme is disturbed in watching this programme, for example by a telephone call, he simply switches over to the next channel after finishing the call, where the same programme is broadcasted with a delay of the above mentioned 15 minutes. The viewer need not to miss parts of the programme. He can 'rewind' the programme in intervals of 15 minutes. The most interesting feature of this services are the multiple start-times of the programme, which nearly allow the user to individually select the time when to watch it.

Up to this point, all discussed video-services were pure broadcast services without any back channel. The introduction of the back channel is the decisive step from a broadcast video-service to an individual video-service.

With a back channel, the subscriber can send data to a service provider or a control center. Then it is possible to introduce a video-on-demand service (VoD). In this case, a large number of movies - say 1,000 - is stored on a video server (large hard disk array). The video server can handle a number of connections and can serve - depending on the configuration - about 20% of the connected subscribers simultaneously. The user chooses a video and the video server serves the movie. Additionally, the aim is to offer full VCR functionality, i.e. the ability for the subscriber, to rewind, to fast forward and to pause or stop the video.

There are a number of technical problems of storing such a high number of videos and to support simultaneously access of dozens of users, possibly accessing the same video. These technical problems are not scope of this overview.

Of course, there is not only the possibility to store videos on the server. Other services include home shopping or information on demand. In the case of home shopping, a catalogue of a mail-order house is stored on the server. The consumer can look up an article, which is presented to him by videos, text and sound. Interactivity enables the viewer to choose the articles and to order them. He can pay by credit card (if the set-top-box is equipped with a card-reader and the system supports a connection to the credit card supplier) or later by using his bank account.

Information on Demand is a service, where information and news are stored on the video server. The consumer can navigate through different categories of information and news (politics, economics, sports, weather, yellow press) and can choose between different multimedia articles with videos, charts, text, sound and still images. At present, there are some discussions about information-on-demand services, which handle this selection automatically for the customer. Then, the customer only has to enter some key words (e.g. 'football results' or 'foreign politics'). A special software called agent automatically chooses the information in relation to the key words. Additionally, he can pay in the same way, if there is the possibility to charge him, as if he uses a pay-per-channel or pay-per-view system.

Tele-Learning, or Distant-Learning, is another example of a content depending Video-service. In this case, educational videos and information are stored on the server and can be accessed by the consumer. Foreign language training courses are a good example for a senseful multimedia application in the field of video-services.

A very important entertainment service of the future may be video games. This means different video games stored on a server. The consumer can play such a game either on his own against the server or together with another consumer, who also wants to play the game, but who also sits in his home somewhere else. The game server coordinates the consumers data links and charges the accounts.

The last stage of the evolving video-services is true interactive TV. The viewer is no longer the passive viewer of a show ('couch potato'), but can influence with his back channel the things happening on the TV screen by communicating with the show master. Interactive TV is in discussion now, but there is a very long way to go.

5   Markets for video-services and their players

There are different possibilities for potential players to enter the market of video-services. The following picture presents an overview about the possibilities (see fig. 3). This picture is an economic extension of the first more technical picture of this chapter.

Regarding the present situation, especially in the USA, there seems to be a bright future for video-services. Companies of the field of telecommunications, like carrier and service providers, are as well engaged as CATV network provider and media giants: British Telecom, single Baby-Bells, NTT of Japan, TCI, Time-Warner and Sega, News Corp., Bertelsmann in Germany - these are only a few names of the large pool. For example, there are about one hundred companies involved in the preparations of the German based Stuttgart trial. All important and international acting companies are establishing contacts, set-up alliances or strategic partnerships and take-over other companies. Also the hard- and software sector with companies like AT&T, Intel, Microsoft, Siemens or Philips is involved.

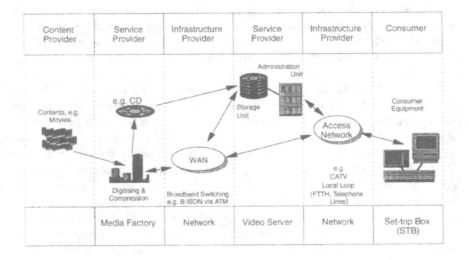

Fig. 3.   Provider scenario

A very good example for the convergence of the telecommunication industry, the computer business and the entertainment sector is the take-over of Time-Warner in the USA by Sony of Japan. This enables Sony to offer all products for all stages of the exploitation of movies. Warner Bros. is a well-known film production company established 1917. Sony is one of three companies involved in the development of digital movie sound, the first development for movie sound since the introduction of Dolby Systems over twenty years ago. The Warner film copies of course are equipped with a digital sound track according to the Sony standard. Additionally, Sony offers with VCRs and TVs all equipment for the later exploitation of movies by video rental or video selling and broadcast by pay-TV or common broadcasting.

The pressure on the different possible competitors is in the meanwhile as high as the stimulus of the possible profits. Theoretically, the mass market is standing on a solid base. At a first glance, it promises advantages for all parties involved:

- Established network and service provider have a new possibility to better utilise their existing infrastructure.
- Media companies find a new possibility to further exploit their magazines, newspapers, movies, shows and other contents.
- Hardware manufacturer hope to sell new types of terminals to the huge market of residential consumers and hope to compensate the break-down of business in the western countries resulting from saturation of present terminals (TVs, VCRs) in private households.
- Software developer want to enter the business because of the important role of coding and compression algorithms and the complex management of video servers and other databases. Consumers can choose from various new types of video-services in the areas of entertainment, culture, and information.

- Especially the network provider has to recognise the important fact, that in the future the money will be made with applications and services, and no longer with simple connections and networks.

So far, it is unclear, which video-services will succeed. Nobody knows, which service will be accepted by the consumer, but experts focus on video-on-demand and home-shopping when discussing the leading services. Another point, which is open, is the question of substitution. Will video-on-demand really influence the business of video-rental? Will there be any influence of home-shopping on traditional mail-order business or local retail business? And what about tele-teaching? Is tele-teaching in a world, where knowledge becomes a key-factor of qualification and professional development, only a cultural fig-leaf in the entertainment dominated chorus of video-services or a real application to make money with?

Similar to other sectors of VANs a structure of content provider, network provider and service provider will arise. The distribution of roles is open from todays point of view and it seems to be a good chance for network providers as well as for content providers also to become a service provider in order to assure this stage of the market.

6 The question of acceptance

The crucial point of success is the acceptance of the new services by the user. The term 'acceptance' includes different aspects: user interface, charging and public control of sensitive contents and personal data. In the discussion, it has to be taken into account, that these points are influenced by the culture of the consumer. This means, that no single solution will be found, but that in different countries different solutions will come up.

The design of user interface of new video-services include terminal handling and use of remote control, styling of commands and screen design. The industry has learned from the fact, that two third of all consumers cannot programm the clock of a VCR.

Charging and pricing is another point. Experts believe, a video may only cost as much as renting a video for a weekend. Apart from that, concepts are being discussed, if the price can be dropped, if the presentation of the movie starts with a commercial or if the movie can be shown free of charge if the user accepts a number of commercials during the presentation, as he is used to today in private TV channels. In the case of tele-shopping, the service provider may think of a service free-of charge for the consumer. Another possibility might be a monthly charge and to set off this charge against an order of the consumer.

Another aspect is the question of charging in the introduction phase of new video-services. Experts agree, that it will be a task of the pilot trials, to examine possible tariffs and to start at a very low level, in order to stimulate the use of services.

Sensitive contents include x-rated movies or violent video-games and possible premium rate services. The public might expect a kind of control by authorities or voluntary control by a group of service providers. Additionally, the consumer wants to be secure, that the number of his credit card in the card-reader is not directed to somebody else than the service provider. Furthermore, a central organised service such as video-on-demand - in contrast to a decentral system like video rental - enables the service provider to set up consumer profile, which could be used for further marketing activities.

The human society cannot stop technological development on its way to the information society, but the society must take care of a human interface, a decent charging and of a common control of contents and private data.

7   Outlook

Throughout the world, many field trials will start in 1995 with different services, different technologies and different groups of users. Some target the privat consumer exclusively, others also include business services. Some trials are quite small with only 30 or 50 households and some are extensive market trials with 4,000 or up to 10,000 households. Most of the trials are scheduled to end after 18 or 24 month, but some executives of the trial organising companies already announced plans to 'export' the technical concept and service profiles after a successfull trial to other areas. In some areas, the trials are very ambitious, with a large number of households connected and wide a variety of services for business and residential customers. This may lead to a delay of start, because problems are more difficult and need more time to be solved than expected.

Of course, user acceptance can only be tested in trials with a number of significant households. Industry so far has shown worth mentioning interest only in trials with more than 1,000 true interactive households. A number of 5,000 households is considered as ideal, as well as regarding costs for such an extensive trial, but also regarding the results of market research and user acceptance tests.

Acceptance tests mainly have to answer two questions: Which service is the killer-application, that finally will establish video-services as regular services? Experts state, that video-on-demand or home-shopping are likely candidates, followed by information-on-demand. The second question is the question of the costs. How much money will the private consumer spend for additional entertainment and information?

Apart from user acceptance, another important question is the problem of the terminal. Will the TV-set change more and more until it finally becomes a computer? Or will the PC become the first choice and will develop to a multimedia-station with the ability also to work as a TV-set? This problem involves the development of the set-top-box, which is not yet standardized. At present, there are different set-top-boxes from different equipment providers. Slowly some key parameters for set-top-boxes come up, like MPEG II as compression standard, but many problems remain unsolved: Should a set-top-box include a smart

card reader for credit cards? What about a key board interface? Which software is stored in the set-top-box and which tasks are processed in the set-top-box and which are directed through the back channel to the server?

The unsolved question of the set-top-box, i.e. missing standards and compatibility, may be an obstacle for a wide introduction of video-services.

Video-services are - after online-services - the second step for private households on their way to the Information Highway.

Information Technology and Applications for Elderly and Disabled People

J. A. van Woerden
TNO Institute of Applied Physics, The Netherlands

1   Introduction

With continually improving health standards, elderly people tend to live longer and lead much longer active lives. The future elderly also tend to live more independently and are generally economically better off than previous generations so constituting an important group of (new) users of assistive devices.

The proportion of elderly people in the population is growing rapidly. Predictions of the increase of people aged over 65 years in Europe being 12% of the population in 1980 expect 16% in the year 2010 and 22% in the year 2040. Disabilities are coming sometimes with age. People are regarded as disabled if they suffer from impairment to the extent that they have difficulty in leading independent lives without additional help in the form of personal assistance, specially adapted environments or practical aids to daily living.

Many older people do not see themselves as disabled yet may have a combination of minor impairments and may require some support with daily functioning. Technology in general, and especially information technology can directly improve the quality of life for older people and people with disabilities. It can improve the efficiency and effectiveness of the services provided to older people and people with disabilities. However, technology is a double edged sword since it can also exclude and disadvantage elderly and disabled people by failing to take their needs into account.

Access by elderly and disabled people to generally used technology and technology based services is a major issue in enabling and facilitating their integration. In order for technology to serve the needs of older people and people with disabilities it is important that their requirements are taken into account throughout the technology development process and incorporated into the development of all equipment and services available in the market. This involves the application of the *design for all* principle. Application of the principle can help ensure that general consumer products and services can become accessible to and usable by as large a grouping of people as feasible, including disabled people and people with disabilities.

In addition to products and services available in the general market which can service the needs of older people and people with disabilities, sectors of these user groups create a demand for specialised technologies which address specific or particular needs. This requires the development and production of so-called *assistive devices* which are of two main types. Firstly devices, interfaces, and specific adaptations applied to products and services available in the general market and which allow the disabled and elderly user access to mainstream facilities, despite his/her specific functional limitation. Secondly, products, services, and stand-alone systems for the specific compensation of limitations in vision, hearing, mobility, speech, and cognition experienced by some people with disabilities and older people in their daily lives i.e. at work, study, leisure, communication, in the home.

A recent trend, currently gaining momentum, is the increased recognition of the need to integrate disabled people into society rather than caring for them in specialised institutions. These people will be to a high extend dependent on technology to be able to lead independent lives.

2   Information technology

Information technology (IT) is among other disciplines of importance for advancement and innovation. Both in the *design for all*, most of the time communication related consumer equipment and in the design of assistive devices.

In the field of innovation and research the European programme TIDE (Telematics for Improving the Quality of Life of Disabled and Elderly People) is playing a major role. It brings together valuable knowledge and experience from all over Europe and because of the cooperation, economy of scale is improved.

The objectives of the TIDE programme are presented in chapter 3. Also an overview of all the running projects in the bridge phase is given to illustrate the research and development lines covered in this initiative.

In chapter 4 an example of the application of information technology is given in the description of a defacto standard for integration of assistive equipment. Both end-effectors (powered wheel-chairs, manipulators, environmental controllers, communication devices) and control devices (joystick, keyboard, scanner, headmovement sensor, optical pointing devices, trackball, sip and puff, tongue controller, speech recogniser) are integrated and connected in a standardised manner.

Finally in chapter 5 an example of a sophisticated device, heavily based on information technology is described namely the manipulator (robot) *Manus*. Very important and specialised items in IT for disabled and elderly people are:

- Access: Both cognitive and physical thresholds are apparent in proposed solutions withholding the access.
- User interface: Feed back devices need to be multi modal. Visual impaired persons have no need for displays and auditive impaired people not for buzzers.
- Users: Users do not like hardware. Users do not like software. Users like *Useware*.

3   European Union Technology Initiative for Disabled and Elderly Persons

To put the TIDE initiative it its proper context a brief overview of the research and technology development policy of the European Union is given as well as some information about the objectives of TIDE.

3.1   European Union RTD

The European Union organises according to its Treaties all its research and technology development (RTD) work in a 5-yearly plan, which is called the Framework Programme. For the next few years this is going to be the Fourth Framework Programme (IV FP). The objectives are generally to help the European economy to be competitive on the work and to secure the best prospects for its future growth for the benefit of its citizens. Keywords are therefore industrial competiveness, sustainable economic growth for the benefit of its high level of employment. A key phrase is also quality of life. Specific emphasis is given in the IV FP to the modernisation of the European economy through information and communication technology, aiming at the so-called Information Society, to ensure access of small and medium enterprises to advanced technologies and to the coordination and complementing with respect for the subsidiarity principle, of national efforts and European Union wide efforts (see Commissioner M. Bangemann communication 8/4/1994).

The IV FP is organised into four activities: firstly research, technological development and demonstration projects, secondly cooperation with third countries and international organisations, thirdly dissemination and valorisation of research results, and finally stimulation of training and mobility of researchers.

3.2   Telematics

Telematics is an RTD programme of applications of information and telecommunication technologies, that takes into account the opportunities offered by for example multi-media, HDTV, and interactive TV.

Telematics in the IV FP contains 12 areas or subprogrammes: telematics for researchers, for education, for libraries; telematics for administrations, for transport, for health care; telematics engineering, language engineering, information engi-neering; telematics for urban and rural areas, for the environment, and finally the subprogramme on which we will focus here: TIDE - which in full stands for telematics for improving the quality of life of disabled and elderly people. The preliminary budget breakdown of telematics provides TIDE with a budget of 65 million ECU.

3.3   TIDE's objective and approach

TIDE's objective is to promote RTD to meet a social and an industrial goal, namely to improve the quality of life for disabled and elderly persons, *and* to improve the European industry and market in products and services that meet the needs of disabled and elderly people.

3.4   Rationale for TIDE

Why is it necessary to do more research and development in technology for disabled and elderly persons and why do we need a programme like TIDE?

The major imperative for action: the European market in this field is extremely fragmented. Although it is a sizable and growing market it consists mainly of small to very small enterprises that operate a national scale at most and are often focused on a single product and a single disability. As a consequence of not achieving economies of scale prices are generally high. Lack of competition is detrimental for the quality of products. European-wide marketing is hampered by national preferences and regulations in the provision of assistive devices and services. At the same time US companies are able to enter and capture the European market aided by their large homogeneous home market, and by progressive legislation like the Americans with Disabilities Act that forces accessibility of all kinds of products and services, thereby creating effectively a market for assistive technology. There is therefore sufficient reasons for coordinated European actions in this field.

3.5   Implementation of TIDE

This has been achieved by TIDE, through research and development projects and horizontal actions like sector studies. These activities are funded 50% by the European Commission following a Call for Proposals which is based upon a workplan, composed through a wide consultation of experts from the field. TIDE has been initiated with a Pilot Phase of 18 million ECU, followed by a Bridge Phase of 42 million ECU that is currently running. The next phase is TIDE in the IV FP, with a budget of 65 million ECU. A call for proposals can be expected in 1995. The new workplan is expected to contain the following areas of RTD work:

- access to communication and information technologies
- information and communication systems for enhancing the efficiency and effectiveness of services supporting independent living
- integrated systems supporting the activities of independent living, education, work, leisure, mobility and training
- applications of manipulation and control technology
- technology supporting assessment, restoration and enhancement of function

as well as horizontal activities and accompanying measures. The second area is a new area in the IV FP compared to the Bridge and Pilot Phases.

3.6   Application domains within TIDE Bridge Phase

To give an idea of the scope of the projects within TIDE we here provide an overview of the application domains that are addressed by the current Bridge Phase TIDE projects:

Educational and vocational support

Many disabled persons require special provisions to integrate in the working environment or to participate in education. Examples are the Bridge Phase projects running from early 1994 until 1996:

- MATHS: representation of mathematics in tactile (Braille) and auditory format for computer supported teaching/usage of mathematics by visually impaired (1033)
- WORKING AND TEST PLANS: symbolic user interface for mentally impaired persons to help them in the workplace (1088)
- VICAID: palmtop vocational support and teaching aid for mentally impaired persons, for example to instruct them about work procedures (1199)

Access to telecommunication

Accessibility of telecommunication services, which is an essential element of modern life, is difficult for many disabled persons, for example blind or hearing impaired persons.

- IBIDEM: deaf persons video communication by lipreading and sign language across normal telephone lines using "retinal" focusing of the lip of sign video image (1039)
- INSIDE: assisted telephone access to health and social information databases supporting the specific capabilities of disabled and elderly (1150)
- SPLIT: conversion of speech to lip readable animation of mouth (for remote hearing persons to deaf person communication) (1215)
- HARMONY: increasing awareness among publishers about European Interchange Format for electronically published material for visual impaired persons (1226)

Teleworking

Telecommunication offers new possibilities in particular for employment of for example mobility impaired persons. Examples are the Bridge Phase projects:

- HYPIT: software for assessing teleworking opportunities and disabled users' capabilities (1175)
- COMBAT: expert system for matching job profiles and IT equipment and profile of disabled users (1135)
- AVISE: information dissemination and awareness creation about telework possibilities for disabled persons (1251)

Computer environments and public terminals

It is well-known that special provisions are required to enable blind persons to work with computers, especially with todays' graphical programmes. However, many more people have difficulty interacting with computers or public terminals, for example people with cognitive problems, and manipulation impaired persons. Examples of Bridge Phase projects in this domain are:

- ACCESS: software tools to design and adapt user interfaces of terminals for different disabilities (1001)
- ETRE: Braille and graphics printer with reusable plastic foils (1021)
- TACIS: Braille printer and tactile panel for active input/output between computer and visually impaired user (1229)
- LAMP: skin reflection of laser light to replace a mouse, for severely mobility impaired users (1249)
- SATURN: contactless smart cards for e.g. mobility-impaired and elderly people (1040)

Home systems and integrated systems

High expectations are held regarding the potential of intelligent home systems to improve the independent living of disabled and elderly persons. Examples are found in the Bridge Phase projects:

- DEFIE: intelligent multimedia user interface techniques for access to services delivered to the home for elderly (and disabled persons) (1221)
- HELPME: multimedia service center hardware and software for remote monitoring of home appliances and health of elderly and disabled at home (1105)
- IMSAS: architecture for multimedia social alarms and support services (1078)
- HS-ADEPT: special interfaces for disabled and elderly persons to home systems with a focus on domestic security (1102)
- CASA: integrated access solutions for the services environment in the home in general (1068)

Localisation and remote support

Telecommunication offers new possibilities to localise and provide remote support to disabled or elderly persons in need, for example in case of disorientation or acute health problems. An example is provided by the Bridge Phase project:

- SCALP: safety call and localisation in sheltered environments using a microwave based communication system for disabled or elderly persons (1002)

Advanced wheel-chairs

Electric wheel-chairs can provide greater mobility especially for severely impaired persons if they could to some extent be self-navigating, as well as be suitable for a variety of environments, for example in-doors and out-doors. Examples are the Bridge Phase projects:

- OMNI: omnidirectional wheel-chair with intelligent navigation (1097)

- SCENARIO: auto-navigation, risk-avoidance and path-teaching modules for electric wheel-chairs (1045)

Integrated controls

In many cases the user has to control a series of devices, for example a wheel-chair and an environmental control system and home appliances. Issues are the match between user capabilities, complexity, safety, and affordability. Examples of work in this area are found in the Bridge Phase projects:

- HEPHAISTOS: user interface architecture for home systems control by disabled and elderly persons (1004)
- FOCUS: wheel-chair/environment control bus (M3S standard); components and integration (1092)
- AURORA: portable control system for sensing and detecting intrusion, and leaks integrated in home environment with a user-friendly interface for a wide range of disabled and elderly persons (1027)

Robotic systems

Increased manipulative mobility can be provided through the application of "intelligent assistants" or in other words: through robotics. Examples are the Bridge Phase projects:

- MOVAID: mobile platform with robotic arm to control the environment including interfacing to and interacting with domestic appliances (1270)
- EPI-RAID: robotic workstation with sensors for simplified programming and M3S compatibility (1024)

Orientation and public environment navigation

Orientation and moving around, especially in public environments like railways poses severe problems for many elderly and disabled persons. These problems are addressed in the Bridge Phase projects:

- ASMONC: orientation and navigation systems for visually impaired persons (1228)
- OPEN: hand-held aid with audio-output for moving around in the subway, for visually impaired persons (1182)
- MOBIC: journey planner using databases with travel information combined with a GPS-based audio-output navigation aid for visually impaired persons (1148)
- TURTLE: analysis and design of providing public transport information to elderly persons (1194)

Speech

Restoration and enhancement of speech capability is addressed in the Bridge Phase projects:

- HARP: computer generation of images of lip movements and speech analysis for speech training of deaf persons (1060)

- DICTUM: interactive multimedia home based for speech and sign language training of deaf persons (1189)
- VAESS: synthetic speech enriched with emotion indicators and word prediction on a portable BLISS touch pad for speech and manipulation impaired persons (1174)
- ALADIN: analysis of conversation models and speech-output software to support interpersonal communication for speech-impaired persons (1035)

Sign language

For hearing impaired persons sign language often is a major form of communication. Many possibilities exist to make use of computer technology and especially of multi-media to teach and use sign language. Examples are the Bridge Phase projects:

- SIGNBASE: CD-based interactive, multimedia sign language dictionary (1282)
- ESLI: CD-I phrase books in sign language for deaf persons and their parents or carers (1242)
- SIGN-PS: graphical font for sign language with data glove and video analysis for input and a sign editor (1202)

Hearing

Hearing aid is an established domain of assistive technology, in which nevertheless advances in technology can provide enormous additional benefits. In particular for the severe hearing impaired persons that were excluded until now from using hearing aids, but also to provide improved hearing aids for moderate impairments. Examples are the Bridge Phase projects:

- OSCAR: acoustical/tactile/visual wearable hearing aid with speech information extraction for severe/profound/totally deaf persons (1217)
- SICONA: multiple FM microphone based aid with tactile or acoustical output (for conventional hearing aids) to participate in group discussions for moderate to severe hearing impairment (1090)
- HEARDIP: integrated system for auditory modelling, fitting and digital signal processing in an acoustical hearing aid for mild to moderate hearing impairment (1094)
- PROSOUND: miniaturised cochlear implant with improved selectivity for profound/severely deaf persons (1230)

Vision

Persons with reduced vision may benefit from advanced in image processing. An example is the Bridge Phase project:

- POVES: spectacle like vision enhancement system with portable image processor for persons with various kind of visual impairment (1211)

Augmentive communication

Persons with communication difficulties (mentally and/or physically) benefit from special communication aids. However, these aids need often individual adaptations, depending upon the disability and the development stage of the persons. In order to reduce the cost of these adaptations common platforms and tooling needs to be provided. This is exemplified by the Bridge Phase projects:

- FESTIVAL: programmable, real time, Electromyogram (EMG) based closed loop Functional Electric Stimulation system for upper limb motion stimulation (1250)
- EPCES: electrical stimulation for controllable wrist movement with EMG feedback loop supported by a mechanical orthosis (1083)
- AMBLE: movement analysis based on solid state gyroscope for lower limb impairment assessment (1064)
- MULOS: intelligent powered orthosis with position and force feedback for upper limb support (1057)
- VETIR: virtual environment technology for assessment, restoration and enhancement of motor dexterity (1216)

AT awareness

Information on user requirements, policy, and markets is fundamental to the TIDE initiative. Examples are the Bridge Phase horizontal activities:

- MARTEL: increasing awareness about rehabilitation technology in the care sector through video and television programmes (1058)
- MART: analysis of relationships between user requirements, telecommunications and social policy (1113)
- TT-RT-SMEI: piloting technology transfer between R&D and SME's with a focus on technology for older people (1144)

Assessment and evaluation tools

Tools for collecting and modelling users' requirements and assessing benefits, and technology transfer are needed to support the R&D projects. Examples are:

- CERTAIN: tools for cost-effectiveness/cost-utility assessment of rehabilitation technology products and services (1264)
- USER: rehabilitation technology usability handbook and newsletter for product developers and designers (1062)

4   M3S, a general purpose interface for rehabilitation application

4.1   Introduction

Integrated solutions are gaining popularity, they can help severely disabled persons to improve their quality of life in independent living, supported living and supported employment.

Emerging intelligent assistive devices like mobility aids, manipulators, environmental controls, multimedia, wide area communications and other end-effectors are becoming more and more available.

Today's integration of these function often lack a structured method of compiling systems together and have no organised control method, while safety is debatable. What is needed is an "open", "modular" and "safe" systems approach. M3S is a bussystem having these features and more. It is a standard communication and control architecture for rehabilitation applications (see fig. 1). Tests and evaluations indicated the validity of the M3S integration method. FOCUS is the TIDE project where extra functionality, based on user requirements, is going to be realised and where key elements (chips) will be designed. Cases are defined to test the validity of these features.

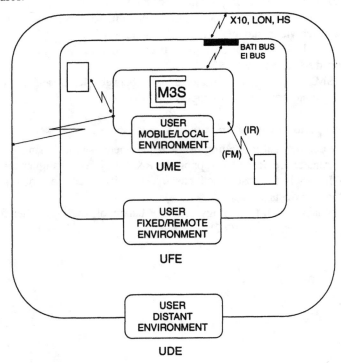

Fig. 1.   Standard communication and control architecture

4.2   Integration technology

Control and communication starts with the user in the centre (see fig. 1). *UME* means M3S control and communication bus, *UFE* means home busses, M3S or telecom communication buses and *UDE* means GSM, POTS, wide area networks or alarm systems.

The user in the centre needs to control his mobility and extra functionality in a safe manner (M3S) and needs to control and communicate with the fixed environment (M3S) wit infrared ECS, homebusses (M3S to batibus, EI bus), and needs to communicate to the distant environment (general purpose telephony).

4.3   M3S architecture

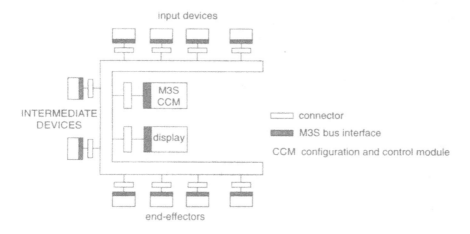

Fig. 2.   M3S architecture

A general M3S system is shown in figure 2. There are three types of devices that can be connected to a M3S system, namely input devices and end effectors and intermediate devices. Examples of input devices are joysticks, switches and speed recognisers while wheel-chairs, robotic manipulators, and speech synthesizers are environmental controllers are examples of end effectors. An example of an intermediate device is a navigator unit. Each system includes a configuration and control function (CCF), usually in a separate module known as the CCM. If the CCF can be integrated into an existing device on the bus the overall system costs will be reduced. The CCM is responsible for configuring the system and for safety monitoring. It also contains a menu structure from which the user can select any of the options available on the system. The M3S architecture was designed so that devices can be added to a system at a later stage without any complicated adaptations. This implies that devices on the system cannot have any knowledge of the other devices present prior to being connected. It also means that devices must be able to communicate via the bus in a generic way. All the devices on a M3S bus therefore contain internally stored configuration information which describes the specific behaviour of the device in a format that can be understood by the CCM. On connection to the system, the CCM uploads the configuration information from the device. The CCM is then aware of the device and is able to establish a method of linking the device to other devices on the bus.

The data that devices can send or receive on the M3S bus are described in terms of input or output actions and are referred to as device degrees of freedom (DOFs). Each DOF may either be sent to the bus, in which case it is called an input DOF (IDOF), or it is read from the bus in which case it is an output DOF (ODOF). Each device is therefore characterised by the number of DOFs and the capability of each DOF.

4.4   M3S background and message structure

The M3S serial communication bus is based on CAN (Controller Area Network) which was developed for use in the automobile industry. The application is within rehabilitation engineering and started with electrically driven wheel-chairs.

4.5   Standardisation and realisation of key elements

The viability of the M3S method has been proved in the demonstrator evaluations in the M3S project. The importance of having a standardised protocol, defacto as well dejure, is considered to be essential for extended market acceptance. Standardisation is regarded to be important for the following reasons:

- Integrated control of assistive devices is the future for the benefit of handicapped persons.
- "Openess" is needed. Particularly while closed systems are coming to the market.
- For safety reasons in control and communication standardised safety rules must be applied.
- The innovative configuration method has to be regulated via standardisation.
- Standardisation helps to harmonise national and international regulations and to lower trade barriers.
- It opens OEM possibilities, re-use of equipment and guarantees faster replacement and efficient maintenance.
- It stimulates innovations in SMEs to develop equipment to be "M3S ready".
- The intended "chip design" is only justifiable for a stable specification.

M3S is a defacto standard. Assistive devices with the interface are available in the market, as are starter kits and the protocol description. The process for standardisation as dejure standard is running in ISO.

4.6   Communication from the mobile base

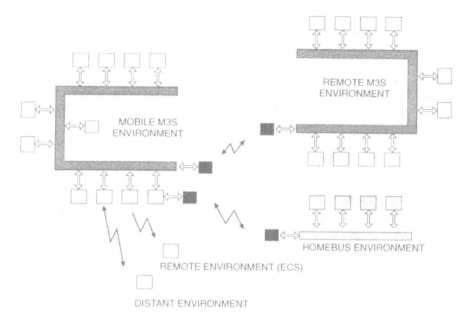

Fig. 3.   Communication from the mobile base

Communication interfaces from the local environment (M3S on the mobile base) will be designed to the remote environment (FST, James) and to the homebus environment (Batibus, EI bus). These communication interfaces are evaluated in the demonstrator platforms.

4.7   Demonstrator platforms and evaluations

Two demonstrator platforms are going to be constructed and configured for individual users for evaluation. These platforms are integrated systems consisting of powered wheel-chairs equipped with the M3S bus, robotic aids, environmental control systems, navigational control with safety zone indication, a choice of input devices (joystick with the new chip, sip and puff sensor, finger sensor made M3S ready and switches, joysticks, keyboards, scanners, headrest control sensor etc, already available for M3S) together with user interface hardware and software for integrated control.

   Homes will become nodes on international information networks. Householders (also people with disabilities) will have a need for services which give them more convenience, more knowledge, more fun, more independence. The inside of homes will be installed with electronic communications and control means and with communication means to the outside world. Various examples for smarthomes, and superhomes are reported.

   In Europe developments in Integrated Home Systems are concentrated around the HS concept (Home Systems) and one of the TIDE projects HS-ADEPT.

5   MANUS

MANUS is a robotic aid designed to increase the independence of severely disabled persons. The manipulator is compact and mounted on electric wheel-chairs. The user has control over the manipulator through input devices which are selected and adapted to his or her abilities. With MANUS, the user can pick up and lift objects up to 1,5 kg from any position and move them to any other position desired. Eight motors ensure smooth motion of the arm. The motors are installed inside the manipulator's main shaft, resulting in a slim, elegant construction.

5.1   Electronics

Cost efficiency and compactness are achieved through an integrated design and ASICs. Motor drivers and joint-angle encoders are fitted to a pair of printed circuit boards. MANUS is controlled by two microprocessors housed in a box mounted on the wheel-chair. The main processor, an 80C187, is used to control the arm. A second processor, an 80C552, is utilised solely for the user interface. A proprietary two-wire serial bus (M^2S) allows for communication between the various parts.

5.2   Control structure

Obviously, the user cannot control all eight degrees of freedom simultaneously. For this reason, a patchboard mechanism has been installed which enables the user to choose from several modes of operation. These modes are based on Cartesian, cylindrical and pilot transformations. The servos, transformations and user commands are processed every 10 ms.

5.3   Safety

Since the user is sitting within the direct environment of the manipulator, high demands are made on safety. Exerted forces are limited, both mechanically and electronically. Thanks to MANUS special construction, inertia of the arm is kept low. In the event of unexpected situations the manipulator can be stopped immediately.

5.4   The project

MANUS is the result of a collaboration between three Dutch Institutes:
- TNO Institute of Applied Physics (TPD Delft) for the electrical design, software and control engineering
- TNO Institute of Product Development (PC Delft) for the mechanical design
- TNO Institute of Rehabilitation Research (IRV Hoensbroek) for the user interface and other user aspects

The project was funded by various government and private sources. MANUS is now being fabricated by Exact Dynamics in Zevenaar, the Netherlands.

Part Four

Current Projects

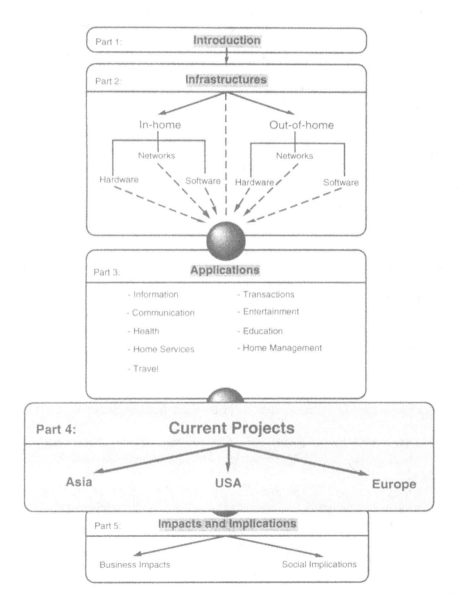

Part Two and Part Three provide the basics needed for our framework proposed in the book's introduction (Part One), namely infrastructures and applications. This section describes a combination of infrastructures and applications: projects and trials that are undertaken to evaluate the modern concepts, the new technology and innovative applications under more or less real life conditions.

After the initial failure of the videotex services all across Europe ex post-analysts claimed that there has been too little testing and involvement of the private end user in the conducted trials. Other critics say that the trials taking place lacked any real life situation and were conducted like laboratory experiments. The same mistake should be avoided this time. Therefore, trials are underway on a larger (Time Warner Full Services Network) and smaller scale (agent based communication in the Munich traffic system).

These differences between actual status of the trials and wishfull-thinking of the marketing department, notwithstanding, the contributions in this part of the book show the future direction. They draw a picture how the private life could look like in the information society. This comprises projects aiming at in-home networking (Goethe-University) and further more at the 'smart home' as well as external out-of home connections to content and service providers (Silicon Graphics, Berner & Mattner Systemtechnik). After two introductory comparisons by a consultant to the EU and a researcher from the Goethe-University of Frankfurt/Main, Germany, representatives of the Asian (NTT), American (Silicon Graphics) and the European (Burda, Berner & Mattner) market offer information about their approaches:

- A *consultant to the European Commission* compares the strategies towards the information society in the Triad. He focuses on the comparison of the different backgrounds and national approaches.
- *Goethe-University* does the same comparative study for the in-home market of home automation and smart homes. It examines the conditions under which the projects in Europe, Japan and the US have been developed and compares installation-, computer- and consumer electronics-based approaches.
- *Nippon Telephone and Telegraph (NTT)* analyzes how the private use of daily time in different life phases can be supported by information services and digital devices.
- *Silicon Graphics* provides an overview to the Time Warner/Silicon Graphics interactive TV trial in Orlando/Florida, USA. After a short introduction to digital networks the characteristics of the Full Service Network (in its future fully operational stage) are stated.
- *Burda New Media* describes how a traditional publisher house extended its operations into the business of electronic media and online services (Europe Online).
- *Berner & Mattner Systemtechnik* summarizes the deployment of smart agents for a municipal traffic service using wireless communications and enhanced personal intelligent communicators (PIC).

However, one may not believe any optimistic press release or marketing announcement. Most of the trials in interactive TV are lagging behind the schedule because of problems in technology, costs, and commitment. For instances, the Time Warner Full Service Network, Orlando/USA, suffered from technological problems and started with a delay of about one year in early 1995. Instead of the projected 4,000 participants only 5 are connected (but Time Warner is making a big PR fuss about it!). Something similar applies to other trials, e.g. by telecommunication companies in the US. In addition, all projects in the area of home automation have failed to exploit a sufficient market or to create considerable demand.

This part compares the distinctive approaches towards the Information Superhighway and makes it clear that cultural, political and regulatory differences are crucial factors for market development. This is valid for the external services rendered via cable, satellite or radio waves as well as for the in-home networking of household and entertainment appliances. Projects from the triad markets may help to understand this issue and provoke further discussion.

The Information Society - Developments in the Triad of Europe, North America and Japan

Roger Longhorn
Senior Expert in Information and Communication Technologies consulting the
European Commission's DG III and DG XIII, Luxemburg[*]

1   Introduction

The driving force behind the Information Society is the desire of governments
worldwide to improve the use of Information and Communication Technologies
(ICT) products and to make the best use of the opportunities they create. This will
lead to an increase in competitiveness, create new jobs and improve the overall
quality of life for all citizens. Example applications which are already available as
pilot systems in many countries can be found in areas as diverse as health care and
tele-medicine (Wall Street Journal 1994), on-line access to public information
services provided by local and national governments, new leisure and entertainment
opportunities (direct broadcast satellite digital TV, virtual reality games played over
the Internet on powerful 64-bit games consoles, interactive TV, direct access to
travel agents for viewing and booking holiday options are just a very few of the
possibilities which already exist today), tele-working, and tele-shopping from home
via a normal telephone line.

This article compares differences and similarities in the various approaches taken
by governments and industry to implement the Information Society in the triad of
major economies composed of the USA, Japan and Europe. Dramatic improvements to telecommunications infrastructure and regulatory issues are now common
themes in the proposals of all the countries involved. These infrastructures will
have to be interconnected and the basic services available on them must be
interoperable, requiring a global policy set by government and agreed by all major
organisations involved in the implementation.

The movement towards an Information Society involves numerous small steps in
many different areas, only some of which involve technology. Many issues being
raised are philosophical or cultural, regarding ethics and legal frameworks, rather
than technology. Also, quite different structures in national or regional forms of
government are to be found in these three major trading economies. These

---

[*]   This article was prepared by the author while employed by the European
Commission's Directorate General III (Industry) in the capacity of research staff in
the Brussels based IT Policy Analysis Unit (A.5). A major extract first appeared in
print in the Winter 1994-5 issue of I&T Magazine, published jointly by the EC's DG
III and DG XIII. The author is now on assignment with DG XIII/E in Luxemburg.

differences in culture, government and degree of readiness are likely to result in different solutions being proposed.

A reassessment is taking place of existing legislation on media ownership, authority to offer various types of services, and the rights and limitations of new service providers. Such legislation was originally put in place to protect consumers from monopolistic practice, but may no longer be appropriate. Rapid resolution of legislative issues is required due to the speed with which industry is responding to commercial opportunities made possible by new technology.

Issues relating to copyright and intellectual property rights require new legal frameworks, on a global basis, including the strengthening of current procedures for detecting misuse of data and enforcing appropriate penalties. Technological advances are making it more difficult to police existing agreements to reward legitimate copyright holders, while at the same time opening up vast new potential markets for the illegal and inexpensive dissemination of copyrighted works (The European Council of Ministers 1995).

But technological innovations, modified legislation, increased spending on infrastructure are *not* causing a quantum jump in the ability to provide information to all members of society. Ordinary citizens will not notice great differences for some years yet. Many pilot services targeted at consumers, such as video-on-demand for movies and tele-shopping, will not reach the mass market for some time yet.

2 The National Information Infrastructure in America

America's formal recognition of the importance of the Information Society was defined in the *Agenda for Action on the National Information Infrastructure (NII)* published in September 1993. The NII was *not* seen as "a cliff which suddenly confronts us, but rather a slope - and one [which] society has been climbing since postal services and semaphore networks were established" (Committee on Applications and Technology 1994).

The US administration moved very rapidly to begin wide ranging consultation with the industrial and commercial actors who were expected to pay for creating the electronic Superhighways needed for an Information Society. The US Advisory Council on the National Information Infrastructure was created by Executive Order in December 1993 to oversee recommendations relating to the US President's NII Initiative.

International attention was further focused on the Information Society as a result of wide-ranging policy statements made by American Vice-President Al Gore, at the Superhighway Summit held in California on 12 January 1994. Mr. Gore's speech emphasised new legislation for national telecommunications reform and a broad plan for the US NII. This speech followed earlier public statements made in the latter part of 1993 relating to "Information Superhighways", a term to which Mr.

Gore claims ownership from 15 years ago. Such high-level government support led to formation of the Information Infrastructure Task Force (IITF), chaired by Secretary of Commerce, Ron Brown, and comprising many separate Committees and Working Groups. The IITF is extremely active today, using the global Internet as its main vehicle for communication among members and with the public and business.

Very large industrial and commercial associations in America began to focus on the problems and the potential for new business of an enhanced information infrastructure. Typical of these were the American Electronics Association (AEA) (AEA 1994), the US Electronics Industry Association (EIA), the Telecommunications Industry Association (TIA) (EIA/TIA 1994), and the Computer & Business Equipment Manufacturers Association (CBEMA) (Interoperability Standards 1994). Because of the size of their member organizations, many of which are major international players in the ICT sector, their experiences will be applied globally, as opportunities present themselves.

At *government* level there was heavy emphasis of deregulatory issues regarding telecommunications, media ownership, media distribution rules, and content production and ownership. From the earliest days, the US administration stressed that industry would have to pay for the information infrastructure and that government's role would be to help "pave the way". There was intense lobbying in Washington, DC, by industry regarding proposed changes to the regulatory environment in the telecommunications industry.

At *industry* level, there was already wide support for this approach. Chief executive officers of major American computer companies had already formed the Computer Systems Policy Project (CSPP) in 1989, producing their first NII vision document in January 1993 (CSPP 1993). They were thus well positioned to provide immediate input to the government's plans, as evidenced by the rapid publication of their joint view on interoperability (CSPP 1994). Also in 1993, the US Council on Competitiveness, founded in 1986, through its Competition Policy Working Group produced both vision and action plan documents (Council on Competitiveness 1993). Industry attention was initially focused on those ventures which would most likely earn an early return for investors, such as "video on demand" services (see fig. 1) and tele-shopping, but business applications have not been forgotten.

Supported by partial funding from the US government's National Information Infrastructure Testbed (NIIT) (National Information Infrastructure Testbed 1993) initiative, various trials are underway, testing the business implications of access to a widespread, high-speed information infrastructure. Pilot applications exist in areas such as just-in-time manufacturing and delivery (Electronic Commerce Network, EC-Net, collaborative NIIT project of DEC, Times-Mirror Cable Television, Arizona State University), electronic publishing, remote collaborative working and linking businesses together on a national (or global) basis (Business Week 1994a). Formal structures for co-ordinated dialogue between public authorities and the private sector are now in place.

Company/Service Provider	Service Locations	Connections
Ameritech (Chicago)	Chicago	501,000
	Detroit	232,000
	Columbus, Ohio	262,000
	Indianapolis	115,000
Bell Atlantic Corp. (Philadelphia)	Eastern US cities	2,032,400
GTE Corp. (Stamford, Conn.)	Ventura, Calif.	122,000
	Honolulu, Hawaii	296,000
	Manassas, Virginia	90,000
	Tampa, Florida	476,000
Nynex Corp (NY)	Providence, R.I.	63,000
	Boston, MA	334,000
Pacific Bell (San Francisco)	Orange County, Calif.	210,000
	San Jose, Calif.	490,000
	Los Angeles, Calif.	360,000
	San Diego, Calif.	250,000
U.S. West Inc. (Englewood, Colorado)	Denver	300,000
	Portland, Oregon	132,000
	Minneapolis, Minn.	292,000
	Boise, Idaho	90,000
	Salt Lake City, Utah	160,000
Total	20 cities	6,807,400

Fig. 1. Major video-on-demand service proposals from the six largest players in the market

Progress towards the Information Society has not been smooth in America. Some of the largest business alliances ever announced in the ICT industry, such as the US$ 23 billion TCI/Bell Atlantic merger, were never completed. Others that were completed have yet to prove that they will be successful in financial terms. The stock value of partners in some alliances has had a disturbing tendency to drop in value following announcement of the mergers.

It soon became evident that not all the required technology *was* readily available, too little information was available on real market sizes for various types of services or products, and no one quite knew just how the new technologies would be received by the average consumer. Of 28 interactive TV trials announced "to begin in 1994" by 21 different operators or consortia in 30 US cities, fewer than 20% actually started that year (TechMonitoring 1994). Most interactive video-on-demand trials have been delayed by as much as a year - with the result that much needed marketing information will not be available until late in 1995.

Uncertainty for American companies concerning regulatory issues remains high. Conflicting signals regarding regulation have been received. Rulings from the Federal Communications Commission (FCC) on lowering cable TV charges had an adverse effect on more than one planned strategic alliance. Anti-competition rulings from the US judicial system and other federal watchdog bodies have also slowed the pace at which the larger companies will be able to fully participate in the Information Society outside their traditional areas of expertise. In fact, contrary to popular opinion, America remains a highly regulated environment in many areas relating to ICT, especially in telecommunications and media distribution.

The changing political power base in US government has also changed the rate at which new initiatives are being proposed. Additional government funding for Information Society related projects is becoming more and more difficult to secure. Congress defeated, in September 1994, the Administration-backed Hollings Telecomms Deregulation Bill that would have permitted regional Bell operating companies (RBOCs) to enter into cable television services and would have enabled cable television companies to more easily offer telephone services, creating new infrastructure opportunities for consumers and more competition.

However, many positive steps have also been achieved. Congress passed two important legislative packages, one permitting radio frequency spectrum auctions, which have proven highly successful in the US, and another to establish regulatory parity for wireless-based telecom services. Many US states have successfully established major intra-state, high-speed, fibre-optic networks linking schools, universities, hospitals and state and local government offices. These are well beyond the pilot stage and have become accepted tools in providing information services to US citizens (Business Week 1994b).

In fact, some of the "hype" surrounding the Information Society seems now to have disappeared in the US and people are looking at practical problems and new services which give genuine benefits (not just 500 movie channels!).

3   Japan watched the USA and EU

Progress was slower in Japan than in the US, and the impetus came from different sources, primarily MITI (Ministry of International Trade and Industry), MPT (Ministry of Posts and Telecommunications) and NTT (Nippon Telephone and Telegraph). Other players in the Japanese vision of the Information Society include the numerous cable TV (CATV) companies, now operating at a loss due to government restrictions on ownership and distribution, plus telecommunications equipment suppliers (including those from the US and Europe) and media owners.

MITI's Information Industry Sub-committee of Industrial Structure Council published its report on improving social infrastructure for the Information Society in June 1993. Later that year, the giant NTT announced the grand plan to put optical fibre throughout the whole of Japan by 2015 - at a cost of approximately US$ 400 billion. Also during this period, MPT was developing its new approach to policy on regulatory issues surrounding the Information Society. A May, 1994, report from MPT's Telecommunications Council on the vision for Japan's high-technology future, including its national information infrastructure, predicted that Japan would be well advanced into the Information Society by the year 2000, with 20% of the population connected to fibre-optic cable for fast, two-way communications. The entire population is to be interconnected by fibre-optics in three stages over 17 years - first connecting the largest cities (20% of population), then cities with populations over 100,000 (60% of population), achieving nation-wide coverage by 2010.

Compared to Europe, Japan *should* have been in the communications vanguard, having privatised NTT in 1985, only two years after the AT&T break-up in the USA. Markets were liberalised to allow more competition. But Japan lost ground compared to the American model, for example falling far behind in cable television by restricting cable businesses to narrow geographic areas, resulting in small operations that lose money. NTT was late in introducing new telephone and data services. Monopoly control of key markets by NTT and KDD increased the cost of everything from microwave transmission to database hook-ups.

In reality, Japan is several years behind the US in high-speed infrastructure, in mobile communications, and in other key areas. Even Japanese sources generally agree that the US has a considerable lead over Japan, citing PC penetration in the US at 42% compared to 10% in Japan, with 56% of US computers already connected to networks compared to 13% in Japan (figures from IDC). Cable TV reaches 70% of homes in the US and only 2.9% in Japan (figures from Jardine Fleming). Yet industrial leaders respond with a few observations of their own. Namely that much of America's cable TV system is now old and will not provide the same capacity as the new systems being installed in Japan and elsewhere and that Japan leads in many of the technology areas which will enable the Information Society, including CD-ROM production, compression techniques, interactive cable systems, display technology.

Japan expects the ICT industry to be generating from 5% to 6% of GDP (gross domestic product) by 2010, and 2.4 million new jobs will have been created (more than in the auto industry) (Financial Times 1994). Japan sees ICT as the "next wave" for substantial growth, following its spectacular post-war performance first in heavy industries, then in automobiles and consumer electronics, were competition is now fierce. The Electronic Industry Association of Japan (EIAJ) expects new business related to the Information Society to grow as large as that of the electronic appliance or automobile industries by the year 2000 - that is, as much as US$ 527 billion. MITI stresses that added value in economic activity will not come from manufacturing, but from intellectual property, such as software, media content, and a high-technology, widely available, communications infrastructure will be crucial to developing this new industry.

Because of its size and near monopolistic position, NTT plays a more dominant role in the future of the Information Society in Japan than do national PTTs in most European countries, or any single RBOC or international carrier in the USA. NTT's 12 research centres have an annual budget of US$ 3 billion to help them focus on the latest technology for the 21st century. NTT is also entering into more foreign collaborations than before. For example, NTT and Mitsubishi joined the "Smart Valley Concept", a California-based experiment of next generation information network using large capacity optical fibre, considered to be a model case for the "Information Superhighway".

NTT does not intend to enter the CATV market itself, but simply to provide the network and related services to the service operators. It will use its Intelligent Network and introduce optical fibres and digital equipment on a massive scale.

Competitors should *not* underestimate what NTT can achieve for the Japanese Information Society in those areas where it chooses to focus attention. In December 1993, NTT created a special multimedia department integrating their video communications department, human-computer interface laboratories and technological study sections, among others, in order to better carry forward the extensive R&D targeted at the multimedia market, which is already well underway. For example, in 1994 NTT announced an ATM switchboard operating at 2.1 Giga bits per second (Gbps), 30 times faster than conventional switchboards, with a final target speed of 1 Terabit per second. They also achieved super high speed optical transmission in a 100 Gbps optical multiplex transmission experiment using 50 kilometres of optical fibre and optical signal processing technology developed in-house.

Financially, however, NTT earnings fell dramatically in 1994 and pre-tax profits fell 66% compared to 1993. Nearly 15% of NTT's staff (33,000) were laid off as of March 1995. This was mainly due to increased competition from its three new long-distance carrier rivals, DDI, Japan Telecom and Teleway Japan. To counter the competition, NTT's new strategy is to refine its market segmentation system, prepare different packages for various segments of users, cut down rates to match those of NCCs, provide discount services to discourage LCRs (Least Cost Routers), and to provide total service packages to maintain customers and secure new business.

In 1993, MPT responded to criticism that it was not doing enough by introducing policy changes to permit broadcasting and telecommunications markets to converge, hopefully in a more orderly manner than in the USA. MPT acknowledged early in 1993 the need to adopt its policy-making to the rapidly changing environment and dynamism of the business sector. To counteract existing problems, they took a 'hands-on' approach to industry regulation, to establish a new framework for competition in the Japanese telephone market.

The reformulated policy focused on developing new services, restructuring the industry, and expanding the total market size. MPT feels this latter point is crucial to the carriers and their suppliers and offers opportunities for foreign players in the market place. In order to change the focus of competition from prices to services, MPT approved lower rates for NTT and KDD long-distance calls from September, 1993. NTT & KDD now aggressively promote their services to residential and business users, with all carriers engaged in heavy advertising and promotional campaigns.

MPT then drew up a plan to connect the country's fragmented cable television operations into a nation-wide network which could provide a full range of multimedia services, believed to be worth nearly US$ 1,000 billion by the year 2010. The proposed network would enable advanced services to be made available, as well as providing significant competition for NTT. In March 1994, Tokyo Electric Power, the country's largest electric utility, plus Tokyu, a railway company, and two trading companies with cable TV interests, created an alliance to provide multimedia services on cable.

MPT recommended in December 1993 that cable companies should be permitted to expand geographically, permitting them to achieve the critical mass of subscribers necessary to survive. Cable companies would also be able to enter the telecomms business and sell more than 20% of their shares to foreign investors. Telecom companies could enter the CATV business. From April, 1994, users were permitted to purchase cellular telephones rather than lease them.

MPT also submitted proposals to government to lift the restriction on non-INTELSAT satellites and to permit usage of private satellites for international leased line services. Finally, at the end of 1993, they announced a firm policy for digital broadcasting into the 21st century in order to let industry know its future operating parameters.

Not to be overshadowed by MPT, in October 1994, MITI launched the "Advanced Computerization Program", its own version of the NII. This is in "competition" with the programme of MPT, its traditional rival in the communications arena. MITI's programme has five basic objectives:
- encourage involvement of computer and network information systems managers
- accelerate technical convergence of telecom technologies
- review existing systems and practices to evolve towards an Information Society
- encourage interaction of users and technical vendors
- formulate a "grand design" in cooperation with other Ministries

MITI focuses actual policies on corporate applications, not consumer services, e.g.:
- image document handling, video-conferencing and e-mail in the office
- real-time production management and intelligent manufacturing systems (IMS) in the factory
- EDI and joint developments between companies
- database R&D, simulation programs, and other measures to reduce development time and cost

In the public sector, MITI has plans:
- for schools, to get students to use computers, not simply learn about them
- to promote supercomputer installations and establish a Research Information Network between organizations
- to encourage electronic transfer of medical images between hospitals
- to set up a New Industry Creation Database Centre and information systems on government statistics and publications
- to interconnect 20 public libraries and develop electronic library systems

Japanese policy makers are now just as committed as are the Americans to the concept of the digital Superhighway and the benefits it will reap for modern societies. They admit that CATV has *not* made the in-roads into Japanese life which would have helped create the infrastructure needed for a broad based Information Society. MPT acknowledges that the telecommunication network is one of the most important parts of the social and industrial infrastructure for Japan's future development. Japanese industry now looks to multimedia and digital video applications to take the place of VCR sales, using a much expanded CATV network to pump large volumes of data into new, low cost, home multimedia PCs. This would greatly assist the PC manufacturers, consumer electronics industry, and the CATV services suppliers/network operators.

Business use of ISDN has been very slow to catch on. The carrier rate structure in Japan still leads to inequalities. As in Europe, there is fear that insufficient telecom services will affect the competitiveness of Japanese business. Part of the problem is with limitations of the NTT network itself and high charges (even though NTT operates ISDN at a significant loss). Japan Telephone Company applied over two years ago for permission to connect its long-distance network to NTT's local networks in order to offer frame-relay data transmission data services. The frame-relay technology is said to be about one-tenth as costly as traditional data transmission services. As of the end of 1995, NTT had yet to reach an agreement on interconnection to JTC's lines. The largest initial potential users of broadband facilities in Japan are expected to be the games and leisure industry, including Sega and Taito (karaoke systems specialists), who complain that the cost of ISDN is still far too great to permit its use in the entertainment area.

Because of the enormous cost of installing high-speed optical fibre to the Japanese populace (versus the US, where 60% of homes already have some cable connection), emphasis is placed on compression technologies and new infra-structure models which combine very high-speed trunks, capable of supporting massive data volumes, with local distribution via existing cable, telephone wires (using ADSL, Asymmetric Digital Subscriber Loop) or radio links at frequencies only now being tested. Greater attention is also being paid to the possibilities of satellite communications.

A new vision for an advanced Information Society was created by Prime Minister Murayama's Advanced Information and Telecommunications Society Promotion Headquarters, launched in September 1994. The objective of this new initiative is to prepare comprehensive measures for social awareness, deregulation, and better definition of the private and public sector roles in the Information Society, including social impact. Senior members include Ministers from MPT and MITI, plus 18 other ministries responsible for areas in which applications will be developed, plus 12 members from the commercial and academic communities and numerous advisors from large businesses. The Japanese government fully recognises the importance of co-operation on these issues and welcomes contacts such as those offered by the proposed EU-Japan "Information Policy Working Group" (IPWG) in the framework of the EU-Japan dialogue on industrial cooperation.

Where is Japan today in regard to the Information Society? As in America, the nation is still struggling to reach a consensus on the way forward, given the huge sums needed to invest in the telecommunications infrastructure. Even with Prime Minister Murayama's initiative, several large government agencies are all still fighting to play a major role in developing the Japanese Information Society. Industry is taking up the challenge and forging ahead with massive new R&D efforts, including novel attempts at "outsourcing" much needed new innovation by investing in R&D facilities in America and Europe (Scientific American 1994).

4   Europe moves towards the Information Society

In Europe, attention was focused on the importance of electronic information by publication in December 1993 of the European Commission's *White Paper on Growth, Competitiveness, Employment - the Challenges and Ways Forward into the 21st Century*. Key elements of this vision of the future for Europe included dramatic improvements in trans-European infrastructure networks, greater use of technology, especially information technology, and co-ordinated implementation of a European Information Society. From an early focus on telecommunications issues, attention has now shifted to the various ways that electronic information will impact on the whole society.

In February, 1994, as mandated by the European Summit of Brussels (December, 1993), Commissioner Martin Bangemann of the European Commission formed a special working group of high-level experts drawn from European industry, including both users of information and providers of products and services. Their task was to examine the issues facing Europe regarding implementation of a European Information Infrastructure to match that of the US. Their goal was to produce recommendations for a practical way forward, including specific application areas, to ensure Europe a rightful place in both the global Information Society and in the marketplace.

This group, known as the Bangemann Task Force, published their report "Europe and the Global Information Society - Recommendations to the European Council", in May, 1994, for presentation to the Corfu summit meeting of late June 1994. The main conclusions were that "the EU should put its faith in market mechanisms ... to carry us into the Information Age", by "fostering an entrepreneurial mentality" and "developing a common regulatory approach". Ten priority application areas were identified for immediate action, ranging from tele-working and distance learning, to university research centre networks and telematic services for SMEs, road traffic management, air traffic control, health care networks, electronic tendering, public administration networks and city information highways. The only public support requested by the group was that EU governments were to establish a pan-European regulatory framework which would permit competition on a level playing field within Europe and with non-EU competitors.

The European Corfu Summit requested a plan to establish a clear framework for actions relating to the Information Society. This led to the communication called "Europe's way to the Information Society: An Action Plan", published in July 1994, covering four areas:

- the required regulatory and legal framework
- networks, basic services, applications and content
- social, societal and cultural aspects
- promotion of the Information Society

The first official mention of a European-level authority to "manage" Europe's entry into the Information Age did not appear until the July 1994 Action Plan responding to the June 1994 Corfu summit meeting of Council. Even today, in Europe, the diverse climate of readiness for the Information Society at national level within the 15 EU Member States results in a lack of consensus concerning many issues, ranging from telecommunications monopolies to audio-visual, copyright and privacy policy. Late in 1994, the European Commission issued a Green Paper on audio-visual policy and proposed orientations to improve the European programme industry. Early in 1995, the Commission's DG XV issued a Green Paper on the rights of authors and "neighbouring" rights in the Information Society.

Similar to the earlier actions in the American NII plans, initial attention in Europe was focused mainly on telecommunications issues. Special emphasis was placed on privatisation of nationalised PTTs and deregulation in other areas, which would eventually lead to reduced costs of telecommunications services to consumers via increased competition. Similar to the Japanese approach, attention later changed focus from pure pricing issues to those of new service possibilities. This led to consideration of the much more thorny issues of standardisation, interoperability, cross media ownership, intellectual property rights, privacy, protection of electronic data, legal protection, potential liability related to supply and use of data and security of data. Due to the geo-political reality of the EU, solutions to these issues will be more complex than in the single-government environments of the USA and Japan.

The European approach to the Information Society places less stress on new technology *per se*, and more on wise, innovative use of existing technology or near-future developments. The assumption is made that broadband networks will be available, at affordable prices, when needed. Sufficient technology already exists to deliver the planned services. What is needed are extensions to infrastructure, such as higher cable penetration to homes and innovative means (such as Euro-ISDN and ATM broadband networks) to enable high-speed connections from the final telecom operator's node to the home or business.

Due to differing national policies, telecommunications deregulation was (and remains) uneven throughout the European Union. Markets available to the companies making possible the Information Society are more diverse because of cultural and linguistic differences among the citizens of the Member States. If the Information Society policy is a strategic creation applicable to the whole Union, then these challenges will be overcome and European cultural richness will be a great asset.

In Europe, the diverse state of readiness for the Information Society at national level within the EU brings additional challenges for industry and Member State governments. As one example, the ACE2000 Forum was formed by BT (UK), Deutsche Telekom (D), France Telecom (F), STET (I) and Telefonica (ES) to jointly support the development of information highways in Europe, investing a total of 500 million Ecu in R&D for broadband technology from 1994. Another 100 million Ecu will fund a pan-European ATM pilot network. The French government postponed funding its ambitious national Superhighway infrastructure from public funds after a study revealed that costs would be around US$ 100 billion over 20 years. Further analysis was recommended to build confidence in the likely return on such an investment on untried markets such as tele-shopping, and interactive TV.

5   What are the basic differences between the US, Japan and Europe?

The different technology, regulatory, government and cultural environments which exist within the USA, Japan and Europe have many implications for the manner in which the Information Society may develop in these regions, as figures 2 and 3 illustrate.

Japan is similar to the USA in offering vendors and developers a single national market, without the multicultural and multilingual problems faced in Europe, and a partially deregulated telecommunications industry. As in America, telecom liberalisation and trade issues can be effectively addressed through the legislative processes of a single government. However, Japan also has similarities to Europe, especially in infrastructure, where cable TV and high-speed communications links have made only limited inroads to citizens' homes. Japan is also weak in software development compared to both the USA and Europe.

In America, extensive cable penetration to homes is a fact of life and major investments are already underway, by industry, to complete the interconnection of all American homes and businesses. Computer literacy is generally higher and computer usage in the home and in secondary schools is higher than in Europe. Also, more emphasis is being placed on personal communications services than in Europe or Japan. Yet even in the USA, awareness and education about technology and its uses are still problems (Associated Press 1993). Much of the US Administration's NII expenditure will be on projects or initiatives which act as a catalyst in various ways, e.g. special R&D projects in critical technologies, public awareness campaigns or resolving legal and standards issues.

As US citizens become more aware of the possibilities offered by wider use of electronic information, and of the dangers of misuse, they are beginning to ask more informed questions of industry and government, and demanding a greater say in how the Information Society will develop in America. As of 1995, a true consensus on the way forward has yet to be reached in the USA, but because of their earlier start, they are probably further along than either Japan or Europe. In both America and Japan, government intervention has centred mainly on the regulatory arena and in helping industry to focus its resources on a structured set of Information Society issues.

Indicator (Source: Nikkei Business, 21.3.1994)	USA - %	Japan - %
Cable TV penetration (% of households)	60.0	20.0
Information service industry (as % of GDP)	1.9	1.2
Software market (as % of hardware market)	1.7	1.0
Database industry (as % of GDP)	0.16	0.04
PCs connected to networks (as % of all PCs)	66.0	17.0
Government employees per one "small" computer	4	36
Central government informatics budget (as % of total budget)	1.9	0.3
Students per computer at schools	19	38

Fig. 2.   Indicators of readiness for the Information Society in USA and Japan
(The European Institute of Japanese Studies)

In Europe, however, because of the multi-national aspect of the market place, even more preparatory work remains to be done. Common EU Member State objectives range from basic IT or Information Society awareness activities through to deregulation, increased efforts in applied R&D and finding ways to overcome the inhibitors to reaching a European wide "critical mass" for information, i.e. multicultural and multilingual issues arising from the political structure of the European Union.

The Action Plan for Europe published following the June 1994 Corfu summit of the European Council focuses attention on similar issues which need to be addressed by EU industrial and national government initiatives. It is important to rapidly identify the most critical areas where improvements are needed now, and in the near future, in order to facilitate the rapid increase in market size needed to encourage the large expenditures needed in infrastructure. Japan faces similar problems. It would obviously be advisable to develop an international framework of cooperation in which common issues could be identified and concerted action taken. Just such issues were the topic of the special G7 summit meeting on the Information Society held in Brussels in February 1995, and which has been widely reported in the European press.

Because of these many differences, we should not expect that the Information Society will develop in all three regions of the trio along identical paths. Emphasis, methodologies, goals and priorities will differ based on variations in political, cultural and business climates. There are, however, issues which face all nations equally. These include creating awareness of the possibilities offered by the Information Society on how to use information infrastructures and co-ordination of effort on global issues such as standardisation, IPR, privacy or competition rules. What steps can be taken at international level to ensure best use of resources?

Similar trends are appearing in all three regions of the Triad. For example, deregulation, especially in removing or reducing the power of monopolies, is now part of all regional plans. Deregulation is also facing stiff opposition, albeit from different sources, in all three regions. Key issues are no longer only those relating to national telecoms infrastructures and access to international lines. Topics such as intellectual property rights, cross-ownership of media, privacy, censorship, and security of electronic information are all *global* problems requiring cooperation and co-ordination at global level. In fact, many of these issues cannot be resolved in a globally interconnected society except by wide, international agreement.

Regardless of the level of uptake by the general public on the new computer and communications technologies and services, business use will increase rapidly because there are financial reasons to adopt new procedures and methods. Unlike private consumers, businesses can more easily afford to pay for the new technology. For example, integration of services and working methods, via electronic data interchange (EDI), or tele-working, can reduce cost of doing business while widening business opportunities.

Similarly, government departments, especially those which are information intensive and must maintain a direct dialogue with the public, can benefit from embracing new information collection, processing and dissemination technologies. Many of the pilot applications now under test in various parts of the world involve attempts by local governments to better inform citizens of their rights, to streamline procedures, to speed up the process of government and to better execute the mandate of government *viz a viz* the needs of citizens.

Similar infrastructures to enable policy and implementation consultation are needed in all *three* regions of the Triad in order that:

- global cooperation can be facilitated, since discussions could then take place at the relevant level, with similarly empowered authorities, across the range of G7 countries, in a common framework, and
- global (commercial and marketing) opportunities could be more readily addressed by *all* actors in the implementation of the Information Society, regardless of their physical, geographical location (which would enhance trade opportunities).

A typical example for global co-operation is the agreement under discussion by the Japan Electronic Industry Association (JEIDA), the US Computer and Business Equipment Manufacturers' Association (CBEMA) and the European Association of Manufacturers of Business Machines and Information Technology Industry (EUROBIT) to find ways forward to promote the Global Information Infrastructure, a high-tech global Information Superhighway project (JEIDA/CBEMA/EUROBIT).

	In the USA & Japan	*In Europe*
Information content	Content is national in character. Single-language market predominates in most mass communications arenas. Large, integrated media companies exist with huge investment power for new technologies. Content sellers are mostly selling to a large single market.	Multinational & multicultural in character; "critical mass" is a problem. Multilingual market. Smaller national media producers need to combine forces to approach the size and financial strength of single American media producers. Sales of information products are to national and European-wide markets.
Network structures	Manufacturers and users have access to basically a singe set of standards, which have evolved in place over many years. Nevertheless there are inter-operability problems. Most technologies are "home-grown", and developed as a result of direct national R&D programmes. Wide distribution of basic infra-structures exists such as telephone, cable TV, inexpensive high-speed networks. This is less true in Japan.	Great success in mobile telephony (GSM). Multiple standards exist at many levels; many foreign suppliers and purchasers are more familiar with the US standards. Often competing technologies exist, developed as a result of national R&D initiatives; innovation is widespread. Distribution of basic services is complicated by national differences in both coverage and regulatory issues. Modern telephone basic infrastructures.
Applications & software	In the USA, a large, aggressive, software product industry rules in critical basic software areas. In Japan, the software product industry is weak.	Specialist developers; many excellent niche market applications, e.g. in areas such as virtual reality systems, compression technologies
The "people" element	Users, especially in business and industry, are technology-oriented and are reaching a level of technology maturity which increases their awareness information use possibilities. Information producers, whether entertainment media, educational material, or simply personal communications, are familiar and at ease with the various technologies and applications. Awareness of information technology and of the Information Society is becoming much more widespread.	The historically lower level of penetration of ICT applications in business and industry, in the home and in secondary and advanced education, is now being rapidly remedied. Relatively late arrival of many information services to Europe means users and producers have not reached the level of their counterparts in the USA; yet Europe has some of the largest publishing groups in the world. Awareness is increasing considerably, but must be carried out in 15 Member States simultaneously.

Fig. 3.   The Information Society - differences between the USA, Japan and Europe

A consultation infrastructure should exist at three levels

Level 1 would consist of contacts in public authorities, i.e. the senior government officials in charge at ministerial or cabinet level of consultation on interoperability, telecom deregulation policy, monopoly control, social impacts, and other high-level issues.

Level 2 would more closely involve the companies through contact with practical work groups examining specific implementation issues and applications areas, for example the Bangemann Task Force in the EU, or the NII Advisory Council in America, or MITI's Information Infrastructure Sub-committee in Japan.

Level 3 would constitute all implementation actors, e.g. the CommerceNet project teams or the digital library programme co-ordinators in the USA, electronic publishers or multimedia fora in Europe and commercial pilot project leaders in Japan.

Dialogue and exchange of information between actors of these three levels at the national and international level is a prerequisite for a successful emergence of a global Information Society.

References

AEA, The AEA Survey on the National Information Infrastructure, March 1994, University of Southern California, Center for Telecommunications Management

Associated Press, a 1993 Associated Press poll in the USA showed that over 40% of adult Americans feel that information technology is *not* helping them. Among the 60% who believe that it is, one-third felt that they are not keeping up for reasons varying from lack of knowledge (36%) to lack of money (24%), lack of time (21%), and even desire to do so (16%).

Business Week International, CommerceNet, doing business on the information superhighway, 18.5.1994a

Business Week, The states swing into I-way construction, 22.8.1994b

Committee on Applications and Technology, What It Takes to Make It Happen: Key Issues for Applications of the National Information Infrastructure, Information Infrastructure Task Force, January 25, 1994

Council on Competitiveness, Vision for a 21st Century Information Infrastructure, May, 1993, and Competition Policy: Unlocking the National Information Infrastructure, from the Publications Office, 900 17th Street, NW - Suite 1050, Washington, D.C., USA

CSPP, Perspectives on the National Information Infrastructure: CSPP's Vision and Recommendations for Action, published by the CSPP on 12 January 1993

CSPP, Perspectives on the NII: Ensuring Interoperability, published by the CSPP in February 1994

EIA/TIA, EIA & TIA White Paper on National Information Infrastructure, February 1994

Financial Times, 13.6.1994

Interoperability Standards and Intellectual Property in NII, March 1994

JEIDA/CBEMA/EUROBIT, JEIDA has 180 member companies, including Hitachi Ltd., Toshiba Corp., NEC Corp., Mitsubishi Electric Corp. and Fujitsu Ltd. CBEMA has over 25 corporate members, including International Business Machines Corp., AT&T Corp. and Compaq Computer Corp., while EUROBIT comprises industrial associations from nine European countries.

National Information Infrastructure Testbed - Vision Becomes Reality, September, 1993, NIIT, 1377 K Street, Northwest, Suite 820, Washington, DC 20005, USA

Scientific American, April 1994: Japanese companies realise that they can no longer simply import ideas and develop them onwards. They must get directly involved in the basic research game and opened nearly a dozen research laboratories in the US by 1991. Facilities such as the NEC Research Institute (with 40 PhD-level research staff) were asked "to be doing Nobel-quality research" in five years time - no mention of products was made. The Mitsubishi Electric Research Laboratories (MERL) in Cambridge, Mass. has 21 senior investigators from some of the best American universities, and chose as its head Laszlo A. Belady, former head of software engineering at IBM's John Watson Research Centre and head of the US advanced projects research company Microelectronics and Computer Technology Corporation. Matsushita, Ricoh and Canon also fund major R&D activities in the US.

TechMonitoring, Fibre-Optic Communications, July 1994, SRI International Tech-Link

The European Council of Ministers agreed on 6 June 1995 the wording for a Commission Directive on protection of electronic databases, following three years of wide debate on the original text and initial discussions which began in 1990. The final text was much reduced in scope compared to the initial text and must be confirmed by European Parliament on 29 June 1995. Assuming acceptance, it will go into effect throughout the European Union not earlier than 1997.

The European Institute of Japanese Studies, Stockholm School of Economics from "Info-Society in Japan - Why still slow onto the "Info-Bahn", W. Pape, Forward Studies Unit of the European Commission

Wall Street Journal, The reality of tele-medicine is rapidly approaching, with total US federal support for trials allocated US$ 85 million in 1994 alone. Individual US states are developing their own networks - up from three systems in 1990 to more than 70 in 1994. An Arthur D Little Inc. study forecast that "broadly implemented, tele-medicine would reduce annual health-care costs by at least US$ 36 billion, or 3% of this year's estimated US health bill," major savings coming from video-conferencing, reducing the time required to travel between consultations while permitting greater opportunities for wider consultation on difficult cases. Beneficiaries will be rural populations and workers in remote sites such as mines or ships. The purpose of current US trials is to make existing products and services work together in new ways. In: Wall Street Journal, 20.9.1994, Computerworld, 26.9.1994, International Business Week, 3.10.1994

Home Automation - Recent Developments in the Genesis and Diffusion of Intelligent Home Technology in Europe, Japan, and the USA

Thomas Heimer
Johann Wolfgang Goethe-University Frankfurt, Germany

1   The research done in Frankfurt

Let us start with a short presentation of the research-project the research is associated with. In 1987, an interdisciplinary research group was founded at Frankfurt University. Within that group researchers from the departments of economics, political sciences and sociology started to investigate the process of the emergence of new technologies. At the moment, the group works in four different fields (Fleischmann 1993). One project concentrates on the genesis of tele-communication technology. A second project is concerned with the genesis of production technology. A third project is engaged in the field of the genesis of traffic technologies. Last but not least there is the project which is concerned with the genesis of Intelligent Home Technology. This project has started to make an international comparison of the Intelligent Home approaches in Europe, Japan and the USA.

On a first view it might not be obvious why it is of any interest for social scientists to investigate the genesis of a new technology. As one will know, the traditional theories of technology claim that the invention and construction of a new technology is only driven by technical factors. According to those traditional theories the genesis of new technologies is independent from social influences.

That notion has been under fierce attack recently. Accordingly, all projects in Frankfurt have in common that a 'technological determinism' is rejected. Therefore, we hypothesise that it is possible to identify the social factors that influence the process of the emergence and genesis of the Intelligent Home Technology (Fleischmann 1994, Hack et al. 1991, Haddon 1995, Heimer 1993, Heimer 1995). To make that point clear: We do not claim that solely social factors shape the genesis of a technology. Technical influences are also of relevance. However, we claim that we can show for the genesis of the Intelligent Home Technology the social *as well as* the technical factors which create the different trajectories of the various international Intelligent Home research projects.

2   A description of the Intelligent Home

Before we show the empirical results of our research, we would like to give an illustration of what is called Intelligent Home Technology. It is nowadays a rather common practice that some 'intelligence' is embedded in modern household appliances. For instance, the washing machine is already available that automatically detects the fabrics you want to wash. Furthermore the programming of VCR's is frequently done by some kind of intelligence. Thus what makes the Intelligent Home Technology different from these technologies? Although the Intelligent Home Technology is not yet on the market we can identify three aspects that all Intelligent Home approaches have in common. Figure 1 gives you an illustration of these aspects as it has been realised by the ESPRIT-approach.

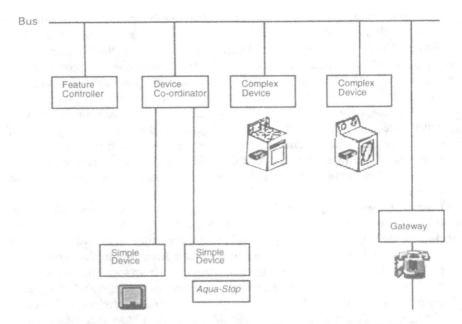

Fig. 1.   Illustration of the Intelligent Home System (ESPRIT-Bus)

Firstly, they all believe the Intelligent Home Technology should be able to connect *all* appliances, devices and systems in the private house that have been independent until now. The purpose of the connection is integration, control and processing of the functions provided by them. In the case of private households we can think of an interconnection among voice sensors, heating systems, security systems, TV-sets, and other appliances and systems at home. Furthermore, it provides the connection between the private home and the environment. This is extremely important for applications like tele-metering. *Secondly*, all projects have in common that microelectronics should provide the connection between the appliances and the systems. *Finally*, the technology in mind should include software programming which is able to extend its capabilities by learning. As we shall see, these quite general aspects in common will end up with some quite heterogeneous technological proposals which in future will compete on the market for acceptance.

3 State of the art in the emergence of Intelligent Home Technology

Let us move now to the empirical results of our study. As already mentioned we have compared the developments in Europe, Japan and the USA to filter out the social factors which influence the genesis of the Intelligent Home Technology. In these countries, the research on Intelligent Home Technology is mostly done by research cooperations. Figure 2 gives you a comprehensive perspective of the projects, their relations and starting points.

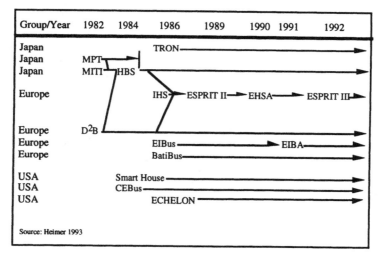

Fig. 2.   List of projects, their relations and starting points

Our research has shown that despite the heterogeneous social and cultural contexts among the Triad countries we can identify three different Intelligent Home approaches in these countries. The three approaches differ with regard to the problem definition and the selected technological proposals (see fig. 3). These varieties are also the basis for differences in the various projects' feasibility to open up for the use in homes.

Thus for the problem-definition we can identify four general questions, which laid the foundations for the differences among the various approaches. These questions are:

- Where should the intelligence within the network be located?
- Should a specific network-technology for the private household be developed and what functions should it provide?
- Who should have access to the computer-network and how large is the influence of the consumers?
- Which voltages should be integrated?

I should mention once more that the questions above are mainly decided by socio-economic considerations. For instance, the decision to include a plug & play function has to be seen on some projects' limited access to installers. However, on the basis of these questions we were able to distinguish world-wide three different kinds of Intelligent Home approaches. Figure 3 gives you a comprehensive description of their characteristics (to be continued on next page):

Approach/ Problem-definition	Consumer-oriented approach	Installations industries approach	Computer-hardware approach
Where should the intelligence within the net be located?	The project members look for a decentralised computer-net where the intelligence is located in the connected appliances and systems.	The intelligence is placed in the installation hardware - for instance, bus-connectors, plugs and switches. Centralised and decentralised net-structures exist.	The intelligence is preinstalled by Chip producers. There are centralised and decentralised net-structures, depending on the capabilities of the participating actors.
Should they develop a specific computer-net-technology for the private household and what functions should it provide?	The approach is only concerned with dwellings and multi-unit houses. Intelligent Buildings are not taken into account. It aims at higher safety and security and more convenience.	They attempt to create a computer-net for dwellings and for functional buildings, but exclude the Audio-Video- parts (BATIBus, EIBus) or work with gateways. Light control is dominant.	The computer-net technology is constructed for all kinds of use, including dwellings and functional buildings. It aims, for instance, at computernets for cars and complete cities.

Who should have access to the computernet and how large is the influence of the consumers?	The target of this approach is to give the private users complete access to all parts of the net. This goes along with a high complexity of the computernet-structure and a plug & play capability of the system.	Electricians have exclusive access to the computer-net and the user can only change a few variables. The advantage of limited user access is a rather low complexity of the net-structure. A plug & play capability of the system does not exist.	The access of the users is rather limited. A plug & play feature of the inter-connected appliances is not taken into account.
Which voltages should be integrated?	Only the alternating current available in these countries is taken into account. The rising need for direct current by low-voltage devices in the house is not taken into account.	Almost all approaches supply AC and DC to drive the appliances and systems connected to the net. This goes along with an increase in the share of small appliances in the home driven by DC.	Only the already available ac has been taken into account for dwellings and functional buildings.
Projects and main actors	Europe ESPRIT: AEG, Philips, Thomson among oth. Japan HBS: Industry Ass., Kansai Industry Dev., MITI, MPT USA CEBus: Electr. Ind. Ass	Europe Batibus: Landis & Gyr, Merlin Gerin Europe EIBus: Siemens USA Smart House: National Ass. of Home Builders	Japan TRON: Japan. Computer Manufactures, Ken Sakamura USA ECHELON: Privat Company with Quantum and Motorola as main share holders

Fig. 3.   De-Contextualization - problem definition

It might be surprising that no direct functions and products are listed which are directly connected to the use in homes. However, we think that the process of problem definition is mainly a process to exclude certain functions and applications so that the project can pass the process of selection by the company and the environment. For instance, the decision of EIBus to exclude the coax-medium has to be seen on the background that the main actor Siemens AG has no strong ties in the brown goods sector. Therefore the coax medium is an impediment to Siemens company that reduces the project's chance to pass the inter-company selection.

On the basis of these three different problem-definitions we started to investigate the differences in the construction of the upcoming technologies. This goes along with our hypothesis that the problem definition is the outset of the work primarily done by engineers (Heimer 1993). Nevertheless, even engineers take socio-economic aspects into consideration. A "one best way" based solely on technical aspects does not exist.

Approach/ Technological proposal	Consumer-oriented approach	Installations industries approach	Computer-hardware approach
What standard is used for inter-connectedness and on what topology is the net structure based?	For their decentralised Bus topology, they use the Open System Interconnection model (OSI) which is standardised by the International Electrotechnical Commission (IEC) as the standard for the message exchange structure.	Some projects use the OSI and some non-OSI models. There is a stronger tendency towards non-OSI-models. We can find star- and bus-topologies, depending on the skills of the electricians in the triad.	The use of OSI and Non-OSI models as well as the Star- and Bus topologies, depending on the know-how of the participating computer companies.
What medium is used for the transport of messages?	Because it is important for the actors of this approach to minimise the installation cost of the computer-net technology, the power-line cabling is the core medium.	All projects use twisted pair wiring as the medium for the transport of mes-sages. On a scientific basis the probability of errors in this medium is low.	Twisted pair wiring is generally used as the medium. ECHELON has recently released a power line system.
How complex are the requirements for the micro-electronics components used by the projects?	The requirement for the hardware is low. The requirement for the net software is high. This stems from the possibility of integrating a feature controller.	The requirements of microelectronics components are rather high. A pre-programmed bus connector has to be used at any connection point.	The requirements of the microelectronics components in use are very high. That is an outcome of the multi-functionality.

Fig. 4.   Technological proposals as a result of the problem definition

Three questions are relevant for a categorisation:
- What standard is used for interconnectedness and on what topology is the net structure based?

- What medium is used for the transport of messages?
- How complex are the requirements for the microelectronics components used by the projects?

Again we can identify three different paths of development which go along with the differences identified in the problem definition (see fig. 4). All projects within the three approaches have developed first prototypes and products. Figure 5 gives an overview:

Project	Approach	Products/Prototypes
BatiBUS (Europe)	Installation industries approach	Electrical installation products available; still low intelligence products. Prototype house in the Netherlands
CEBus (US)	Consumer-oriented approach	No products, no prototypes
ECHELON (US)	Computer-hardware approach	Chips and development tool available - first products on the market. First installations in France
EIBus (Europe)	Installations industries approach	First installation products on the market. Siemens AG and ABB train electricians in company's training centre. White & brown products are hardly included. Prototype in Norway available
ESPRIT-Home Systems (Europe)	Consumer-oriented approach	Prototypes in Germany and Holland - heating system and power-line control-system for white goods will be soon on the market. Development tool and net-hardware available
Home Bus Systems (HBS) (Japan)	Consumer-oriented approach	First products available
Smart House (US)	Installations industries approach	Prototypes in many cities. But mostly Smart Reddy Houses with no intelligence
TRON (Japan)	Computer-hardware approach	Prototype available

Fig. 5.   Intelligent Home projects and their products/prototypes
(not a complete list)

We have tried to list new consumer goods and services which are intuitively attractive for the customers. But there are just a few applications available at the moment. Honeywell, for instance, sells his ECHELON based TOS-Master Systems that controls electrical appliances via power-line. EIBus also sells his system that controls electrical appliances via twisted pair. Additional a EIBus member has announced to present a compatible power line system which is based on the American X10 system. We already mentioned the load management system for white goods that will be offered by an ESPRIT member. That system will also use power line for message transport. Additional an ESPRIT member will sell a single room controlled central heating system later this year. However, these examples show already that the development of products and, in particular, of new applications that will raise the value gained from stand-alone goods is rather slow.

However, the eight technological proposals within the three approaches compete for standardisation. As suggested by the term technological proposal, up until now we have no answer to the question which approach will win the "battle of standardisation".

4   Standardisation and diffusion of Intelligent Home Technology

At the moment the process of standardisation is still an ongoing process. Although most projects have already developed fixed trajectories there is still some flexibility so that the shaping of the technology can still be influenced. However, before we discuss in greater detail the ongoing process of standardisation of the Intelligent Home Technology a brief jump into the year 2010 may be helpful. Imagine you are a scientist visiting a small town where 50% of the citizens live in their own homes using a sophisticated Intelligent Home Technology. Further assume, that the people are quite happy with the Intelligent Home Technology. However, interviews show that some parts of the system work in a way the inhabitants do not appreciate. Most people complain about the low speed of the information-line. On some days it takes about 5 minutes to get a connection. Others complain about the low quality of the picture on the Videophone. However, aside from these complaints, people in general appreciate the technology. The small disadvantages are seen as inevitable. "That's how technology is - you can't change it!", they say.

In the light of contemporary theories of technology we know that the point is not, how technology is, but how we make it. The low speed of the information-line, for instance, can be the result of a decision to choose the power-line medium which minimises the costs of the network. The low performance of the Videophone could be the result of a missing integration of audio-video in the standard. Therefore the audio-video connection has to be realised by a gateway which might produce losses in quality.

You might raise the objection that the technology selected is superior in the light of the relevant economic *and* technological criteria or restrictions. Unfortunately, the modern economic theory of standardisation (Arthur 1989, David/Greenstein 1990, Fleischmann 1994, Heimer 1995) shows that there is no guaranty that a standard which is superior in economic and technological respects will be pushed through.

Let us discuss that point in greater detail. A set-up of a standard in general can be obtained either by a voluntary standard body or by the market. The telecommunication standards are a good example for a standardisation by negotiation while the VCR-standard stands for a standardisation via market. In the past ex-ante standards have mostly been discussed in voluntary standard bodies like CENELEC. That also happened with the Intelligent Home Technology in Europe. At the moment three projects have submitted their proposals (BatiBUS, EIBus and ESPRIT-Bus) to the European standard body CENELEC. However, up until now the different projects represented within CENELEC TC 105 have not been able to agree on a common standard. The situation in Japanese and American voluntary standard bodies is absolutely the same.

The reasons for that world-wide problems lay in the heterogeneous interests the projects pursue. The EIBus project, for instance, aims mainly at new lighting features and other installation goods whilst the ESPRIT project is dominated by white and brown good suppliers. Additionally, differences in profit appropriabilities connected to the different proposals have been impeding an agreement on a common standard. Accordingly all projects attempt to establish their standard proposal on the market. However, we should emphasise that an agreement on a common standard for Intelligent Home Technology within the voluntary standard body would be very efficient. The reason for that comes from the problems which are related with the de facto standardisation on the market.

As we have already mentioned even the standardisation on the market is no guaranty for a "survival of the fittest". In contrary, we know the phenomena of the standardisation of an inferior technology. We call this a lock-in (Arthur 1989, Cowan 1992, David/Greenstein 1990). The QWERTY-keyboard and the VHS-standard for VCR's are frequently quoted examples (the validity of the examples but not the theoretical context has been criticised by Liebowitz/Margolis 1990, 1994). In these cases early users influenced the adoption of competing technologies in a certain way so that the diffusion ended up in a lock-in (Heimer 1994, 1995). The lock-in into an inferior technology is always possible if the technologies under consideration show increasing returns to adoption (Arthur 1989, Hanson 1985).

Figure 6 gives you an illustration of a lock-in. The Figure shows - for the case of two technological alternatives - the adoption probability curve. The diffusion illustrated in Figure 6 represents the case in which two stable and one unstable equilibria exist. The stable equilibria are so called corner solutions. That means that the illustrated technology A either gains a 100% market share or nothing.

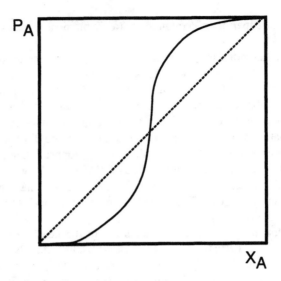

Fig. 6.   Adoption probability function for 2 alternatives with high increasing
returns and low functional utility

What can we learn from these cases for the diffusion of the Intelligent Home
Technology? As is quite obvious the Intelligent Home Technology possesses
attributes which make it very likely that a lock-in into an inferior solution can
happen. In particular the relation between the functional utility and the increasing
returns to adoption created by the number of users of that technology has to be
explained. Let us give you an example to illustrate this rather complex problem. If
a consumer buys, for instance, a washing machine he gains all the utility created by
it. Quite different is the situation in the case of the telephone. Here the consumer
does not gain any return from buying a single telephone. The utility is produced by
the number of people whom he or she can call. In the case of the Intelligent Home
Technology, the network itself as well as the standard for interconnection does not
deliver any returns. Therefore, the returns from installing interfaces, cabling etc. are
the outcome of positive feed-backs gained from new products and services. In
addition, the consumer gains positive feed-backs from the upgrades of already
available products and systems by the network.

   Thus, for the process of diffusion of the Intelligent Home Technology, we can
state that all projects have problems in reaching the critical mass - that is the
number of users - which is necessary for gaining first positive returns from
adoption (Rohlfs 1974). Only if the different approaches are able to integrate
products and services with an high direct benefit to the users in the network, the
market will gain the momentum the producers need to succeed on the market.
Furthermore, it is very likely that only one technology survives on the market.

5   Conclusion

The article, on the one hand, has shown the state of the art in the genesis of Intelligent Home Technology. We showed that we can identify three general approaches. We have emphasised that the differences among the different projects are mainly stimulated by socio-economic factors. Afterwards we illustrated the diffusion of Intelligent Home Technology. We mainly discussed some theoretical aspects that influence the diffusion. We like to cease the article by a brief discussion of the question: Can we proof these theoretical results by our study? Let us discuss that point for Europe because the diffusion in Europe is more advanced than in Japan and the USA. In Europe we find two different issues that might influence the adoption probability of the different approaches. On the one hand it is well known that the ESPRIT consortium negotiates with the BATIBus Club to gain some compatibility. If they succeed the ESPRIT Bus's chance to gain the qualitative majority within CENELEC will increase. We should mention that an european CENELEC standard for Intelligent Home Technology is binding for the european countries. On the other hand attempts exist to gain compatibility among EIBus and ECHELON. Although ECHELON is not passed to CENELEC for standardization the rational behind that cooperation has to be seen in the attempt to gain market power. This is the result of the fact that ECHELON and EIBus are market leaders by the number of installations in Europe.

A different empirical result of our study is the analysis of the market shares the different approaches gained in the european countries. We were able to identify France and Germany as two key markets for Intelligent Home Technology. The situation in Germany shows the EIBus as the leading company. Neither ESPRIT nor ECHELON have gained remarkable market shares. The situation in France is totally different. Here the ESPRIT project has gained momentum when EDF decided to use the ESPRIT Bus for its load management. Nevertheless ECHELON also has gained some momentum in France when the SILD company got the order to install their ECHELON based TIPI system in 7,000 flats in Chateroux (Phillips 1994).

On the background of this empirical results we see two alternative directions towards the future market for Intelligent Home Technology. The first alternative is that an agreement in a standard body as well as compatibility among the european approaches is not realised. That may lead us to a heterogeneous market for the different European countries. It also will impede the rapid diffusion of the new technology because increasing returns to adoption can not be realised. The second alternative is an agreement in CENELEC or an intensive attempt of the different projects to realise cross-compatibility. If that will happen both the suppliers and the users will have an advantage. The suppliers advantage can be seen in the realisable economies of scale and in the reduction of the critical mass problem. The users' advantage can be seen in lower prices and the greater product variety. Therefore, on an economic perspective the second way will produce higher welfare than the first way ever can do.

References

Arthur, B. W., Competing Technologies, Increasing Returns, and Lock-in by Historical Events, in: The Economic Journal, Vol. 99, 1989, pp. 116-131

Cowan, R., High technology and the economics of standardization, in: Dierkes, M., U. Hoffmann (eds.), New Technology at the Outset: Social Forces in the Shaping of Technological Innovations, Frankfurt/Main, New York, 1992, pp. 279-299

David, P. A., Greenstein, S., The Economics of Compatibility Standards: An Introduction to Recent Research, in: Economics of Innovation and New Technologies, Vol. 1, 1990, pp. 3-41

Fleischmann, G. (ed.), Interdisziplinäre Technologieforschung-Diskussionsbeiträge, Arbeitspapier 4, Frankfurt/M., 1993

Fleischmann, G., Ökonomische Theorien der Standardisierung inferiorer Technologien, in: Schlosser, H. D. (ed.), Gesellschaft Macht Technik: Vorlesungen zur Technikgenese als sozialer Prozeß, Frankfurt/M., 1994, pp. 95-115

Hack, L. et al., Technologieentwicklung als Institutionalisierungsprozeß: Stand der Forschung, Lage der Dinge, gemeinsame Überlegungen, in: Fleischmann, G. (ed.), Interdisziplinäre Technologieforschung-Diskussionsbeiträge, Arbeitspapier 1, Frankfurt/M., 1991

Haddon, L., The Home of the Future Today: The Social Origins of Intelligent Homes, in: Esser, J., Fleischmann, G., Heimer, T. (eds.), Soziale und ökonomische Konflikte in Standardisierungsprozessen, Frankfurt/M., Campus, 1995

Hanson, W. A., Bandwagons and Orphans: Dynamic Pricing of Competing Technological systems Subject to Decreasing Costs. Dissertation, Standford University, 1985

Heimer, T., Zur Ökonomik der Entstehung von Technologien: Eine theoretische und empirische Erörterung am Beispiel des "Intelligent Home", Marburg, Metropolis Verlag, 1993

Heimer, T., Elektronische Hauswirtschaftssysteme können Energie sparen und den Wohnkomfort erhöhen, in: Blick durch die Wirtschaft, 24 January 1994, p. 10

Heimer, T., The Genesis of Intelligent Home Technology, in: Esser, J., Fleischmann, G., Heimer, T. (eds.), Soziale und ökonomische Konflikte in Standardisierungsprozessen, Frankfurt/M., Campus, 1995

Liebowitz, S. J., Margolis, S. E., The Fable of the Keys, in: Journal of Law and Economics, Vol. 33, 1990, No. 1, pp. 1-25

Liebowitz, S. J., Margolis, S. E., Network Externality: An Uncommon Tragedy, in: Journal of Economic Perspectives, Vol. 8, 1994, No. 2, pp. 133-150

Phillips, T., Welcome to the computerised home, in: The Guardian, 10 March 1994, p. 19

Rohlfs, J., A Theory of Interdependent Demand for Communications Service, in: Bell Journal of Economics and Management Science, Vol. 5, 1974, pp. 16-37

Multimedia Application Services

Sadami Kurihara
Nippon Telephone and Telegraph (NTT), Japan*

1   Introduction

Progress in the field of semi-conductors and LSIs has made the size of computers smaller and smaller and brought us very powerful workstations (WSs) and personal computers (PCs). Digital switching and transmission technologies have realized an ISDN that provides various attractive telecommunication services. These computers and communication networks have become one of the most important social infrastructures for the 21st century. Computer systems were initially limited to character-based information, but recent WSs and PCs can easily manipulate multimedia information such as characters, figures, sound and image data. B-ISDN, which will be realized by ATM switching and optical transmission technologies, can effectively transmit multimedia data include audio and video.

When we use computers and communication systems as tools for our work or daily life, it is important to chose the most suitable media. In order to make this choice, we should clarify the relationship between the tools available and our life space. Telephon es, facsimiles, TVs and PCs/WSs are already being used widely in our life space as tools. TV games, which mainly entertain young people, have recently impressed many people with the impact of multimedia technologies on various business fields. Multimedia technologies can also be effective in using computers and communication systems as tools for our work and daily life.

There are two types of multimedia applications. To add advanced functions to existing tools is the first type. To offer new tools which create new work styles is the other. Personal Multimedia-multipoint Teleconference System, PMTC, shown as an example of the first type, adds the video conference function to PCs or WSs already used for many purposes on the desk. TeamWorkStation (TWS) and ClearBoard (CB) are examples of the second type, and can offer a cooperative work space on the desk top by applying video communication functions.

In the future, we will use computers and communication systems more often as information referencing tools. In this case, multimedia presentation techniques must be most effectively utilized. The Hypermedia Book System is one example of the multimedia presentation methods on PCs or WSs for our network operation

*   Main parts of this paper have already been published in the NTT Review, 6(1994)5, pp. 24-30. The editors thank the NTT Review for the permission of republication.

services. The ISDN Visual Information System has been developed to offer the
visual information service over video phones. The Digital Video Response System,
which stores and delivers digital video information, has been developed to offer
video information services such as the video on demand services that can transmit
any video programs at any time.

2   Life space and multimedia application services

It is very important when examining advanced multimedia application services to
clearly define who will use them and what their purpose will be. To clarify the role
of multimedia application services, let us look at our life space: it includes our
business life, community life, and personal life. We can divide a person's life into
three ages as shown by figure 1.

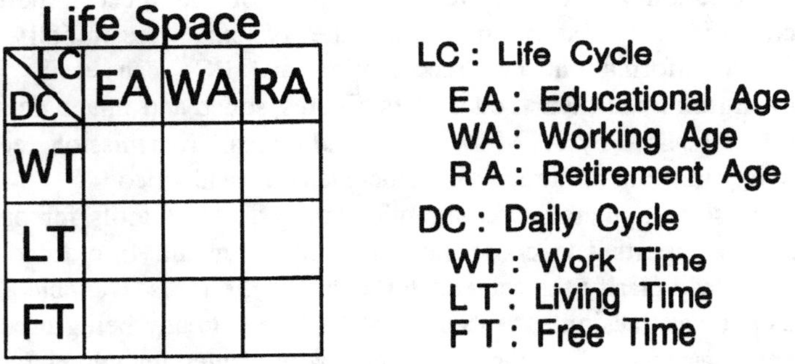

Life Space

LC DC	EA	WA	RA
WT			
LT			
FT			

LC : Life Cycle
  E A : Educational Age
  WA : Working Age
  R A : Retirement Age
DC : Daily Cycle
  WT : Work Time
  L T : Living Time
  F T : Free Time

Fig. 1.   Application area in life space

First the education age, say up to 20. This is the first part of our life cycle. The
second age involves social activity through work, our working age. And third, after
retirement, we should enjoy our own life. That is to say, the third part of the life
cycle is the enjoyable post retirement age.

These three ages can be subdivided into three daily periods. First, we must spend
some time fulfilling social responsibilities, the working time. The second time is
for daily living and covers activities such as shopping. Last, but not least, is the
free time that we can use at our own discretion for pastimes, hobbies, and so on.
Let us now consider the usage of typical existing media. Figure 2 shows the
relationships between our life space and existing media.

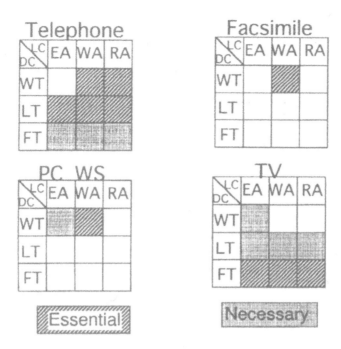

Fig. 2.   Role of existing media in life space

First, telephones. As we can see, telephones are widely used in almost all fields. It is unlikely that telephones will ever be widely used for education purposes. Facsimile is for static image communications. It is mostly used for business purposes. Next is the television which can be found in every household. It is most commonly used for living time and for free time. Finally, let us take a look at personal computers and workstations. They are used most often in the working space. They are essential in business and necessary in education. We believe that multimedia application services will be computer-based, but several blank portions remain. The combinations of telephone functions, facsimile functions, and video functions suggests a clear definition of multimedia application services.

3   Examples of multimedia application services

Multimedia application services should achieve two things in the work place. The first is to improve work efficiency by using tools that already exist in our work places. The second is a revolution in work styles by using new multimedia application systems.

Some examples of our latest multimedia communication systems and their main targets and aims for improving work efficieny are shown in figures 3 and 4.

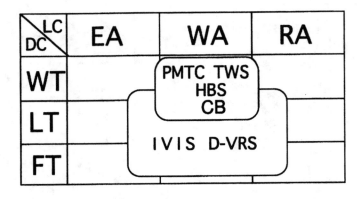

Fig. 3.   Targets of new services

To realize more powerful business communication functions, we developed the Personal Multimedia-multipoint Teleconferencing System (PMTC), TeamWork-Station (TWS), and ClearBoard (CB). To more accurately understand the information necessary to cary out of work, we developed the Hypermedia Book System (HBS).

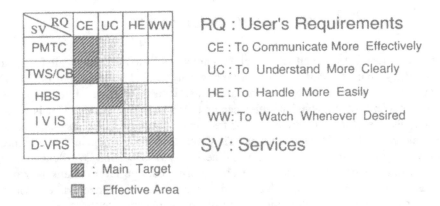

Fig. 4.   Targets of the multimedia services

In daily life, we need to get the most appropriate information in the most efficient manner. To achieve this, we created IVIS, an ISDN Visual Information System, and D-VRS, a Digital Video Response System. Some of those systems are described below.

3.1   Personal Multimedia-multipoint Teleconferencing System (PMTC)

PMTC is based on four design concepts. The first is to offer new conference locations. This system enables a person to participate in a multipoint teleconference from his/her own desk by using his/her own personal computer or workstation. This significantly improves work efficiency. No dedicated teleconferences facilities or systems are needed.

The second concept is to create virtual conference spaces modeled on the activities that occur in actual conferences. The shared space is for all participants. Side conferences can be established by groups of conferees in the closed spaces. Each conferee has his own local space. These three virtual conference spaces significantly enhance communication efficiency.

The third concept is able to apply multimedia information technologies to make documents for conferences. Teleconferences can be made more effective by making it easy to exchange various types of data. Each conferee can freely utilize parts of the images, data, or video information stored in files, that he can access. The material may include characters, speech, diagrams, motion pictures, handdrawn pictures, and pointing tools.

The fourth concept is to offer a new environment to group works. This system provides a common work environment. We are able to use the three virtual conference spaces which support not only teleconferencing services but also multipoint cooperative work such as distributed software development and cooperative document editing.

3.2   Hypermedia Book System

We developed the Hypermedia Book System to realize the effective use of multimedia presentation functions on PCs and WSs. We took a guide book that we had previously created for developing human interfaces design methods and converted it into a Hypermedia Book System. The Hypermedia Book is user friendly and permits several powerful functions to be realized. It is very easy to retrieve any page by using several kinds if index information. For example, if we want to access the textbook using the keyword 'multimedia', what happens? All text associated with 'multimedia' is displayed. From this listing we can select the entry desired. The system contains multimedia information structured as the most effective combinations of characters, speech, diagrams and motion pictures.

3.3   Visual Information System

The ISDN Visual Information System was developed to offer visual information services by using visual terminals through ISDN. This system is composed of a visual information center system and visual terminals such as video phones or teleconferencing terminals. Figure 5 outlines the services offered by the system.

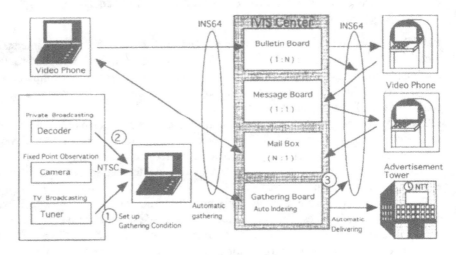

Fig. 5.   ISDN Visual Information System and services

Examples of the services include bulletin board services, message services, mail services, and gathering board services.

The video information center is composed of a general purpose workstation, video information storage equipment, and video information transfer control equipment. The maximum number of channels for simultaneous connections is 50. Terminal speeds range from 64 kbit/s to 1.5 Mbit/s. The center can hold audio visual information equivalent to 500 hours of video. This system is actually aimed at video phones and teleconferencing systems.

3.4   Digital Video Response System

A more advanced system, the Digital Video Response System (D-VRS), has been developed. The Digital Video Response System provides retrieval-based video with broadcast or video quality. Figure 6 shows the outline of the Digital Video Response System configuration which is composed of a video information center and B-ISDN and visual terminals.

The functions of the center include video information storage and delivery control to realize the same services as video-on-demand services which are very popular now. The control equipment installed in the center accepts requests through the communication network and delivers the digital video data through B-ISDN. It offers various video handling functions such as start-stop, slow-quick and forward-reverse for each user.

Hierarchical memory control technologies achieved with optical disk libraries and array disks have been adopted in the storage system to realize multimedia services economically. For example, public news or town information will be held on array disks, whereas video libraries will utilize optical disk files.

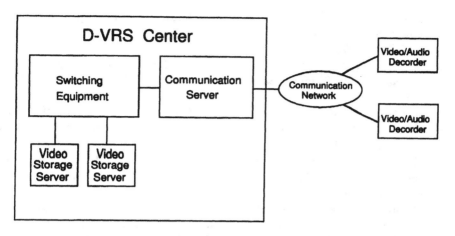

Fig. 6.   System configuration of D-VRS

4   Conclusion

The recent progress in multimedia technologies allows us to offer easy-to-use information systems, improve job efficiency, and supply needed information any time anywhere. In this paper I described the multimedia service design concept based on the relationships between our life space and multimedia application services.

Personal Multimedia-multipoint Teleconferencing System, TeamWorkStation and ClearBoard will make collaborative work more effective. The Hypermedia book System supports our understanding of many things such as manual documents because it uses the multimedia display function. The Visual Information System and the Digital Video Response System can offer visual information services easily and economically. I believe that these effective multimedia application services will solve many of the problems we will meet in the 21st century.

References

Ishii, H., Arita, K., Yagi, T., Beyond Videophones: TeamWorkStation-2 for Narrow-band ISDN, in: Proceedings of Third European Conference on Computer-Supported Cooperative Work (ECSCW'93), Kluwer Academic Publishers, Dordrecht, Netherlands, Sept. 1993, pp. 325-340

Ishii, H., Kobayashi, M., ClearBoard: A Seamless Medium for Shared Drawing and Conversation with Eye Contact, in: Proceedings of CHI'92, ACM, May 1992, pp. 525-532

Ishii, H., Kobayashi, M., Gurdin, J., Integration of Inter-personal Space and Shared Workspace: ClearBoard Design and Experiments, in: Proceedings of CSCW'92, ACM, Nov. 1992, pp. 33-42

Masaki, S., Yamaguchi, H., Tschihara, H., Shimamura, K., A Desktop Teleconferencing Terminal Based on B-ISDN: PMTC, in: NTT REVIEW, 4(1992)4, pp. 81-85

Nakamura, O., Matsuda, C., Tsuchiya, H., Ohiyama, M., Nakano, H., Video Message Handling System using Visual Telephone, in: Proceedings of the 41th IPS Conference, 1990

Nishimura, K., Ishibashi, Y., Nakano, H., Multiple-Access Methods for Digital Video Programs, in: Proceedings of the 1992 IEICE Fall Conference, Sept. 1992, Part 6, D-196

Nishimura, T., Masaki, S., Yamaguchi, H., Ichihara, H., Sakatani, T., Ishibashi, S., System Design of Personal Multimedia-Multipoint Teleconference System for N-ISDN, in: Proceedings of the 1993 IEICE Fall Conference 1993, D-220

Ogawara, K., Kimura, S., Asano, Y., Designing the Book Metaphor Interaction, in: Proceedings of the Eighths Symposium on Human Interface, the Society Instrument and Control Engineers, 1992, pp. 283-286

Sakamoto, H., Nakano, H., Video-on-Demand Service System, in: Tokai Section Joint Convention Record of the 6 Institutes of Electrical and Related Engineers, 1993

Tamura, K., Matsuda, C., Tsuchiya, H., Maruyama, M., A Study of the Data Channel Control Method in Visual Message Handling System, in: Proceedings of the 1992 IEICE Spring Conference 1992, B-696

Time Warner Cable Full Service Network - Silicon Graphics Technology and Architecture Overview

Gary Sager
Silicon Graphics, Inc., USA

1 The dawn of a new age

Sixty years after Philo T. Farnsworth first demonstrated a television system, his amazing invention remains in some respects exactly as he left it. Though television has received wide spread distribution around the world and the quality of the picture has steadily improved, it remains for the most part a passive display system for broadcasting images into the home. Even telephone technology has experienced more evolutionary development than television, with individualized, interactive services such as voice mail, call waiting, conference calling and others. Television is about to undergo a revolutionary transformation, with the introduction of the Time Warner Cable's Full Service Network (FSN), the world's first digital, interactive television network.

Debuting in Orlando, Florida, the FSN includes movies-on-demand, home shopping in a "video mall", interactive multiplayer video games, the ability to print material via a color printer, and much more. In 1995, expected additions to the network include the "News Exchange", from Time Inc., HBO (pay-TV channel) on demand, the Magic Music Store, a virtual supermarket and drugstore, other interactive shopping and services, interactive educational services, and other new world innovations.

Time Warner Cable selected Silicon Graphics to develop this extremely complex system because of Silicon Graphics' unrivaled experience with visual computing and distributed network operating systems. This paper will examine the Silicon Graphics technology that lies at the heart of the FSN, and show how Silicon Graphics' adherence to a standards-based, open, scalable, system architecture positions the FSN as the basis for a solid standard for the entire interactive television industry.

2   Interactive Digital Networks (IDN): What are they?

The widespread digital distribution of interactive information, services and entertainment is a technological development as significant and exciting as the introduction of personal computers (PCs). Both interactive television - which channels digital information and services to home televisions-and interactive digital media - which pipes information to workstations, PCs and other devices - blend elements of computing, telephone and television technologies. When these technologies are woven together in an expansive network that links consumers, businesses and government agencies with massive and powerful data repositories, the average household or business soon will have access to information services and compute power previously limited to a privileged few.

Yet these new solutions promise to reach even further into people's lives than PCs: interactive digital networks (IDNs) will transform the way people view the world from their living rooms, offices and laboratories, providing them with a simple-to-use and affordable window into the powerful Information Superhighway.

To live up to the much-touted destiny of the interactive age, architects of the Information Superhighway will have to pave the communications landscape with technologies capable of delivering useful applications today and 20 years from now. The scope of these applications must stretch from simple consumer video-on-demand services to other, more fundamentally significant deployments: delivering interactive 911 emergency medical services to rural areas, for example, or teaming powerful supercomputers around the globe to collaborate on the world's most perplexing and critical scientific problems. To reach subscribers using all types of today's information tools - from televisions and personal data assistants to PCs and supercomputers - governments, businesses and consumer services providers will likely access the same overarching digital network (see fig. 1), a network that must be designed with enough technological headroom to evolve and expand its services into the next century.

2.1   Consumer

Today, the video rental business is a $12 billion industry. The idea of supplying home viewers with movies on line has provided a catalyst for investment in interactive television (ITV) - the primary vehicle for delivering interactive services to consumers. While video-on-demand will likely be one of the first home applications, the industry's most advanced technology suppliers understand that video-on-demand is among the simplest of services to implement. Those who comprehend the significant investment required to erect the IDN infrastructure also realize that delivering video to the home will play only a part - and perhaps a very small part - in defining the importance of ITV, and justifying its very existence.

When implemented properly, ITV's first mission is to serve the consumer, and that service will take many forms. When the consumer wants to be entertained, such entertainment services as video-on-demand, interactive games and customized sports programming will be readily available. But when the consumer has a more specific goal in mind, ITV will deliver such services as interactive shopping, news-on-demand, travel planning, custom traffic updates and on-line postal services.

Business	Government	Consumer	
Private Medical Networks	Entertainment	Entertainment	Services
Training	911 Services	Video-On-Demand	News-On-Demand
Collaborative Computing	Municipal Services	Games	Concierge
Service & Entertainment	Research Networks	Sports	Weather
Private Entertainment Networks	Security	Programming-On-Demand	Value-Added Advertising
Location-Based Entertainment & Amusements	Defense	Home Shopping	
Retail Distribution			
Point-of-Purchase Kiosks			

Fig. 1. Information Superhighway applications

Interactive television also encourages remarkable enhancements to today's already lucrative network and cable television business models. While the public consciousness seems fixed on the entertainment aspects of interactive services for the home, IDN deployment brings an opportunity for service providers to reach customers and constituents in more efficient and targeted ways than ever before. Today, television advertisers already spend millions of dollars in attempts to target their message at specific audiences: sporting goods manufacturers advertise heavily on sports networks, for example. When ITV is deployed from coast to coast, advertisers (with the appropriate permissions from viewers) will know - down to the name and address - which individuals spend time watching sports, or which potential customers have an affinity for classic motion pictures. Interactive television will take much of the guesswork out of targeting customer demographics, providing advertisers with the most focused marketing vehicle in history - a dynamic, on-line database whose research can be updated with an individual's programming preferences and purchasing habits daily, and even hourly.

The advantage is dramatic for the consumer as well. A new car advertisement can offer viewers an option to receive copies of the latest auto magazine reviews of the car. Or, with a mere click of the remote control, viewers can shedule a test drive at the auto dealer nearest them. Suddenly, a product advertisement can itself become a service, and advertising - today the bane of the television experience for many viewers - becomes a useful tool for both advertiser and viewer.

2.2   Business

Involving business is a critical step in building the global data infrastructure, and businesses are certain to reap similarly dramatic benefits from its use. By plugging into the Information Superhighway, commercial users will be able to enhance their existing approaches to doing business. For instance, by accessing massive databases stored centrally or regionally, corporate users can collaborate on projects that demand participation from separate departments, buildings, campuses, even geographical regions. Today, those same users must depend on telephone communication or, in some cases, expensive proprietary videoconferencing systems, but with the advent of IDNs, collaboration and communication can happen with desktop computers, or even PDAs (Personal Digital Assistants). Only those users with powerful media workstations such as Silicon Graphics' Indy workstation are able to collaborate in real time today.

Health care, racked by skyrocketing costs and facing greater medical challenges than ever before, can make critical use of IDNs. Physicians, who today use the traditional communication vehicles of phone, fax and overnight shipping to consult, communicate and deliver data, will soon exchange information and guidance in more effective, media-rich environments. Using televisions, PCs or 3D workstations linked by IDN-based private medical networks, hospitals all around the world can instantly and interactively share X-rays, MRI output or patient data. The result is clear and instant communication, more effective consultation, and better and more efficient health care.

The prospects for expansion in the entertainment industry are intriguing as well. Location-based entertainment today is defined by amusement centers and hotel closed-circuit concierge services. These types of services can burgeon under the options available through IDNs. By accessing distributed databases, amusement centers can deliver dozens of "virtual worlds" to a single site. The same model applies to hotels, who today either subscribe to strictly scheduled video broadcasts or video-tape based motion picture services. With IDNs, hotel guests - or even cruise ship passengers - will access interactive services that span for beyond watching a simple motion picture, thus expanding revenue streams for lodging concerns and their suppliers.

2.3   Government

The groups that may gain the most from accessing IDN services are educational institutions, municipalities and other government agencies. In the face of shrinking budgets and heightening demands to improve services, these institutions are voraciously seeking new ways to modernize and streamline their operations. IDNs hold more promise for this class of user than any single technological development since the advent of computing itself.

Take education, for instance. Interactive networks will give financially strapped schools access to the kinds of on-line services that for years have been held up as the ultimate promise of modern education. Guest lectures by leaders of government, sciences or the arts; access to on-line film and video libraries; video teleconferences with school children in other areas; on-line multimedia encyclopedias that can be updated daily; virtual laboratories stocked with the latest and most expensive equipment; and interactive news services enhanced by analysis and comment: all of these services could be accessed via low-cost television/set-top devices, PCs or workstations. Government agencies also are in line to garner the rewards of IDNs. Municipalities will expand their ability to communicate with city, state and federal government, as well as with citizens. For instance, police will be able to access photographs, fingerprints and other data about crime suspects from police departments in other areas. They can also use interactive network technology to quickly and efficiently pinpoint locations when responding to 911 emergency calls. City, state and federal governments can leverage existing IDNs to transact routine business: motorists, for example, can register their automobiles or renew their drivers licences through the IDN, reducing traffic both on the streets and in motor vehicle departments. The prospects are just as positive for large federal offices which currently transact business over the telephone or through the postal service.

Full deployment of interactive digital networks will occur as technology evolves and conforms to user interests. Communication and computer companies are already testing their systems in trials throughout the world, and these tests are likely to continue for years. With computing performance relative to price increasing 10-fold 3 1/2 years, companies pursuing the interactive market must invest today in advanced technologies that will keep pace with future price/performance structures.

2.4   Paving the Information Superhighway

The potential applications of interactive digital networks are limitless. While many have focused on video-demand and other entertainment applications, the real implications are much more profound. The Data Superhighway promises people a new way to communicate and unprecedented access to information. Some observers believe interactive networks will lead to sweeping changes in society. Without question, it will alter the business landscape, perhaps leading to fundamental ways in the way people work, and even learn.

The manner in which interactive technology evolves and how it will be used are matters that are bound only by the imagination. Any attempt to define technology based solely on what is currently known is perilous indeed. What is important is to understand the elements necessary for the broadest, most flexible infrastructure, and to realize implementations and trials are the only means to progress. Therefore, one of the most advanced trials, the Time Warner Full Service Network in Orlando, Florida, will be described in detail.

3   The Full Service Network system software

The Full Service Network (FSN) is controlled by a system software environment developed by Silicon Graphics for current and future interactive television systems. It offers many features - here and now - that are far more advanced than those found in systems under development. This technology is a natural outgrowth of Silicon Graphics' recognized leadership in developing advanced:

- MIPS® RISC microprocessors
- 3D graphics computing systems
- symmetric multiprocessing system architecture
- supercomputing servers
- real-time operating system software
- distributed computing environments
- 3D graphical user interfaces

The FSN system software is much more than a continuous media delivery system for video-on-demand. Its modular architecture encompasses all aspects of an interactive television operation, from the underlying hardware up through the applications and creative content available to subscribers.

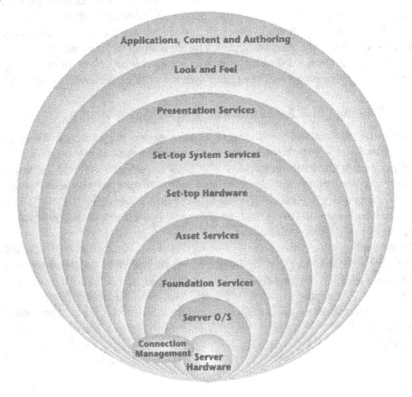

Fig. 2.   The modular architecture of the FSN system software

The FSN system software architecture can perhaps best be understood by imagining its modular construction in the form of a layered "onion". As this image suggests, modular layers can be peeled away so that network operators, system integrators, and service providers can take advantage of as much - or as little - of the functionality as they wish (see fig. 2).

The key benefits of the FSN system include:

- *Recoverability* - The FSN system software has been designed to recover instantly and gracefully from hardware and software failures.
- *Scalability* - Both the FSN system software and the underlying Silicon Graphics hardware platform offer an open architecture and can be scaled to a level of performance no other system currently can obtain.
- *Flexibility* - The FSN system software is designed to incorporate off-the-shelf third party solutions wherever possible.
- *Network neutrality* - The IRIX operating system at the heart of the FSN system software allows for a variety of network connectivity solutions.
- *Security* - The FSN system software protects network resources while maintaining the privacy of users.
- *Autonomy* - The FSN system software allows service providers to create autonomous "domains" within the system that can be managed independently from those belonging to a network operator. The boundaries of these domains are completely invisible to network subscribers.
- *A deterministic environment* - IRIX features built-in REACT real-time extensions for deterministic performance. Silicon Graphics' Challenge XL media servers provide the supercomputing performance needed in a demanding real-time environment.

For application developers and content providers, key benefits include:

- *An open and accessible architecture* - The FSN system software was designed to be open and accessible to developers of services and programs.
- *Authoring Tools* - Innovative software authoring tools are available to enable developers and content providers to create compelling applications and services. A Style Guide is available.
- *Media Integration* - Advanced media integration tools provide a complete library of media - audio, video, animation, images, 2D graphics, 3D graphics, and text - with built-in synchronization and MPEG support.
- *Data management* - The FSN system software features the UNIX-based IRIX operating system as well as information management and database management software tools.

4   Welcome to the Full Service Network

Time Warner Cable's Full Service Network in Orlando, Florida, will offer subscribers a vast array of interactive applications in addition to video-on-demand and the programming currently found on existing cable television systems.

The Full Service Network is perceived by the viewer not as a simple sequence of channels, but rather as a cyberspace world complete with a shopping mall, a movie theater, a news center, a game arcade and several other venues.

The viewer is presented with a dazzling 3D graphical interface carefully designed and thoroughly tested to provide intuitive access to all available services. The interface is built around a network navigator known as the Carousel, which presents the viewer with a beautiful, 3D, rotating "location selector." The viewer selects a location on Carousel with a special remote control device, and can quickly jump from location to location within the world of the Full Service Network.

Each location the viewer visits exists in a time frame determined by the viewer's activities on the Full Service Network. For example, a viewer might experience the following scenario:

1. The viewer goes to the movie theater and selects a movie.
2. The viewer watches the movie, and can pause, fast forward, and rewind it at will.
3. During the movie, the viewer decides to play a game, so he or she pauses the movie and jumps to the Playway Games center.
4. If the viewer chooses to exit the game, he or she quits the game and jumps to the Shopping Mall to browse for new clothing.
5. After selecting a new outfit and paying for it by entering a credit card number, the viewer decides to go back to the movie theater and finish the movie.
6. When the movie is over, the viewer goes to the Program Guide and identifies programs of interest.
7. During the next few days, the viewer periodically calls up the Program Guide and then jumps to the desired programs.

The Carousel is but one possible interface that might be implemented with the flexible FSN system software. As the FSN grows, a viewer might travel through gateways to different networks and encounter a new, standards-based interface with a slightly different look-and-feel for each network - much like the experience of traveling to a foreign country.

5   Major components of the Full Service Network

At the highest level, there are three major hardware components that make up the Full Service Network (see fig. 3):

- the *server complex* where the bulk of services available over the network are provisioned
- the *distribution network* which provides connectivity between the server complex and the set-top installed in subscribers homes
- the *set-top* which consists of a computer that's interfaced into the network, the television, and a hand-held remote control.

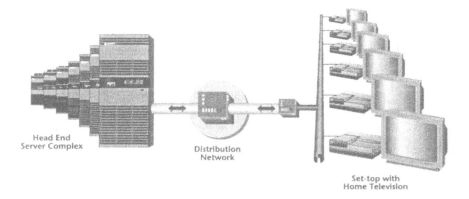

Head End
Server Complex

Distribution
Network

Set-top with
Home Television

Fig. 3. Components of the Full Service Network

5.1 Head-end server complex

The head-end server complex in the Full Service Network consists of server computers, storage systems, and an interconnection network that provides high-speed, two-way communication between different elements of the complex (see fig. 4).

The complex is built around the Silicon Graphics' Challenge XL line of symmetric multiprocessing (SMP), media servers. The Challenge XL server is based on a general purpose MIPS RISC processor and an open, scalable architecture - a very important feature in a system that's expected to grow rapidly in terms of both services and subscribers. Each Challenge server provides 1.2 gigabytes per second of sustained system bandwidth and can be configured with up to:

- 36 MIPS R4400 64-bit processors 200MHz
- 16 gigabytes of main memory
- 6 terabytes of disk storage

Networking connectivity includes Ethernet, FDDI and ATM. The Challenge media servers are capable of automatic recovery and isolation of failed elements so they can provide a high degree of unattended service.

The architecture of the FSN server complex allows services to reside on any server or combination of servers. In order to permit introduction of services that do not have to meet stringent real-time requirements, the architecture partitions servers into front-end - those that must provide real-time interactive services to the viewer - and back-end - those that indirectly provide services such as billing through the front-end systems. This partitioning permits more flexibility in connecting a rich set of services to the network, including the ability to interface existing service provider information management systems.

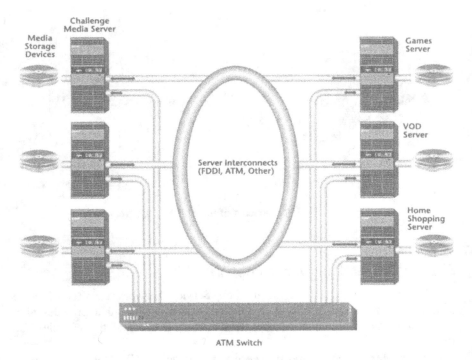

Fig. 4. Head-end server complex

5.1.1 IRIX operating system

To achieve the responsive performance that interactive television requires, the network architecture is designed as a single integrated system. The Silicon Graphics head-end servers use the IRIX operating system that is used throughout Silicon Graphics' entire product line.

IRIX is an adaptation of the UNIX® operating system and offers a feature-rich software environment and an extensive collection of programming tools and libraries. It is designed to run on multiprocessor systems and is able to support multiple threads of execution which significantly enhances the capacity of the system and application services.

Some of the key benefits of IRIX include:

- IRIX provides an industry standard operating system, and a rich and time-tested set of applications and development tools. Additional disks drives, memory, and different network interfaces can easily be added to the network without modifying the software.
- Silicon Graphics developed a new file system - XFS - to expand the UNIX file size limit to 264 bytes, a number so large that file size is virtually unlimited. The total amount of data space that a single IRIX-based device can manage is now 289 bytes. XFS is fully compatible with NFS and existing applications.

- The IRIX file system provides an abstraction of the contents of the storage system so the entire disk array is treated as contiguous data space. Data can be broken up and laid across multiple disks to provide the most efficient use of resources. For example, this allows the use of "data striping" to provide the highest possible I/O access.
- IRIX provides real-time features (REACT extensions), including flexible schemes for processor, memory, bus bandwidth and file input/output allocations that can guarantee the delivery of time critical services even while the system is being used for background tasks.

5.1.2 Foundation services

The basic mechanisms for participation in the FSN are provided by the system software foundation services. The implementation of foundation services is based on the industry-standard Object Management Group (OMG) and Common Object Request Broker Architecture (CORBA). Silicon Graphics intends to make the specifications and implementations of these services available to vendors who desire to add higher level services.

Resources and services in the FSN system software are implemented as objects, thus adding a layer of abstraction that hides underlying implementation details. Access to resources and services is provided by Application Programming Interfaces (APIs), which are defined using the industry-standard OMG Interface Definition Language (IDL). This makes it possible, in spite of any differences in underlying hardware or system software, to access any of the services from any part of the network. It also enables the development of distributed services capable of accommodating devices as diverse as legacy systems, PCs, telephones, and pagers, in addition to a spectrum of set-tops ranging from very simple devices to very sophisticated ones.

Object oriented design also provides for future improvements by shielding application and tool interfaces from any changes that are made as the underlying technology continues to evolve. Network applications, moreover, can be extended simply by adding new types, versions, and implementation for services on a continuing basis.

Object communication is designed to be flexible; the underlying interprocess communications mechanisms and networking protocols can be tailored to fit the needs of the systems being connected.

The object management layer provides a naming service by which objects can identify themselves and locate each other. By obtaining an object reference to a service from the naming service, a client can invoke the service through the IDL-defined APIs without having to know the location of the service or the protocols by which communication is effected. Furthermore, the object management system communications system provides secure communications.

5.1.3 Asset services

Asset Services build upon the Object Management layer to provide the generic services needed to support applications. In addition to the basic function of constant-bit-rate media delivery, services are provided to manage the media and to distribute service loads across multiple server systems as well as across resources with the systems. Some generic services, such as filing, are also provided for use by set-top applications to manage their own assets.

The prime considerations in the design and implementation of Server System services are:

- Scalability/Capacity
- Service Guarantees
- Reliability/Recovery
- Configurability

Generally, these goals are achieved by providing for distributed operations within the head-end server complex. One of the most obvious advantages of this approach is that it allows for some of the systems in the head-end to be highly specialized. This means, among other things, that third parties and independent service providers can introduce new servers and systems to a working network without disrupting already established services.

5.2   Distribution network

The distribution network carries information between the head-end server complex and the set-tops belonging to network subscribers (see fig. 5).

The FSN system software has been adapted to a number of network distribution architectures. It hides the details of the network from services and applications with a general interface for connection management.

The Full Service Network is based on ATM switching, RF modulation, and frequency multiplexing over fiber optic and coaxial cable. A switch routes information between servers and "MOD/DEMOD" boxes which multiplex, modulate and demodulate signals for each of the neighborhoods served by the Full Service Network. It is not economical to run fiber all the way to the home, so at some point between the MOD/DEMOD and the home, a Neighborhood Area Node (NAN) converts signals between AM light signals carried by the fiber and the AM electromagnetic signals carried by coaxial cable.

Typically, coaxial cable is used to carry signals to and from up to 500 homes in a single neighborhood. Because this last run of cable is rarely longer than one to three miles in length, it's generally referred to as "the last mile."

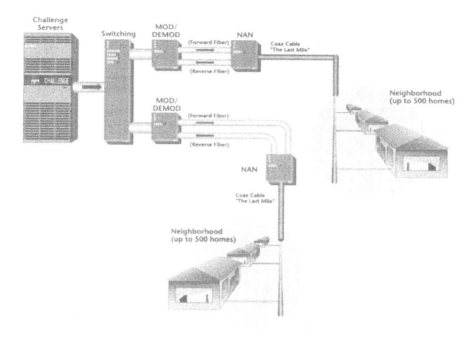

Fig. 5.   Distribution network

5.3   Set-top

The set-top is the element of the system that conveys media in both directions between the FSN and the subscriber's television. The set-top is located with the television and is controlled by an infrared remote control device that allows the viewer to make selections on-screen (see fig. 6).

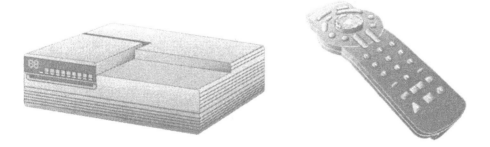

Fig. 6.   Set-top equipment

5.3.1 Set-top hardware

The set-top developed for the FSN is an integration of pre-existing and new components from Silicon Graphics and Scientific Atlanta. Through MIPS Technologies, Inc., Silicon Graphics has provided the high performance media microprocessor technology that is at the core of the set-top.

The set-top requires significant compute power to deliver the decoding, rendering, image compositing, decryption, and real-time 2D and 3D graphics - all of which provide a highly intuitive, visually compelling, and responsive viewer environment.

The set-top:
- provides high-bandwidth two-way connectivity with the head-end server complex for reliable delivery of data
- decodes the digital audio and video media sent by the head-end server complex and then re-encodes the signal into an analog form that can be interpreted by the television
- provides "upstream signaling" to the head-end for navigating through the available services
- provides the graphical user interface

In progress is a new media microprocessor design from MIPS Technologies, Inc. that will integrate many of the important functions into silicon making it possible to produce robust, fully functional set-top systems at a very attractive consumer price.

5.3.2 Set-top operating system

A key element of the set-top is the real-time micro-kernel operating system that provides a set of services sufficient to support multimedia applications on a dedicated single processor. The kernel supports drivers that can interface a wide variety of peripherals to the set-top, such as a printer.

5.3.3 Presentation services

The FSN system software multimedia resources include libraries for every media type:
- Audio
- Video
- 3D Graphics
- 2D Graphics
- Animation
- Text

The multimedia resources provide content developers with the tools to seamlessly integrate different media types and include built-in synchronization mechanisms and MPEG support.

The graphics library provides the functionality for constructing, manipulating, and displaying graphics objects. Each element within the presentation services layer is treated as a separate object, meaning that any presentation services that are added - whether developed by Silicon Graphics or by third parties - will be easy to integrate with existing services.

6   Applications, authoring, and content production

Application programs in the FSN are generally implemented as client-server programs. The client executes on the set-top, and makes use of the set-top and server services described above. The application may include a server portion that executes on the IRIX operating system and makes use of Foundation Services to communicate with its client.

Applications in the FSN system software can draw on services available from one or more servers in the head-end complex. Because of the system's object-oriented design, the location of these services can remain transparent to the applications.

To produce compelling applications, developers must have access to affordable platforms supporting a full range of multimedia capabilities and authoring tools. Silicon Graphics has provided FSN content developers with a powerful set of authoring and development tools. These tools enable developers to rapidly prototype media rich interface designs, integrate diverse media, simulate the FSN network environment, and test their applications.

Through Silicon Studio, Inc., Silicon Graphics provides a full digital production environment based on Silicon Graphics workstations, video products, and third party applications. This integrated solution spans the entire content production cycle from storyboards to animation to final post production.

6.1   IRIS Performer

IRIS Performer is a software development environment that provides high-level support for graphics-intensive tasks. It simplifies the process of scene generation and streamlines the use of simulation databases. As an economical and productive starting point for application developers, Performer includes advanced image-generation functions layered above the IRIS GL.

6.2   ImageVision Library

The ImageVision Library toolkit is an object-oriented extensible library for creating, processing, and displaying images. Its robust core set of image processing functions includes color conversion, arithmetic functions, radiometric and geometric transforms, statistics, spatial and non-spatial domain transforms, and edge, line and spot detection. These functions simplify the extension of standard function sets to suit specific image processing needs.

6.3   CASEVision

CASEVision provides a unique approach to programming by providing tools to visually represent complex development issues. For example, CASEVision includes the Array Visualizer to simplify debugging with a unique 3-D interface; Structure Browser to graphically indicate pointers to linked lists and data structures and highlight dangling or incorrect pointers; Heap View that graphically displays dynamic memory and highlights memory leaks and errors and many others.

7   Summary

The Time Warner Cable Full Service Network architecture and the technologies described in this document represent an ambitious and far-reaching vision for the future (see fig. 7).

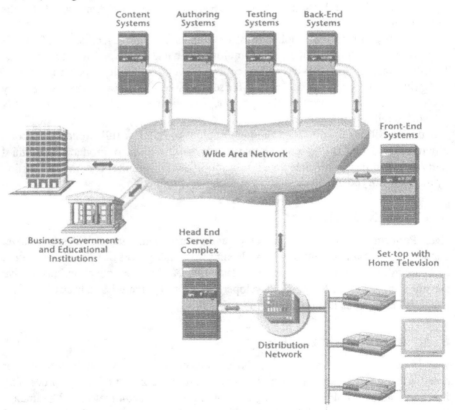

Fig. 7.   Growing into the future

Where most other interactive television trials or deployments are satisfied with delivering only movies to the home, the FSN is truly delivering on the promise of interactive television. The FSN architecture and technology is the first to put television viewers in complete control of the information and entertainment they want and need. And it provides the technological headroom that will allow application providers to enhance interactive services over time, making them more compelling and interactive and, ultimately, more valuable.

Time Warner Cable's Full Service Network represents the new standard for interactive television. It is a solid and significant deliverable. But it is only the beginning, both for consumers and for the companies that have invented powerful new interactive technology for the Orlando trial. To maintain this momentum of innovation, two FSN technology partners, Silicon Graphics and AT&T, created a joint venture, Interactive Digital Solutions, based in Mountain View, California. Interactive Digital Solutions was formed to develop and deliver large-scale, fully integrated, interactive video server solutions for telephone company networks and cable TV systems. Interactive Digital Solutions develops middleware and application frameworks and tightly integrates them with hardware and open systems suppliers to provide complete solutions for interactive services.

The achievements of Silicon Graphics, Interactive Digital Solutions, AT&T, Scientific-Atlanta and the other FSN technology partners will allow the creative community and content authors to produce compelling interactive programming services for potentially millions of television households nationwide. In the final analysis, the FSN and its underlying technology provide the infrastructure that enables commercial and educational communities to reinvent themselves, create new opportunities, and thrive in the emerging Interactive Age.

References

MIPS is a registered trademark of MIPS Technologies, Inc.
UNIX is a registered trademark of UNIX System Laboratories Inc.
Full Service Network is trademark of Time Warner Cable
Carousel is a trademark of Time Warner Cable
IRIX is a trademark of Silicon Graphics Inc.
REACT is a trademark of Silicon Graphics Inc.
XFS is a trademark of Silicon Graphics Inc.
IRIS Performer is a trademark of Silicon Graphics Inc.
ImageVision Library is a trademark of Silicon Graphics Inc.
CASEVision is a trademark of Silicon Graphics Inc.
IRIS GL is a trademark of Silicon Graphics Inc.

Acknowledgments

The Full Service Network design and implementation is the integration of many technologies developed by numerous people within Silicon Graphics and at partnering companies. The list of persons who made significant intellectual and personal contributions to the Full Service Network would itself be as long as this overview.

Burda New Media's Multimedia Activities for Private Customers

Hubertus Hoffmann
Burda New Media GmbH, Germany, and
Europe Online S.A., Luxemburg

1   Introduction

In December 1993, when we set up the independent business area, Burda New Media within our Munich publishing company, you could say we set off in a VW Polo on the communication highway. Very soon, however, this proved to be a country lane full of potholes, an adventure, the realisation of a new idea, like the construction of the railroad between the east and west coast of America in the previous century. It is very easy to get lost in the fog on the communication highway, and to misjudge the bends.

We feel rather like Otto von Bismarck, who once wrote to his wife saying that his foreign policy was not somehow predefined or amenable to planning. He often felt like a small child in a dark room, slowly feeling his way forwards. In other words: only as an active participant, a part of the whole, is it possible to learn from experience. If you don't jump in the water, you can never learn to swim.

The information highway appears to any new driver like the Leverkusen motorway junction, where it is always a huge relief to discover that you've found the right exit, otherwise you end up somewhere else. The multiplicity of new English terms is confusing. It is a completely new world.

It is fascinating that whole sectors of industry are branching out into completely foreign business areas via the new media. The big power supply companies, VEBA, VIAG or RWE, consider themselves the civil engineers for the information highway. This brings them closer to the suppliers of material, the media companies.

The telephone companies, too, such as AT&T in America or Deutsche Telekom, are also involved. Retailing, via the marketing of CD-ROMs, is also part of the scene. The first major trading companies have already sent their lorries and bulldozers onto the information highway to stake their claims. But let us not be deceived by the euphoria: the chances of making money are as high as the chances of losing it.

At Burda New Media we are delighted to have implemented seven concrete projects within a few months. But we are just as pleased to have rejected twice as many after detailed examination. This has certainly saved us 20 million DM of bad investment.

There is a euphoric gold-digging atmosphere on the information highway. But as cool, calculating businessmen we must analyse the situation soberly and in proportion, and very carefully assess the chances and risks.

2   The new Information Society: The second industrial revolution

On the basis of data for the European Union the trend is unmistakable. In the year 1800, 70% of all people employed worked in agriculture; in Germany it is currently only 4%. Agriculture was then far and away the biggest employer in Europe, and is now far and away the smallest.

As a result of the industrial revolution 100 years ago, and the first and second world wars the numbers employed in production rose steadily until the 1950s. The crises in steel and coal on the rivers Rhein and Ruhr in the 1960s provided early evidence that ever fewer jobs in the production industries could be sustained. The numbers employed in the service industry rose only slightly in the last century. This sector is now second in terms of numbers employed. The information sector (telecommunication, media, computing) grew only very slowly in the 19th century and up to the second world war, but has for some years been experiencing a period of dynamism.

We are currently living through a period of transition from the industrial to the information society. After 100 years, this is Europe's second industrial revolution, with enormous implications for all sectors of the economy. In the year 2000 the information sector will be the biggest employer. No-one can avoid this trend.

The information market is global. There is no longer territorial protection or closed markets. In many areas of entertainment and computing the market is dominated by America; this certainly does not provide a good prognosis for the German economy. Europe must stake its claims now, and become strong market players. In the media business we need to position ourselves between two extremes: "the early bird's eaten by the cat", and "come too late and life will punish you". It is essential to avoid both of these extremes.

If you carry the management responsibility for 530,000 employees and control 19 million square metres of space in 19,000 sales outlets you cannot afford to either back the wrong horse in an excess of euphoria or miss the train of destiny.

We believe that in the information era it is not the large that will eat the small, but the quick that will eat the slow. There are many new players in this economic sector. An important aspect of the New Media strategy is risk dispersal. The market is only in the process of becoming. It is not yet there. You can compare the situation with that of the private television stations, Sat.1 and RTL, ten years ago. It has taken nearly a decade for these stations to become profitable for their owners. But now they represent goldmines.

Risk dispersal means not making large investments in one or two projects, but planting one or two dozen saplings along the information highway. We don't yet know which will grow into strong oak trees. The multimedia market is slowly establishing itself. Here too it is important not to have any illusions. In Germany, the core areas, online and CD-ROM, will only become of interest to us sales people in autumn 1995. In this sense it is a good time to get involved.

We will need a lot of creativity. However, creativity is difficult to develop effectively in large-scale organizations. Consequently we have spun off our projects into subsidiaries with suitable partners. We prefer small, dynamic teams. If they are successful they will be extended and given international links.

It is important to be internationally competitive, especially with respect to our mighty US rivals. And to this end we favour strategic partnerships. In Europe Online, we have entered into partnership with the world's largest tele-communication company, AT&T, which has an annual turnover of 108 billion DM. Navigo Multimedia and Navigator TV involve cooperation with the Pro7 television group in Munich.

In boom the chances are high. The German Economic Minister, Rexrodt, expects the multimedia sector to have a turnover of 1.5 billion DM and 10 million new jobs in Europe by the year 2000. The renamed Prognos-Institut in Basel estimates that media consumption in Germany, which was 100 billion DM three years ago, will rise to 160 billion DM in five years, and 280 billion DM in 15 years.

This means that our customers will be spending more money on information and entertainment. That is the big opportunity for trading and media companies.

3 The Burda New Media projects on the communication highway

Using the example of Burda New Media's projects, I would like to describe in more detail how we are feeling our way forward along the information highway.

We have chosen to split the business area of Burda New Media GmbH into two: first the "interactive television" area, and second the "PC material" area.

It is not yet clear whether the PC or interactive television will be favoured by the consumer 10 years from now. But for some time we have had the feeling that the trend is towards the PC. The PC is interactive. The TV is inactive. We estimate that television will continue to be regarded as a passive entertainment instrument by the Germans.

3.1 Interactive television

Let me describe a few projects in the interactive television area.

3.1.1 Klartext/Navigator TV

Together with the Pro7 television group in Munich, which is run dynamically, successfully and with vision by Dr. Kofler and his team, in 1994 we established the Klartext/Navigator TV Partnership. Along with the Grundig Multimedia Solution

GmbH in Fürth we developed a three-stage system for interactive programme management. Since June 1994 Pro7 has been transmitting the teletext "Klartext", which is the first electronic television magazine in Germany. It provides an overview of the television listings of over 30 TV stations.

This summer at the Broadcasting Trade Fair in Berlin we will for the first time transmit the second stage, the so-called "Megatext" from Siemens-Grundig. This makes use of improved graphic resolution possibilities.

Our objective is stage three: an intelligent, interactive programme manager. It will require a digital television signal and a set-top-box. This independent television station will provide viewers in the year 2000 with an on-screen interactive overview of the wide range of television programmes. It will be the Navigator through the 100 or more television stations in the digital era.

3.1.2 X-Base.Computer Future Club

On ZDF we have been transmitting "X-Base.Computer Future Club" daily, an interactive game show for the generation of computer kids, with weekly viewing figures of 2 million. In the most successful computer gameshow on German television we get to know the generation of computer kids, and can inform our customers about our CD-ROM and online products.

3.1.3 TV Specials

For media companies the material in interactive television is particularly important. The large number of television stations will increase the demand for software, i.e. television shows and films, even further. From our hallmarks BUNTE and ELLE we are developing television concepts such as "BUNTE-TV" and "ELLE-TV". At present we are filming a 45-minute special with Henry Kissinger on "World Power Diplomacy".

3.1.4 Blockbuster Video Deutschland GmbH

A few weeks ago Burda New Media GmbH, together with the US company Blockbuster International from Fort Lauderdale, USA, formed Blockbuster Video Deutschland GmbH based in Munich.

With its 3,500 outlets Blockbuster is the most successful video chain in the world. Now the company is also part of the second biggest US media concern, the Viacom Group, which includes the Columbia Film Studios, the television stations MTV, VH-1 and Nickelodeon. With Blockbuster we will open 20 independent video and multimedia outlets in Munich and Berlin. The first will be opened in July. In the second step we intend to open a further 220 outlets on a franchise basis throughout Germany.

Blockbuster's success concept is: No sex or violence, i.e. a family-friendly video library. A satisfactory selection of all top films, and an extensive range of about 6,000 films. In addition, the sale or loan of video games and CD-ROM titles. We believe in this successful family entertainment concept consisting of videos, games and CD-ROMs. It is in line with the lifestyle of tomorrow's customers in the information and entertainment era.

We are dubious whether for the mass public "video on demand" will represent a cheap alternative to the video library within the next ten years. The Telekom reckons that by the year 2000 only 3 million set-top-boxes will have been sold. This means that only every tenth television household will be able to call up video on demand. The set-top-boxes must be paid for by the customer. The current price lies between 1,000 and 5,000 US$ each. The customer is scarcely willing to pay so much money for this new technology.

3.2   The PC area

The following sections describe our projects in the PC area. Here we have established a clear emphasis.

3.2.1   Europe Online S.A., Luxemburg

Our main project is the creation of Europe Online. On 1 June 1994 Dr. Hubert Burda and the Luxemburg partners established Europe Online S.A. in the presence of the then Minister President, and current President of the EU Commission, Jacques Santer. Why?

The Luxemburg government supports this new visionary company. Alongside SES/Astra and the CTL television group, it is to become the third foundation of the media industry in this European country. We receive 30% of our net investment back directly from the state of Luxemburg in the form of tax certificates. Comparable start-up conditions are not available in Germany.

The partners include the former German Postal Minister, Dr. Christian Schwarz-Schilling, four Luxemburg investors, Meigher-Communication from New York, the Matra-Hachette concern from France, and Pearson from England (Financial Times, Economist, etc.).

Europe Online is pursuing three business ideas:

First we are renting 30 transmission capabilities for audio, video and data on the SES Astra satellites. *In addition* we are offering charge collection possibilities for interactive television, the so-called "conditional access", together with the US technology concern, General Instruments. The *main objective* is to create an online service with a European flavour in Germany, England and France in the year 1995. The software for this large online service is provided by our technology partner AT&T Interchange from Boston. Europe Online will offer the customer communication via e-mail, access to the Internet, and many new services. In Munich the German partnership has been founded with many famous German names.

Will Online become a business?

Turnover in the online area for the USA in 1988 were, at 160 million US$, very modest. Within three years they are estimated to have rocketed to a provision 3 billion US$. To this extent a mass market is also being established there at present. Online penetration is currently only 8% of US households. This will rise significantly in the next few years. Last year more PCs were sold in America than televisions. At present every third US household has a PC. It will soon be every other one.

Something similar is beginning to happen in Europe. At present conservative estimates suggest there are 43 million PCs. Half of these are in small companies and households. This constitutes the group that we are aiming at. This potential will double within five years. Of course, the gap between Europe and America will still exist: Whereas last year 35% of American households already owned a PC, in Europe it will only be 24% in five years time. The reason for this is the relatively insignificant PC penetration of France and southern Europe. There is a gaping hole.

What can be offered online?

The US market shows that for current online users communication from computer to computer is most significant, accounting for 40% of the usage. 40% of the supply is made up of computer fora, i.e. all information relating to hardware and software. Only 20% of the time is used for information. This breakdown will change once online becomes of interest not only to a narrow group, but is opened up to the mass market.

Using telephone cables, signal relays, modem and PC a multiplicity of information and services can be offered. Of great importance are the areas of online banking and financial information, telephone information, travel and recreation information, online newspapers, lexica, the school and education fields, games, job markets. Gateways to other new databases will constitute components of the new services.

3.2.2 Metroconnect New York

In New York we are currently trying out a local online service called Metroconnect Inc. in the largest, most dynamic online market in the world. There is a wide range of useful local services, e.g. information about a jazz club, property advertisements, information about New York city hall politics, travel and recreation opportunities. In other words: all the local "news to use".

3.2.3 New World Vision Ltd.

As well as the online area, offline is also important for PCs, i.e. information and entertainment stored on some data media, cassette or CD-ROM. Together with the famous British publisher, Lord George Weidenfeld, in September 1994 we established New World Vision Ltd. in London. This will create high-quality CD-ROMs, whose calibre will be obvious from the products. We want to distance ourselves from the cheap CD-ROM image. At present, certainly 80% of the CD-ROM titles available in Germany are simply trash. The customer is being ripped-off. From outside he cannot see how bad the brightly packaged contents are.

In October our CD-ROM "Jerusalem Interactive" will be ready, a multimedia journey through the history of this interesting city. At the same time our "Goethe in Weimar" will also be available, visiting the city of classicism on the trail of Johann Wolfgang von Goethe. We believe that in this way we can lead computer kids in an entertaining fashion into the world of Goethe's ideas and books.

Together with the National Gallery of Art in Washington D.C. we are producing three titles on artists, their famous works and their times. With Pavarotti we are planning a "Pavarotti Interactive", an interesting mixture of private reminiscences.

Agent Based Communication in Traffic Telematics

Christoph Mayser, Martin Römer, and Georg Zimmermann
Berner & Mattner Systemtechnik GmbH, Germany

1   Introduction

The need for mobile communication grows with the increasing mobility of our society. A good example of this is the wide acceptance of mobile phones since the introduction of GSM-services. For road users mobile access to static and dynamic information gets more and more important with growing traffic. Mobile gets an advanced meaning - similar to mobile phone calls this implies not only within the means of transportation but everywhere. Complex data communication replaces voice communication for instance in trip planning or navigation applications.

The provision of static traffic information is already available today. Access to dynamic information is the goal of different research projects. The access to this huge amount of information has to be economical and efficient (Take less bits, but the right ones). The main point of these projects is not the technical feasibility, but the solution of conflicts of political interests.

Applications from the home and office area, such as are available today, are based on an online connection. The user has to control a data connection to a server for the whole time of the request and he has to know the retrieval mechanism of the service. Both are not suitable for the mobile access to information. Online connections via GSM are expensive and road users need simpler access mechanisms than those provided by the services of today.

For applications within the field of traffic telematics there have to be more extensive technologies. Agent based communication is a very interesting approach to create mobile, complete and intelligent access to existing information.

2   Properties of agent based communications

Agent based communication is a revolutionary idea for communication in the future. The idea is based on software objects which we call agents, because they are acting on behalf of the sending computer even while in the receiving computer. An agent contains data and procedures and is carried by the network. In the host computer it is executed, that means its procedures are performed in the context of the data of the agent. This new approach to networking is called *Remote Programming*. Remote Programming has two properties which are important for traffic telematic applications. On the one hand it is possible to separate the networking and application part of service provider and application user. On the other hand low level tasks are processed by intelligent software in the network. Most low level tasks like navigation in the network and tasks for reserving or buying something are common to more than one application. Agents can process these tasks without any input from the user, even if results the agent produced before are needed to process the current task. Self-reliant processing is possible because reacting on events is a principle of agent based communication.

Agent based communication is independent from existing network infrastructures. Therefore it is possible to connect already established databases or information services to an agent based communication network. An external methods interface is used for the connection to the access mechanisms of the existing services.

There are high requirements for security on agent based communication because agents are travelling in the network. A basic part of the concept of an agent is that agents are not directly executed, they are interpreted. The only interface to the outside world is the external method interface and because of that agents have controlled access to resources and information on host computers. Every agent has to identify its author and permits before it can access any resources. The host computer still has the control and so the ability to refuse an agent if the identity is not proven. Any kind of damage can be prevented using this concept.

3   Applications for traffic telematics

Agent based communication provides the means to make existing in-car applications more efficient. Furthermore it delivers the base technologies to configure these and new applications and give them mobility.

With the properties mentioned above the creation of new applications becomes possible. Agents can compare different offers for a journey (trading) or they can organize whole scenarios (orchestrating). Furthermore agents are able to monitor the traffic situation or the adherence to flight plans.

3.1 Intermodal trip planning

Intermodal trip planning is an ideal application for agent based communication. Most travellers, when planning a trip take into consideration only their prefered or habitual means of transportation. This is due both to lack of access to information as well as lack of awareness.

The mimimum input for trip planning using agents is the start point, the destination point and the selected departure or arrival time. An agent then goes to the electronic marketplace to meet other agents. It gets the information from databases of airlines, railways or car rental companies. Using a personal profile it estimates the time and cost of a trip with the different means of transportation.

The agent returns and offers the user different possibilities to travel to the destination, including information about the location of restaurants or hotels. The user can just use the information or in a more complex application he can select one possibility and send another agent to organize the whole trip with all reservations.

It is now that the monitoring functionality of agent based communication is a big advantage. The agent leaves a child agent at the service provider, which monitors the constraining conditions of the trip. If there is a change to these conditions, for example an already booked flight is cancelled, the child agent goes back to the user and alerts him about the changed conditions. Going back, the child agent can even present a new alternate trip to the user. In case the conditions are stable the child agent just disappears after the trip.

3.2 City and tourist information

There might be an application giving the user all the information about events, hotels and restaurants in a city. This application makes it possible to organize a whole night on the town using an agent. First the agent reserves tickets for a theatre, then it looks for a restaurant nearby and reserves a table there. Last of all it arranges a surprise for the companion of the user, such as a bouquet of flowers at the table, perhaps.

3.3 Dynamic navigation

Some car manufactors install a navigation system in their upper class models. These systems are based on static road information. They lead the driver of the car to a previously selected destination.

The information for the driver is the information which was available at the day it was stored on the CD-ROM. The driver cannot get any information on the actual traffic situation, since the application is not communicating. This is a big disadvantage of the systems which are currently used.

Using agent based communication it is possible reorganize the available systems into dynamic navigation systems. The concept of RDS/TMC and the SOCRATES project is compatible to technologies used for agent based communications.

The next step is to expand the dynamic system to an intermodal navigation system. In this case the road user needs additional information about park and ride facilities and the time table of the public transport system. This idea is one of the goals of the EUROSCOUT-System from Siemens. Agent based communication is independent from special hardware. That is the reason why it is possible to access these information from outside a car. In electronic market places, which still have to be implemented, the access to traffic information could be decentralized and economically.

3.4   Fleet management

Intelligent agents can replace low level voice communication in fleet management applications. Furthermore available applications based on data communication can be enhanced with agents technology. The monitoring functionality lifts the burdon from the driver and the supervisor, without causing high costs for online communication.

A supervisor could check technical data of the vehicles from his office even if the trucks are on the road. This is another interesting point of view using agent based communication in a fleet management application.

4   Devices

We call devices for applications based on agents technologies *Personal Intelligent Communicators* (PIC). They are a combination of a fax, a phone and a mini computer. There is a difference between PICs and *Personal Digital Assistants* (PDA). A PDA is mobile device with the focus on organizing. A PIC is the window to the world of information. Data and application programms can be downloaded over the network.

Two different devices are available on the US market. One is the *MagicLink* device from Sony, the other the *Envoy* from Motorola. Both are coming out of the office area and have smart messaging as a standard application.

In the field of traffic telematics the devices are called *Personal Travel Assistant* (PTA). PICs and PTAs have different Man Machine Interfaces. A driver has to be concentrated on the traffic and because of that there are other concepts for the MMI of a device used within a car. The integrated GSM-Modem has to be deactivated for this time and the device has to be connected with the communication interface of the vehicle.

5   Key technologies

May 1994 Berner & Mattner Systemtechnik GmbH started a project to evaluate available technologies in the field of agent based communication. As a result of this evaluation Berner & Mattner identified *Telescript* and *Magic Cap* as the only suitable technologies. Both technologies are developed by *General Magic*. General Magic is a US company with partners like Apple, Motorola, Sony, Philips, Matsushita, Fujitsu, Mitsubishi Electric, OKI Electric, Sanyo Electric, Toshiba, AT&T, NTT, France Telekom, Northern Telekom and Cable & Wireless.

Telescript is an object oriented programming language with the focus on communication. Agents and electronic market places are developed in Telescript. The Go-Command is a basic concept of Telescript and gives an agent the ability to navigate in the network.

Magic Cap is on the one hand a platform, on the other hand it is the graphical user interface. It is based on the use of metaphors. Telescript is included in Magic Cap, which means Magic Cap applications can use the concept of agent to communicate. General Magic announced Magic Cap for Windows and for Macintosh within 1995. A Windows or Mac version of Magic Cap brings the technologies to a huge number of computers. It also links the mobile and stationary usage of application using agent based communication.

Philips Advanced Communication Enterprise (PACE) represents General Magic in Europe. PACE is an organisation within Philips which collaborates with Berner & Mattner Systemtechnik GmbH in the field of agent based communications.

6   Development of a PTA-Demonstrator

After the evaluation project BMW Research initiated a Personal Travel Assistant (PTA)-Demonstrator. Get expierences with Magic Cap was the goal of the project. Berner & Mattner extended the Magic Cap user interface adding a new building on the *Downtown* of the Magic Cap user interface (see fig. 1). This building contains an information service for the time table of the public transport system in Munich.

Fig. 1.   A new building on the Magic Cap Scene Downtown

In the next step Berner & Mattner connected this application as a prototype to the existing time table information service of the public transport system in Munich. BMW Research, the public transport system of Munich (MVV) and the software company Mentz Datenverarbeitung were consultants on this project. With the technical support of PACE, Berner & Mattner developed the first application using Telescript and Magic Cap in Germany. This application was part of the demonstration scenario PACE presented with Berner & Mattner at the CeBIT 1995 in Hannover.

7   Prospects

Agent based communication is a technology with useful concepts. Not in short term but in medium term this technology will be part of our communication. For establishment on the market three main players have to collaborate:

- Service providers have to establish interesting services with agent based communication as base technology
- Network operators have to establish an agent based network for smart messaging
- Software and hardware developers have to develop interesting applications and cheap devices

There have to be managers with agent based communication as a vision. They have to focus the interests of the different main players to create a pilot project.

But in short term the decisions will be made for technologies of tomorrow. The list of partners in the alliance of General Magic shows that agent based communication is an important topic. Mobile access to information is one of the main topics within the booming communication industry.

Research departments are able to evaluate new technologies do without having a return on investment in short terms. That is the reason why agent based communication has to be pushed by these departments.

Some regional, national and international research projects are working on devices like Personal Travel Assistants. Members of these projects are universities, engineering offices, companies of the car industry or the public transport systems and the Deutsche Bahn AG. These projects should show the benefits of agent based communication and, if so, they will fasten the development of networks and services using this technologies.

8   Summary

Agent based communication is a convincing approach for mobile access to information. The decoupling the networking and application part of service provider and application user and the processing of low level tasks using agents, which are carried by the network, are important properties, especially for traffic telematics. Dynamic navigation, intermodal trip planning, tourist information systems or fleet management and diagnosis system are possible applications in the field of traffic telematics. We call the devices for agent based communication Personal Intelligent Communicators (PIC), or where they are used in the field of traffic telematics Personal Travel Assistant (PTA). Magic Cap and Telescript are the only suitable technologies to develop applications and networks. They were developed by General Magic, a US company. Berner & Mattner Systemtechnik has designed and implemented a PTA demonstrator using General Magic technologies. This project was initiated by BMW Research and supported by Philips Advanced Communication Enterprise (PACE).

Part Five

Impacts and Implications

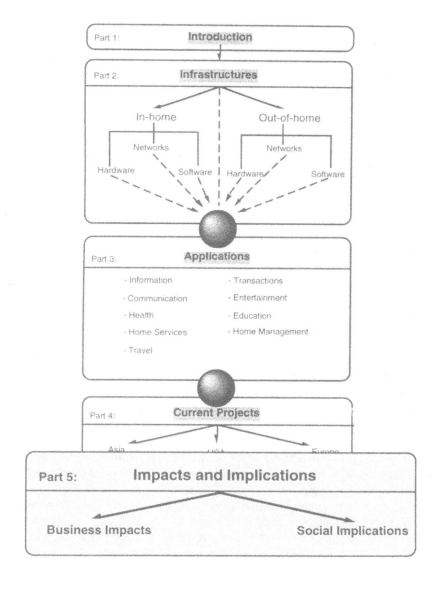

After description of infrastructures (Part Two), applications (Part Three) and projects (Part Four) this section analyzes the main social and business implications of information technology in the private home and for private uses.

The following contributions try to shed light on the difficulties in identifying, stimulating and exploiting the new home-IT market. The central questions addressed by all these theoretically based and strategically focused papers are: 'How can we the providers take advantage of these enormous new market arising at the horizon?' 'How to avoid risks?' 'How to retain the largest market share?'

- *Multimedia Software GmbH Dresden* summarizes - from a interactive multimedia application provider's viewpoint - facts and obstacles essential to the provision of IT-related products and services for the private home.
- *University of California et. al.* examine the implications for advertising and marketing communications in the post-modern home-IT world defining a new paradigm for advertising and marketing.
- *Roland Berger & Partner's* concern is the market development for integrated home systems, i.e. home automation. Products are available, but there is a lack of standards and as an expert puts it 'a solution awaiting a problem'.
- *Booz, Allen & Hamilton* analyzes the multimedia market that is based on stand-alone devices (in comparison to ones provided by online services) and showed that this market - favored to be the most profitable in the short run - is of economic importance.
- *Andersen Consulting* gives advice for strategic management under the context of converging industries and the emerging information society, i.e. the entry of IT in the private home.
- *KPMG* makes some critical comments on the ongoing discussion of multimedia which is characterized by hype and PR activities. Projections of future revenues (e.g. like this one by Ovum cited below) depend on many factors and must be handled with care.
- *University of Rhode Island* examines the different markets for possible application types and discusses the options concerning the race between the PC, TV or game device into the home.
- *Free University of Berlin* claims the specific characteristics of a computer use at home in a broad cultural and social context.
- *Hogeschool van Amsterdam* defines the term home information technology and then reflects on the social implications that the usage of IT in the home might have.

Even if the social contributions are in the minority in this book we would like to highlight the importance of a home technology aligned with social and cultural requirements and conditions.

There are huge market potentials within the reach of providers of infrastructure, services and content. According to a recent Ovum study, by the year 2005 the Information Superhighway will generate revenues of US$ 185 billion, more than 34% of which is predicted to come from the domestic sector. For Germany alone the year 2000 should bring revenues of US$ 5.15 billion of residential Information Superhighway applications.

Further there are the social consequences of information technology in the home. Although in the inplementation process of new technologies social change is always associated the intrusion of IT in the private, most intimate sphere is something owing special consideration and care.

Examples of technologies like the video cassette recorder or the automatic washing-machine show the long period of time (10-15 years) that is needed to reach a penetration rate beyond 50% of households. Resistance to change is one aspect of it (note that private IT will only be used on a voluntary basis and must therefore provide a new or added value). Technology that must be fitted into cultural conditions and the way of life is another one. On the one hand low penetration means high market chances, but on the other hand it burdens the provision of goods and services with the necessity to understand the private user and to customize mass products as if they were made-to-measure. Success stories such as the one of Bang & Olufsen show how to accomplish this task in a competitive market.

The objective of this last section is to prove that well-known institutions and consultants are actually working on the issues and economic impacts of computerized information processing of the private household, but in some cases without particularly emphasizing the fact that it is about *residential* information technology or explicitly separating it from the business applications.

In summary, the topic of home-IT is already on top of many agendas - pursued by either implicit or explicit concepts. The fifth part should pave the way for a business administration-centered research for the issues of home-IT.

Business Impacts

New Products and Services for Private Households on the Information Highway: Facts and Obstacles

Joachim Niemeier
Multimedia Software GmbH Dresden, Germany

1   Information society has been real for a long time

When the topic of discussion is "Information Highway", there are two groups frequently asking to speak. The sceptics refer to the high lead costs and use the absence of social acceptance, the insufficient command of the technological basics and the missing markets as arguments. Their counterparts are the gold-diggers. Whether technology or contents suppliers, both groups see the future in the new technologies. The consumer is frequently uncertain when hearing that multimedia on the Information Highway will change his working environment, his role as a consumer, the information he gets and his leisure time.

The Information Highway and multimedia are considered as keys to information society. The service sector's commercial importance increases more and more, the industrial nations are evolving at an increasing pace into service nations. Competition is increasingly defined by service around a product or as a product per se. In the course of the transition from an industrial to a service society the tangible products are more and more pushed into the background. The service sector is widespread, it includes activities such as information services (e.g. telecommunication, outsourcing, database services), transportation and supply, public services (e.g. education, public health services), financial services (e.g. banks, insurance companies), technical services, trade, management consulting and employee counselling etc. The pioneers for service nations are the USA and Japan, since service markets are largely deregulated in these countries.

If one considers the number of jobs in the various economic sectors, one will see that in the Federal Republic of Germany already more than 50% of those in gainful employment are working in the information-based service sector (see figure 1). For the year 2000 it is expected that this sector will have more employees than the entire automobile industry.

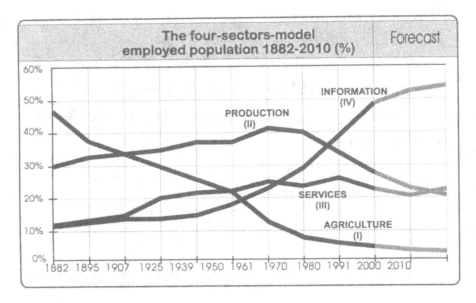

Fig. 1.   Development of the employees structure as a function of the sectors of
economy in Germany (see Dostal 1993)

2   New realities, expectations and illusions

The first ones to be asked on the topic of new products and services on the
Information Highway are the market researchers. Definite results for Germany are
not yet on hand. A study performed by B.A.T. Freizeit-Forschungsinstitut (Leisure-
Time Research Institute), Hamburg, dated 1995, for instance, dampens the
multimedia euphoria. Only eleven per cent of 2,000 interviewees believe that the
private use of the new technologies will yield vocational benefits as well. All the
same, 24 per cent reckon with new jobs. But media consumption costs time. 22 per
cent believe they cannot afford this time. Just each tenth anticipates a gain in time
from multimedia.

The results of a study carried out by IRES by order of the DM commercial
magazine (see DM 1995, 5 pp.) are quite different:

- 33% of the West Germans asked are acquainted with the term of "multimedia"
  today, with this figure being 96% for the private PC users. Especially the
  private PC users are very interested in this topic.
- The term of "interactive TV" is meaningful to 43% of the private PC users, they
  would like to select videos from home and use the services offered as active
  participants. Almost 66% of the interviewees would even participate in a field
  trial.

With regard to the topic of multimedia, Arthur D. Little management consultants see "Europe at a cross-roads". Europe needs the multimedia market of the future, since it might have an impact on 10 to 11 million jobs. According to this study, multimedia is of a twofold decisive importance for the welfare work as well as in leisure time (see Arthur D. Little 1994, p. 3):

- "Creation of new jobs through the development of new products and services for the business world and leisure-time use.
- Re-structuring of industries, organizational cycles, performance processes and jobs by employing interactive multimedia system technology, with the effect of cost savings, faster and more direct market assess and frequent circulation of capital."

Politicians turn into visionaries about this topic. Even leading businessmen who are otherwise rather realistic - not limited to those of the media industry - fall into raptures in the face of "getting realistic". In this regard the industry in the USA is already one step ahead. One believes at least that the challenges which the industry is faced with and which will have to coped with on a realistic path in the future have been identified:

"Of course, the holy grail of the "Information Highway" will permit us to finally get enough bandwidth to get media to move around the world as easily as words today on the Internet. Despite the intense hype, I now believe most people understand the flash point for these applications is five to ten years away" (Braun 1995, p. 27).

3   Facts about the multimedia world of today

So let us follow the call to "getting realistic" and try first of all to get a picture of the facts.

3.1   Fact 1: Explosive growth of on-line services

According to "Die Zeit", 1995 will become the year of the most tremendous expansion of the "on-line world". Internet is still considered as the major Information Highway. This is evidenced by plain figures such as number of users, transmitted data volumes or number of hosts within Internet.

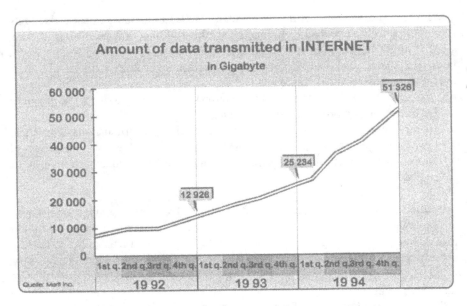

Fig. 2.   Data volumes transmitted via Internet

World-wide, the number of the network-connected computers is still doubling each year, also in the case of the commercial service providers "CompuServe", "America Online" or "Prodigy". Comparisons made between the member counts in Germany show that "T-Online" has reached a top position in Germany in this sector (see figure 3). Microsoft Network, as a newcomer, is expected to acquire 700,000 members world-wide as early as by the end of 1995.

The companies offer on the online services is at present mainly limited to information and advertisement. Where as in Germany the companies offers are typically created under their own control and without a strategic overall concept by individual enthusiastic "technology freaks", this medium has long been picked up by the public relations, marketing and distribution sectors in the USA. The address of the "homepage" has become more important than the business card. The set-up of the first "virtual shops" illustrate the enormous potential in the range of commerce ("electronic commerce"). Software, hardware, books, trips and tickets for music or sport events are increasingly ordered via the network.

The main focus of the providers of new products and services on the Information Highway is on the number of subscribers. At present the only critical mass besides T-Online with 2,500 providers is Internet. Owing to the new market opportunities the longstanding borders between commercial and non-commercial applications are presently vanishing more and more in the case of Internet. Besides the number of subscribers, criteria such as security, response-time behaviour, user surface and, last but not least, costs have become a major argument for the commitment.

The manifesting growth in on-line services characterizes the second wave in the multimedia business. Depending on the multimedia applications, it is expected that wideband will not become a commercial success before 2000 (see figure 4).

Service	Supplier	Members worldwide	Members Germany	Growth rate
Internet	Eunet	40 millions	several millions	15% per month
CompuServe	CompuServe	2,5 millions	70.000	8% per month
America Online	Joint Venture with Bertels-mann	2,5 millions	Target: 1 million members in the year 2000	
Prodigy	IBM/Sears	2 millions		
T-Online	Deutsche Telekom AG	-	850.000	4% per month

Fig. 3.   Comparison between on-line services (status as of November 1995)

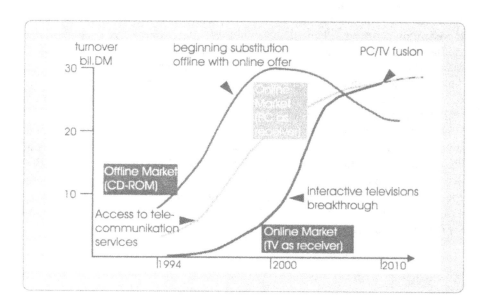

Fig. 4.   Market development for multimedia

3.2   Fact 2: Market convergence and strategic alliances

There are a lot of "communities of prey" wishing to conquer the Information Highway. There is no other commercial sector with as many alliances as in the square made up of the contents providers, the services providers, the network carriers and the hard- and software manufacturers. The final goal of all these alliances is to win customer groups for new products and services. The points under discussion within these alliances are questions relating to financing, the ultimate-consumer access, independence and standardization.

In fact everyone agrees: The only way to win customers is via contents and make-up. However, customized offers are also depending on suitable order-political setting conditions. This includes licensing authorities and procedures, advertisement regulations and restrictions, youth, data and consumer protection, but also the solution of multiple and cross-ownership issues.

The following citation describes the current situation very well: "The tussle over the best starting position in the business of new media technologies is reminiscent of exhibition bouts: An enormous hustle and bustle in the foreground, while the protagonists and coaches are working hard in the background in order to come up to the expectations" (n. a. 1995, p. 15).

3.3   Fact 3: Innovation cycles come thick and fast

The statement from the publisher environment saying that everything can be traced back to "Gutenberg" has meanwhile lost its validity even for the media sector. In the past, companies had enough time to adapt themselves to new technological developments and to wait for the most favourable time to introduce products and services suited for the market. Today, this situation has dramatically changed. In increasingly short periods of time the market is accessed by new computerized media which can be grasped and turned into a product or service (see figure 5). In many cases the providers are faced with the entrepreneurial opportunity of "inventing" a new market. At the same time, this situation bears the risk that with the more and more short innovation cycles the time window for refinancing on the marketplace will not be sufficient.

Not only the technologies, the market turns "online", too. As a consequence, only those companies will be successful who manage to build up such core competencies as enable them to create a new product or service within a short time, test it on the market and adapt it to the customers' desires. Long development times, e.g. 6 up to 12 months in off-line multimedia production in the case of video-centered applications, are equally detrimental as a too low consumer number for new services within the framework of pilot testing.

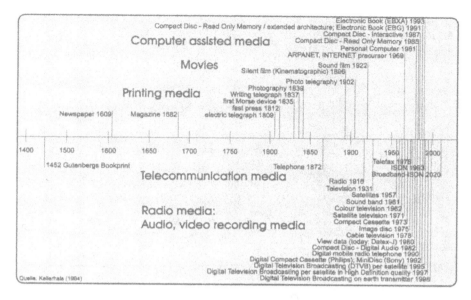

Fig. 5.   Innovations in the media technology sector (Source: Kellerhals 1994, p. 124)

3.4   Fact 4: Computerization of the households has begun

More and more sectors of everyday's life will make use of the opportunities of information and (tele-)communication technologies. Following the computerization of the world of business through corporate information processing, the future private households will also become integrated via networks in a heterogeneous environment from which they will procure their services (see Brenner/Kolbe 1994):

- The so-called "in-home infrastructure" covers the entirety of the hardware, software and networks such as home computers, CD players, TV-sets and telephone PBXs.
- The "out-of-home infrastructure" includes the entirety of hardware, software and networks such as telephone lines, servers or mobile communication systems which are installed outside the private household and can be used by it.

   This information-technological infrastructure forms the basis of numerous types of applications in the range of "computerized information processing of the private households" (see Brenner/Kolbe 1994, 373 pp.):

- health and sports
- dwelling and supply
- travelling and mobility
- shopping
- entertainment
- initial and further education

- communication
- information
- household management

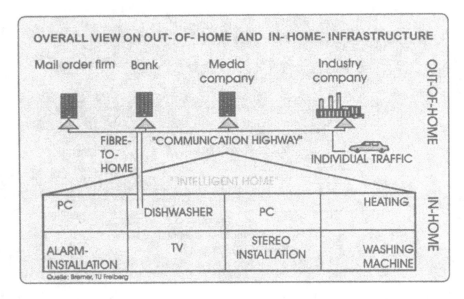

Fig. 6.   Overview of out-of-home and in-home infrastructure (Source: Brenner/Kolbe 1994, p. 370)

4   Obstacles in the way to new products and services on the Information Highway

If one looks at the four facts above together, the preconditions for a transition from technology-driven business to market-driven business are set. There are, however, still some obstacles in the entrance to the Information Highway.

4.1   Obstacle 1: The lack of creative products and services

A lot of products and services become pretty soon boring after they have been tried out for the first time. Every owner of a CD-ROM drive will realize after a short time that his collection of silver plates is growing continually but that, with a few exception, he will not use them ever again. The exceptions are on the one hand products with highly standardized contents such as reference works, or on the other hand offers with a high level of topicality, or which are continually updated when used via the net. This can lead to the derivation of the following fashioning guidelines for the contents design of creative products and services on the Information Highway:

- to actualize something other providers cannot offer,
- to offer the customer a cost benefit or a value addition in return for the use,
- to present highly topical contents, or to integrate them in standardized product, or
- to enable customer-specific products or services.

One of the decisive factors for the success of a new product or service for private households is the issue of carefully adapting them to the respective customer group (see figure 7).

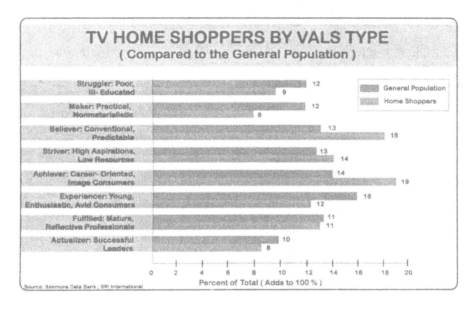

Fig. 7.   TV home shoppers by vals type (Source: Simmons Data, SRI International)

4.2   Obstacle 2: The customers' household budget is limited

Besides the nature of the offer, the price to be paid for the product or service plays an important role, too. Considering the tight private household budgets the portion which can be spent on new products and services will be very limited. Online services which make the meter rattle will certainly not cause too much joy.

The conceivable substitution market is also very limited. Before the setting of the American video-on-demand field trials, Kagan's Media Index 1994 determined that the households lend an average of 3.9 movies from the video-tape library per month for which they spend just under 10 dollars rent. Even with generous assumptions it would be very difficult to come to a Return On Investment (ROI) for a "full service network".

The following financing strategies can help to create the acceptance for new products and services under economic aspects:

- The existing budgets on the provider side, for instance in the marketing or distribution sector, have to be diverted in proportion to the new products and services.
- Existing contents must be used in multiple ways and in a purposeful manner. Within the framework of a media-assets management one could, for instance, couple archived information with up-to-date information:
- The private end customers may be interested, since they occur in large numbers. However, owing to the limitation of the private household budgets, products or services may also become attractive for business applications.

Within this discussion it is often overlooked that no consumer-oriented application will do without commercial applications, and that there is an overlapping between them (see figure 8).

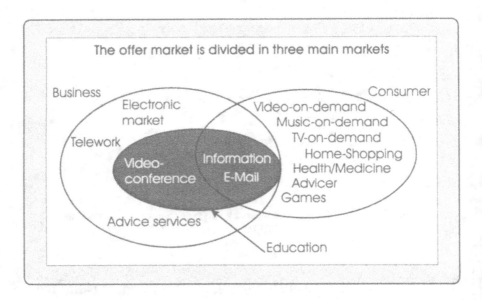

Fig. 8.   The offer market is divided in three main markets

4.3   Obstacle 3: Inefficient development processes in the production of multimedia products or services

The best market is useless if the company's costs of production are too high. This statement also applies to the multimedia sector. Today, the creation of multimedia products and services is like an attempt to introduce a new automobile class using the procedures of craftsmen.

Therefore, "content centers" are required for the efficient production of multimedia applications on the basis of concepts, contents and ideas which the provider makes available. Such "content centers" may be organized as profit centers of their own or as independent companies.

For the sole reason of the required infrastructure for the hardware and software (author tools, 2D/3D animation, digitalization, compression) the production of multimedia products and services involves high costs. The required technologies are on the first stage of development and will remain there even in the mid-term future. Considering that a mass market does not exist so far, the costs of these technologies are very high. Other cost drivers are the individual development processes and the missing concepts for the reusability of contents.

For content providers, the production of a multimedia application is a critical access step. In the previous business environment these technologies were often unnecessary, which means that sometimes not even the terminology is known. As a rule, a content provider does not have the required qualification basis. In addition to special know-how, new knowledge and skills will become necessary, which are frequently still in their infancy even on the free market. The first market opportunities will therefore be open to those companies who are producing multimedia products and services.

4.4   Obstacle 4: The degree of maturity of the technologies is still low

The user expects that he can use products and services on the Information Highway without extensive installation efforts. But even in the range of CD s comprehensive installation routines are still a must. In addition, a large portion of the innovative technologies is only available as a lab prototype, if any. For instance, the video-on-demand applications which were exhibited in 1995 on trade fairs are often still controlled by a standard computer rather than by a set-top box. Navigation was via a mouse or a trade-fair-suited keyboard rather than via a remote control.

5   Factors of success for providers of products and services in the Information Highway

The provider's success will be influenced by the following factors:
- Availability of contents
- access to the coverage medium
- management of the customer relations

Only if the company manages to realize all these three factors at favourable costs, its products and services will succeed on the market. Cyber Companies and

Cyber Markets: These catchwords show that the corporate and marketing identities will have to be redefined before the background of the Information Highway. Existing company structures will have to be scrutinized. There are new possibilities of direct market access and new distribution channels. The entire chain of logistics will be restructured.

Companies desiring to become active in this field will have to find the clarification of the required core competencies and their structure. The qualification of the staff potential and the kind of the make-up of the business processes will have to change. The starting pints for these are:

- Modern marketing strategies require to enter in close contact with the customers. The consumer evolves from a "sheep-like" message recipient into a partner. He defines the depth of the information level and the detailing degree of the information as a function of the selection level.
- The creation of multimedia products and services requires knowledge and skills which are frequently absent within companies and cannot be accommodated within the framework of the existing corporate culture.

Co-operation with other companies in the framework of value-creation partnerships will first have to be learned in many companies. Lacking co-operation ability is the most frequent cause of the projects' failure.

References

Arthur D. Little, Multimedia: Europa am Scheideweg. Wettbewerbsfähiger Mitspieler oder Konsument und Gebührenzahler, 1994

Braun, M. A., The Multimedia Industry - From Real to Realistic, in: Glowalla, U. et. al. (eds.), Auffahrt zum Information Highway, Heidelberg, 1995

Brenner, W., Kolbe, L., Die computergestützte Informationsverarbeitung der privaten Haushalte als Herausforderung für Wissenschaft und Wirtschaft, in: Wirtschaftsinformatik, 36(1994)4, pp. 369-378

DM, Multimedia '95. Ergebnisse einer repräsentativen Grundlagenstudie, 1995

Dostal, Informationstechnik und Arbeitsmarkt, working paper at the Institut für Arbeitsmarkt und Berufsforschung, Nürnberg, 1993

Kellerhals, R. A., Neue Medien und Gesellschaft: Totale Unterhaltung oder intellektuelle Herausforderung? Computergestützte Medien (IV), in: technologie & management, 43(1994)3, pp. 123-128

n. a., Multimedia. Ohne Maus wirkt Arnold mikrig, in: DM Extra, 1995, pp. 6-16

New Visions of Information Technology and Postmodernism: Implications for Advertising and Marketing Communications

Alladi Venkatesh
University of California, Irvine, USA, and
Ruby Roy Dholakia and Nikhilesh Dholakia,
University of Rhode Island, USA

1   Introduction

Although volumes have been written on information revolution and much writing continues at this very moment, it is rather surprising that this has not made an impact on the academic field of marketing communications or advertising (Katz 1991). Even within the broader field of marketing, the writing is limited - for exceptions, see Blattberg/Glazer/Little (1994), and current authors' contributions from 1984 through 1994. In the world of marketing practice, there is no question that the information revolution has had an impact on various marketing activities such as, channels of distribution, networking of global markets, product design and new product development, customer data management, home shopping, home banking, real time manufacturing and marketing, to name a few. Although the world of marketing practice is being revolutionized because of new information technologies, the field of advertising seems to lag behind. In a recent speech to the Advertising Foundation, Edwin Artzt, the Chairman of Procter and Gamble lamented profoundly about the state of the advertising field, pointing to the fact that it has yet to show any initiative in capitalizing on new technologies. Here is a quote from his speech:

"...[T]he industry [advertising] is too slow to react to rapid technological changes in the way information is delivered to the consumers...From where we stand today, we can't be sure that ad supported TV programming will have a future in the world being created - a world view of video-on-demand, pay per view and subscription TV...These are designed to carry no advertising at all, and as a result, mass marketers like P&G will have a hard time achieving the reach and frequency we need to support our brands...The absolute key is to create ad-driven programming that suits the many new forms of media that are evolving...Interactive technology can be used to engage consumers in commercials...If a consumer wants to know which Cover Girl nail polish matches the lipstick she saw in our commercial, we can tell her on the spot...Targeting of not just demographic segments but individual households...[A]gencies and clients should use interactive advertising to engage consumers in commercials and provide direct consumer response...If a family has a new born baby, we can make sure that they get a pampers commercial....Ad agencies must embrace today's new media opportunities just as the industry so swiftly adapted to changes brought by the coming of radio and then TV." (Ed Artzt, Chairman of Procter and Gamble - Quoted in Yahn (1994)).

A similar observation has also been made by Blattberg/Glazer/Little (1994, p. 27) in their recent book, The Marketing Information Revolution, "perhaps the greatest casualty of information revolution will be advertising".

Although the field of advertising or, in general, the academic scholarship in marketing communications has not addressed the nature and impact of information technology, there is a lot that is happening in the diffusion of information technology across all sectors of the society that has relevance to the field of marketing communications and advertising. In this paper, we critically evaluate the rapid transformation of our society into information culture, or cyberculture as some authors prefer to call it (Escobar 1994), and the implications of this transformation to the field of advertising and communications. To capture the full impact of the information revolution, we use a postmodern framework.

The study is based on our own investigation of the impact of information technology on American consumers and households, which has been in progress for nearly a decade, as well as our writings on postmodernism. Our work, both empirical and theoretical on these two subjects, has been reported over the past few years (Dholakia/Dholakia 1989, Dholakia 1994, Dholakia/Dholakia 1994, Dholakia/Mundorf/Dholakia 1995, Venkatesh/Vitalari 1987, Venkatesh 1994, Venkatesh/Vitalari 1990, Venkatesh/Vitalari 1992). Funding for the technology-based studies were provided by the National Science Foundation, and AT&T. The primary focus of these studies is on the diffusion of computer technology into the home and their actual use by the members of the household.

In the last ten years, three major technological innovations have entered the American home and each has represented a different development. The first was the arrival of the VCR (the technology of entertainment), the second, almost simultaneously, was the arrival of the personal computer (the technology of information), and the third is an ensemble comprising the answering machines, fax machines, voice telephones (the technologies of telecommunication). The fourth which is the most recent and at a rather rudimentary stage of development is the interactive technology or the multimedia. All these developments are far advanced in nature compared to the previous technology of the home, the television set, an enduring technology in its own right but ready for change.

In addition to these new technologies of hardware, there have been other developments in the service oriented technologies of information and telecommunication, such as cable TV, database services, and integrated technologies such as World Wide Web, Prodigy, America Online, video services, home shopping and home banking. All these use existing hardware, the telephone, the television, and the computer.

It is true that not all these services are well developed. On the other hand, collectively, they represent a sea-change in the way the new technological environment is emerging.

More concretely, we are reminded that the era of information highway may have just begun (Brody 1993, Davids 1994, Egan 1991, Lee 1993, Ziegler 1994) and we are now in the world of multimedia (Fetterman/Gupta 1993, Goble 1994), virtual reality (Biocca 1992, Taubes 1994, Warwick, Gray/Roberts 1993), and interactivity (Davids 1994, MacDonald/Shneiderman 1994). The placid setting of the home to which we escape from the pressures of the outside world may no longer remain the same as these technologies make a concerted effort to change its interior and link it electronically to the exterior (Bjerg/Borreby 1994). Speculative as some of these visionary schemes are, they are being viewed as serious possibilities in the years to come.

The purpose of this paper is to address various issues raised by the developments in information technology and postmodern practices and examine their implications to the field of advertising. The paper will proceed as follows. In Section I, we discuss the existing communication paradigm in advertising. The next section will examine some empirical findings on home computer use based on our research. This will be followed by a discussion of more current developments in new technologies such as multimedia, virtual reality and interactivity. Following this, we provide a brief but focused analysis of postmodernism and its relationship to the emergence of new technologies. In the final section, we propose a new paradigm for advertising based on our discussions in the previous sections.

2   Existing paradigm for advertising

The field of marketing communications and advertising, in particular, as it is currently understood, operates under a modernist paradigm (see figure 1). Modernism is defined here as a cultural/philosophical position which regards human subjects in cognitive terms as opposed to viewing them in semiotic or symbolic terms (see Domzal/Kernan (1993) for elaboration of these ideas in the context of advertising). Advertising encompasses the domain of mass communication, is involved in information transfer from producer to the consumer, and is a uni-directional system of communication from the sender to the receiver. The technologies of mass communication on which advertising relies are the print media, radio, and TV which are primarily designed to reflect this model of unidirectional communication. The characteristics of the existing paradigm as shown in figure 1 may be described in the following terms:

1. The underlying theoretical model of communication involves four primary elements, the message sender, the message, the message channel, and the message recipient (Belch/Belch 1990, pp. 128-132). This scheme is also more popularly known as "who says what to whom with what effect". This is a unilinear model which in practice translates into what we shall label as the one-to-many model. This model of sender-to-a-passive receiver is extremely fundamental to the way advertising has been conceptualized in both academic scholarship and actual practice. This model has been found useful in the era of mass marketing and mass advertising and has been in force for nearly half a century.

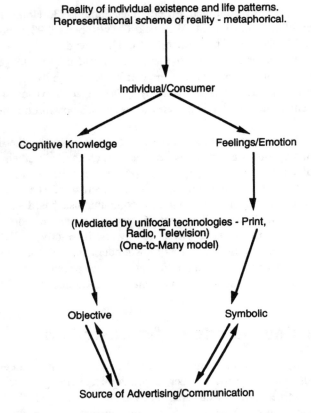

Fig. 1.   Old paradigm for advertising/marketing communications

2. In this model, advertising is viewed as an activity of information transfer and system of communication preceding product sale.

3. The dominant media for advertising are print, radio, and television. The history of modern advertising coincides with the development of these three media (photography and color print, film, and wireless transmission of audio and video messages). These media are independent in that they are not connected to each other technologically (as multimedia technologies are). However, they are linked strategically by the marketer who tries to complement each medium with the other for advertising purposes. These three media are designed to reflect the theoretical model mentioned earlier.

4. Advertising operates under the important assumption that mass communication is ephemeral and perishable. Advertising campaigns last a limited number of weeks and a specific advertising message is repeated only a few times. Hence the research technologies of advertising - reach, frequency, response measures - are developed to reflect this particular aspect of advertising.

5. The advertising messages operate on a metaphorical scheme of representation which is also the modernist view of representation. It means that the goal of

advertising is to capture and present the world of reality as it exists or to capture its idealized form, although the contexts and situations surrounding the reality might vary. Advertising models, both marketing strategy models and consumer response models, are designed to correspond to this framework of reality.

Why is this model inadequate? In what sense does it need to be reevaluated? Our position in this paper is that the communication environment in which the established models of advertising have operated for years is radically changing. The primary engine for this change is the emergence of new technologies. In addition to the communication environment, our notions of reality and how the individual subject is constituted are also changing. These changes are captured in a postmodern framework.

Our proposed model of advertising (see figure 2) is indeed based on different assumptions of reality and the nature of communication environment shaped by the emergence of new technologies. We discuss the proposed model in detail in the last section of the paper following a critical and comprehensive examination of the emerging technological picture. In the next section we present some key findings of our research on the impact of computing technologies.

2   Empirical work on computers

When we began studying computers for home use in the early eighties (Dholakia/Dholakia 1989, Venkatesh/Vitalari 1987), this was an uncharted territory. As we were entering the field, in the broader field of computers, the transition had just occurred from large scale to mini computers and then on to personal computers (PCs). We started our study with the beginning of the PC era. Against all speculative predictions that a PC revolution was afoot in the home front, we were cautiously optimistic about the changes that were likely to occur, claiming that there was nothing quite approaching a revolution. We conceded that computers and computing technology had the potential to transform many sectors of society including the American home, but this was not going to occur suddenly and the conditions needed for computer take over were not yet available. To avoid speculative forecasts, we decided to study the phenomenon of home computing empirically and systematically and launched multiple long term projects beginning in the mid-1980s and continuing to the present time to study the actual use of the computer in the home. Our studies are one of the very first to investigate computer use in the home and they are certainly the most comprehensive.

During the first period of our projects, roughly coinciding with the later half of the 80s' decade, the talk of home computer revolution began to slowly fade. Instead of computer "revolution", people were talking about computer "bust". Many pessimistic articles began to appear in the press, manufactures were totally confused, and popular writers stopped talking about computers in the home as a major development. There was much silence.

We found that the pessimism of the late eighties was as unjustified as the heightened hype of the early eighties. We are now in the nineties, things have changed dramatically, optimism has returned with a tinge of realism, aided by a decade of actual experience to back it all up. This is not to say that the speculative cycle has not returned, but this time it has assumed a different character - speculation seems inevitable in the technological game.

Our studies which began in the mid-to-late mid-eighties included longitudinal surveys, cross-sectional surveys, regional and national surveys of American household studies. The primary focus of the study was the use of computers in the home as stand alone units, and more recently, this has expanded into the use of computers in a multimedia context. Our various studies revealed that there was no justification for early hype or later pessimism. Computer revolution may not have occurred in the precise manner predicted, but there certainly was a quiet revolution. The popular press was imprudent in predicting the early revolution as it was in diagnosing the later demise. Our job throughout, as researchers, was to separate fact from fiction and establish the knowledge needed for continued exploration.

The following is a summary of important findings. Before giving the actual findings, some general observations based on our research will be in order.

2.1   Some general observations

1. Technological environment moves faster than the capacity of human beings to adapt to them. This asymmetry of technological production and consumption needs careful evaluation. However, once the consumers are familiar with the technologies, and well-versed in their use, the consumers become the prime movers of technological acceleration. In this sense the consumer is both a consumer and producer of technology.

2. It was a mistake to generalize the success of information technology from the commercial/industrial sector to the household sector. Success cannot be easily duplicated if the domains are not equivalent. Companies which manufactured commercial information technologies had no experience in the household consumer market, nor did they understand the dynamics of the household behavior. There was much ignorance in this area and when failure struck, the companies they simply withdrew, closed shop, and did not exhibit any desire to learn. Although they finally realized that technological prowess in one area does not automatically translate into another domain, they were not interested in finding out why.

3. In the eighties, the computer technology lagged very much behind its promised potential, particularly in the area of software development for home use (e.g. multimedia). There were many constraints on what computers could do and the software capabilities were rather limited in terms of what the households would need. Although claims were made that computers could do several things, their technical capabilities were rather primitive. However, because computers were already well established in work environment, the software technology was more developed for job related uses.

4. In order to understand why technologies succeed or fail, we need first a theory of technology, second a theory of household behavior and third, a theory of household-technology interaction. After years of our own empirical work, and a growing body of knowledge resulting from the work of other researchers, we believe such theoretical frameworks are available.

5. To call a PC a home computer does not guarantee its acceptability in the home environment just because the prefix "home" is attached to the word "computer". It is not the label that one gives to the technology that counts. Second, the fact that PC can be used in the home and is in fact used in the home does not guarantee its acceptability.

6. Instead of labeling the 1980s the decade of failed revolution, it is more accurate to describe it as the decade which laid the foundations for the home-information revolution that was due to begin in the 1990s.

7. The time is now ripe to study contemporary developments, to record and critically analyze the events as they are unfolding in the context of home-information technology scene.

2.2 Specific findings of our studies

1. A majority in our first set of samples viewed computers as job-oriented technology. It did not matter that computers were used inside the home, but they were still perceived as tools that facilitated job related work. Close to seventy percent of computer use in our sample was for job related purposes. In other words, computers were primarily viewed as technology which facilitated work at home. But they were also viewed as establishing a link between the place of work and home.

2. The above result needs some elaboration. On the positive side, computers can facilitate teleworking or telecommuting. Those people who want to work at home for any number of reasons, part time or full time, may be able to work at home if the nature of their work (i.e. transportability of work) permitted it.

3. A related finding was that computer use for work at home was high among those with telecommunications facility (e.g. multimedia) compared to those who did not have this facility and where the computer operated as a stand alone unit. This additional finding leads to interesting possibilities for the 1990s. Respondents were interested in multimedia capabilities of the computer rather than computer as a stand-alone unit. In the 1980s the telecommunication facilities were rather rudimentary and had not reached a high degree of sophistication until the 1990s.

4. Computers are appealing if they can be linked to other media. This explains why for example, the diffusion and penetration of VCRs which came into the market roughly about the same time as PCs, was faster and deeper. The penetration rate of computers in the mid-eighties was about 10% and has inched to 33% in recent months (Shiver 1994). The VCR penetration rate is now any where between 75% to 85% and was already close to 35% to 40% in mid-eighties. More than the computers, VCRs were viewed as part of the family

entertainment scene. VCRs were also used to record family events and were, therefore, treated as family electronic album.

5. As mentioned earlier, it is clear that as long as computers were stand alone units, their potential usefulness was limited. This does not mean that there are no stand-alone technologies in the household. In fact, almost all domestic technologies are uni-functional stand alone units (refrigerators, vacuum cleaners, microwave oven or television). But these technologies are well integrated into the household environment. They were originally developed as household technologies and did not derive from industrial applications. They were all designed to assist in the performance of several household tasks such as food preparation, house cleaning, family entertainment and the like. Computers did not fit this scenario. In addition they are very complex machines and require skills that are not commonly accessible to most household members.

2.3   New developments

We have already mentioned that the environment of the 1990s is very different from the 1980s. The following are some key developments that differentiate the two decades.

1. The whole development in the software is unprecedented. The software developments have reached extremely sophisticated levels which means that we have the technology available that addresses consumer needs.
2. The development of multimedia which was not even mentioned as a technological possibility in the 1980s. Multimedia possibilities are the direct result of cross-over technologies.
3. There is now a sudden realization that "home" is where new technologies can achieve their full potential. No more is it necessary to assume that technology needs to be transferred from the commercial site to home site. Home itself has become the main site for many technologies. Most technologies are being developed with home as the main target site. Four different industries are now viewing home as their target of attack - the telecommunications industry, the information industry, the computer industry, and the entertainment industry.
4. Development of the concept of smart home or intelligent home. The development of prototypes makes this a new reality within the grasp of residential architects, technology developers, and town planners. The 21st century has suddenly become a reality.
5. Why has the home become the main target? There is no one single or main reason. There are many forces and some key ones are mentioned here.

2.3.1   From the technology side, what was considered˜ speculative or idle fancy (fantasy?) has suddenly become a real possibility

The convergence of many technologies is rapidly occurring. It is now possible as never before to link computers, communications, telephone, and entertainment technologies. As a result of cross-over technologies, new possibilities have emerged.

New information technologies have been introduced into the home successfully - e.g. the answering machine and the fax - paving the way for similar introductions. New electronic services are also becoming available, video-on-demand, home shopping, home banking, and home financial management (see excursus below for a full description of the emerging technologies). As a result of cross-over technologies, we find that companies are leaving their traditional business areas seeking unfamiliar territories for exploration. Apple (computers) is now getting into multimedia, AT&T (telecommunications) is getting into entertainment, Philips (entertainment and consumer electronics) is now moving into smart homes, CBS (Broadcasting) is trying to move into home shopping and so on.

Excursus: **Information Highway, Multimedia, Virtual Reality and Interactivity**

Note: This section is based on a review of selective recent literature: Biocca (1992), Brody (1993), Davids (1994), Egan (1991), Fetterman/Gupta (1993), Goble (1994), Grant (1991), Lee (1993), Macdonald/Shneiderman (1994), Schatz/Hardin (1994), Science (1994), Taubes (1994), Warwick/Gray/Roberts (1993), Ziegler (1994).

Information Highway

The information highway is a powerful electronic network capable of delivering vast amounts of data and entertainment to businesses, households and other publics which in turn can be inter-connected. An ultimate global connection will link various national markets on a real-time basis. The highway is in the early stages of planning but some existing links will form the foundation for a full-fledged construction that might take anywhere from ten to fifteen years for completion. As part of the information highway, multimedia, interactivity, and virtual environments are the mechanisms for delivering image, text and sound data in which the user interacts with the databases using a combination of the television, the telephone, and the personal computer.

The information high way consists of many facilities and systems; data compression and storage, servers, the conduit (e.g. fiber optics), the user interface (TV or PC), the set top box (multimedia converter), and communication systems for correspondence, voice mail and video images.

Below are some brief descriptions of multimedia, virtual reality, and interactivity. These are not mutually exclusive and highly inter-dependent in terms of their structure and scope.

Multimedia

Multimedia refers to electronic data processing technology that can combine several functions: text processing systems to format and prepare text documents; text retrieval systems to find a document from a set of documents; database management systems to store and retrieve a structured data; special systems to handle animations, images, video ands sound. Usually, the access to such technological functions involves a computer with telecommunication facilities (telephone, cable TV). In the absence of a computer, a television set can be used as the main interface for accessing these various functions. From the technology side the construction of multimedia requires an infrastructure that is at its very elementary stages of development. This is the reason why the Information superhighway has been proposed. Multimedia resources are very expensive to produce and require capital expenditures that only a few organizations can make. They also require the expertise of several disciplines. For example, in a smart home project now in progress in Copenhagen, Denmark, over a hundred companies are involved. They require highly specialized tools. Systems that integrate various multimedia functions are still under development, but the technology is moving very fast.

Multimedia technologies can combine the elements of the artificial world with the elements of the real world. The elements of the artificial world are text, graphics, and animation. The elements of the real world are audio, image and other sensual experiences.

Multimedia industry is extremely fragmented. One can see small operations of ten people to 500 people. There is nothing to say that the bigger organizations have an advantage in this industry. Conventional organizational theories do not hold in terms of growth and sustainability. New theories are not available to suggest what patterns work and which ones do not. Therefore, there is a lot of experimentation in both practice and theorizing.

Virtual Reality

Virtual reality is a set of computer technologies which, when combined, provide an interface to the computer with which the user can believe he or she is actually in a computer-generated world. This computer-generated world could be model of a real-world object such as a house not yet been built or currently existing, or it might be any abstract world or simulated real world. The computer interface provided by virtual reality is three-dimensional. The world or model to be viewed by the user is apparently real, completely surrounding the user, and responds appropriately to the user's natural motion and interactions. The user is led to believe that the model being viewed is real.

Two key concepts of virtual reality are immersion and interaction. The user must feel immersed in the virtual environment, and must be able to interact with the world using hands, arms, head and legs. Without both immersion and interaction, the user will not readily believe that the world is real, and will not gain the same depth of understanding of the model or data. Virtual reality incorporates much human aspects engineering which maximizes its impact on human senses and perceptions. The technology was born from the merging of many disciplines including psychology, cybernetics, computer graphics, data base design, real-time and distributed systems, electronics, robotics, multimedia, and telepresence.

Interactivity

Interactivity refers to the active participatory role of the individual in computer-based virtual and multimedia environments. The traditional electronic media, radio and television are non-interactive media. The first interactivity began with the introduction of VCRs and remote control switches for the TV. But they are interactive in a very limited sense for they do not change the environments in any significant way. Another early example of interactivity are the video games but games are not real environments although they are very interactive. Telephone is the only true long-standing interactive technology but it is limited to voice-to-voice interface.

Fetterman and Gupta (1993) have identified four types of interactivity based on space-time displacements. The spatial displacement model defines interactivity when it takes place at the same time but across different spatial zones. The best example of this is the telephone. The second model is the temporal displacement model where interactivity takes place at different times but within the same space. This is a shared communication environment. The third type is both temporal and spatial displacement where messages are stored and forwarded through electronic media. All kinds of computer based communications fall into this category. The last type is where there is no displacement of either space or time. The best example of this is the face-to-face communication. This type of communication is also is being incorporated into shared electronic space and real-time environments. The digital technology can now accommodate virtual environments as if the participants are communicating face-to-face.

Interactivity in current parlance means the real world participation of the individual by establishing simultaneous or sequential communication with the source of communication in the context of multimedia. The word source of communication is somewhat meaningless because the initiator could be at either end of the communication chain.

According to various industry sources and academic researchers the following areas have been identified as having an impact because of the new technologies and electronic media: Teleworking/telecommuting, Home Entertainment, Education, Tele-shopping/Home shopping (Grant 1991), Telecommunications, Home Computing/Home Management. In no sense are these areas to be considered mutually exclusive or exhaustive. Here is a brief description of how these areas are developing and will continue to develop.

Teleworking: This refers to work at home. Our own research (1990, 1992) shows that this a growing activity largely aided by computers at home. In our research, we identified five different types of teleworking, telecommuters who substitute working at home for commuting to work, moonlighters who work on different jobs from their primary employment during weekends or evenings, supplemental workers who work at home in addition to full time work, self-employed people who use the home as their business, and part-timers who work at home for outside organizations on contract work.

Home Entertainment: Includes two principle services, movies-on-demand and video games. Many industry experts believe that this will be the most commercially successful market among interactive services. The reason for this is that home entertainment via TV and VCR is already well established and also because of the low level effort involved by the user.

Teleshopping: Teleshopping promises consumers the ability to purchase goods and services through the TV set. This is still in a development stage although some companies are quite successful in the home shopping business, Home Shopping Network and QVC. There also have been some failures, as evidenced by the closing down of J.C. Penney's interactive shopping system and Sears Roebuck's joint venture with IBM on Prodigy Services Corporation.

Telecommunications: This is a rapidly growing area especially with possible integration of the telephone, personal computer, and television. Some already existing facilities include, computerized fax systems, electronic mail, and telemedicine.

Computing in the Home: This was a promised land in the eighties and while the growth has been slow, it seems to be coming on its own. Currently, computer services, such as, Prodigy, America On-line, and Compuserve are pushing their services aggressively.

Internet: This refers to electronic networking of individuals with other individuals and organizations on a one-to-one basis or simultaneously.

Home Management and Intelligent Home Systems: The user is granted convenience and control over appliances and electrical equipment in the home through interactive systems, thus minimizing manual operations. There are three functional categories in the home system: interactive smart products, intelligent subsystems, and central home automation systems. This is at a very experimental stage and requires the integration of computers, fiber optics, multimedia capabilities, where data, voice, and visual communications come together.

2.3.2 Globally speaking...

The idea that the world is becoming a global village, (an idea 10-15 years ago was an idle chat) has now become less fanciful. It is now possible for any two sites in the world, however remote they might be and however undeveloped they might be in terms of their industrial profile, to establish contact with each other, and to transmit symbols and images across the globe. Many communities which have remained isolated and technologically primitive are suddenly brought into the electronic age without having to tread the conventional technological paths.

Many information technology oriented companies or information technology dependent companies are able to move freely across the globe and set up their production facilities wherever they wish. Information technologies require information oriented labor. Information labor was historically expensive because it required high degree of technical skills and specialized university training. In the past, that is, in the 80s, in advanced industrial countries, such labor was most expensive and although companies may have had the technical feasibility it was not easy to employ such labor. Or, they had to import labor and that was also expensive because they had to comply with local industrial wage standards.

Now things have changed. First, a majority of technical skills are now available in low wage countries - e.g. China, India, Mexico, and Eastern Europe. Second, there is no need to import labor from these countries. The companies can themselves move their operations and easily establish them in many of the developing countries. With the collapse of communism and the cold war, countries which were not accessible to American/Western companies are now available with their technical talent. With old political ideologies disappearing and with them, all kinds of barriers, the so called closed societies are opening up for new international cooperation and business ventures.

Companies like Motorola and Texas Instruments which are pioneers in information technologies are setting up facilities in these new markets. Companies which are not producers of information technologies but major users are also taking similar steps. For example, Swissair and Singapore airlines are moving some facilities to developing countries for similar reasons.

2.3.3 New commercial possibilities

In order for technologies to develop, there must be a potential for commercial success. Many companies and large transnational corporations are now entering the information technology business or information business. With new realities, the meanings of the terms, information technology and information are changing dramatically. First the character of their business is changing because of the developments in the information technologies. It is becoming an imperative as well as attractive for many companies to link their future with the development in information technologies. First, the commercial opportunities are opening up in ways hitherto unforeseen. Second, the costs of technology are dropping dramatically and this is making it attractive for companies to enter the business.

2.3.4 People's use of information/communication technologies as everyday experiences...

The general public is now exposed to greater computerization than ever before. Whether it is the work environments, schools, airports, shopping malls, supermarkets, banks, all kinds of everyday activities are now performed using computer based technologies. The convergence of information and telecommunication technologies is now taking place without much fanfare, with much more of it to come. The 1990s are appearing more and more like the information society discussed in the speculative literature of the past. The information revolution has arrived unnoticed but bringing fundamental transformation in our society.

We are also seeing a whole generation of young children growing up with computers. There are many two year olds and three year olds using computers as if the computers are part of their world of toys and play accessories.

2.3.5 The government has joined the fray...

The US government has also stepped in to develop a new industrial policy around information technology. The "information highway" which was recently declared by no less a person than Al Gore (US Vice-President) as the next technological frontier is the first sign that there is a collective pressure to generate and nurture a new public culture of information. This may sound a bit like the "space exploration to the moon" project of the 1960s, but it also demonstrates how communities or societies make conscious decisions regarding their goals and objectives and how they marshal their collective resources towards achieving them.

Driven by global competition and other economic pressures, both domestic and from abroad, coupled with the realization that technological resources and talent are available at unprecedented levels, the decline of cold war and the freeing of resources, the concerted move toward creating an information society is to be viewed as the most serious effort to date in this direction.

As a historical comparison, we can liken this new scenario to the development of the automobile industry and the telephone industry, both of which have revolutionized American life styles and culture. In sum, in the ten years since we started our early studies much has happened and much is happening. We are strategically situated to investigate these changes as reflected in the new technological culture.

3   Postmodernism

Although this is not a place for a long discussion on postmodernism, some key ideas will be presented here with implications to marketing communications and advertising. Readers are referred to recent articles (Domzal/Kernan 1993, Firat/Venkatesh 1993, Firat/Dholakia/Venkatesh 1995, Sherry 1991) for elaborate treatment of postmodern concepts.

In many ways marketing represents the essence of the ongoing transition to postmodernity. As we discussed in our earlier work (Firat/Venkatesh 1993, Firat/Dholakia/Venkatesh 1995), in postmodernity, the boundaries between the market organization-customer, consumer-worker, individual-institution have begun to blur. The period of modernist dichotomies is coming to an end as we begin to enter the postmodern era. The long established dichotomies that separated the production processes from the consumption processes, work from leisure, economy from culture, male from female (as a socially gendered category although not a biological category), functional from the symbolic, center from the margins, domestic from the global, real from the artificial, and substance from form, are all dissolving either into new dichotomies are new forms of postmodern realities. The earlier social order and our cultural experiences were predicated upon these dichotomies. We are now witnessing some fundamental changes in our society. For example, the male-female distinction is changing with the changing roles. This has also altered the shape of our work force and our notions of work culture. With the new technologies of information and telecommunication our work and leisure processes are also changing. With the emergence of virtual reality and virtual environments, our concepts of reality are also changing. Postmodernists use the term hyperreal for our new visions of reality. Similarly, the categories of producer and consumer are being altered as more and more consumers are producing and reproducing new symbols of consumption and reconstructing their roles as consumers. The distinction between private and public is also subject to change as our social mores undergo modifications. Finally, the whole movement toward globalization in production and consumption patterns are effacing national boundaries and cultural barriers.

Many of the above changes are being accelerated by the emergence of new technologies of information and telecommunications. Computers are making it possible for people to work at home or from remote locations. Here we see both spatial and temporal displacements never encountered before. Because of the new technologies, new forms of culture are emerging. MTV is a case in point. The entire MTV revolution has altered our conceptions of entertainment for entertainment has become both hypervisual and televisual. MTV has no parallel in real life and is the best definition of a virtual environment. Recent developments in Las Vegas using extremely powerful cinematic-technological effects to produce new vistas of historical detail have received much attention not only because of their tourist interest but because of their virtual character.

Underlying the relationship between postmodern consciousness and information technology is a profound relationship between ontology (our view of reality) and technology. One feeds on the other incessantly. As technology creates new realities, virtual and interactive, postmodernism provides a framework within which such realities can be grasped and understood. Many of our postmodern sensibilities are concretized through technological possibilities. The fragmented subject which is a constant theme in advertising images is not simply a technological gimmickry but a redefinition of our notions of the individual subject. Similarly, the postmodern notion of hyperreality - which is a paradoxical notion that there are things which are more real than the real - is possible because the technology of multimedia and visual environments have realized it. In a remarkable way, our cultural ethos, the social order and economic behaviors are shaped simultaneously by the products of our postmodern sensibilities and technological possibilities.

4   A new paradigm for advertising

In figure 2, the proposed model looks at advertising in postmodern terms. The whole picture of communications changes because of the assumptions we have to make based on new realities.

With the arrival of new technologies of communication and information and the postmodern conceptions of reality, a new paradigm needs to be considered.
1. Instead of considering the individual on two dimensions, cognitive (information processing) and emotional, we introduce two more dimensions, the semiotic or linguistic dimension, and the interactive-experiential dimension.
2. Instead of viewing the communication model based on one-to-many (the producer of the product to a mass of consumers), we consider alternative models such as one-to-one, or many-to-one, or many-to-many.
3. The mediating technologies in the earlier model were print, radio, and television which basically reflected the one-to-many model. With the introduction of multimedia, virtual reality, and interactivity, we should be able to accommodate more participatory models of consumer response.

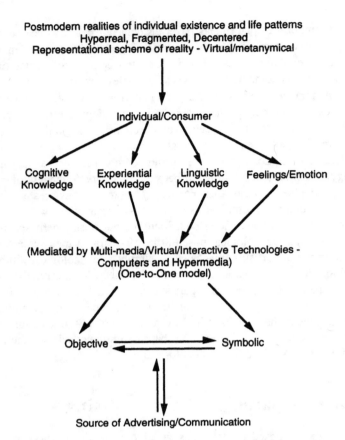

Fig. 2.   New (postmodern) paradigm for advertising/marketing communications

4. In the previous model (see figure 1), it is assumed that the source of communication is the producer but in the current model, the source can be the consumer.

5. The previous model also assumes that advertising is a companion function to marketing that in that it stimulates interest in the consumer to purchase the product after being exposed to the ad. There is thus a spatial and temporal displacement of purchase, where as in the current model no such implicit or explicit assumption exists. The product advertisement can appear at the same time that the purchase is also influenced. The best current example of this model is the infomercial where a number of products are advertised and the consumer is given the opportunity to buy the product at the same time. Thus the advertising function is combined with the sales and distribution function in an interactive mode.

6. Virtual reality environments can also make it possible for consumers to engage in certain product experiences as if they are real-world experiences.

7. The proposed model has a different symbolic scheme. Instead of the representational scheme of the earlier model where advertising attempts to

represent reality but in an idealized fashion, in the proposed model advertising operates metanymically where images and messages are interspersed in a world of virtual reality. Virtual reality is an "as if reality" and unabashedly so. The consumer enacts the virtual environments. The traditional technologies of mass communication are based on metaphorical representational schemes where reality is meant to be represented by the mediating technologies as realistically as possible. But with the changing notions of the real and the artificial, the models of consumer response cannot remain the same.

8. The technological environment is changing fast. Technologies are personalized instead of being massified. They are also democratized as in the case of Internet, fragmented and decentralized in a postmodern sense. In fact the best embryonic model of the new technology is the telephone and not the traditional radio or television, but it never realized its potential, until now. The personal computer has come into the picture as the new personal communication technology par excellence. Coupled with telephony it has assumed a key position in the new technological development. Secondly, the earlier model of advertising was based on the notions of perishable information partly because of the nature of the media. But now, we find that information is more archival, data-base centered, non-perishable, and storable.

The computers are networked which means individual consumers can communicate with many other consumers electronically, via bulletin boards and Internet. In fact computer networks are being replaced by networking in an information space.

5   Conclusions

In this paper, we have attempted to show that our ideas of advertising need to undergo radical revision in view of the emerging technologies. Apparently, this feeling is shared by many practitioners who have come to realize that business cannot go an as usual. As academic researchers, we can contribute to this process of change with new ideas and paradigms.

References

Belch, G. E., Belch, M. S., Introduction to Advertising and Promotion Management, Homewood, IL, Irwin, 1990

Biocca, F., Virtual Reality Technology: A Tutorial, in: Journal of Communication, Vol. 42, No. 4, August 1992, pp. 23-72

Bjerg, K., Borreby, K. (eds.), Home Informatics and Telematics & Automation, Proceedings of the Home Informatics Conference, Copenhagen, June-July 1994

Blattberg, R. C., Glazer, R., Little, J. D. C., The Marketing Information Revolution, Harvard Business School Press, 1994

Brody, H., Information Highway: The Home Front, in: Technology Review, August/September 1993, pp. 31-40

Davids, M., The Interactive Evolution, in: The Journal of Business Strategy, Vol. 15, No. 4, July 1994, pp. 52-54

Dholakia, R. R., Even PC Men Won't Shop by Computer, in: American Demographics, May 1994, p. 11

Dholakia, N., Dholakia, R. R., The Challenge of High Technology to Marketing, in: McTavish, R. (ed.), Linking Marketing and Technology Strategies, Chicago, American Marketing Association, pp. 29-32

Dholakia, R. R., Mundorf, N., Dholakia, N. (eds.), Information Technology in the Home: Demand Side Perspectives, Lawrence Erlbaum Associates, 1995

Dholakia, R. R., Dholakia, N., Multimedia Technologies in the American Home: Prospects and Challenges Ahead, in: Bjerg, K., Borreby, K. (eds.), Home-Oriented Informatics Telematics & Automation, Copenhagen University Press, 1994, pp. 29-42

Domzal, T. J., Kernan, J. B., Mirror, Mirror: Some Postmodern Reflections on Global Advertising, in: Journal of Advertising, Vol. XXII, No. 4, December 1993, pp. 1-20

Egan, B. L., Information Superhighways: The Economics of Advanced Public Communications Networks, Boston, MA, Arttech House, 1991

Escobar, A., Welcome to Cyberia: Notes on the Anthropology of Cyberculture, in: Current Anthropology, Vol. 35, No. 3, June 1994, pp. 211-231

Fetterman, R. L., Gupta, S. K., Mainstream Multimedia: Applying Multimedia in Business, Van Nostrand and Reingold, 1993

Firat, A. F., Venkatesh, A., Postmodernity: The Age of Marketing, in: International Journal of Research in Marketing, Vol. 10, September 1993, pp. 227-249

Firat, A. F., Dholakia, N., Venkatesh, A., Marketing in a Postmodern World, in: European Journal of Marketing, Vol. 29, 1995, No. 1, pp. 40-56

Goble, C., Multimedia Information Systems: The Confluence of Technologies and Disciplines, in: Information and Software Technology, Vol. 36, 1994, No. 4, 195-196

Grant, A. E., Guthrie, K. K., Ball-Rokeach, S. J., Television Shopping: A Media System Dependency Perspective, in: Communications Research, Vol. 18, No. 6, December 1991, pp. 773-798

Katz, H., How Major US Advertising Agencies Are Coping With Data Overload, in: Journal of Advertising Research, Vol. 31, No. 1, Feb./March 1991, pp. 7-16

Lee, J. K., Towards the Information Superhighway, in: Telecommunications Policy, November 1993, pp. 631-635

MacDonald, L., Shneiderman, J., Interacting With Virtual Environments, New York, John Wiley & Sons, 1994

Schatz, B. R., Hardin, J. B., NCSA Mosaic and the World Wide Web: Global Hypermedia Protocols for the Internet, in: Science, Vol. 265, 1994, August 12, pp. 895-901

Science, Vol. 265, 1994, August 12, Special Issue on Computer Networks and Modeling

Shiver, J., Survey Finds 1 in 3 Homes Has a Computer, in: Los Angeles Times, 1994, May 28, pp. D1-D5

Taubes, G., Taking the Data in Hand - Literally - With Virtual Reality, in: Science, Vol. 265, 1994, August 12, pp. 884-886

Venkatesh, A., Cultural Dimensions of Household Technology Adoption, in: Bjerg, K., Borreby, K. (eds.), Home-Oriented Informatics Telematics & Automation, Copenhagen University Press, 1994

Venkatesh, A., Vitalari, N., Computing Technology for the Home: Strategies for the Next Generation, in: Journal of Product Innovation and Management, Vol. 3, No. 3, September 1986, pp. 171-186

Venkatesh, A., Vitalari, N., A Post-adoption Analysis of Computing in the Home, in: Journal of Economic Psychology, Vol. 8, June 1987, pp. 161-180

Venkatesh, A., Vitalari, N., A Longitudinal Analysis of Computing in the Home, in: National Science Foundation Report, Center for Research on Information Technology in Organizations, University of California, Irvine, 1990

Venkatesh, A., Vitalari, N., An Emergent Distributed Work Arrangement: An Investigation of Computer-Based Supplemental Work at Home, in: Management Science, Vol. 38, No. 12, December 1992, pp. 1687-1706

Warwick, K., Gray, J., Roberts, D. (eds.), Virtual Reality in Engineering, The Institution of Electrical Engineers, UK, 1993

Yahn, S., Advertising's Grave New World, in: Advertising Age, 1994, May 16, p. 1, p. 53

Ziegler, B., Building the Highway: New Obstacles, New Solutions, in: Wall Street Journal, 1994, May 18, p. B1

Seven Theses on Successful Market Development for Home Management Systems

Kai Howaldt and Mirko-Stefan Jeck
Roland Berger & Partner GmbH, International Management Consultants, Germany

1   Introduction

Roland Berger & Partner have worked in the area of home management for about three years. Two issues have always come up during the intensive discussions with companies involved in this sector:

- The technical problems of home automation have more or less been solved.
- Nevertheless, the discussions within and between companies have been carried out almost exclusively on a technical level.

In Roland Berger & Partner's opinion, the time has come to shift the focus of discussion to marketing and sales, in order to develop the market for existing technical solutions.

There are great chances for the companies involved. However, for successful market entry, a number of factors have to be taken into consideration.

We have summarised the most important ones in seven theses:

1. Despite many similarities, facility management and home management are not comparable businesses.
2. The market for home automation must be created - in this connection it is not the technical feasibility but the customer benefits that are decisive.
3. The market for home automation will polarise: only simple or comprehensive modular systems will be successful.
4. Standardisation will be achieved by establishing de facto standards.
5. Intensive internal and external collaboration with clear system leadership is a fundamental requirement for success.
6. The necessary marketing structures for market penetration still need to be developed.
7. Service providers and innovative appliance manufacturers will be the winners.

2   Thesis 1: Despite many similarities, facility management and home management are not comparable businesses

The technology of the building automation of the 90ies cannot be compared with that of the past. Development in industrial and commercial buildings has progressed tremendously fast. The rapid advances in microelectronics have revolutionised the installation, use and operation of electrical facilities and the technical fittings. During the course of building automation, the various systems have been integrated into a superior control and monitoring system. These include the heating, air-conditioning and ventilation systems, lighting, blinds, elevators and security systems. In this area the process control system assumes the central monitoring, control and optimisation of all technical installations. This requires modern bus systems which make two-way communication possible between the various subsystems.

When external services, such as maintenance, cleaning, security and administration are included, building automation changes from being an integrated system into an integrated problem solution. Building automation becomes facility management.

Since the mid-80ies, similar concepts have been under discussion for use in the private sector: home automation. Home automation is the name given to the communicative networking of the most varied kinds of appliances and systems in the private household, their software controlled programming and intelligent control. In addition to the systems mentioned above which are the focus of automation in industrial and commercial buildings, there are additional integration fields in home automation such as household appliances, consumer electronics and telecommunication.

External services also play an important role within the wider concept of *home management*, which involves more technical services such as load management and telemetering as well as service hotlines and maintenance services. Additionally, other services such as security and emergency services, interactive entertainment services, home banking, home shopping and home office applications are gaining ground.

Whilst building automation is being increasingly used in industrial and commercial buildings, home automation is still in the early stages of development. It is necessary to reckon with a lag of approximately five to ten years between the two. This is due to business-specific differences, which hinder similar marketing methods for the two applications.

Despite their common technological basis, namely intelligent networking via modern bus systems, home automation and building automation fall into two clearly different business categories, due to the different areas they serve. Whilst building automation primarily shows the characteristics of an custom-made orders business and a commercial buyer structure, home automation shows definite characteristics of classic system business as well as a predominantly private buyer structure.

The two business categories demand individual marketing strategies that differ accordingly. By means of a generally closed system, building automation systems provide an individual problem solution for large buildings predominantly in the industrial and commercial sector. The development of specific systems is done jointly by several manufacturers. Sale is mostly direct, without using a distribution agent.

Building automation systems are marked by their investment-type character. For the investor, operational efficiency and complexity reduction are of prime importance. Professional personnel, who have comprehensive access possibilities to the system, are usually in charge of its operation.

Home automation systems are mainly conceived as open systems. They are based on equipment compatibility (all brands) and can easily be upgraded by integrating additional functional modules. Home automation, with its standardised modular system concept is aimed at a mass market which with the relevant volume allows for cost degressive effects. For the penetration of a mass market, wide distribution through various forms of sales agents is necessary.

However, the home automation systems are consumer goods. The manageability of the system is of great significance, since unlike the professional operators of building automation systems, no comparable technical competence can be expected of private users.

They are marked by their multidimensional benefit concepts. A difference should be made here between functional benefits such as operational efficiency, safety and comfort and emotional aspects, such as prestige or ecology. As a consequence, targeted end user communication will represent an important success factor. It will be necessary to convey segment specific benefit concepts to each of the target groups using specific communication strategies.

3   Thesis 2: The market for home automation must be created - in this connection it is not the technical feasibility but the customer benefits that are decisive

The integration of technical applications, systems and services in home automation offer the consumer a wide range of benefits, both functional and emotional. The development of home automation systems must be orientated towards these advantages, or needs of the consumer. The mistake often made by developing everything that is technically possible is, that it ignores client needs and leads to the creation of unmarketable products.

Although varying according to the applications, first user surveys have on the whole already shown very positive results concerning the various benefits (see fig. 1). Nevertheless, the needs and preferences differ significantly in Europe, depending on the countries and the various user groups.

Application	Evaluation
Lighting and blind control	+
Heating and ventilation control	+ + +
Load management	+ + +
Monitoring / Malfunction indication	+ +
Small device control	+
Entertainment system (A/V)	+
Closed-Circuit-TV / Entrance control	+
Security system	+ + +
Remote control (external)	+ +
Services (home shopping, home banking, Information)	+ +

Source: Roland Berger & Partner

Fig. 1. Evaluation of home automation applications by the user

Whilst the average consumer is still unaware of the multidimensional benefits, social trends indicate that there will be an increasing demand for home automation applications in future.

Hence, it is expected that the rise in the number of single and double income households will produce a greater interest in the possibilities of external remote control of individual systems in the household, since there will usually be nobody at home during the day. In the growing seniors' segment, it can be supposed that, due to the restricted mobility of old people, there will be a particular demand on their part for operating facility and remote control of technical applications in the household. At the same time, the sensitive health and the special need old people have for security will provide a demand for the relevant emergency systems.

In addition to these demographic developments, another trend is becoming apparent: the home will gain new importance as a social centre. This will be linked to a withdrawal to one's own home (cocooning). On the one hand, this will lead to demand regarding comfort and a comprehensive supply of entertainment and information in the house, on the other to requirements regarding prestige as the house gains in importance and becomes an object to be shown off. The wish for multimedia entertainment or effective lighting systems could also be seen in connection with a growing need for action and adventure.

Growing ecological awareness will strongly affect considerations regarding the introduction of energy management systems. Finally, the rising crime rate will lead to a greater demand for security systems.

All these trends will slowly break down the unquestionable resistance the majority of consumers has at present to increased technology in the home. What is more, a generation is now growing up, whose familiarity with technology and in particular computers is quite different from that of today's generation of buyers.

Therefore, if home automation is linked to the clearly growing benefit for the user, although this is not yet perceived by the average consumer, the market can be developed by supplier activities.

The reasons explaining why this growing benefit is not yet being perceived are rather obvious:

- Since the current systems only cover rudimentary applications, the current additional benefit which can be achieved is low.
- Details of the additional benefit are not being communicated and the issue of home automation is not associated in any way with a positive image or prestige value: The end user has insufficient information as well as a negative attitude.
- The current systems are only distributed through a small number of outlets.

It would consequently be possible for the manufacturers to develop the market by rectifying these deficiencies:

- A closed technical solution has to be offered.
- Comprehensive, consistent market preparation and communication has to be provided.
- The manufacturers have to combine efforts in marketing and distribution.

In other words: the market has to be created.

4   Thesis 3: The market for home automation will polarise: only simple or comprehensive modular systems will be successful

The decision of the users for or against a home automation system will be determined by a cost-benefit calculation. On the cost side, the application-related and current costs (hard- and software and maintenance respectively) and especially the system fixed costs of planning and installation, the installation material and the network components (control units and user interfaces) will be the main deciding factors.

On the other hand there are the additional functional and emotional benefits. The network itself does not provide any benefits for the user. With the integration of different applications, systems and services, the entire benefit of the system is the sum obtained when adding together all realisable application-related partial benefits.

The cost-benefit analysis provides differing results regarding the various system categories.

Simple systems mainly include on and off functions. They do not normally require any specific network installation. The communication tends to be between equipment and a central control unit via the existing electricity supply. The system configuration goes into operation automatically after the equipment has been plugged into the main netline ("plug and play"). These simple systems enable comparably high realisable benefit increases with minimum system fixed costs and show overall a positive cost-benefit result.

In comparison, *limited systems* offer extended performance capability in the form of complex and flexible control and optimisation programmes. However, they are limited to individual applications and demand a specific installation, which has to be carried out by specialists. This system-related installation needed for limited systems entails considerable costs, which may not be compensated by related benefits.

Comprehensive systems also demand a specific network and its professional installation. They integrate a variety of technical applications and external services like those already mentioned for home management. Therefore, they involve considerable initial investment and corresponding costs. However, based on the variety of applications which can be integrated there is, after addition of the partial benefits, an overall positive cost-benefit result, irrespective whether many partial benefits are realised straight away or integrated later as part of a modular system.

The above-mentioned observations show that simple or comprehensive systems have the best market chances, whilst the limited systems have to be regarded more critically (see fig. 2).

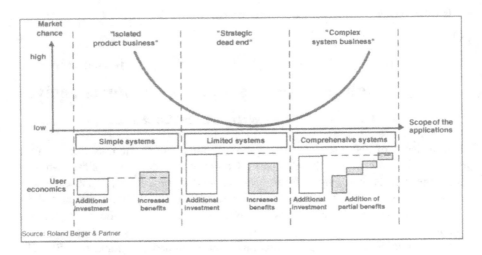

Fig. 2.   Market potential by system categories

5   Thesis 4: Standardisation will be achieved by establishing de facto standards

The ability to communicate between different appliances and systems demands a uniform communication protocol. The interoperability of the appliances of various manufacturers can only be guaranteed on the basis of a joint standard regarding the format of the data transfer and the kind of commands to be transferred. In the triad markets (America, Europe and Japan) individual companies and consortiums throughout all branches of industry have developed various standards (see fig. 3).

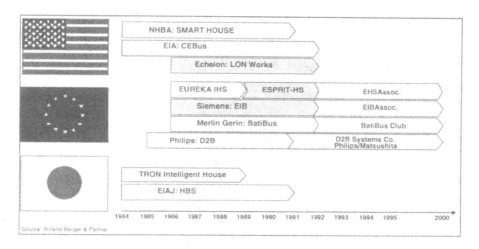

Fig. 3.   Examples of home automation standards in the triad markets

As yet no uniform standard has been able to establish itself in any of these triad markets. In Europe, there are currently three important stardardisation approaches being used for home automation: the ESPRIT Home Systems (HS) Standard, supported mainly by consumer electronics and appliance manufacturers and promoted by the EU, the EIBus Standard, favoured by electricians, already used - like Bati Bus- in building automation, as well as the LON Works standard developed in the computer industry, which is also used in other application fields besides home automation such as industrial production and automotive electronics.

Since all the efforts by the standards' commissions to define a uniform European standard have been unsuccessful till now, not in small part due to the opposing interests involved, the European standard will probably not be determined by these commissions. The diffusion of standards is more likely to be carried out by the establishment of de facto standards.

Examples of this can be seen in various branches, for example the establishment of the VHS Video standard or the MS-DOS operating system. These examples show - as does the as yet unsuccessful attempt to establish the digital compact cassette or the HDTV - that a few important success factors have to be taken into account when establishing de facto standards.

The fusion of markets in the home automation market which have mostly been quite separate until now will alter the rules of the game in the market and lead to uncertainty on the part of all market participants, especially the users. It will only be possible to diminish it with the clear commitment of all the companies involved.

The successful establishment of a standard therefore requires the prompt development of a system platform and a comprehensive application package as well as the implementation of first reference installations. It is only with the collaboration of companies from various industries that a comprehensive system can be established.

Fast market penetration demands intensive and coordinated market processing of all important decision makers. In the case of home automation, besides trade and users, these include in particular installers, planners and architects. As the VHS example shows in particular, the establishment of a de facto standard is also supported by general licencing. The conception of a home automation system as an open system and the granting of licences to component manufacturers and software providers will consequently play an important role.

A pioneer position reached in this way would create high market entry barriers: first, the companies involved would dispose of strategic contacts to important influential parties and decision makers. Secondly, switching between different home automation standards generally entails considerable costs for the end user. With the first system installation, therefore, a close client tie would be achieved.

6   Thesis 5: Intensive internal and external collaboration with clear system leadership is a fundamental requirement for success

In order to exploit the market potential of comprehensive home automation systems, tremendous inter-company collaboration is necessary.

It is only with the collaboration of companies from various industries that a system can be developed which offers adequate consumer benefits in return for the required investments and related costs for the customer (see fig. 4). Additionally, the necessary research and development costs and unavoidable investment risks would be unacceptable for one company even if it had the necessary competence available.

The companies involved in the development of home automation systems can be divided into four categories: the appliance manufacturers, the manufacturers of network intelligence, the component manufacturers and the service providers.

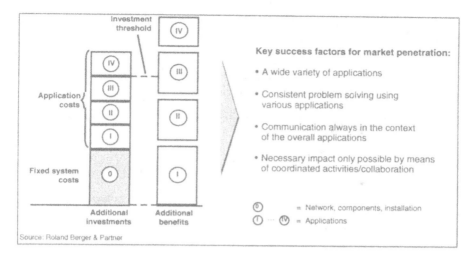

Key success factors for market penetration:

- A wide variety of applications

- Consistent problem solving using various applications

- Communication always in the context of the overall applications

- Necessary impact only possible by means of coordinated activities/collaboration

Fig. 4.   Principle of the addition of partial benefits

The appliance manufacturers include the suppliers of heating, air-conditioning and ventilation systems, security and alarm systems, household appliances, consumer electronics, telecommunication terminals and personal computers.

The group of manufacturers of network intelligence include micro-chip producers and other hardware suppliers (feature controllers) as well as software suppliers.

Component manufacturers primarily supply installation material and measuring instruments (sensor technology).

Among the service providers, there are a variety of heterogeneous branches and companies such as energy suppliers, security services, charity associations, customer service centers, department stores, publishing houses, banks and collection services.

The individual groups are involved in the developing and marketing process in the most varied of ways. These encompass five main fields of cooperation: the basic concept, research and development, marketing, sales and customer service.

Whilst all the groups are to be involved in the R&D process, the customer-related functions of marketing, sales and customer service as well as the formulation of a basic concept will demand the closest collaboration of appliance manufacturers and service providers. These already have direct access to the end users and offer the real benefit with their applications in the system network.

Finally, it will be necessary to assign a system leader in order to coordinate all the activities. The function of a system leader can only be carried out by a large and diversified company (see fig. 5).

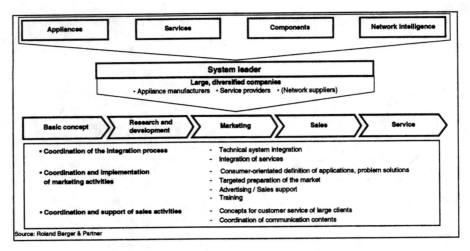

Fig. 5.   Tasks of the system leader

For the successful development of the new market of home automation, it is not only external cooperation that will be necessary. There will also be a considerable need for interfunctional coordination within the companies involved as well as cooperation between the product and business areas involved, especially in very diversified corporations. The entry into system business will demand a rethinking process on the part of all the staff. They will have to think in terms of integrative problem solutions instead of product concepts and the organisational structure of the company will have to take this into account.

There are three main organisational forms which would be appropriate: project organisation, system head organisation and system divisional organisation.

Project organisation will involve a temporary merging of key managers into an interfunctional and interdivisional project team. In addition, the project team will be able to involve relevant staff from the company. The project organisation presents a flexible organisational form, which will be particularly attractive in the initial stages.

The *system head organisation* encompasses critical functions such as development and marketing in one independent organisational unit. Relevant staff from "non critical" functions will be temporarily involved. The system head organisation controls the system design and the preparation of the market entry concept like an internal system manager. It is therefore particularly suitable for the market development phase.

All the system-related functions such as R&D, production, marketing, sales and service will be brought together within the *system divisional organisation* as one business area: home automation. Interdependences vis-à-vis other product or business areas are to be internalised as far as possible, in order to guarantee the required autonomy. The divisional organisation assumes the further development of system-related marketing strategies and their operative implementation. In this respect, it is the best choice for the marketing phase, in particular for the penetration of the mass market.

7   Thesis 6: The necessary marketing structures for market penetration still need to be developed

Successful marketing vis-à-vis the end user demands a closed market appearance in the form of *one* contact partner for the potential clients. It is not acceptable for the client if he/she has to bring together all the necessary services connected with consultation, planning, installation and the operation of a home automation system. For this purpose, a system integrator will be required to organise a product and service pack of the various market participants such as the appliance manufacturers, the service providers, the architects and installers. He provides the application support, the system configuration and installation, the customer service as well as the administrative operating functions (see fig. 6).

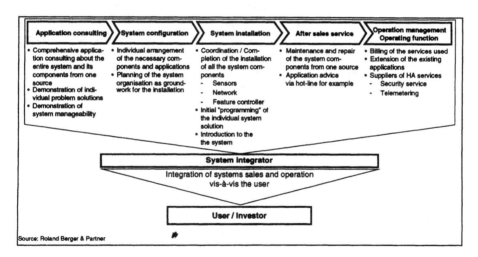

Fig. 6.   Value added chain of the system integrator

With a view to the creation of marketing structures, it must clearly be defined who is to assume the function of a system integrator vis-à-vis the end user in future. Basically, all of the market participants mentioned until now could be considered as well as completely new service providers such as companies specialised in customised packages in these tasks. Whoever assumes these functions is going to need considerable support from the supplier, the system manager. The development of the corresponding tools, ranging from the hot-line and planning support right to the training course, is an important basis for the successful work of the system integrator.

8   Thesis 7: Service providers and innovative appliance manufacturers will be the winners

Home automation involves linking together partial markets for products and services to obtain an integrated problem solution. This results in a very varied market potential for manufacturers and service providers.

There is only limited additional sales potential for classic appliance manufacturers. They will mainly profit from users buying early replacements. On the one hand, they will be forced to take an active role in the design and market introduction if they wish to avoid too much of their product intelligence being transferred to other suppliers such as the computer industry. On the other hand, the initial investment in the development of the market will be very high for the appliance manufacturer, considering the limited market potential. This could prove to be a strategic trap for appliance manufacturers.

However, in the partial market for appliances capable of home automation, there is considerable differentiating and image potential for innovative appliance manufacturers. Also the existing business would benefit from such a positive image.

There is more sales potential for the manufacturers of network intelligence and components, although even in installation, substitution effects between conventional components and components capable of home automation have to be taken into consideration.

The largest market is actually in the service area. There is tremendous potential for the suppliers of professional support, installation and servicing as well as for the application service providers in the areas of energy supply, security, home banking, home shopping, interactive entertainment and information services.

In fact, this area will also provide appliance manufacturers offering innovative services with a good chance to benefit from the tremendous future potential of this market.

Stand-alone Multimedia in the Private Household

Felix Goedhart and Thomas Künstner
Booz, Allen & Hamilton, Germany

1   Introduction

For almost two years now *multimedia* has been the key "buzzword" within the Communications, Media, Computing and Electronics industries. The discussion originally started with the announcements of the Clinton/Gore administration to actively support the creation of the "Information Superhighway" as well as industrial mergers such as the one between Viacom and Paramount. Today several possible developments are discussed under the umbrella of multimedia. Whereas corporate strategic planners and marketing specialists envision an enormous market potential for new products and services, social scientists paint the dark picture of "couch potatoes" and social isolation. In order to go beyond such superficial statements it is necessary to at least roughly define what multimedia or the multimedia-market is and which applications and technologies will presumably drive the market.

There are three main characteristics for multimedia applications:
- the opportunity for interactive usage which means that the user can actively influence the usage process
- the integration of different media types which means that static (text, pictures and data) and dynamic (video and audio) media can be combined
- digital technology and data compression which enable the storage and alteration of all data and therefore build the technological base for all the multimedia applications

Clearly this definition is neither scientific nor fully exhaustive but rather a first framework to understand what differentiates multimedia applications from "regular" products and services within the communications, media, computing and electronics industries. While screening currently discussed applications with this definition in mind it becomes obvious how heterogeneous the multimedia landscape presents itself. The range of products and services spans from video games and interactive homeshopping to multimedia databases and video conferencing. Furthermore it becomes clear that some of the applications now classified as multimedia, e.g. video conferencing already existed long before the term multimedia had been created.

In order to analyze the drivers of the complex and heterogeneous multimedia marketplace it should be simplified by defining market segments which can be looked at separately. Figure 1 shows the multimedia market segmentation developed by Booz, Allen & Hamilton.

Seg-ments Net-working	Business	Private
Stand-alone	• Personal Digital Assistant (PDA, e.g. Newton) • Multimedia Learning (CD-ROM) • Multimedia Presentation • Multimedia Information (CD-ROM)	• Edutainment (CD-ROM) • Infotainment (CD-ROM) • MM Games (e.g. Gameboy) • MM Videos (CD-ROM)
	Migration	Migration
Networked	• Point-of-Sales (PoS) • Point-of-Information (PoI) • Teleworking • Video Conference • Video Telephony • MM Information Online • MM E-Mail • MM Telelearning	• Interactive Pay-TV (PPV, PPC, enhanced PPV) • Video-on-Demand (VoD) • Games-on-Demand (GoD) • Interactive Homeshopping • Home Services (e.g. Electronic Banking) • Video Telephony • MM Information Online Services • MM Telelearning

Fig. 1.   Multimedia market structure

Four market segments can be identified using a combination of customer and technologically oriented criteria. On one side it should be differentiated between stand-alone (off-line) and network-based (on-line) applications on the other side most of the applications can be classified as either privately used or applications for business purposes. Looking at the four market segments it becomes clear that network oriented applications for private consumers such as interactive video services and interactive homeshopping obtain most of the attention in today's public and corporate multimedia discussion. But a short look behind the curtains reveals that today the multimedia market takes place in the stand-alone segments where "real" products such as video games and point-of-information kiosks meet "real" demand from consumers who are willing to spend "real" money. Especially the network-based private segment is still characterized by technologically oriented field trials some of which regularly have to be postponed due to difficulties in the area of server technology and systems integration. The emergence of a mass market in this area before the year 2000 seems to be rather questionable.

This paper focuses on the already existing and prospering stand-alone segment of the multimedia market for the private consumer. This part of the multimedia market will also have strong impact on the use and very nature of computing in the private household. This article describes the status of this market in Europe (Germany, France and the UK). Two strongly interdependent parts of the stand-alone market, hardware and software, have to be considered. We will first focus on the software side of the business, which is the driving force of the market and represents about 60% of total sales now. Then we will discuss the hardware-segment and show the interdependence between both parts. The analyses of the market structure, the value chain and important players show how the market trends are going to shape the evolving business system. Besides being a very interesting market on its own the analysis of the dynamics in the stand-alone market helps to understand key drivers for most of the developments within the network based segment. As a closing remark we will show which developments within the stand-alone market should be closely observed and analyzed as a means of supporting the prediction of network-based applications.

2 Market segments and development in the stand-alone software market

The software-side of the stand-alone multimedia market for private consumers can be divided into three market segments: video games, edutainment and infotainment. The video games segment includes both the jump & run games i.e. Mortal Kombat and the strategy games i.e. Myst. Edutainment are software-titles combining educational material with game-elements. The idea is to bring playing and learning experiences together. These titles are targeted at children in the school and preschool age. An example is the French "Adi" series from Coktel Vision. Infotainment titles are aimed at an age range from 15 to 45. This category combines entertaining elements with information. All the electronic encyclopedias like Microsoft's Encarta fall in this category. Figure 2 describes the status and potential development of the three segments over time.

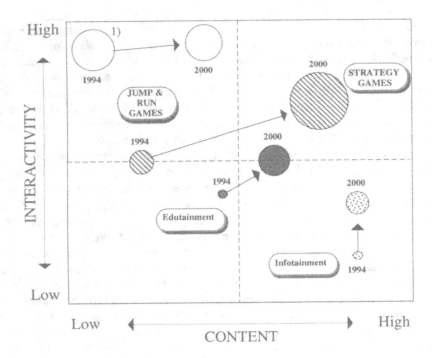

1) Area of circles represents relative size of segment; not drawn to scale

Fig. 2.   Development of market segments in the consumer stand-alone market

Clearly games dominate the European market with their 90% plus share of the overall volume of about US$ 2 billion in 1994. Compared to a US$ 15 billion European book market the stand-alone multimedia market looks rather small. However, substantial growth rates in the range of 40% across all segments already indicate the markets future potential and significance. Bertelsmann for example expects this business to grow into similar dimensions as their music business within the next few years.

Whereas games by nature offer a high degree of interactivity to the user but relatively little content, edutainment and infotainment products such as encyclopedias offer substantially more content but relatively little interaction, so far. Analyses of consumer demand indicate that a trend towards more content and more interactivity becomes visible across all three segments. Moreover, the analysis of the three segments reveals other substantial differences. Figure 3 shows these differences such as geographic coverage, target consumers, shelf life, marketing support and turnover.

The video games market, for example, clearly is a global business which shows great similarities to Hollywood. The video games market is very much Blockbuster driven: The 20 best selling titles accounted for over 80% of 1993's software sales in the UK. The marketing budgets for these titles are enormous. Nintendo placed over 700 TV ads in Germany to support the Christmas campaign for its Blockbuster title 'Donkey Kong'. One increasingly important success factor of games is the use of well known characters. Some of the characters are own productions like 'Super Mario' by Nintendo or 'Sonic the Hedgehog' by Sega, but very often they are taken from Blockbuster movies such as Jurassic Park. Acquiring rights for these characters substantially adds to the production cost of video games. This large up front investment for the production and marketing of the titles favors large, globally operating players.

Edutainment and infotainment titles, on the other hand, contain a much higher degree of local content. This includes language as well as cultural preferences. A multimedia sports dictionary will be quite different in the USA and in Europe, for example. Also within Europe there will be substantial differences - the space attributed to the Cricket section is only one example. This makes it much more difficult to produce and market titles globally within these segments.

Market Segment		Current Size	Platform	Geographic Coverage	Target Market	Growth Potential	Shelf Life	Marketing Support	Turnover	Degree of Content	Degree of Interactivity
Games	Jump and Run, e.g. Mortal Kombat	Large	Mainly cartridge	Global	Boys (12-14)	Stable	Short	High	Fast-moving		
	Strategy, e.g. Myst	Large	PC floppy, CD-ROM and CD-i growing	Global	Older children/ adults	Medium to good	Medium	High	Fast-moving		
Edutainment, e.g. ADI Series, Asterix Learns French		Small	CD-ROM, CD-i, PC Floppy	National	Children (school age), some adult titles	Good in medium term	Long	Low	Slow-moving		
Infotainment, e.g. Cinemenia		Small	CD-ROM, CD-i	National	Adults and teen-agers	Good in long term (but less than edu-tainment)	Long	Medium to low	Slow-moving		

Fig. 3. Characteristics of market segments

3 Hardware platforms

Hardware platforms and the software side of the business are strongly interlinked. High quality software titles are an important prerequisite for hardware sales. Consumers are not interested in the hardware themselves, but mainly in the content that plays on it. On the other hand, a high installed base of hardware platforms offers an excellent basis for a prospering software business. If the hardware producer stays in control of his platform he can charge royalties for every title sold. The profits of Sega and Nintendo in the early 90ies show how successful this business model can be.

Today the consoles and handhelds for games offered by Sega and Nintendo with around 20 million units installed across Europe clearly dominate the platform landscape. However, the cumulative number of consoles and handhelds has peaked in 1993 and since then has fallen by about 5% annually. This trend is reflected by the substantially decreasing number of software titles sold for these platforms. Consoles as well as handhelds are platforms for video games and due to their data storage limitations not suited for movies or edutainment and infotainment titles.

A wide range of new competitors are trying to break in this duopolistic domain with the next generation of CD based consoles. Between them are well known names of the consumer-electronics and computing world. For example Philips with its CD-i console which has recently been relaunched supported by a major marketing campaign and numerous cooperations and licensing agreements with software developers. Other examples are 3DO developed by Matsushita, the PSX backed by Sony Corporation and Jaguar by Atari. Also Sega and Nintendo launch their CD formats with Sega CD, Saturn and Project Reality.

A third category is the combination of standard PC/Mac with CD-ROM drives. The installed base of these 'multimedia-machines' is growing rapidly across Europe and is evolving as an important platform for all segments - games, edutainment and infotainment. This is driven by the decreasing cost of the initial purchase and the growing number of software-titles including games for this category. Figure 4 shows an overview of the different platform concepts focusing on the main characteristics of the PC/Mac and the other CD-based platforms.

Hardware suppliers seem to understand that the business in general moves toward software and that eventually the software available determines the success of a hardware platform. Hardware wars like the one which took place in the field of VCR help neither the consumer nor the industry. Therefore licensing agreements with software developers are key to the penetration of platforms. Software developers are interested in producing software for as many users as possible in order to make up for their substantial costs and refuse to be restricted to a platform with a limited installed base. This makes it very difficult to sign up good software titles for newly launched platforms. New technological developments, especially the increased standardization, make it easier for title producers to transfer their titles from one platform to the other. Another important factor for software producers are the royalty fees which have to be paid to the hardware producers for each title sold for a specific console. The absence of such royalties is a strong incentive for title developers to support open platforms like PC/Mac and CD-ROM. This is already leading to a power-shift between hardware producers and title developers. It is becoming more and more difficult for Sega and Nintendo to get exclusive contracts for successful games and titles.

	PC/MAC CD-ROM	CD-I	CD-32	3DO	Sony PSX	Sega CD/CDX	Sega Saturn	Nintendo Project Reality	Jaguar
System developers	Various	Philips Sony	Commodore	3 DO	Sony	Sega	Sega Microsoft JVC Hitachi Yamaha	Nintendo Silicon Graphics	Atari
Active manufacturer	Various	Philips Goldstar Samsung Daewoo	Commodore	Matsushita AT&T Sanyo	Sony	Sega Sanyo	Sega JVC Hitachi Yamaha	Nintendo	IBM (OEM)
Launch date									
U.S.	Well	Oct 91	Mar 94	Oct 93	Nov 94	Nov 92	Nov 94	Autumn 95	Nov 93
U.K.	established	Apr 92	Sep 93	Jun 94	–	Apr 93	–	–	Dec 93
Japan		Apr 92	–	Mar 94	Nov 94	Dec 91	Nov 94	–	–
Europe (other)		Sep 92	Oct 93	Summer 94	–	–	–	Autumn 95	–
Hardware prices									
Launch	£	$1,000/£599	$399/£299	$699	–	–	–	–	–
Lowest now [1]	£1,000	$399/£399	$399/£399	$499	–	–	(under £200)	(under £200)	–
Global installed base	10 Mn	300 K	140 K	30 K	–	1,140 K (170 K Eur)	–	–	30 K
Architecture	8/16 bit	16 bit	32 bit	32 bit	32 bit	16 bit	32 bit	64 bit	64 bit
Disk speed	1, 2, 3 X	1 X	2 X	2 X	2 X	1 X	4 X?	Cartridge only	2 X
Video CD compatible	√	√ ($249/£150)	√ (£199)	√ ($200)	X	X	(likely)?	N/A	Later in 94
Software titles available	abt. 6,000	150	60	31	–	35	–	–	20 +
Average software prices	£50	$15 - $60 £15 - £60	£30	$45 - $80	–	$60	–	–	$39 - $69
Software types	Entertainment Children's Education Reference	Games Entertainment Films Children's Education Reference	Games Movies	Games Films Entertainment Children's Education Reference	Games	Games	Games	Games	Games

1) August 1, 1994

Fig. 4. Overview of stand-alone hardware platforms

As a consequence from the factors described above the prospects for many of the proprietary platforms mentioned are more than questionable. Booz, Allen & Hamilton estimates that in addition to the already installed Sega and Nintendo platforms and the fast growing PC/Mac CD-ROM combination only one or two other CD-based platforms will survive.

4 Supplier structure

The business system for stand-alone multimedia products for private consumers is rather complex. Figure 5 describes the different components of the business by using the multimedia value chain developed by Booz, Allen & Hamilton. The business process starts with the creative concept which is the major part of the product development process. The eventual quality of the product is determined by this creative concept. The optimal use of the different media types is essential for the optical attractiveness of the title. Many titles lack "true" multimedia content and are not more than a relatively simple combination of mainly static media types. Prerequisite for a good creative concept is a new form of creative talent. The next step, the provision of content mainly done by acquisition of rights is both, one of the major success factors and a substantial cost driver. Programming represents a major bottleneck within the whole business system in the moment. Only a few companies in Europe of which quite a few are relatively small start-up companies are capable of programming complex multimedia products across various platforms. Most of these companies are located in the UK. The manufacturing which means the pressing of the CDs is already a commodity business with great similarities to music CD pressing. Three players dominate the European market with

Bertelsmann´s Sonopress being the largest supplier. The remainder of the multimedia value chain looks very much like the one for "regular" packaged consumer goods.

Product Development	Content Provision/ Acquisition	Program- ming	Manu- facturing	Marketing	Dis- tribution/ Whole- saling	Sales	Retailing
• Product planning • Editorial research & design • Script-writing • Storyboard • Database design • Visual design • Building develop-ment tools	• Content cataloguing • Film/photo research and selection • Acquiring rights • Audio recording • Animation • Images/ design	• Digitizing video/ photos • Integrating media • Creating hypertext/ media links • Creating game sequences • Testing • Documen-tation • Licensing	• Production of master copy • Pressing disks • Packaging	• Packaging design • Public relations • Budgeting • Media strategy • Trade show design and management • Trade and consumer pro-motion • Setting price to distributor • Branding • Marketing and sales to distributors/major retailers	• Ware-housing • Logistics • Shelf displays • Customer base man-agement • Setting price to retailer	• Distribu-tion strategy • Distribu-tor/reseller support • Customer service • Handling of returns • Mainte-nance of warranty	• Shelf space manage-ment • Merchan-dising • Stock man-agement • Promotion • Setting retail price

Source: SIMBA, BA&H analysis

Fig. 5.   Multimedia value chain for stand-alone titles

Within the market for stand-alone multimedia products for private consumers two major player roles are emerging: publishing and distribution. These two roles incorporate different parts of the multimedia value chain. Publishers very often develop ideas for products and then are involved in the product development either by building up in-house capacities or by funding small multimedia production houses which can not afford to come up with the necessary up front investments. Publishers usually bear the financial risk of a title production. One of the major tasks of publishers is the acquisition of rights. Many publishers are major players in either book, music or magazine publishing and therefore already own substantial amounts of relevant content. For theses publishers the multimedia market represents the opportunity to both naturally extend their product lines and to reach new customer segments. Leading German book publishers estimate that between 10 to 20% of the book market will migrate to electronic/multimedia formats within the next five years. This makes clear that the multimedia market development does not only represent a chance, but much rather a necessity for diversification for book publishers. In order to do this they need to acquire a new set of capabilities covering the product development and the programming for multimedia titles.

Whereas most publishers try to do the product development at least partly in-house, they generally tend to outsource the programming of the titles to small programming houses who are capable of handling state of the art equipment. However, some publishers like for instance Bertelsmann build up significant in-house capabilities after having realized that programming is still a bottleneck within the overall production process. As a key function the publisher takes over most of the marketing for the products. This includes the packaging design, promotional efforts as well as pricing for distributors and key accounts. In addition the publisher is creating a brand name, e.g. by organizing product catalogues. The other key role in the multimedia market is distribution. Distributors generally control all wholesaling and sales activities including warehousing, logistics, shelf displays, return handling, retailer support, maintenance of warranty as well as pricing to retailers. Figure 6 illustrates these different roles and shows in which parts of the value chain the most important players in Germany, France and the UK get actively involved. Although generally existing, the boundaries between the two roles mentioned above vary reflecting national practices. The chart also indicates that Bertelsmann through its numerous subsidiaries follows a strategy of full integration in the field of stand-alone multimedia for private consumers.

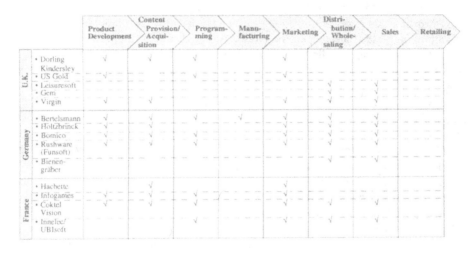

Fig. 6.   Activities of major players

As mentioned above network-based multimedia applications such as video-on-demand, games-on-demand and interactive homeshopping attract most of the attention within today's multimedia discussion. A close look at the developments in the stand-alone market could in many ways help to understand key drivers and to create possible scenarios. The following examples briefly illustrate the relevance of one market for the other:

- sales figures across the different market segments and product categories could serve as an indicator for customer demand for network-based applications. Games will presumably be one of the key service offerings among network-based applications. The development in the edutainment and infotainment segments could serve as an indicator of future network-based service offerings such as telelearning.

- the platform developments will have a direct impact on the network-based applications. The PC/Mac will be a well established platform in private households by the time network-based interactive services will be offered on the marketplace. On the other hand all suppliers of TV-oriented CD-based platforms see their products as being the first step towards intelligent set-top boxes.

5   Summary

In contrast to the actual status of the multimedia market most of the attention within today's discussions is drawn to network-based applications for private consumers such as interactive video services and interactive homeshopping. Looking only at applications for private consumers it can be clearly stated that most of the network-based applications are still in their early stages which in most cases means that they are technologically tested within regularly postponed and discouraging field trials around the world. Although not in the center of attention the stand-alone multimedia market for private consumers has already reached a substantial size representing sales of about US$ 2 billion in Europe. The market is clearly dominated by video games which account for more than 90% of all sales. The two other market segments edutainment and infotainment are in their early stages but will grow substantially in the future. The games segment is dominated by two companies, Sega and Nintendo which established their consoles and handhelds as the major technological platform over the last years. However, recent market data indicates that these platforms have peaked in 1993 and are constantly declining. Although comparatively small in numbers the combination of PC/Mac and CD-ROM seems to be evolving as a major platform for games as well as for edutainment and infotainment software titles. The battle for a TV-oriented CD-based platform has not yet been decided. The production process of multimedia titles is rather complex and incorporates several steps. Most important are the creative concept which basically means the arrangement of the different media types, the user-interface and the acquisition of content rights. The programming across different platforms is still a major bottleneck of the entire process. The market will be driven by two kinds of players. Publishers either existing publishers or specialized multimedia publishers will fund the product development and programming, acquire the necessary content rights and take over most of the marketing responsibilities including the pricing to distributors and key accounts retailers such as large retail chains. Distributors on the other hand take over the warehousing, physical distribution and logistics as well as retailer support and the pricing to retailers. However, due to the early stage of the market no clear market structure has evolved across Europe. The analysis of the stand-alone market reveals many issues that are also relevant for predictions regarding the network-based market for private consumers. Particularly the development on both, the demand and technology side could serve as indicators for trends in the market for on-line-services of any kind.

References

BIS Strategic Decisions, Interactive Video Games-Market Report 1994, London, 1994

Booz, Allen & Hamilton (ed.), Zukunft Multimedia-Grundlagen, Märkte und Perspektiven in Deutschland, Frankfurt, 1994

Booz, Allen & Hamilton, The Globalization of Hollywood, London, 1991

Dataquest, Multimedia Market Trends 1994, UK, 1994

Glen, D., Sega of America, Interactive Entertainment on the Information Superhighway, presented at the IIR conference on the Information Superhighway, Frankfurt, May, 1994

Glowalla, U., Multimedia '94-Grundlagen und Praxis, Heidelberg, 1994

InfoTech, Optical Publishing Industry Assessment (OPIA), London, 1994

SIMBA Information, The Economics of Multimedia Publishing, Wilton, 1994

Teletech NRW, Landesinitiative Telekommunikation, Band 18: Interaktive Medien-Multimedia, Düsseldorf, 1993

TFPL Publishing (ed.), Facts and Figures 1994, London, 1994

Strategic Management and Transformation in Converging Industries - Towards the Information Society

Thomas Baubin and Bernd W. Wirtz
Andersen Consulting, Strategic Services Group West Europe, Germany

1 Information market evolution and the virtualization of corporate structures

The use of multimedia technologies as the core driving element of converging markets and virtual corporate structures will impel considerable economic and social change. Sound strategic management which takes into consideration the basic transformation processes of this sector will be a substantial success factor in securing a competitive advantage within this deciding future market. The related change from an industrial to an Information Society will above all else be affected by the dynamics of technological developments. The underlying principal of these developments can be explained with the Contratief Cycle Theorem (Nefiodow 1991). Accordingly, technological innovations are the substantial determinants of economic growth and social change. Today's transformations are driven by information technologies, in particular multi-media based technologies, much like the steam engine, railways, the telephone, radio and the automobile (Contratief Cycle factors) have changed mankind's daily existence in the past. Following the Contratief divisions of the model, our present post-modern industrial society is in the midst of a transformation towards an Information Society (the transition from the fourth to the fifth Contratief Cycle). The fifth Contratief Cycle will be strongly influenced by emerging multimedia technologies, which will act as catalysts towards the Information Society.

The absorption of communication and information technologies in a growing number of economic and social areas has increased significantly in recent years (Denger/Wirtz 1995). This diffusion process is at present driven substantially by the American Government's National Information Infrastructure Program, the European Union's Program towards the Information Society and the Multimedia Initiative of the Japanese Ministry for Industry and Commerce (MITI). All of these programs envision the expedited expansion and effective use of the so-called Information Superhighway as a deciding competitive advantage for individual companies, entire industrial branches and even economic spheres within the Triad of global competition. The Information Highways are thereby expected to become the central driving force of future economic and social development. The rapid establishment of virtual corporate and industrial structures is the final goal of such forced activities. It is within this context that one often speaks of electronic markets and virtual value chains (Benjamin/Wigand 1995, Miller/Clemons/Row 1993), wherein the term "virtual" actually implies that all the essential characteristics of an object are present without the object itself - in essence, it defines the possibility of a situation ("as if") which cannot be found in reality. The understanding "virtual" is used in many possible constellations, such as, for example, virtual products, virtual company, virtual value chain or virtual market (Davidow/Malone 1993). This manifold usage may be confusing at first glance, but despite this, all of the applications of the term virtual share a basic and defining attribute, the understanding of which is mirrored in the (pars pro toto) definition of the virtual organization.

A virtual organization may be understood as a temporary network of independent companies (suppliers, co-producers, distributors, but also clients or competitors) which are tied together by modern communication and information technology in order to exchange knowledge and know-how, to supplement abilities, to share costs, and beyond this, to tap into new product spheres and markets (Byrne/Brandt/Port 1993). Ideally, all of the stakeholders contribute complimentary core competencies. Virtual value chains or virtual markets represent the macro level of virtual company relationships which form the transaction framework for various material and immaterial exchange processes. The transaction characteristics and possibilities of these new technologies, which determine the true virtualization of structures and processes, are fundamental for the understanding of virtual market relationships. The virtualization, or rather the virtualization potential, can thereby constitute, for example, the gradual elimination of an entire distribution step within a value chain, or rather within a transaction relationship. At the same time, however, it is possible to subsume a technology induced change of the consumer relationship within the concept of virtualization. Or in other words: Virtualization represents the dynamic transformation of transactional market relationships and types of coordination based on the use or effects of modern information and communication technology. The retail sector is a good example of the impact of virtual developments. Through the use of Information Highway infrastructure, producers will be able to establish direct connections with consumers and vice versa. The possibility of ordering merchandise directly through intelligent home ordering services and the use of newly emerging logistic companies, which will carry out the immediate delivery of the merchandise, will make traditional retail functions and trade stages at least partially obsolete. Virtualisation as such can therefore lead to the elimination of entire industry branches, or steps within value chains.

The market, however, remains in its early phases of development, eventhough the idea of virtualization and multimedia has become a topic of discussion lately, especially through such catchphrases as the Information Highway and a variety of new products and services, the full impact of which will not to be felt for another 10 to 15 years. Since the multimedia market is not fundamentally forming from scratch, but is much more a combination of already existing products and applications based on differing converging markets, this convergence itself represents an important prerequisite.

The emerging multimedia market is already branded with a high market dynamism. Ideally, one could describe the further development of the market as follows (Denger/Wirtz 1995): The emerging phase will essentially be shaped by attempts to establish standards for proprietary multimedia systems. The increasing process of diffusion, technological development and the establishment of a limited number of proprietary systems in the marketplace will motivate further competitor compatibility strategies during the course of continuing developments. In the end, standardization and compatibility strategies will lead to the assertion of a uniform industry standard. During the course of the later market phases of multimedia development, invention and innovation will necessitate an evolution which will once again force this established industry standard into obsolescence (see fig. 1).

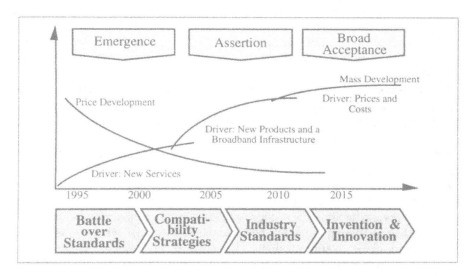

Fig. 1.   Market evolution cycle

The convergence of component markets such as telecommunications, computer hardware and software, entertainment electronics, and media is of consequence for the developing multimedia market and closely tied to the themes of innovation and establishing standards. Broad corporate and consumer application driven mass markets will not emerge until the convergence of component markets, which will create generally accepted standards and affordable products, and its transformational effects on related industries and sectors have occured. However, a broad acceptance of multimedia applications is not to be expected before the year 2010, since mass markets will not emerge until the combination of corresponding technological infrastructure, products and services at affordable prices is achieved. The home shopping experience reveals a suitable example, since the required TV intelligence is not yet available and only the integration of PCs and TVs into intelligent and user friendly devices at acceptable prices will change home ordering into a broad mass market.

2   The emergence of new markets and economic structures

Convergence processes will not, however, affect a complete merger of these basic sectors. The fundamental new structure of this market will form an entirely separate entity, which itself, however, will consist mainly of heterogeneous component markets. A fitting example of this development is found in the emerging integration of personal computers and intelligent televisions and the herewith associated developing new market for intelligent broadcasting. Herein we are dealing with a product driven transformation process which will be caused in large part by a change in private household consumer behavior. When one considers new developments within both of these product markets, it is possible to determine, for example, that more multimedia capable PCs were sold in the US in 1994 than television sets.

The entertainment electronics industry is increasingly responding to this evolution by expanding its traditional TV-systems with computer know-how and developing intelligent television sets which also have PC functionality. As a result, large entertainment electronics conglomerates like Sony, Philips or Matsushita are considering acquisitions specifically in the field of computer know-how. In a similar vein, the computer industry is clearly in a trend to augment its traditional offering with multimedia components. Beside this transformation of the end user device industry, telecommunication carriers (through their cabel infrastructures and intelligent network design) and mobile communication providers (through their packaging and organization services) will unite within an emerging market segment in intelligent digital broadcasting to combine entertainment, education and home shopping services. As this example illustrates, companies from within at least four separate industries (media, telcommunications, computers and entertainment electronics) can create a new multimedia market segment through transformation and convergence processes. The fundamental directions of influence of these transformation processes are exhibited in figure 2.

In figure 2, three different sector rings are presented (core ring, middle ring and periphery ring) in which different transformation processes will transpire. The convergence and transformation processes within the core ring will produce completely new value chains and value constellations, which in turn will lead to the emergence of entirely new markets. The exclusion of entire value added fields and steps in the middle ring due to their migration into the core (core migration) will force the reformation of traditional production structures (reshaping industry).

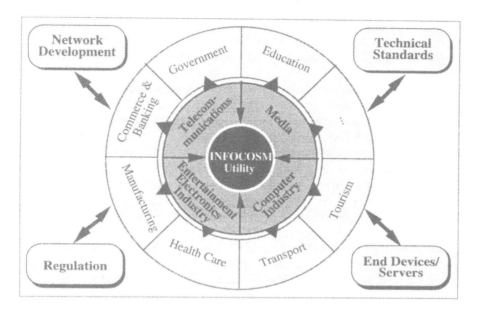

Fig. 2.   Convergence ring model

The emergence of the core ring will therefore have considerable cannibalization effects on the essential business of the industries within the middle ring. Herein also exists the great substitution potential and the therewith associated market selection processes. The availability of new applications, products and services from within the core and middle rings can be seen as the driving force of changes in the outer ring. The digital information highways in commerce, for example, will give consumers fast and increased access to a vast selection of goods, but will also cause an evolution from retail channels to electronic markets. The virtual products offered will be ordered on screen and delivered direct to the home. Large process changes will not only affect commerce by means of home ordering - the tourism industry, for example, can entirely change its processes with travel agencies through the use of new electronic distribution possibilities.

This example illustrates that even within the outer ring, fundamental transformation processes within industrial structures are possible, even if shaped to a considerable extent by the willingness of households to change their demand behavior. In considering the basic branches in which future convergence processes are expected, it becomes apparent that two of the four industries (telecommunications and media) exhibit a high degree of regulation. The future liberalization of these fields is a considerable prerequisite for convergence. In the US, for example, a consequential deregulation and an industrial-political consensus over the expansion of the Information Highway have established a corresponding climate for the breakthrough into the multimedia age. In Europe, however, the liberalization of voice and network monopolies is not planed until 1998 (Wirtz 1995a).

Because of this, a large number of European companies run the risk of losing their association with the expanding multimedia field. Thus, for example, MCI, a major American long distance provider, entered into a partnership with British Telecom (which has long been exposed to open competition) instead of Deutsche Telekom, despite the fact that contracts had been negotiated and were awaiting signatures with the latter. The reason for this was not so much because of a more attractive financial offer, but much more because of the lead which British Telecom had gained as a private corporation in its interaction with competitors. The disadvantage which most European companies in the telecommunications sector have to endure rests on a long tradition of regulation within the European communications markets. Market regulation in the form of government monopolies, especially in telecommunications and radio, brought forth mostly large and inefficient organizations, which can adapt to rapidly changing competitive conditions only with the greatest of difficulty.

Moreover, such intensive regulation hinders the rapid development of a European multimedia market, because of the multitude of governmental entry barriers and conditions which it presents. The multimedia market structure and the competitive conduct of its participants is at present still largely determined by regulative intervention and control to the disadvantage of competitive companies. A rapid and fundamental deregulation is therefore a substantial requirement for the creation and maintenance of competitiveness and a conditio sine qua non for a comprehensive diffusion of multimedia applications. First signs of a fundamental change in the regulatory behavior on the level of the European Union can be seen in the findings of the so called Bangemann Report, which provides for a comprehensive liberalization (Bangemann Group 1994).

The necessary deregulation of these areas should, however, not be allowed to lead to a complete liberalization, as economic, social and anti-trust considerations must be taken into account. In this regard, it is necessary to establish a type of regulation which sensibly and efficiently organizes the competitive activities within the different market layers. Figure 3 illustrates a basic model which may be used to further explain substantial organizational principals.

The treatment of vertical integration within the value added stages of figure 3 depicts the considerable regulatory problem. The open and competitive organization of the information and communication sector is of special significance in light of its influence on the formation and maintenance of a multitude of societal opinions. For this reason, vertical strategies within these value added stages, which lead to market closure effects and promote anti-competitive behavior, must be fundamentally understood and restricted (Wirtz 1995b). Competitive discrimination, such as, for example, a preferred or exclusionary accessibility to combined organization and transport services, can be prevented in large part by the separation of market dominating firms within the program organization and network structure levels.

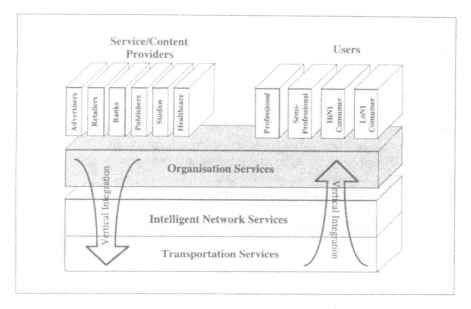

Fig. 3.   Sector model

A recent example of a prevention of this type of vertical integration by dominant firms was the attempted collaboration between the Deutsche Telekom, the Bertelsmann AG and the Kirch Group. In November 1994, the European Commission ruled against the formation of this Media Services consortium because of its fears of such vertical strategies establishing anti-competitive structures and behavior. The effective restriction of vertical integration cross sector strategies therefore represents a sine qua non for open, competitive structures within these newly developing markets.

3   New value constellations

The multimedia market can be fundamentally divided into four different competitive, or strategic fields. This division is based upon differing application or need categories that are inherent within multimedia technologies. All multimedia services can therefore be subdivided into the following four categories: transaction, information, communication, entertainment/education. Essentially, it is the communication and information aspect which stand in the foreground of the business application market segment. On-line databases will become more user friendly for business use through the application of multimedia elements such as sound and graphics. Videoconferencing and teleworking represent typical communication simplifying media.

Educational programs will be applied in corporate environments for employee training and development, as well as in the public sphere, within universities for example. The entertainment aspect dominates within the private user market segment, where services such as Interactive Pay-TV, Video-on-Demand and computer games will make individualized entertainment possible. The consumer information and transaction aspects, relate to services such as home shopping, electronic banking and information kiosks.

It is critical for the success of multimedia pioneers to convince both the private and business consumer of the usefulness of new multimedia products and services, for in the end, they will decide the fate of such new technologies beyond an initial introductory phase. Three points are especially significant for this:

- developing experience with consumer behavior through pilot projects
- establishing simpler transaction structures
- creating simple and user friendly interfaces

A combination of different value stages will be necessary for the successful supply and marketing of these multimedia services and products. The multimedia value chain allows itself to be divided into five stages: *Content Creators* generate information and entertainment. *Content Packagers* combine various contents to create programs together with *Providers of Value Added Services*. The most important role in the future will be that of the *Content Organizer* who packages different types of content like education, shoppping offers, and entertainment according to market target user segments. Lastly, *Content Distributors* undertake the transmission of the contents to the consumer. Figure 4 elucidates the multimedia value chain.

Content creation

The Content Creators in their role as information suppliers constitute a core component of the value chain. The Hollywood majors, such as Time Warner and Columbia Pictures, but also TV and media conglomerates such as the German Kirch Group and Rupert Murdoch, and news agencies such as Reuters and dpa, count among the most important companies of this value stage.

Content packaging

Content Packagers combine various contents into segment specific packages and/or channels. These are then purchased by suppliers of comprehensive programming and incorporated into their total offerings. The US media giant, Viacom, for example, combines a variety of diverse music videos and its own commentary to create the music channel MTV, which it in turn offers to cabel TV supliers such as TCI Inc. (other examples include movie channels such as HBO or Premiere, news channels such as CNN and ntv).

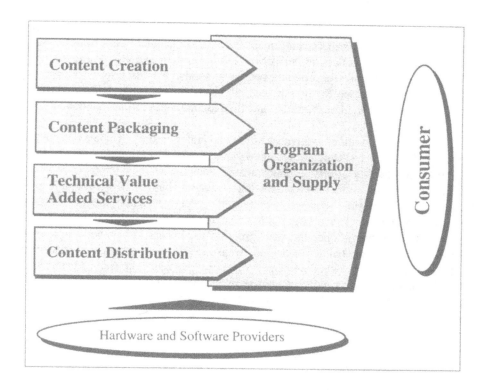

Fig. 4. Multimedia value chain

Technical Value Added Services

Technical Value Added Services use existing carrier services, such as the telephone network, to provide such diverse products as billing assistance, development, construction and operation of server platforms and agent systems. The AT&T and Lotus Developments joint venture which aims to offer a private, virtual Notes network, is an example of a Technical Value Added Service using an existing infrastructure. The various Internet access providers which are riding the Internet wave are a further example of such a service.

Content distribution

Transmission, switching and network management are among the central functions within this value stage. Carrier services in Europe are provided to a large extent by state owned telecommunications companies.

Program organization and supply

The Program Suppliers are customer oriented with their central task being the organization of a program. In so doing, they move within the recipient as well as the content procurement and advertising markets. The Program Providers organize the compilation of targeted contents and functions and market the product. Their activities include subscriber management (advertising, contract design, performance assurance, billing, collection, subscriber administration and update service), the development and supply of program specific equipment (end user soft- and hardware systems), the development or purchase of contents, technical functionality and transmission and switching capacity and the integration of product components.

The "digital revolution" motivated fusion and "intermixing" of affected industries and the therefrom resulting entirely new value constellations create the necessity among multimedia pioneers to fundamentally reorientate their strategic behavior. Consequently and similar to the market structure changes, a quantum leap in competitive strategies becomes necessary in order to capture the new growth potential of the market. An example of this is the future change in the competitive positions of network operators and program organizers. The legally protected network operators are being substantially weakened through continual deregulation. At the same time, growing product complexity and rising consumer demand for individualized solutions will emphasize the program organizers' marketing and packaging competences. Figure 5 illustrates the basic transformation processes which clarify the need for strategic reorientation within these branches.

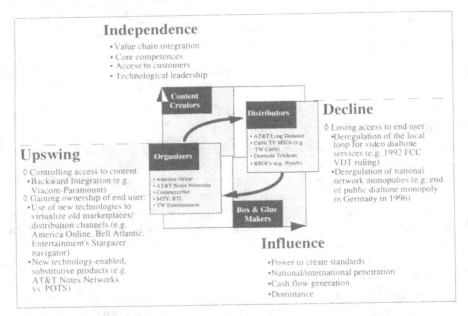

Fig. 5.   Competitive grid

Many companies from different origins (Telecom, Media Industry, Electronic Industry) will attempt to take a favoured position within the grid. Successful organizers therefore need to carefully define a strategy that provides an optimal combination of independence and influence based on their traditional core competences. For example, content based companies that want to provide mobility services (e.g. automotive producers) need to extend there competences in designing telecom modules for cars and in maintaining direct customer links in order to build the high entry barriers of market independence and influence.

4   Competitive strategies and corporate transactions

Participants in the multimedia market must prepare for the threat to their traditional business posed by newcomers arising out of the convergence activity in electronic distribution, end user device manufacture and the media industry. In addition, considerable infrastructure investments and the costly creation of customer acceptance and preference are necessary for entry into the multimedia market. A multitude of cooperative arrangements is emerging within the multimedia market since the risks of an independent technological leadership are relatively high. Experts estimate that in the United States alone there are already in excess of 350 alliances with the goal of participating in the creation and eventually demanding control of at least a part of the newly evolving business through cross sectoral cooperation.

Strategic alliances in the form of capital integrations, joint ventures and long-term contracts and agreements are being closed in order to secure know-how and dominate important new business fields. The merger of the Bell Company and Time Warner Entertainment represents one of the most speculative of these alliances. This regional telephone service provider purchased a 2.5 billion US$ share in the highly indebted entertainment and cable television giant in order to develop a "full service network" in several US states.

A further example of capital integration is the share which Deutsche Telekom together with France Télécom have taken in Sprint, the third largest US long distance telecommunication provider. For the Europeans, this alliance represents one of the last possibilities of cooperating with a large American partner, since AT&T has already entered into a multitude of alliances and the second largest possible partner, MCI, has already enlisted in a joint venture with British Telecom (Weißenberg 1994). Perhaps the most consequential joint venture was formed by AT&T, Singapore Telecom, Telecom New Zealand and Unisource (the state owned telephone companies of Switzerland, Sweden and the Netherlands). The particular significance of this consortium is a result of the inclusion of an Asian partner and the strong position of the global player AT&T within all telecommunication markets.

The majority of strategic alliances are preferred in the form of capital integrations and share purchases. This path will be chosen to efficiently expand the spectrum of possible action in response to the time constraints placed on an internal business expansion. In orienting their multimedia strategies, market players pass through differing strategic development stages and bandwidths of the value chain processes. These reach from a focusing strategy through a cooperative strategy all the way to an integration strategy (see fig. 6). A consequential expansion of the action spectrum above and beyond the pure production of contents and services to include electronic processing and the organization and preparation of programs up to and including their transport to the customer is executed in several strategic stages. An integration strategy aims to accomplish a commanding position within all stages of the value chain and thereby hopes to secure the largest possible market domination for the players involved.

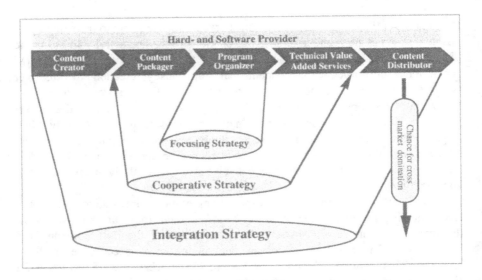

Fig. 6.   Value chain and competitive strategies

A focusing strategy is only of limited strategic value for a global player. These instead attempt to expand their core business and establish a lead position through cooperation with a large number of suppliers from different value added stages. At present, a multitude of companies may be found in the stages of developing such cooperative agreements. Such a strategy makes possible the rapid expansion of business fields with limited financial commitment. An expansion of the cooperation strategy throughout the entire value chain eventually leads to the integration strategy which offers the possibility of dominant market control. Time Warner and AT&T can be seen as pioneers of such integration strategies. AT&T's declared goal to "offer business and private customers everything out of one hand, from the telephone network, through the related services, up to and including end user devices" (Palaß/Preissner-Polte 1994) has motivated it to take a world-wide leading position in the Content Distributor value stage. However, due to continuing market deregulation and growing competition, margins are shrinking considerably in the traditional business of voice and data communication services, especially for long distance carriers such as AT&T. Hence, AT&T is striving to expand their position by developing Value Added Services and incorporating intelligence (on-line services and software, groupware services in a joint with Lotus Development). The necessary software for achieving an added value for the customer must provide both the choice of and access to contents, as well as their administration and distribution. Correspondingly, AT&T is striving to complete a multitude of cooperative agreements with market participants from the different value stages.

For this reason, Content Creators such as film studios, TV companies, publishers and video producers, who possess one of the most profitable value adding stages, are the most attractive cooperation partners. Especially the movie industry offers yield opportunities unlike any other entertainment branch, through box office receipts, soundtracks and TV and video rights. Consequently, the pure production of contents will often be the core building stone of integrated value chain strategies. The control of the Content Creator and Content Distributor stages of the value chain will not, however, be sufficient for a dominating role in the future multimedia market. The cooperation with Content Organizers represents a further contingency for a successful integration strategy. Program contents will in the future be mere commodities (much like hardware in today's PC market), in which consumers will only be interested if they can filter through the bewildering quantity of information, that is, if these contents are specifically oriented to their particular needs. The attainment of a corresponding customer value added through the administration and preparation of information is therefore a further crucial asset.

Of all the value added stages, the Hard- and Software Providers (see fig. 6) are perhaps most urgently in need of partnerships. These manufacturers can hardly continue to amortize their high investments despite rising demand for multimedia end user devices, because of ever shortening product life cycles and a price erosion within the entire hardware sector that varies betweeen 10 and 50%. Information contents have therefore become the main revenue bearers. It is no longer technology which represents the deciding success factor, but the achievement of an added value for the consumer. For the Hard- and Software Providers, the cooperation with the Content Creators and Distributors thus becomes an unavoidable necessity.

Despite the fact that the integration of the value chain stages is sensible from a market dominance perspective, the management tasks which arise therefrom should not be underestimated. It is true that the network operators have sufficient capital and know-how at their disposal for the control of single value added stages, however, a corresponding integration-know-how and a tuned organizational flexibility are necessary for the pursuit of integration strategies. Yet it remains evident that no single market participant can capture the multimedia market alone. Integration strategies make possible a minimization of risk within the process of capturing the market through an efficient bundling of resources and a dispersion of the capital raising responsibility among several market participants. For the global players, it opens a broad window on the market and its rapidly developing technologies and services.

5   Perspectives

The need for integration strategies and the desire of all companies to dominate markets create, of course, significant regulatory issues. It is understandable that large media companies, who estimate that they will conduct 30% of their business in electronic form by the year 2020, will want to build their own technical platforms. Yet the danger that, due to the immense investments required, a few large media conglomerates will reign over our world's information supply is obvious.

Two perspectives should be considered in attempting to control this danger. Firstly, regulatory authorities need to monitor the market behavior and market share growth of media companies. Meaningful guidelines will have to be established to provide a stimulous for all publishers and media companies while still allowing for the necessary multitude of opinions and fragmentation of the industry.

Secondly, providers of technical infrastructure, i.e. content distributors and Value Added Services providers, will have to build platforms that can also be used by small publishers and media companies. Very similar to the Internet, this technical infrastructure will have to evolve as an open platform for information and communication, thereby enabling the unrestricted and unbiased dissemination of knowledge, entertainment, and commercial interests.

Only by these means will the media industry continue to guarantee freedom of opinion and become a governor of our cultural heritage as we move towards the Information Society.

References

Bangemann-Group, Europe and the Information Society, Brussels, 1994

Benjamin, R., Wigand, R., Electronic Markets and Virtual Value Chains on the Information Superhighway, in: Sloan Management Review, No. 2, 1995, pp. 62-72

Byrne, J. A., Brandt, R., Port, O., The Virtual Corporation, in: International Business Week, February 8, 1993, pp. 36-40

Davidow, W. H., Malone, M. S., Das virtuelle Unternehmen - Der Kunde als Co-Produzent, Frankfurt/Main, 1993

Denger, K., Wirtz, B., Die digitale Revolution, in: Gablers Magazin, No. 2, 1995, pp. 20-24.

Miller, D. B., Clemons, E. K., Row, M. C., Information Technology and the Global Virtual Corporation, in: Bradley, S. P., Hausman, J. A., Nolan, R. L. (eds.), Globalization, Technology and Competition, Harvard Business School Press, Boston, 1993, pp. 283-307

Nefiodow, L., Der fünfte Kondratieff, Wiesbaden, 1991

Palaß, B., Preissner-Polte, A., Odysse 2000, in: Manager Magazin, No. 7, 1994, pp. 107-113, here p. 112

Weißenberg, P., Information-highways ohne Tempolimit, in: Top Business, No. 8, 1994, pp. 74-75

Wirtz, B., Strategische und organisatorische Transformationsprozesse in der Telekommunikationsindustrie, in: Zeitschrift Führung und Organisation, 64(1995a)2, pp. 90-94

Wirtz, B., Strategischer Wettbewerb im Televisionsmarkt, in: List Forum für Wirtschafts- und Finanzpolitik, No. 2, 1995b, pp. 225-236

The Multimedia Marketplace in the Private Household - Some Observations and Comments

Georg Rainer Hofmann
KPMG Unternehmensberatung, Germany

1 Introduction

If there are no waves, you can't be paddling.

Writing an article on the multimedia marketplace of the private households, one is confronted with the readers expectations. These might include to read chapters on a comprehensive description of the status quo of the multimedia applications of the private households, a glance of the current technological discussion, and finally a - quantitative - forecast of the future shape of the market. This contribution is different: It simply states some observations that the author picked up during the first quarter of this year, and it tries to show that even the topic of the article is fuzzy in nature. Instead of a in-depth analysis of the terms "multimedia" and "private", the article immediately leads to the illustrations of some "waves", the reader might wish to draw his/her own deductions regarding the shape and size of the "paddles".

2 Forecasting the multimedia market: Very likely, everything that can be said will be wrong

The German weekly newspaper "Die Zeit" (Zeit 1995a) recently published an interesting comparison between telecommunication market forecasts of some years ago and what became today's telecommunication market reality.

The listed examples were about the following services:
- Teletex
- Telefax
- BTX
- Mobile phone

For *Teletex*, the forecasted market volume has been for 1987 and for 1993 some 40,000 and some 130,000 users, respectively. The real market volume for the years 1987 and 1993 has been some 18,000 and some 10,000 user, respectively. Here, not only the quantitative forecast has been significantly wrong, even the qualitative forecast was not quite and exactly correct. Instead of an *increase* of 325%, the market faced a *decrease* to 55% in 1993, compared to its volume in 1987.

The *BTX* service forecasts have a special history. This service, in the mid 1980ies forecasted at some 2,000,000 users for 1990, had only 260,000 users at that year. For those companies which did invest massively in the development of, e.g., BTX terminals, wrong forecastings of the market volume had some bitter consequences. Some of the so-called market forecasting institutes were forced to correct their number from one edition of their "market reports" to the other - a fact that seems as interesting as well as funny. As commonly known, the main error has been the overestimation of the allowable individual prices for a private BTX access. Today, since prices for BTX came drastically down, the BTX user community is increasing, reaching at some 700,000 - and more - in Germany today. Certainly the opening of BTX to the Internet and other services ("Telekom Online") will give BTX an additional push.

But, on the other side, some other telecommunication market segments were massively underestimated.

The forecastings of the *fax* user community, for exampe, were by far to low. Today, in Germany some 3,000,000 fax machines are in usage by both, private and commercial applications. Forecastings at the end of the 1980ies might have expected some 500,000 users at maximum.

Quite the same picture shows the *mobile phone* market. Forecastings issued in the early 1990ies did expect some 80,000 users in 1992, and some 450,000 users in 1994. Instead of these numbers, we have had about 210,000 mobile phone users in 1992, and some 1,600,000 users in 1994. No doubt, it has its good sides for investors, when the real market development reaches over 350% of the market forecastings.

Now, forecasters of the multimedia market volume are more cautious, indeed. Booz, Allen & Hamilton (BAH), for example, recently rolled-out two numbers on the occassion of the publication of a multimedia market study performed for the Deutsche Bundestag (Handelsblatt 1995b): For the multimedia market volume, BAH estimates for the year 2000 some 10,000,000,000 DM for commercial applications, and some 6,000,000,000 DM for private applications; *if* - BAH said - the acceptance of new services by the users and the deregulation of the telecommunication market will not influence the future market developments in an other direction, and thus the resulting market volume will be different to the forecasts.

For example, Philips Consumer Electronics pointed out (Handelsblatt 1995b) that the crucial multimedia market issue is whether the private client is realizing the benefits of new multimedia applications, and, subsequently, accepts to pay for them.

The latter thought leads directly to a basic question: Could one identify a basic criterium for the sucess or the failure of a telecommunication and/or multimedia service, compared to the forecasts and expectations?

3   Trendsetting the multimedia and telecommunication market places: The private household sector is way ahead

Due to our own research in the field, we think the criterium for "product success" in this sense is whether a product has been accepted by the private users and the private households or not. Looking back in history of the last ten years, a newly developed high-tech product became a real success for the industry and the manufactures, when it has been accepted by the non-commercial, private sector. A list - illustrative vs. exhaustive - would be in the historical order of average appearance:

- Pocket calculator
- Video tape recorder
- Video game
- CD player
- 1st generation PC
- Satellite dish
- Game boy
- 2nd generation PC (multimedia features)
- PC modem and online service access
- Private fax machine
- Mobile phone

The private users' decisions on the buying of these specific high technology products were always, and will be in the future as well, not depending on a comprehensive cost/benefit analysis, and certainly not on bare monetary factors.

Instead, the success of a high-tech product has been always depending on factors like

- cheapness - can the user afford to buy it?
- commodity - is it easy to learn how to use it?
- luxury and life style - does it impress the user's friends?
- fun - can the user (or the children) use it alone at home?

Based on considerations as outlined above, how will the "multimedia marketplace for the private household" look like, and on what factors does its further development depend on?

Based on KPMG's research, we would stress the following points.

Firstly: The *target hardware* for private multimedia usage will be the second generation *Personal Computer (PC)*. This PC features a larger colour screen, huge masses of storage capacity of all kind, a sound hardware, all kind of disk drives including a double-speed CD-ROM drive, a modem (for data transfer based either on PSTN, ISDN, or even GSM). Clearly, the high standardization expectations of the private consumer will prevent any special multimedia hardware solutions, e.g., so-called set-top boxes for receiving video-on-demand, to become a economical success. Recently reported numbers (Welt 1995a) say that about 12% of all households in the United States do possess an advanced PC with a modem and do have potential access to network services.

Secondly: The *target software* basis for multimedia applications will be highly standardized. The basic system will be cheap, if not available for free in the public domain. For example, successful tools for the multimedia information services access will likely be public domain and be based on the WWW/Internet.

Thirdly: The basic carrier service will be Internet-based. Not only the Internet community is clearly in advance in terms of its - currently roughly estimated - some 40 million users, the Internet world will also "integrate" other services, like Compuserve or BTX. The latter ones have to provide smooth interfaces and gateways to the main-stream Internet. The basic Internet access will likely be for free (Welt 1995b); Internet service providers will not be able to sell the basic access to the net, but need to give it away for free.

4   Multimedia advertising on nets: The analogon to the print media and TV

The private household, once being well-equipped with a multimedia PC, and having access to a multimedia service, will face the commercial side of the multimedia information society. It has been reported, for example, that the impact of the newly emerging online services will massively influence the consumer markets (Handelsblatt 1995a). Private households will base their decisions how and when to buy specific goods more and more on electronically available information. A questionaire did address some 3,500 WWW users in Europe and North America. The WWW users did answer that would *buy* computer software, books, computer hardware, and music CDs over a WWW online service. On the other hand, the study did also proof, that WWW users would rather *inform* themselves on certain products than to *buy* actually these products. For example, more expensive goods, like cars, household furniture, or the like, will hardly be bought over the WWW. Nevertheless, advertising these goods over the WWW works very well. The study concluded that for the preparation of selling goods to the "WWW/Internet households", the WWW meanwhile became the most but one important medium. Just the print media still perform better in the discipline of forwarding product information to the prospective consumers in the private households.

When it comes to multimedia advertising on nets, the analogon to the print media is obvious. No wonder that the traditional print media enterprises try to claim their market shares as early as possible. The market target is clearly the segement of the private households. The media company Bertelsmann, for example, has formed an joint venture with America Online (Handelsblatt 1995c). Bertelsmann bought shares that equal 50,000,000 US$, and the commonly formed joint venture will invest another 150,000,000 DM for the preparation of the technological multimedia online marketplace in Europe. But Bertelsmann is not the only player in this special market. The Burda group (Germany) joined recently forces with the French Groupe Matra-Hachette and the British Pearson to form the media enterprise Europe Online S.A., based in Luxemburg. The German Telekom AG will broaden and re-position its DATEX-J service to become the "Telekom Online" service.

All the above-listed activities aim at the same target, which is the preparation of the technical and commercial infrastructure for the electronic-commerce-based market place. The applications on the market place will include
- News and information services of all kind
- Railroad, bus, and air traffic schedules
- Product cataloques of all kind, especially bulky ones
- Phone books, including yellow pages
- Electronic banking
- Games and entertainment software on a pay-per-use basis
- Messaging services including voice mail features

Highly specialized electronic commerce companies will provide the technical infrastructure, the dissemination of software and hardware necessary for using these services, and, finally, the accounting and billing mechanisms.

However, there is still a long way ahead. Crucial issues are, among others, the construction, establishment, and the shaping of a "professional electronic commerce service firm". The functionality of "electronic cash" systems is also under intensive discussions (Zeit 1995b).

5 Teleworking: Some workers will stay at home

Whether the further development of the information society will affect the way we work at our offices or not - this seems no question: It will. But in which way? Arthur D. Little's (ADL) recent study (Zeit 1995a) said that some 10 million working places will be *involved*. In fact, by some politicians, this result is quoted often wrongly. Instead of what has been written by ADL, some say that the information society will *create* some 10 million working places (Zeit 1995a).

Information technology, and multimedia technology is a part of it, is destroying millions of jobs. The hope is, that is will create more than it destroys, as John F Kennedy said: "If men have the talent to invent new machines that put men out of work, they have the talent to put those men back to work." (Economist 1995).

But, as being more pervasive, the outcoming technologies of the multimedia information society are being introduced much faster than earlier new technologies were (such as, e.g., the mechanised loom or the spinning jenny). That means that there is less time to replace the jobs that are lost and to train and adapt people to the new circumstances.

It seems reasonable, that multimedia information technology will influence the *private working situation*, since it makes works more portable. In some services, physical contact to clients and working colleagues becomes unnecessary at a very high degree. Multimedia-based teleworking enables firms to move jobs elsewhere, even to the private homes. In this sense, two effects will occur - or even have occured:

Firstly, new multimedia technology not only reduces the demand for labour, it also increases its supply.

Secondly, the concentration of work to a few skilled persons will massively increase. The workload will swap over to those to can't detract themselves from work, because their work follows them to everywhere they are. The exploding market for accessoires for portable work, such as mobile phones, laptop computers, portable fax systems etc. tells a clear story.

And there is a dark side of it all: "Well, the new technology has made it possible for me to work at home full time. - I've been laid off", said the home-coming husband to his wife in a magazine cartoon (Economist 1995).

References

Economist, Technology and Unemployment, in: The Economist, Febr. 11, 1995

Handelsblatt, Kommerzielle Nutzung wird forciert, in: Handelsblatt, March 8, 1995a

Handelsblatt, Markt wird sondiert, in: Handelsblatt, Febr. 17/18, 1995b

Handelsblatt, Wössner will ins Online-Geschäft, Bertelsmann steigt bei America Online ein, in: Handelsblatt, March 2, 1995c

Welt, Zahl des Tages, in: Die Welt, Jan. 27, 1995a

Welt, Auf dem Marsch in die Info-Gesellschaft, in: Die Welt, Febr. 28, 1995b

Zeit, Starker Glaube, schwache Fakten, in: Die Zeit 13/1995, March 24, 1995a

Zeit, Wo Geld nicht mehr stinken kann, in: Die Zeit 13/1995, March 24, 1995b

Information Technologies in the Home: Policies and Markets

Norbert Mundorf
University of Rhode Island, USA

1   Introduction

Computers and telecommunications have experienced steady growth in the business sector since the 1950s and have boomed during the past decade. Business applications of information technologies (IT) were discussed in the trade press and in academic publications (Dholakia/Mundorf/Dholakia 1995). Diffusion of IT in the home was delayed by decades and has only recently gained momentum. As the business sector experiences some degree of saturation with a somewhat predictable replacement cycle, home IT is thought to be the growth market of the 1990s and beyond. In addition, the home and business markets are increasingly intertwined (Mundorf/Zoche 1994). Media, industry, and government officials have announced the multimedia revolution and the Information Superhighway with much fanfare. We have seen much supply-side driven enthusiasm. However, the demand side of home IT-adoption is not well understood.

This chapter explores some of the key issues of home IT adoption, in particular the role of information and entertainment. It analyzes the market potential for VoD as well as some VoD trials. Revenue potential of VoD is seen as limited. Other applications of interactive technology will need to supplement VoD in order to provide adequate economic and social benefits.

In particular, the focus on film entertainment is misguided as more and more players attempt to divide roughly the same consumer dollars amongst themselves. After analyzing prospects for video on demand, business and work applications for the home are analyzed. Finally, the chapter discusses existing access devices used in the home, and their prospects of being adapted to emerging technologies, systems, and software.

2   Video dialtone and video on demand

While advantages for voice services have become apparent, telecommunications suppliers are now looking for additional revenue sources, in part to offset lost revenue from shrinking regulated monopolies. One of the widely discussed options for revenue enhancement is video on demand. Banking on the success of home video and presumably added revenue potential of a faster, more convenient method of delivery, various companies have announced plans to implement this service.

Several industries have lined up to provide advanced video services into the home: the seven regional bell operating companies (RBOCs), the cable industry, long-distance providers, independent phone companies, as well as content providers (major studios etc.). These industries are going through a period of consolidation and mergers. As each industry has different roots, different regulatory concerns, and different customer perceptions, the playing field is far from level. Local telephone companies are still heavily regulated and the cable industry is going through reregulation. While the cable industry has few actual regulatory constrains keeping it from entering the telephone business, customer perceptions of this industry are poor (Landler 1995). Phone companies have a positive customer image, but many regulatory constraints and lacking expertise in the area of entertaining content. A large number of trials were announced during the past two years, but only a few have actually been implemented, and usually late and with a much smaller scope.

Much of the current discussion of advanced interactive services for private households on the "Information Superhighway" has revolved around "video on demand (VoD)." More specifically, VoD is often used to refer to "movies on demand (MoD)." Since the late 1970s we have witnessed vigorous growth in the market for feature films. At first, the expansion of basic cable and the addition of pay-cable provided numerous additional outlets for such films. By the mid-1980s, video rentals created the unprecedented development of a home video market. Towards the late 1980s and early 1990s, pay-per-view as well as Direct Broadcast Satellite (DBS) generated yet another layer of channels for filmed entertainment. Home video in particular experienced vigorous growth in the past decade and has evolved into a mature industry. DBS has grown rapidly in Europe and in parts of Asia, while the high cable penetration in the U.S. makes such growth less likely.

Because of the phenomenal success of home video and its popularity with most consumers, and because of the easy availability of thousands of feature films, these trials have focused primarily on video on demand. Typically, VoD permits the viewer to choose a film or other video and view it instantaneously on the TV set (or other device) at home. Usually, viewers have the option to interrupt the movie and continue viewing at a later time.

A less costly alternative is near video on demand (NVoD), in which a dozen or so currently popular movies start in 15 or 30 minute intervals. Twelve 2-hour movies starting every 30 minutes would require 48 channels of NVoD (Auletta 1994, n. a. 1993). Compression technologies will soon permit appropriate channel numbers. NVoD obviously can be implemented using the current tree-and-branch structure of existing cable TV systems. Limited upstream messaging could use the phone lines or other existing stuctures.

We will initially discuss technology, content, and cost related challenges facing the implementation of VoD from the vintage point of the service provider before we address additional uses of interactive technologies in the home.

2.1 Supply-side issues: Technology, content, and cost

2.1.1 The network

Several alternatives are currently being discussed regarding the technical implementation of VoD. Fiber to the home (FTTH) was seen as the only alternative by many until recently. Although fiber in the backbone has been installed by telephone and cable providers, the cost of installing fiber in the 'last mile' to the customer premise is currently prohibitive. Most agree that within the next twenty years fiber will replace copper; a vastly accelerated replacement cycle seems impractical, however (Andrews 1994).

Most VoD pilot projects currently utilize hybrid fiber/coax lines. Fiber is run to the neighborhood or the curb; coaxial lines are used to connect individual homes. This combination is currently thought to cut cost in half ($800/HH) compared to $1,600 in electronics and labor needed for a fiber-only solution (Sager/Gleckman 1994).

Another alternative used to limit the cost of the "last mile" is video–dialtone sending compressed video over existing phone lines aided by ADSL technology. The critical bottleneck is the bandwidth of twisted-pair phone wires. Video over twisted-pair is still considered unacceptable in quality and reliability.

2.1.2 Set-top box

The need for intelligent set-top boxes is creating another hurdle regarding the rapid implementation of VoD. This box must be able to process downstream and upstream signals, and decompress or compress them. Also, there will be a need for digital/analog conversion while consumer equipment is still analog. According to some estimates, the cost prototypes is still around $5,000. For purposes of mass marketing, this equipment needs to be available for around $300.

2.1.3 Video server

Large servers are required to store enormously memory-intensive digital video. Two main problems are the need to deliver the same movie to many households with overlapping starting times, and the requirement to store and retrieve thousands of more or less popular movies on demand. Currently no satisfactory system for mass usage has been employed. The digital systems used in the trials serve only a few families, while others have installed manual solutions for the transition period. For instance SNET, the independent telephone company in Conneticut, is currently running a trial of 350 households. The video on demand operation utilizes employees who manually feed videotapes into one out of a hundred VCRs (Wyss 1995). This approach seems adequate for a market test. It is currently not clear when adequate servers will be available, how they will address customer needs, and at what cost per household (Schwartz 1994).

2.2   Content

There has been much speculation as to the content of advanced interactive services. Because of the high visibility of movies, the great public interest in this type of content, and their easy availability, movies on demand has been the offering of choice for many interactive services. Music videos, news, and special interest programming also have their share of attention by the programmers of interactive cable and video dialtone systems. Judging from the experience with pay-per-view, VoD may also cater to special sports, music, or other events at a premium price (pay-per-view charges often reach $30). Interactive game channels are added to some systems. In-home gambling has strong economic appeal; regulatory barriers prevail, however (Mermigas 1995b).

Among movies on demand, blockbuster material is sought after. However, top selling movies usually stay in the theaters for weeks or even months where they generate sales of $7 or $8 per ticket. Although theatrical distribution generates a relatively small percentage of studio revenues (less than 16% domestically), success in the theaters usually spawns success in subsequent exhibition windows. The video rental market reaps the largest profits once video stores are saturated with copies of movies (Mermigas 1995a).

Soft-porn has also proven consistently appealing in late-night pay-per-view. There is a considerable audience. Because operators are reluctant to reserve entire channels for such content, they may lend themselves to a VoD environment. The offering "Private Viewing" at the SNET trial in Hartford, for instance, attracted a positive response from one third of the participating households within the first month (Hunley 1994). While R-rated erotica appear acceptable given appropriate protection of minors, community standards will prohibit VoD distribution of x-rated materials, which are readily available in video stores. The prohibition of distributing obscene content is included in the current congressional tele-communications bill.

Several providers experiment with interactive applications which give the viewer options beyond simply choosing a program. These include game show participation, choice of camera angles at sports games, access to background information for products advertised in commercials, and choice of plot lines and endings in movies. Sega and 3DO are providing interactive games (Kelly 1995). Availability of most applications is very limited, however. They are difficult to produce and require considerable technology. Compared to the massive amount of movies available, true interactivity is still far from any significant availability. Audience demand for this interactivity is not yet understood. While many children and teens feel comfortable with it due to exposure to video games, those in the older demographics are mainly passive consumers of media entertainment.

2.3   Pricing

The pricing of movies on demand needs to be competitive with video rentals, in the $3-4 range. Since there is typically a revenue split with the movie distributor, the revenues generated from MoD will be small initially. Given the existing base of

VCRs, and the dense network of videotape distribution outlets, the transition to MoD could be lengthy.

3   Demand-side issues

3.1   Difficulty assessing demand

Forecasting the demand for new information and entertainment services is fraught with considerable problems. A key issue is that consumers are usually not familiar with the new service or product, thus making it difficult to determine its future use and appeal.

Carey and Elton (Carey/Elton 1995) point out that in estimating demand for new services, we can usually identify the size of the existing market in which the new service may fit, but we often overestimate the market share of the newcomer. Even conservative estimates can lead to misprojections if the share is close to zero.

An even more frequent mistake is made when estimating the point in time when a service will "take off." Screen-based information services are a case in point. Videotex and similar services have existed for two decades. But only now are we seeing sizeable consumer interest as a result of the success of the Internet and the increase in computers in the home. Similarly, the Direct Broadcast Satellite triggered high marketer hopes in the early 1980s, but is only now beginning to gain momentum. Early market entry is not always advantageous, in particular when a complex service cannot be introduced on a trial and error basis.

Often marketers bet on the wrong application made possible by a technology, and the system lacks the flexibility to adjust quickly to the actual demand. E-mail has emerged as the primary use of screen-based information services, while providers were betting on electronic news, travel bookings, and other services which are available more easily and less expensively through traditional channels.

3.2   VoD acceptance

Acceptance of VoD is largely a source of speculation. There are several indications of factors affecting consumer attitude, however: VoD is more popular among younger viewers, who like the combination of convenience and high-tech appeal. The ability to interrupt the film is critical. Some viewers seem to prefer NVoD, simply because it forces them to make fewer choices compared to VoD.

Since MoD is essentially a new delivery method for an existing product, thus adding only limited value, pricing is the key issue. For most movies, only a small surcharge compared to video rental will be acceptable. Current monthly household expenditures for cable and home video are limited to around $30-40. Orme (Orme 1995) reports that customers spent a monthly average of $6-7 on video on demand in a Colorado trial. Other studies report similar figures. Although VoD is far more popular than conventional pay-per-View, annual revenues under $100 would not seem to make it particularly attractive as an investment.

Dholakia (Dholakia 1995) found interest in MoD to be overall modest, but relatively strongest among those who see it as fitting their lifestyle. Besides being younger and more educated, investment in video technology and current movie viewing at home are good predictors of MoD interest.

The overall conclusion from the previous discussion is that entertainment applications may not generate sufficient added revenue to justify implementation of costly interactive systems. However, the combination with business and work applications has greater revenue potential and may present a more realistic venue.

Marketing and regulatory implications differ considerably, however, for these applications compared to the strictly entertainment-based ones. Existing technologies and distribution systems have been adequately providing entertainment services to an increasingly segmented audience. The small viewership for new cable channels, for instance, indicates that there is little added demand for this type of service. Also, private information needs are well served by TV, radio, newspapers, special interest magazines, and telephone services.

4   Business and work applications

An alternate perspective perceives MoD and interactive entertainment as only one subset of applications made possible through an advanced electronic infrastructure. Other applications such as telework, telebanking, teleshopping, telemedicine and distance learning can be used to generate sufficient additional revenues. The same "pipe" can be used to transmit different types of content, possibly resulting in a better return on investment. Often bandwidth requirments are even less compared to video entertainment.

The revenues for non-entertainment applications may be considerable, since the funds will not come from the limited household entertainment budget, but from other sources. In the case of telework, for instance, employers will finance part or all of the expenses needed to connect the employee to the corporate office or the customer. Private households may be able to reallocate part of their transportation budget to telework. Companies will pay for some of the costs of teleshopping, which will partially replace conventional shopping and direct marketing. Home banking, telemedicing, distance learning etc. can lead to additional savings and convenience, which in turn permits reallocation of resources. Social benefits can be realized, as well, through improved access to education, health care, and employment opportunities for the physically challenged or those living in remote locations.

4.1   Work-at-home

The need for an improved infrastructure serving the interface between private households and work and business areas appears more urgent, however. The work-at-home market has boomed in the U.S. and a few other countries after the 1980s corporate restructuring in combination with improved, less-expensive technology and the flattening of corporate hierarchies. According to some estimates, this market has reached close to 40 million people in the U.S. alone, of which 8 million work in corporate telecommuting arrangements.

While corporate investments in information technologies initially failed to pay off in productivity increases, this trend has been reversed. Information technology permits cost savings and it helps smaller companies compete effectively with corporate giants (Sager 1994).

In particular, it permits collaboration relatively independent of location. Individuals or ad-hoc teams are able to work on projects in distant locations. As work becomes increasingly information-intensive, individuals with the right tools can be equally or more effective working out of their home compared to the corporate office.

Most analyses have shown increased productivity and job satisfaction (Sullivan 1992). Other advantages are reduced pollution and traffic congestion, office space savings, the ability to employ people who live too far away or whose circumstances don't permit daily commutes, as well as employee savings in automotive, clothing, and food expenses. Possible drawbacks are isolation, weakened collective bargaining, lack of consideration for promotions. Some professions are not suitable for telework, and individual differences have to be taken into account when selecting employees for telework programs. In spite of some setbacks, the trend towards telework is increasing, and generating strong demand for technologies in the home and adequate software and network facilities. Self-employed home workers with computers also represent a large market for such services and hardware. According to Roberts (Roberts 1995), they generate almost $70,000 in household income.

4.2   Home shopping

Most home shopping is currently still low-tech. Catalog and TV shoppers order by phone using a toll-free number and charging the purchase to a credit card. Catalog shopping is an enormous market, which has grown rapidly in the 1980s due to increasing numbers of double-income families, the growth in direct marketing and specialty catalogues and an improved infrastructure of toll-free phone numbers, voice mail, and computerized order processing.

TV shopping has grown in the early 1990s. However, the growth has been limited by the selection of goods available, by the limited demographic appeal of TV shopping, and by the inconvenience of being able to purchase only products currently advertised.

Computer shopping is available, as well, through online services such as Prodigy, through Videotex type services in Europe, and most recently through the Internet (Castro 1995). MCI has started an electronic mall offered over the World Wide Web. With the possible exception of the French Teletel, all these services are still costly, and limited to the still fairly small number of users with modems who subscribe to the appropriate services. Billing is also fraught with problems. Because of the lack of security, credit card purchases using the internet are considered unreliable. Collection by the online service provider, as found in some European systems is practical only for small purchases, and it doesn't permit purchases by users outside the system (or country).

In order for electronic shopping to capture significant market share from catalog or even from in-store shopping, interactive technology has to be available, which is user friendly, affordable, and permits easy access to desired goods and comparative pricing information. Even then only certain demographic and psychographic segments will prefer this transactional mode. Generally, adoption of technology is positively related to income and inversely related to age. Dual-income households with children may be considered prime targets due to their lack of time, active purchasing behavior, and age and education related technology acceptance. Even within this group, attitudes towards technology will mediate use of electronic shopping. Also, certain product types lend themselves better to electronic shopping than others. Current catalog shopping patterns provide an indication of product viability.

4.3   Telebanking

Conventional banking is very inefficient both for banks due to the high cost of transactions and the customer because of the time and inconvenience involved in writing checks, going to the bank. Telephone banking is gaining acceptance in the U.S., where touchtone dialing is widely available. Some banks have established or joined online systems. Many business customers are tied into electronic banking systems. But the bulk of private bank customers still utilizes conventional means.

The enormous success of automatic teller machines has evidenced great demand for convenient electronic banking. Due to the essentially alphanumeric nature and limited product range of electronic banking, it is easier to implement than electronic shopping. However, user friendliness and security are essential. In addition, banks tend to be conservative and may be resistant to change. Customers may also be skeptical because of recent problems related to computerized trading and break-ins by hackers. As with other technologies, adoption is positively related to income and education, and inversely related to age.

4.4   Distance learning

Because of the increasing competition in the global economy, continuing education is a growing concern. To remain competitive, employees have to improve their job skills; increasingly, they have to aquire a new set of skills to change jobs. Also, education is valued more highly than in the past. Even real estate values in the U.S. are related to the quality of area schools. Finally, the cost of college education is skyrocketing. Distance learning can address these concerns.

While the concept has been in existence for more than a century in correspondence courses, and later through the use of radio, television, and the VCR, the widespread availability of computers in schools and homes (Levy 1995), satellite and videoconferencing technology have lead to the prospect of interactive distance learning accessible to considerable parts of the population (Wallis 1995).

Interactive evening or weekend courses can make it easier for employees to improve their skills without the inconvenience of additional travel. Schools in remote areas can receive similar quality and diversity of educational offerings as those in wealthy suburbs. Finally, distance learning can improve the quality of and lead to cost savings for college education by linking small colleges or remote branch campuses to the educational opportunities provided by research universities. Some schools currently experiment with degrees based on electronically delivered courses. Rather than replacing the current educational system, distance learning is expected to complement it.

4.5   Telemedicine

Like education, cost of health care is rising dramatically. Telemedicine addresses such concerns by providing access to specialists, limiting the need for offices visits, and by making medical information quickly available. Some countries and states with populations in remote areas are experimenting with telemedicine. Norway, for instance, has linked dispersed populations in its northern parts with specialists in Oslo (Bakke 1993). In the U.S. the need to control health care costs and to reach underserved groups is encouraging increased reliance on computers and telecommunications in medicine. Telemedicine also holds economic promise in that it increases the reach of the health care industry beyond the local community. Currently, the strength of telemedicing is in home health care, prevention and diagnostics, although ultimately remote surgery using microrobotics is conceivable. Particularly, health care automation helps shift health care from hospitals to the home through remote diagnosis and by aiding visiting nurses or family members in the administration of drugs (Donovan 1995). Digital communication networks are considered critical in the transmission of medical images and in distant patient-nurse-doctor communication (Kostrzewa 1995).

5   User interface

The question of the preferable mode of access in the private home is gaining importance as increasingly untrained groups of users gain access to information technologies. Several types of end-user equipment are more or less suitable for different functions. Functionality is not the only criterion, however. In particular, cost, availability, ease of use and perceived fit within a consumer's lifestyle precipitate the choice of a particular technology. This section discusses four technologies (telephone, TV, PC, and video game machines) and assesses ho suitable they are for the applications mentioned above.

Ultimately the distinctions between these technologies will vanish in favor some kind of telecomputer (Gilder 1989), and dedicated miniature equipment specific uses. However, because of the enormous installed base of exi equipment, the shift towards such new devices will take years and marketers ne target their strategies to the existing base.

5.1   Telephone

Virtually all consumers are familiar with this device. Penetration is close to 100%. It is inexpensive and easy to use and ties into the most advanced and universal communication network. Portability is high for cordless and cellular phones and newly emerging personal communications systems. Currently the visual component is lacking, which limits certain interactive applications. However, the touch-tone telephone is a key medium for home shopping and banking. Several providers are developing intelligent telephones featuring a small display (Williams 1994) with practical utility for several types of transactions. These are still limited for entertainment applications, but lend themselves to use in practical transactions (shopping, bill paying).

5.2   Television

As the most common audiovisiual medium, TV enjoys almost universal penetration; it is fairly inexpensive and very user friendly. However, interactivity is limited, the TV set has very limited intelligence, and screen resolution is poor for graphic and text display. HDTV is generally not considered an affordable alternative. Viewers are currently used to the remote control as a limited interactive option.

Most advanced interactive trials are planning to use an intelligent set-top box to link the TV in the home to a client-server network. The box serves only one purpose, however, and is of limited use to the consumer. Current prototype boxes are in a price range which is prohibitive for a mass market. Bringing down the price for these set-top boxes is a key requirement for successful large-scale implementation of interactive TV based services.

5.3   Personal computer

During the past decade, personal computers have gained considerable acceptance in private homes. About one third of U.S. households are estimated to own at least one PC. Private ownership of PCs experienced a boost during the recent multimedia wave. Personal computers are becoming more user friendly, attractive and entertaining because of mouse, CD-ROM, audio and video, color monitors and printers. A main strength of PCs is their universal usability. Keyboard and mouse much more versatile input devices than the TV remote control or the telephone keypad. PCs are independent of a central distribution system (broadcast, cable, satellite). Some PCs can now even be used to view video and cable TV in picture quality superior to conventional TV. Among the current drawbacks of the PC are e limited level of diffusion (30+%) vs. TV and phone (90+%); pricing; the need ᐧ special keyboard and programming skills; and the association of PCs with work l learning rather than entertainment and leisure (Markoff 1994). These drawbacks adually losing importance. Interest in PCs and other interactive technologies versely related to age and is thus expected to increase over time. Finally, ᵗ in and ownership of PCs is positively related to that in other interactive

5.4   Video games

Video game machines play the role of an outsider in the discussion of new technologies. But they have a large installed based in households with children and adolescents (Brandt/Gross 1994). The games are interactive already and latest versions offer the option of games over telephone wires. Conceivably such equipment can be modified to serve practical uses, such as home banking. More importantly, their users have conquered fear of technology already, and will have little trouble moving towards more complex applications. Games such as "Doom" make the transition from video games to CD-ROM easy. This, in turn increases acceptance among younger consumers. Video games in their current form are too specialized to become the primary medium of interactivity.

6   Conclusion

This article has analyzed factors influencing the introduction of information technologies in the home. Entertainment will serve an important function. Video-on-demand alone might not be able to generate sufficient revenue to justify the huge investment necessary to implement an interactive network including intelligent set-top boxes and large servers. The combination of entertainment with work and business applications will provide a more solid basis for such investment. As far as the preferred access device is concerned, the PC holds the most flexibility and is likely to be the basis for more complex application such as telework and distance learning. Enhanced telephones with limited video are suitable for home banking, travel information/booking and limited home shopping. The TV-set enjoys the greatest popularity and level of diffusion, and is thus most suitable for mass market applications such as home shopping, VoD, and other entertainment. It is a particularly useful medium in reaching older and less educated consumers, who are often not familiar with PCs (or videogame machines).

Videogame equipment can be used to reach children and teenagers. Based on current applications it will remain primarily an entertainment medium, with some limited use for shopping and communications.

Some authors (Gilder 1989) may find this focus on existing technologies backward. However, many consumers don't feel the urgent need or don't have the means to invest in the newest technologies as soon as they become available. As a result, the transition period of the next ten to twenty years to a fiber broadband network connected to digital user equipment will challenge suppliers to market software, systems and consumer electronics suiting the needs of a diverse population with limited resources, skills, and motivation to adopt new technologies. Consumers will adopt systems which provide tangible benefits at a good cost-benefit ratio. Suppliers need to learn much about consumer needs and attitudes regarding information technologies in the home to avoid large scale errors of judgment.

References

Andrews, P., More realistic view of 'information superhighway' is taking shape, in: The Seattle Times, D2, February 8, 1994

Auletta, K., The magic box, in: The New Yorker, April 11, 1994, pp. 40-45

Bakke, J. W., Contribution to 1993 Honors Colloquium 1993, in: Dholakia, N., Mundorf, N., New Information Technologies: Panacea or Peril. Research Institute for Telecommunications and Information Marketing, University of Rhode Island, 1993

Brandt, R., Gross, N., Sega, in: Business Week, February 21, 1994, pp. 66-74

Carey, J., Elton, Forecasting demand for new consumer services: Challenges and alternatives, in: Dholakia, R. R., Mundorf, N., Dholakia, N. (ed.), New Infotainment Technologies in the Home: Demand-side Perspectives, Hillsdale, NJ, Erlbaum Publishers, forthcoming 1995

Castro, J., Just click to buy, in: Time Magazine Special Issue: Welcome to Cyberspace, 1995, pp. 74-75

Dholakia, R. R., Taking movies-on-demand to market, in: Dholakia, R. R., Mundorf, N., Dholakia, N. (ed.), New Infotainment Technologies in the Home: Demand-side Perspectives, Hillsdale, NJ, Erlbaum Publishers, forthcoming 1995

Dholakia, R. R., Mundorf, N., Dholakia, N., Bringing infotainment home: Challenges and choses, in: Dholakia, R. R., Mundorf, N., Dholakia, N. (ed.). New Infotainment Technologies in the Home: Demand-side Perspectives, Hillsdale, NJ, Erlbaum Publishers, forthcoming 1995

Donovan, W. J., Three trailblazers fill gaps in health care with technology, in: Providence Sunday Journal, A 17, March 12, 1995

Gilder, G., Microcosm, New York, Simon & Schuster, 1989

Hunley, A., Personal interview, October, 1994

Kelly, L., US West sets programers for video trials, in: Electronic Media, February 27, 1995, p. 56

Kostrzewa, J., R.I. health care prescription: Innovation, in: Providence Sunday Journal, A1, March 12, 1995, p. 16

Landler, M., Cable customers unhappy, in: Providence Journal, E1, March 2, 1995, p. 8

Levy, S., TechnoMania, in: Newsweek, February 27, 1995, pp. 25-29

Markoff, J., "I wonder what's on the PC tonight.", in: New York Times, F1, May 8, 1994, p. 8

Mermigas, D., Programming boom spurring co-ventures, in: Electronic Media, February 27, 1995a, p. 24, p. 26

Mermigas, D., TCI: Gaming is 'Killer Application', in: Electronic Media, May 8, 1995b, p. 32

Mundorf, N., Zoche, P., Nutzer, private Haushalte und Informationstechnik, in: Zoche, P. (ed.), Herausforderungen für die Informationstechnik, Springer, 1994, pp. 59-69

n. a., "A Year of Turmoil in Communications", in: New York Times, D11, October 14, 1993

Orme, P., Strategies for broadband communications, in: Dholakia, R. R., Mundorf, N., Dholakia, N. (ed.), New Infotainment Technologies in the Home: Demand-side Perspectives, Hillsdale, NJ, Erlbaum Publishers, forthcoming 1995

Roberts, T., Who are the high-tech home workers?, in: Inc. Technology, 1995, p. 13, p. 16, p. 31

Sager, I., Gleckman, H., The digital juggernaut, in: Business Week Special Issue: The Information Revolution, 1994, pp. 22-31

Sager, I., The great equalizer, in: Business Week Special Issue: The Information Revolution, 1994, pp. 100-107

Schwartz, E. I., Demanding Task: Video on Demand, in: New York Times, F4, January 23, 1994

Sullivan, N., How to save $23 Billion, in: Home Office Computing, February, 1992, p. 96

Wallis, C., The Learning revolution, in: Time Magazine Special Issue: Welcome to Cyberspace, Spring, 1995, pp. 49-51

Williams, F., On prospects for citizens' information services, in: Williams, F., Pavlik, J. V. (ed.). The people's right to know: Media, democracy and the Information Highway, Hillsdale, NJ, Erlbaum, 1994

Wyss, B., TV Heaven: Interactive video coming to a living room near you, in: Providence Sunday Journal, A1, February 12, 1995, p. 14

Social Implications

Computer Use at Home - A Cultural Challenge to Technology Development

Werner Rammert
Free University of Berlin, Germany

1   Introduction

Computerized information processing is a new type of technology. It is not a simple piece of hardware or only a new physical machine, but a technical system in which microcomputers, household machines or communication media are loosely coupled with one another or with a network to allow programmed or interactive use. This type of a high technology system based upon information engineering (Rammert 1992a) does not only change production and control at the private enterprise, but it will also change work and communication at the private household.

Whenever our societies are confronted with new technologies, social scientists are asked to assess their social consequences and to evaluate their cultural impact. That is not only a rather difficult job, because nearly all relevant data are at that time missing: the producers have not yet decided upon the ultimate design of the utilities; the users did not have enough time to make their experience with it, and the politicians had not settled the legal and institutional problems. *Technologies which are in the process of development create a circle of uncertainties.* But the assessment of emerging technologies is also a dangerous task, because one runs the risk of reducing the uncertainty by a technological fix and thereby rectifying the actual technological trend.

2   Visions of computer use in private households

One method to handle with the circle of uncertainty is to construct a set of alternative scenarios. Looking at the literature about the visions of the electroni cottage or of the computerized home we can distinguish two opposite scenarios: "mobile homuter society" and the "information-polluted society".

The *"mobile homuter society"-scenario* unites all the optimistic visions of modernization and technological progress (Homo-Computer-Symbiosis see Haefner/Eichmann/Hinze 1987, Masuda 1981). Under this perspective computer technology realizes an old utopian dream: to rationalize the up to now "irrational" private life. For instance, individual ignorance and personal idleness could be overcome by microcomputers built in household machines to save energy and to take care of environmental impacts. A computer coupled with the car and the traffic regulation system could slow down the speed maniac and would be able to guide the helpless driver through the chaos on the roads. The easily manipulated consumer could only buy things via terminal, if he had chequed a criteria list controlled by a health and a consumer agency. Computerized information processing will enhance people's mobility of body and mind by surrounding him with an "intelligent" environment.

The *"information-polluted society"-scenario* combines the pessimistic visions of industrial and ecological criticism (Steinmüller 1988, Kubicek 1985). Their supporters refer to the unsolved problems of industrial modernization and warn not to subordinate the private sphere and the family life to the imperatives of the economy and the state. They fear for instance, that cable networks would give access to consumer behavior and would open the private households to commercial manipulation. The constant use of computers would promote schematic thinking, and the human capability to live with ambivalence and to be sensitive to fine differences would go to waste (Pflüger/Schurz 1987). The increase of technology-mediated-communication would disturb the "ecological equilibrium of communication" by undermining face-to-face interaction and with that the sensual and moral foundations of human communication (Mettler-Meibom 1987). Finally, the overproduction of data would lead us into the crisis of information pollution.

Both scenarios are basicly technology-driven and supply-oriented. They suppose a soft technological determinism, because they make the assumption that the technological trajectories were given and would challenge social and cultural adaptation. I propose to quit this line of thinking in terms of "cultural lag" or "social consequences" (Ogburn 1922). Let us turn the perspective from consequences of technologies to the cultural challenge of technological development. *Then technological development can be deconstructed to a loosely coupled chain of technological projects influenced by the visions, concepts and strategies of cooperating and competing social groups.* Following this "social shaping of technology" framework (MacKenzie/Wajcman 1985, Rammert 1992b) we restrict our contribution to the following questions:

- How may cultural orientations influence the generation and the design of information technologies?
- Which part play cultural practices in the appropriation and diffusion of information technologies?

3   The cultural construction of information technologies

Technologies seem to be shaped foremost by parameters of technological perfection and economic efficiency; but who knows what it means to be better? Under which aspect? For how long? In comparison to which alternative? *Technological parameters are cultural artifacts and must be defined socially. They are dependent on the vision of use, on the established engineering culture and on the claims of the user groups.* Controversies about the quality or security of a technology indicate the inherent openess and contingency of technological development which can be only limited by a social closure (Pinch/Bijker 1987).

When we move to the inception and generation of new technology, the circle of uncertainty increases and the variety of possible projects augments. *Visions* of how to use a device for which sake give a first orientation to technological development. For instance, the idea to substitute a programmable machine for the disciplined operations of human computers (Turing 1937, Heintz 1993) pointed the way to hard and software development in computer technology. The vision of computers as "augmented knowledge workshops" (Engelbart 1988) and "personal dynamic media" (Kay/Goldberg 1988, Mambrey/Tepper 1992) diverted computer development to the new trajectory of home and personal microcomputers. The big corporation IBM sticked to its elder vision of big central computers because of its technological leadership in this field and of economic calculations. But with the change of the technological paradigm the controversy about the question what is the best computer was reopened, and IBM lost ground. This example illustrates that a cultural change towards an alternative vision of even a weak economic actor can cause an economic giant to totter.

Concepts are elements of engineering cultures and give clearer reference points than visions. They determine the concrete design of a technical system, for instance whether you can interact with the computer via keyboard, natural language or screen contact. That depends on the user model that designers have in their heads. Finally, the technical construction of machines, programs and networks shapes the frames of social relations. For instance, it is fixed, who does the work, the bank or the client; who may intervene, the manager or the employee; who gets access to relevant data, the administration or the citizen. This process of inscribing concepts of use, user models, and supplier-user relations into technical systems can be seen as a cultural construction of technology.

What can we learn from this view when developing and designing new information technologies? Let us discuss some problems!

One actual problem is the difficulty to change the direction of a technological trajectory or to reorientate the development of a large technical system. The "technological momentum" (Hughes 1987) that seems to be the result of an "autonomous technology" can be disguised as an inherent feature of the engineering culture. Engineers stick to their tested concepts and to the established state of the art, even if they are designing new technologies, because they want to keep away the risk of non-functioning. This structural conservatism of the engineering culture (Knie 1989) is one important factor, if new visions loose their variety-enforcing power and are constricted to traditional lines of development. For instance, in the beginning the telephone was seen as one-way media like the established telegraphy. Following this concept it was then used for some years in Germany as a local device for the prolongation of the telegraphy system. The vision of two-way media was later exploited (Rammert 1993). Another example is the development of the computer. Although the vision of an "universal machine" was already existing, for a long time computers were built and improved into one direction: only to do calculations (MacKenzie 1991).

Another problem arises from the fact that information technologies are designed and installed as if there were no differences to mechanical production technologies. But they are not simple machines substituting computers for clerical work, but they are *media* facilitating the communication and control of all kinds of representations (Rammert 1990, Esposito 1993). For instance, expert systems don't substitute a computer program for highly qualified experts, but their use acquires people with high competences to interpret the results and to fit them to the context (Collins 1993). The information systems should not be designed and sold as finished products, but designing and implementation are better conceived of as an evolutionary process (Floyd 1987). Following the media concept it is not a matter of priority to improve the technical parameters, like the speed, the precision, and the memory of the machine, but it would be of greater importance to think about the media qualities, like the design of the interface, the lucidity of programs, and the flexibility of user models.

A third problem is the adequate representation of the user. Every technical artifact incorporates an image of the envisaged user. In industry, production engineers and salesmen are configuring the user (Woolgar 1991). On the national level, we can sometimes find great differences between the cultural constructions of the user. For instance, if the user is - like in most American concepts of engineering - conceived as a person with average knowledge and with a tendency to comfort, technical systems will be highly automatized and completely encapsulated from user's intervention (for a French example see Akriche 1994). If the user is constructed like the engineer himself, that means as a highly rational man and keen to experiment, then we get a technically perfect system like the German interactive videotex which asks too much of the user. The missing user-friendliness turned the technically brilliant achievement to a commercial disaster (Mayntz/Schneider 1988).

We see that the *cultural* construction of information technologies is sometimes more crucial to economic success and social diffusion than the technical *Fresh* improvement alone. *Real new technologies bring up a lot of uncertainties: the choice of technical parameters, the testing of sufficient functioning, the envisionaged user group, and the commercial pay off. This circle of uncertainty is interrupted by cultural concepts which guide the technical development by implicit paradigms and explicit concepts.*

4   The appropriation and cultivation of information technologies by the user

How do new information technologies disseminate into the private households? An engineer of the development department would answer that new devices convinced people because of their technical capacities. A business economist would emphasize that they were selling as goods with a reasonable price. These conditions of diffusion are necessary, but not sufficient. Beyond technical perfection and economic inexpensiveness users must see the meaning and the usefulness of a device and must be able to appropriate it and to fit it into everyday life routines without problems. We will argue that usefulness is always defined in a cultural framework and dependent on shared values and norms. And we will show that the processes of a new technology's appropriation and cultivation are shaped by practices and lifestyles within different subcultures.

The *meaning* and the *usefulness* of a new technology are not self-evident. The visions of the inventors, the concepts of the engineers, and the images of the salesmen are but only proposals for a sensible use of the new technical system, though they have prestructured the prototypes. From the beginning on there is an experimentation about the uses and a negotation about the reasonable use of a new technology. We have seen a continous change of design concepts in the history of computing, ranging from the central big machinery over the decentral workstation to the home computer and the terminal in the World Wide Web (WWW). They were closely interwoven with the visions and practices of different user groups.

Many collective actors participate in this process of defining the meaning and reasonable use of a new technology. No single actor can impose his concept of computer use to the others. For instance, the quick diffusion of micro-computers in American households was mainly caused neither by the persuasive marketing strategies of the producers nor by the political decision to introduce computer education at schools, but by the self-augmenting and self-organizing cultural movement of hackers and computer clubs (Allerbeck/Hoag 1989). The *public* construction of the micro-computer could be observed at three arenas (Rammert et. al. 1991). Producers and sellers of computers on the one side and users clubs and consumer organizations on the other side discussed the price and negotiated about the service and the quality standards in the *economic* arena. Police, government institutions, and databank owners on the one side and hackers and political groups fighting for the freedom of information or the protection of personal data on the other side struggled at the *political* arena for the definition what is a legitimate, what is a legal, and what is a criminal use of computers. Finally, at the *cultural* arena quite different groups, such as artists and marketing people, scientists and computer clubs are competing with each other for creating new applications and cultivating new styles of computing.

This public construction of a new technology's meaning and usefulness functions as a back stage for the *private* construction of a new technical practice. At first, we have to realize the difference between *social places* where these practices are created.

Using an information system at work or at home or at public places, that makes a big difference. At work one can expect that the employee has the professional competence to use it and that he seriously will follow the instructions of use. At home we will meet a great variety of competences and interests: systems should be open for creative and experimental uses and give enough room for emotional needs and amusement (Dholakia 1994). At public places the system designer has to imagine the "occasional user" with low competence and low frustration tolerance. The cultural concept of the "mass user" is fading, if we focus on the new information technologies and the places where they are practiced (Bievert/Monse 1992).

Secondly, we have to look after the differences between *cultural milieus* and life styles. Beyond traditional class divisions sociologists observe "individualization" and "pluralization" processes of life styles (Beck 1986, Schulze 1992). The users at the households cannot any longer be conceived as "passive consumers" who are buying goods with nearly the same motivation and are using the products in nearly the same manner. Especially the new information technologies which are open to flexible and creative use require the "active user" shaping and appropriating the technical system according to his individual needs and personal style.

The micro-computer, for instance, does not move in the household as a fact and finished good, but it is constructed and configured along subcultural images and tastes. As the computer is eminently suitable as a projection surface, like a Rorschach-test (Turkle 1982), it will be quite unreasonable to expect the one-dimensional computer user, the freak with a pale face, or the man with a mechanical character (Weizenbaum 1976, Volpert 1988, Pflüger/Schurz 1987). As our own empirical study about fifty computer users, men and women of all social classes and aged between 18 and 60, demonstrated, one will find different types of defining the computer and different styles of using the computer with different social and cultural impacts (Rammert et. al. 1991).

We called the group "computer avantgardists" or "computer virtuosos", which constructed it as a "life style medium". It cultivates creative programming and graphic programs. This subculture looks for prestige and social distinction from "lay users". Its members belong to the milieu of independent businessmen and young professionals. The group of women who want to get back into the job or of men who want to better themselves in the job define the computer as a "resource of qualification". They try hard to learn programming at home or at computer clubs. The computer is viewed as a vehicle of their vocational career. This necessarily often disappointed illusion is shared by people coming from lower classes or with female gender. "Computing as passion" is the style how "do-it-your-selfers" and "computer pioneers" define their attitude to the machine. They are a kind of "technofreaks" or "software collectors" who are only interested in the technical stuff, but not in practical use. They belong to the milieu of qualified workers and employees whose practical intelligence is not enough demanded in their jobs. A fourth subculture is built by people who love doing puzzles and brain-teasers. They cultivate computer use as an "intellectual challenge". They prefer an experimental and playful style to test their mental capacities. In this group one can only find men from a higher professional milieu having close contact with computer use in the job.

You can even find more or other classifications (Turkle 1984, Eckert et. al. 1991), but this short outline sufficiently demonstrates: *computers are appropriated and cultivated at home in different ways, and these private constructions of the computer determine the practice and the cultural consequences of computing.* From this we can draw some conclusions for a successful implementation of new information technologies in the private households.

5   Conclusion: Conditions of success and failure

In our view new information technologies are extremely rarely failing because of technical imperfectness or mere economic inefficiency. The hesitating diffusion and the economic desaster of a technology at the outset are very often caused by missing the cultural challenge. *If you will introduce and disseminate a new information technology with success, you have to solve the key problem of tuning the implicit user models with the users' practices in everyday life.*

From the point of view of matter, we often observe a wide gap between the engineers' activity to perfect the technical design and the users' drive to cultivate the use of the technical system. The main challenge is not to find and fix a putative "one best way", it is not to fit a device definitely in a technical infrastructure, but the cultural challenge means to keep the technical system open to a multiplicity and variety of user options.

From the point of view of time, frictions and resistancies grow out of the tendency to offer a finished product to the customer or client, whereas users prefer an open process of trying and defining their personal technical practice. Time, money, and trust should not be gambled away, as it is done with the traditonal strategy, at first to develop an information technology under isolated efficiency and profitability criteria, and afterwards to improve the usability, to put an attractive design on it, and to care about the range of sensible uses. Instead of this procedure one can imagine a temporal coupling of the technical engineering and the cultural construction processes, like the stepwise evolutionary system development (Floyd 1987), where time is reserved to learn and to experiment with the system. To keep open this room to move in the process of design and development is a second challenge to information technologies.

From the point of view of social structure, wrong developments of information technologies spring from the social distance between developers and users and from the reduction of their social relations to mere market relations between suppliers and demanders. Engineers are used to design systems with simplified user models in their heads. They follow an universal image of man as a cognitve and rational being. But users do not only differ from oneanother by income, age and gender, but they belong to different socio-cultural milieus with special values and norms.

Within this cultural framework individual users appropriate new information technologies, invent new technical practices, and cultivate typical styles of living with the new devices. In giving up old practices and establishing new practices they are changing and shaping their culture. This cultural change is initiated by the new technologies, but not determined by their technological features.

The market is not any longer a sufficient coordinator between the developer, the producer and the consumer of new technologies. *Therefore it is the greatest challenge to actual information technology development to raise the reciprocal consciousness between designers and users by making the designers sensitive of users' practices, by finding new ways of user participation in the design process, and by stimulating public discussions about the visions and cultural concepts guiding technological development.*

6   Summary

Traditional views of computer use and its social impact are criticized, because they are technology-driven and supply-oriented. A social constructivist and user-oriented approach is proposed that stresses the cultural challenge of technical development instead of its cultural consequences. In the first part, the author explains how technologies at the outset are shaped more by cultural constructs, like visions of use, user models, and engineering cultures, than by economic calculation or technological parameters. In the second part, it is demonstrated how the dissemination of computers depends on the public construction of the computer as a legitimate and reasonable technical practice and how the cultural impact can be explained by different ways of its private appropriation and by the styles of its cultivation in the social milieu. It is concluded that the main challenge to new information technologies is to tune the implicit user models with the users' practices in a more reflexive, participative and discursive way.

References

Allerbeck, K., Hoag, W., "Utopia is Around the Corner", Computerdiffusion in den USA als soziale Bewegung, in: Zeitschrift für Soziologie, 1(1989)18, pp. 35-53

Akriche, M., The De-Scription of Technical Objects, in: Bijker, W., Law, J. (eds.), Shaping Technology/Building Society, Cambridge, MA, MIT Press, 1994, pp. 205-224

Beck, U., Risikogesellschaft, Frankfurt/M., Suhrkamp, 1986

Biervert, B., Monse, K., Creating applications of information technologies in the service sector, in: M. Dierkes, Monse, K. (eds.), New Technologies at the Outset, Social Forces in the Shaping of Technological Innovations, Frankfurt/Bolder, Campus/Westview Press, 1992, pp. 256-276

Collins, H. M., Artificial Experts. Social Knowledge and Intelligent Machines, Cambridge/MA, MIT Press, 1993

Dholakia, R. R., The Plugged-in Home: Marketing of Information Technology to US Households, in: Zoche, P. (ed.), Herausforderungen für die Informationstechnik, Heidelberg, Physica, Springer, 1994, pp. 86-100

Eckert, R. et. al., Auf digitalen Pfaden. Die Kulturen von Hackern, Programmierern, Crackern und Spielern, Opladen, Westdeutscher Verlag, 1991

Engelbart, D. C., Augmenting human intellect - A conceptual framework, AFOSR-3223, Stanford Research Institute, Menlo Parc, reprinted under the title "The Augmented Knowledge Workshop" in: Goldberg, A. (ed.), A History of Personal Workstations. New York, Addison Wesley, 1988

Esposito, E., Der Computer als Maschine und Medium, in: Zeitschrift für Soziologie, 5(1993)22, pp. 338-354

Floyd, C., Outline of a Paradigma Change in Software Engineering, in: Bjerknes, G. et al. (eds.), Computers and Democracy, Avebur, Aldershot, 1987, pp. 186-203

Haefner, K., Eichmann, E., Hinze, C., Denkzeuge. Was leistet der Computer? Was muss der Mensch selber tun?, Basel, Birkhäuser, 1987

Heintz, B., Die Herrschaft der Regel. Zur Grundlagengeschichte des Computers, Frankfurt/M., Campus, 1993

Hughes, T. P., The evolution of technological systems, in: Bijker, W. et al. (eds.), The Social Construction of Technological Systems, Cambridge, MIT, 1987, pp. 51-82

Kay, A., Goldberg, A., Personal Dynamic Media, in: Goldberg, A. (ed.), A History of Personal Workstations, New York, Addison Wesley, 1988

Knie, A., Das Konservative des technischen Fortschritts. Zur Bedeutung von Konstruktionstraditionen, Forschungs- und Konstruktionsstilen in der Technikgenese, FS II 89-11, Berlin, WZB, 1989

Kubicek, H., Kabel im Keller - Satellit überm Dach, Reinbek, Rowohlt, 1985 (2nd ed.)

MacKenzie, D., Wajcman, J. (eds.), The Social Shaping of Technology, Milton Keynes, Open University Press, 1985

MacKenzie, D., Notes Towards a Sociology of Supercomputing, in: de La Porte, T. (ed.), Social Responses to Large Technical Systems, Dordrecht, 1991, pp. 159-175

Mambrey, P., Tepper, A., Metaphern und Leitbilder als Instrument. Beispiele und Methoden, Arbeitspapier Nr. 651, St. Augustin, GMD, 1992

Masuda, Y., The Information Society as Post-industrial Society, Washington, 1981

Mayntz, R., Schneider, V., The dynamics of system development in comparative perspective: Interactive videotex in Germany, France, and Britain, in: Mayntz, R., Hughes, T. P. (eds.), The development of large technical systems, Bolder, Westview Press, 1988, pp. 263-298

Mettler-Meibom, B., Soziale Kosten der Informationsgesellschaft, Frankfurt/M., Fischer, 1987

Ogburn, W. F., Social Change: With Respect to Culture and Original Nature, New York, 1922

Pflüger, J., Schurz, R., Der maschinelle Charakter. Sozialpsychologische Aspekte des Umgangs mit Computern, Opladen, Westdeutscher Verlag, 1987

Pinch, T. J., Bijker, W. E., The Social Construction of Facts and Artifacts: Or How the Sociology of Science and the Sociology of Technology Might Benefit Each Other, in: Bijker, W. E., Hughes, T. P., Pinch, T. J. (eds.), The Social Construction of Technological Systems, Cambridge, MA, MIT Press, 1987, pp. 17-50

Rammert, W., Computerwelten - Alltagswelten. Von der Konstrastierung zur Variation eines Themas, in: Rammert, W. (ed.), Computerwelten - Alltagswelten. Wie verändert der Computer die soziale Wirklichkeit? Opladen, Westdeutscher Verlag, 1990, pp. 13-26

Rammert, W., From Mechanical Engineering to Information Engineering: Phenomenology and the Social Roots of an Emerging Type of Technology, in: Dierkes, M., Hoffmann, U. (eds.), New Technology at the Outset, Frankfurt/Bolder, Campus/Westview Press, 1992a, pp. 193-205

Rammert, W., Research on the Generation and Development of Technology: The State of the Art in Germany, in: Dierkes, M., Hoffmann, U. (eds.), New Technology at the Outset, Frankfurt/Bolder, Campus/Westview Press, 1992b, pp. 62-89

Rammert, W., Technik aus soziologischer Perspektive, Opladen, Westdeutscher Verlag, 1993

Rammert, W., et. al., Vom Umgang mit Computern im Alltag. Fallstudien zur Kultivierung einer neuen Technik, Opladen, Westdeutscher Verlag, 1991

Schulze, G., Die Erlebnisgesellschaft. Kultursoziologie der Gegenwart, Frankfurt/M., Campus, 1992

Steinmüller, W. (ed.), Verdatet und vernetzt. Sozialökologische Handlungsspielräume in der Informationsgesellschaft, Frankfurt/M., Fischer, 1988

Turkle, S., The subjective computer. A study in the psychology of personal computation, in: Social Studies of Science, 12, 1982, pp. 173-205

Turkle, S., The Second Self. Computers and the Human Spirit, New York, Simon & Schuster, 1984

Turing, A., On computable numbers with an application to the Entscheidungsproblem, Proceedings of the London Mathematical Society, 2(1937)42

Volpert, W., Zauberlehrlinge. Die gefährliche Liebe zum Computer, München, dtv, 1988

Weizenbaum, J., Computer Power and Human Reason. From Judgement to Calculation, San Francisco, Freeman, 1976

Woolgar, S., Configuring the user, in: Law, J. (ed.), A Sociology of Monsters: essays on power, technology and domination, London, Routledge, 1991, pp. 57-99

The Home in Transition: Social Implications of Home Information Technologies

Felix van Rijn
Hogeschool van Amsterdam, The Netherlands, and
IFIP Working Group 9.3 HOIT (Home-Oriented Informatics and Telematics)

1   Introduction

Risk-free one may prophesy that new information technologies in the home will have an impact on everyday life and on the functioning of households. Predicting the nature and the extent of the social implications of new home information technologies is more precarious. Even today little insight exists about how every day and domestic lives are being affected by information technologies. Little systematic research has been and most research confines to one or some specific aspects. A clear picture of the whole is hard to get.

The collected contributions to IFIP's Working Conference Home-Oriented Informatics, Telematics and Automation in Copenhagen (Denmark), June 1994, support this observation (Bjerg/Borreby 1994). They form a dazzling kaleidoscope of views, approaches and research results, reflecting the different backgrounds of the authors, who came from business, industry, politics and different scientific disciplines. A main conclusion at the end of the conference was that we see a scattered picture and that an in-depth analysis of the factual impact of information technologies on households and everyday life is still lacking. Another main conclusion was that the consequences of home applications of information technology relate strongly with the - changing - place and role of the household in the social and economic structure of society. From this perspective a prudential assessment of the - future - social impact may make sense. A short retrospective and a concise analysis of the present precede this assessment.

Intermezzo: terminology

In an attempt to avoid confusion and misunderstanding about the terminology used in this article, some terms are defined below:

Information technology stands for all computerized information processing and includes automation and datacommunication.

Home information technology implies all information technology intended to be used in the home or to be used for communication with the home.

Household means private households i.e. any group of persons living together in a social and economic entity.

Home is the spatial habitat of a household including all available equipment and facilities.

2   Retrospective

The history of home information technology starts in the late 1970s with the introduction of videotex (viewdata). It was the first commercial application of computerized information processing in the private household. Also around 1980 many authors published their visions on the future of the 'computerized' society and the 'intelligent' home.

Already in the 1960's MacLuhan had prophesied the Global Village, where people living all over the world would communicate as living in a village by means of the - in those days - new mass medium television (MacLuhan 1964). In this concept of the Global Village one-way mass communications would be the village street, of which CNN is an example.

Martin stated that not television but public response (two-way) telecommunications could have the potentials to create a real global village, where the original practice of democracy could be restored as it flowered in the ancient Greek city-states: government of the people, by the people, for the people (Martin 1978).

Toffler imagined the home as the 'electronic cottage' of the future and forecasted a return to cottage industry with a new emphasis on the home as the center of society (Toffler 1980). I.e. a society that would move toward a 'telecommunity' based upon the benefits of computers and communications.

Williams argued that if society (in particular USA society) should make the right choices with the powerful computer and telecommunications technology, in some future century the history of the late twentieth century, like that of the fourteenth, might mark a great transition of civilization, a cusp between old and new. He called this transition 'the electronic renaissance' (Williams 1982).

These authors (and many others) shared an optimistic view upon *their* world of tomorrow, *our* world of today. They were optimistic, not only about the benefits of computer and telecommunications technology, but also about the rate of introduction and acceptance of these technologies in daily life.

Others were very skeptical about the benevolence of the forthcoming telematics society. For example the monopolization of information supply channels by government and media giants might lead to a demise of traditional freedom of press (Wicklein 1981). The growing imbalance in the distribution of information resources and the growing gap between the information rich and the information poor would contribute to reinforce existing global power distributions (Moscow 1982).

Today we know that the penetration of computers and telematics services into the households did not occur at the scale and the pace foreseen by these visionaries. However, a 'silent' information technology 'revolution' took place during the last decade. A large range of equipment that at large scale found its way to the homes has built-in microprocessors. Most of the electric household equipment has been digitized and people have gotten used to program it (Rijn 1990).

This hidden information technology has been interfering with the changes of social structures in the households. The penetration of easier-to-use and new apparatus contributed to or facilitated changes in division of labor in households. Or is it vice versa? In the 1970's and 1980's changes in social structures in households were driven by changes in thinking about relations and division of roles between household partners. Men became more emancipated to do tasks that traditionally women carried out, such as housekeeping, child care, cooking. Often, emancipated men took the initiative to buy new household equipment such as dish washers and microwave ovens. Concurrently with the arrival such apparatus in households, changes in household patterns took place. For example people are developing more individual eating patterns and the common family meal is becoming less important as the daily meeting moment.

Where is the chicken and where is the egg?

The effect of the market push should not be underestimated, but the market has to be ready for the new product in one or another way. Where households are in transition, with a tendency toward more individuality and privacy for household members, with less self-evidence of roles and division of household labor, people are susceptible to new products of which they feel that these comply with these transitions.

Until now the information technology industry did not really succeed to identify and to answer to this transition. There are few clues for a strong social impact of home information technology since its introduction some fifteen years. However, the hidden information technology, built in domestic equipment has interfered with changes in everyday life.

3   The present

Since a few years the penetration of personal computers in the home has been cascading. In 1988 the percentage of households with a computer in any country did not exceed 15%.

Today two million's Dutch households (30%) possess one or more PC's and this number is expected to increase to 46% of all households in 1995. About 17% of the households with a PC have a modem. The main uses of computer technology in households are text processing, games/entertainment and education (Dholakia/Dholakia 1994).

Electronic communication does not yet play a major role in private households. Only the French videotex system (Télétel) succeeded to realize a reasonable acceptance with some seven millions Minitels installed. The main private use is for consulting the electronic telephone directory. Télétel developed also into a new medium for small ads and anonymous contacts. In particular the 'messagerie rouge' received abundant attention in the media, although it comprises a few percent of the total traffic.

Moreover, the market for 'contact ads' also flourishes in the traditional - printed - media and via the telephone. Other home applications of information technology, such as teleservices and teleshopping, still stay far behind expectations. The poor human-computer interfaces and the costs can only be a partial explanation for this.

More likely people do not see sufficient added values in these applications. Most probably because they do not respond to needs arising from their habits and lifestyles.

Still, today little knowledge is available about the social impact of home information technology. There seems even to be a reverse effect: the intrusion of information technology in the homes is - partly - due to social forces. At least in industrialized countries one is expected to be acquainted with the use of information technology and almost to have a computer at home. School children and students are increasingly expected to prepare papers at the computer *at home.*

The current hype around Internet, World Wide Web, multimedia and other information technology gadgets give people the feeling that they may miss the train if they do not jump on it now.

Not having a personal computer at home and soon not having an Internet account and access to World Wide Web (WWW), starts to be considered as strange as not having a TV, a VCR, a car, a microwave oven, a bicycle (in the Netherlands) and so on. In this way home information technology is a product of social forces that may have a - secondary - social impact in return.

However, the abundant literature gives mainly speculations about the future impact. Some case studies describe the implications for individual households, but these cannot be considered representative. The questions and research issues addressed in 1987 (Rijn/Williams 1988) are still valid and in fact we are not much further than in the early 1980's.

This lead to a first conclusion that the social impact of home information technology as such cannot yet be pointed out, because it only entered the homes at large scale during the last years. The impact of hidden information technology can hardly be appraised, because little research has been on the interference between changes in habits/lifestyles and the adoption of computer-controlled equipment.

Nevertheless the situation is changing: information technology is entering the households at large scale and the connection to the household is considered as a crucial ramp for the 'Electronic Superhighway'. This may make the social impact more visible.

4   A jigsaw in more dimensions

The social impact of home information technologies looks like a collection of pieces of a jigsaw. A jigsaw in more dimensions because there are many perspectives on it and is hardly impossible to get a total view combining all perspectives. The puzzle appears to be unsolvable, but sometimes the solution for an 'impossible' puzzle may be found if it is looked at in a different way.

Where is the clue?

I have already argued that the adoption of home information technologies is - at least partly - a strategic decision of the household itself. The introduction of information technology in institutionalized organizations is - or should be - subjected to management policy and strategy.

Most models for the study on social impacts of home information technology take the technology and its applications as the starting point (Moran 1993, Brenner/Kolbe 1994, Haddon/Silverstone 1994). The household is primarily considered as the target of industry and business for selling technology and new services. The emphasis is on the consumption role of the household, while the household is an economic production unit too. This later is often underexposed or even neglected. In terms of the New Home Economics the private household is a decision-making unit by allocating time and market goods between consumption and private household production (Becker 1975). The interchange between information technology and household production might be a major factor in the adoption process. Private households are more inclined to use information technology if they experience its added, economic value (Lehmer 1993).

The central issue of social impacts of home information technology is not the technology or its applications. The focus should be the home as an organization for production and consuming. An organization that has its own goals, strategy and internal structure, but that also has interferences with external organizations. The social implications of home information technologies are a priori due to changes in the internal organization of the household and in the relations with the outside work. Changes that *may* be facilitated or accelerated by technology.

Take for example teleworking. Teleworking is *not* a consequence of information technology. The necessary technology is already available for many years, including electronic communication. The actual incentives for teleworking may be incidental (like the earthquake in California a few years ago) or more structural (like the development of more flexible labor organizations). Motivations can be reducing of costs, caring for the environment by energy saving, empowering less-advantaged people for the labor market. While teleworking has been the subject of numerous studies since years, it did not yet penetrate has at large scale, in spite of the expectations. Conclusions on the impact of teleworking on the households are still based on case studies with small groups of teleworkers, typically less than 25. Moreover, teleworking households seem often leaders in the domestication of information and communication technologies (Silverstone 1994).

The situation in other fields, e.g. education, shopping, banking, and information services, is similar. Only a few households are involved that can be considered as early adaptors of information technology.

This brings us to a crucial question. If households have not yet domesticated information technology, why would they do in the next future? The answer may be found inside the jigsaw. Because the jigsaw has many dimensions, looking from the outside can give a partial view only. Let us have a look from the focus, the household.

Applications of home information technology fall into three main categories:
- home automation
- home information systems
- electronic communication

Home automation has become an important tool for home management. Households are highly susceptible to technology that attribute to an increase of comfort, convenience and safety. Households have an impressive number of household appliances. Originally (electro)mechanic apparatuses are computer-controlled today and many appliances would not have existed at all without computer technology. Nevertheless the average time spent for basic housekeeping and household management did not decrease since over fifty years (Hagelskjær 1988). As household technology allows for increased flexibility of lifestyles, it also creates more work that often undoes the time savings. The first generation of 'smart houses' will not change much in this respect, because existing prototypes show that little attention is paid to smart solutions for basic tasks like cleaning and washing (Berg 1991).

Home information systems are still mainly used for entertainment and edutainment. Other uses are text processing, data files (e.g., for addresses or recipes) and administration of personal finances. Besides teleworking and home-based self-employment, (pseudo) professional use is growing. Many organizations are stimulating their employees to use the computer at home to get acquainted with desk top computing and the use of application packages.

Electronic communication is mainly used for information services and to a lesser extent for transactions. People using electronic messaging (electronic mail) are mainly computer hobbyists and people who are using it in their office too. Telematics is increasingly applied for monitoring and control from outside the home in particular for remote security and alarm systems and for safety systems for elderly people.

5   Social issues

Home information technology is steadily becoming integrated in the households. It is adopted as is felt to increase convenience, pleasure or time saving. It appears to be of benefit for households and individuals. But it has an other side too.

Households are increasingly dependent on technology that make them more *vulnerable* for failures of the technology. Besides the interruption of energy supply, a breakdown of the automation and information system is becoming a new risk for modern households. In particular if in the future the 'electronic habitat' is being controlled by a central computer system like the 'House Brain' in the experimental Xanadu house (Mason 1988).

Social isolation could be increased by electronic communication. Social contacts form an essential element of outside activities such as shopping, banking, working and learning. Performing such activities from home may save time and costs for traveling, waiting and transportation, but reduces the human contacts. When elderly and other homebound people are becoming more self-supporting with help of information and communication technology, the frequency of visits by family, welfare workers and others might decrease.

Social inequality, the gap between groups having or having not access to home information technology, being or not being educated and skilled to use it, may grow.

New threats for *privacy* emerge. Telemetering of the use of energy supplies and registration and monitoring of the use telematics for communication, consulting information services and remote transactions, enable the building up detailed profiles of households and individuals. Such profiles are very attractive for commercial uses.

These and other social risks will not, and should not, inhibit the progressing domestication of information technology. But, users, developers and suppliers have to be aware of these risks.

6   Scenario's for the future: a new OIKOS?

Thirty years after MacLuhan's vision the Global Village seems to be more near than ever. On the National Information Infrastructure, The Transeuropean Electronic Superhighway, the Infobahn, whatever it is called, everybody all over the world will everybody's neighbor. The World Wide Web opened easy access to the Internet for people that are not computer freaks. The telecom, cable television, media and entertainment industry are joining forces in huge alliances to serve the citizens of the global village. How will the household in this global village look like? Will the future household be a virtual one and part of a virtual community?

Virtual communities with names like WELL (Whole Earth 'Lectronic' Link), TWICS, CIX, CalvaCOM and many others do already exist for many years (Rheingold 1993).

These are typical communities of individuals, not of households. Some argue that information technology will contribute to a further disintegration of the nuclear family (Mowshowitz 1995). Others see a reinforcement of traditional family structures and households becoming postmodern 'farms' (Terreehorst 1994). Probably they are both partly right.

Let us go back for while to the community that gave its name to economics: the *Oikos*.

In ancient Greece 'Oikos' meant not only the house, but also the greater family clan that formed the basic economic entity of society. In this community, people lived and worked together, producing what the community needed for shelter, clothing, food and other commodities. It was the environment for education, leisure and social contacts. The Oikos was the constituting part of the larger community, the town state (politeia). During the centuries politeia became politics and the Oikos became the nuclear private household. Basic functions of the Oikos have been 'outsourced' and institutionalized as formal labor, formal education and even formal holidays. Since the nineteenth century the household is more and more considered as a consuming unit only. Only since the last twenty, thirty years the economic value of household activities has been recognized again.

This coincided with changes in family structures. Roles and division labor in households are not longer not as obvious as they were before. The traditional, nuclear family is not longer the apparently only form of a private household.

Being a nuclear family or not, in today's households people live together that appreciate individuality, privacy, economic independency and flexible lifestyles. Home information technologies may offer new opportunities to meet these requirements. It allows people to make choices what activities they want to do, how, where and when, having access to all resources they need.

It requires more flexibility of the external organizations that are interfering with the private household organization, the employing company, the school, or the bureaucratic authorities. This may lead to a new Oikos where people study, work and produce at home as well as outside the home. Where the Electronic Superhighway allows for distributed, cooperative work and gives electronic access to information and others sources that people need.

References

Becker, G. S., A Theory of the Allocation of Time, in: Economic Journal, Vol. 75, No. 229, 1975, pp. 493-517

Berg, A. J., Gender and the smart house. Paper presented at the GRANITE seminar New information technologies and the changing nature of domestic, Amsterdam, 1991

Bjerg, K., Borreby, K. (eds.), Home-Oriented Informatics, Telematics & Automation, University of Copenhagen, 1994

Brenner, W., Kolbe, L., Future Business Spheres Arising from Computerized Information Processing in the Private Household, in: Bjerg, K., Borreby, K. (eds.), Home-Oriented Informatics, Telematics and Automation, University of Copenhagen, 1994, pp. 105-118

Dholakia, R.R, Dholakia, N., Multimedia Technologies in the American Home: Prospects and Challenges Ahead, in: Bjerg, K., Borreby, K. (eds.), Home-Oriented Informatics, Telematics and Automation, University of Copenhagen, 1994, pp. 29-42

Fedida, S., Malik, R., The viewdata revolution, Associated Business Press, London, 1979

Haddon, L., Silverstone, R., The Careers of Information and Communication Technologies in the Home, in: Bjerg, K., Borreby, K. (eds.), Home-Oriented Informatics, Telematics and Automation, University of Copenhagen, 1994, pp. 275-283

Hagelskjær, E., Bringing modern times into households, in: Rijn, F. van, Williams, R. (eds.), Concerning home telematics, North-Holland, Amsterdam, 1988

Lehmer, G., Theorie des wirtschaftlichen Handelns der privaten Haushalte, Bergisch Gladbach-Köln, Josef Eul, 1993

MacLuhan, M., Understanding Media, New York, McGraw Hill, 1964

Martin, J., The wired society, Prentice Hall, Englewood Cliffs, 1978

Mason, R., Living in tomorrow's electronic home today, in: Rijn, F. van, Williams, R. (eds.), Concerning home telematics, North-Holland, Amsterdam, 1988

Moran, R., The Electronic Home, Social and Spatial aspects, A scoping report, Luxembourg, Office for Official Publications of the European Commission, 1993

Moscow, V., Pushbuttons fantasies, Ablex, Norwood, 1982

Mowshowitz, A., Brave New Marketplace: Information Commodoties and Societal Change, presented at Economie de l'Information, Lyon, France, 1995

Rheingold, H., The Virtual Community, Homesteading on the Electronic Frontier, Reading, Massachusetts, Addison-Wesley, 1993

Rijn, F. van, Interactive telematics comes home: a long way, in: Berleur, J., Drumm, J. (eds.), Information Technology Assessment, North-Holland, Amsterdam, 1991

Rijn, F. van, The Cultural Scenery of Information Technology, in: Berleur, J. et al. (eds.), The Information Society, Evolving landscapes, New York, Springer, 1990, pp. 90-95

Rijn, F. van, Williams, R. (eds.), Concernig home telematics, 1988

Silverstone, R., In the Eye of the Storm, the Domestication of Information and Communication Technologies, Present and Future, in: Bjerg, K., Borreby, K. (eds.), Home-Oriented Informatics, Telematics and Automation, University of Copenhagen, 1994, pp. 263-274

Terreehorst, P., Het Boerderijmode, wenken voor een postmodern gezin, Amsterdam, De Balie, 1994

Toffler, A., The third wave, William Morrow, New York, 1980

Wicklein, J., Electronic nightmare, Viking, New York, 1981

Williams, F., The communications revolution, Sage, London, 1982

Author Profiles

Dr. Thomas Baubin is an international partner of Andersen Consulting and leads the Strategic Services Group in Germany, Austria and Switzerland. Within this function he is responsible for the Andersen Consulting Infocosm Program in the West European region. He holds a Ph.D. in economics and a masters degree in engineering. Before he joined Andersen Consulting he worked for the Stanford Research Institute, where he advised large international organizations in government, healthcare, telecommunications and banking. His primary professional and research areas are information technology management, the convergence of industries and the economic transformation towards the information society. He is author of the book 'Efficient growth strategies for the information industry' and has published several articles on information management.

Prof. Dr. Walter Brenner holds the Chair for Business Administration and Business-Informatics at the Technical University of Freiberg, Germany, since April 1993. From 1989 to 1992 he headed the research programme 'IM2000' at the Hochschule St. Gallen, Switzerland. Prior to that, he worked with the Alusuisse-Lonza AG, Basel/Switzerland, at last responsible for computer application developments. He received an university degree and a Ph.D. from the Hochschule St. Gallen. His research areas comprise information management, business re-engineering and information processing of the private household.

Florian Brody is an international specialist in new media and electronic publishing based in Vienna, Austria. He was technical director of the Expanded Books Project at The Voyager Company, Santa Monica/USA, and before that senior project manager at the Austrian National Library in Vienna. He teaches at the Art Center College of Design in Pasadena and at the Vienna University. Brody is president of the Austrian Society for Virtual Reality, Telepresence and Cyberspace.

Mary Callaghan has ten years experience in the IT industry. Prior to joining Oracle in 1989, she spent four years at Digital, where she managed the company's internal IT systems. She has been new technologies manager since January 1993. Her brief is to position Oracle within new and emerging technologies with particular emphasis on multimedia. Her role includes developing market awareness of the impact of the Information Superhighway.

Prof. Dr. Nikhilesh Dholakia is professor of marketing at the University of Rhode Island (URI) and Partner, Group Disa. In the field of telecom and information technology, he has worked on projects dealing with organization buying of telecom systems, strategies for enhanced telecom services, information technology in the home, technology adoption and diffusion processes, and public policy towards telecommunications. Among his books are 'Consumption and Marketing: Macro Dimensions' (South-Western, 1996), and 'New Infotainment Technologies in the Home: Demand-Side Perspectives' (Lawrence Erlbaum Associates, 1996, forthcoming).

Prof. Dr. Ruby Roy Dholakia is the founder and director of the Research Institute for Telecommunications and Information Marketing (RITIM) and professor of marketing at the University of Rhode Island and Partner, Group Disa. Engaged extensively in research projects on telecommunications and information technologies for the home and the workplace, she has chaired several conferences and special sessions on related topics. Her research has been presented to various audiences in the United States and Western Europe. Articles have also appeared in specialized publications dealing with telecom and electronic industries. She is the editor of 'Marketing Strategies for Information Technologies' (JAI Press, 1994) and a co-editor of 'New Infotainment Technologies in the Home: Demand-Side Perspectives' (Lawrence Erlbaum Associates, 1996, forthcoming).

Heiner Drathen is head of the department 'Multimedia and new technologies' within the debis Systemhaus Dienstleistungen GmbH in Düsseldorf. As project manager of the Quelle CD-ROM project he was responsible for the complete system integration process.

Jonne R. M. van der Drift has extensive experience in international marketing and business development of products and services based on interactive media. He started his career in the travel and entertainment industry at American Express. Later he worked for ITT World Directories as a manager in sales, marketing and new product development for Yellow pages, Europages and the electronic directories. Then, as a business consultant he held general management positions at a Dutch cable-TV news operation and a videotex network for PC users. When the network merged with the videotex network of PTT Telecom he became responsible for marketing their national videotex services. At PTT Telecom he discovered the need for networked multimedia and decided to found CD-Matics.

David G. J. Fanshawe is a graduate of Durham University (UK), a Chartered Physicist and an Associate Member of the IEEE. Since 1986 David has led a team of engineers in Philips Consumer Electronics working on the European Home

Systems specification. He also works closely with the European Commission, evaluating and reviewing projects in the ESPRIT and TIDE programmes.

Winnie Forster works as a journalist on electronic games and new media. He is a co-founder of Germany's premier video gaming magazine 'Video Games' and currently publisher of the multi-format-games-magazine MAN!AC.

Prof. Dr. Wolfgang Glatthaar studied mathematics and physics at the University of Tübingen, then followed by a doctorate in informatics at the University of Stuttgart. He is Director of Research at IBM Deutschland Informationssysteme GmbH and honorary professor at the Technical University of Chemnitz-Zwickau. Memberships: President of the Gesellschaft für Informatik (German Computer Society), member of the scientific board of the German national research center for computer science (GMD), and member of the supervisory board of the Deutsches Forschungszentrum für künstliche Intelligenz GmbH (German artificial intelligence research centre).

Felix Goedhart is a Senior Associate with the international top-management consulting firm Booz, Allen & Hamilton. The focus of his work lies in telecommunications and the media business. Within this focus he concentrates on the subject of multimedia. Mr. Goedhart gained a degree in business administration at the Hochschule St. Gallen in Switzerland and the MBA of the University of Chicago Graduate School of Business.

Dr. Thomas Heimer is research fellow at the Economic Department of the Johann Wolfgang Goethe-University in Frankfurt/Main. His research is mainly concerned with the economic theory of the explanation of the genesis of new technologies. His doctoral thesis is concerned with the explanation of the genesis of Intelligent Home technology.

Petra Höper joined Beate Uhse AG in Flensburg as management assistant in 1990. Prior, she received her diploma in business administration. Since 1993 she has been project leader for the multimedia business area. Here, she is responsible for the coordination of all operations from the development of product ideas through to production, sales, and monitoring the profitability of in-house products.

Dr. Hubertus Hoffmann is a member of the executive board of Burda Publishing, responsible for the 'New Media' area, and Vice President of 'Europe Online SA' (Luxemburg). He studied law, political science, medieval and modern history at the Universities of Munich and Bonn. He obtained his doctorate in political science at the University of Bonn in 1985. Since December 1993 he has been a member of the Burda Publishing executive board responsible for television productions, CD-ROM, online and other media, as well as being manager of the Pan TV Produktionsgesellschaft mbH in Munich.

Dr. Georg Rainer Hofmann, KPMG Unternehmensberatung (Frankfurt/Berlin), is manager for KPMG's business field and programme 'Information and Communication Technology Transfer'. These include, among others, high-technology marketing and scenario-based cost/benefit analysis, the coordination of KPMG's (Germany) engagement in the ESSI programme of the CEC DG III, and consulting for the public sector and gouvernment in Germany. Mr. Hofmann received a diploma in computer science and political economics and in 1991 a doctorate in engineering. All degrees are from Technical University of Darmstadt. He is the speaker of the SIG 'Software and Service Market' of the German Computer Society (GI).

Kai Howaldt studied electrical engineering and business administration at the University of Bremen and the Technical University of Munich. After a two years experience at Siemens AG in Munich he joined Roland Berger & Partner International Management Consultants in 1990. He is now project manager at the Electronics and Consumer Durables Competence Center and currently in charge of the company's home automation activities.

Terry R. Hurley has a first class honours degree in electrical engineering from Imperial College, London. His career includes four years at the Independent Broadcasting Authority (UK), seven years with Sony developing broadcast products followed by a year with VideoLogic before re-joining Sony in 1993 to lead development of new consumer products.

Michaela Jaritz is Product Manager in the Consumer Divsion at Microsoft's German subsidiary has been with Microsoft since 1991. After a year in the Redmond headquarters she joined the German subsidiary where she has been engaged in consumer product marketing since then.

Mirko-Stefan Jeck studied business administration at The Koblenz School of Corporate Management (WHU) in Vallendar, in Barcelona and College Station, Texas. Before his studies he worked for five years in marketing and sales at Hoechst AG in Frankfurt and Buenos Aires. He has worked on home automation since 1993. In 1994 he joined Roland Berger & Partner International Management Consultants as a consultant and expert in home automation.

Niels Klußmann received a diploma in electrical engineering in 1993 and joined the Mobile Applications Laboratory of Ericsson Eurolab Deutschland in Aachen, Germany. He is now working for Eutelis Consult, Ratingen, Germany, and focuses on broadband services, online services, multi-media applications and all other developments of the Information Highway.

Lutz Kolbe works at the Technical University of Freiberg since January 1994 as an academic assistant; currently he is writing his doctoral dissertation about 'Computerized Information Processing in the Private Household'. Earlier, he worked as financial consultant. He has got a professional background in banking and holds a master degree in business-informatics from the Technical University Braunschweig, Germany.

Thomas Künstner is an associate with Booz, Allen & Hamilton. He is specialized on the telecommunications, computing and media industries. The focus of his consulting activities lies on strategy development, technology management and organizational redesign. Before joining Booz, Allen & Hamilton, Mr. Künstner received a degree in business administration from Passau University in Germany.

Sadami Kurihara received the B.E. and the M.E. degrees in electronics engineering from Kyushu University in 1969 and 1971. Since joining the NTT in 1971, he has been active in R&D on communications services. He is now a Executive Manager of NTT Multimedia Planning and Promotion Office.

Roger Longhorn, holding BSc and MSc degrees from MIT (Cambridge, MA, USA), has spent over 25 years in the information technology industry. Since 1989 he has been a senior expert in IT to the European Commission, initially spending four years in Luxembourg, supporting DG XIII's IMPACT (Information Market Policy ACTions) programme. In January 1994 he moved to DG III's Information and Communications Technologies (ICT) Policy Analysis Unit in Brussels, where he spent 14 months as a member of research staff, producing the Commission's Strategic Watch in ICT bulletin. He also provided direct support to the preparatory activities for the European Information Infrastructure, from the beginnings of the Bangemann Task Force through to the special G7 meeting on Information Society issues hosted by the European Commission in Brussels at the end of February, 1995. Roger has now returned to DG XIII in Luxembourg to help prepare a Communication to the European Council and Parliament on creating a European Geographic Information Infrastructure (EGII).

Norbert Maassen, born in 1961, studied telecommunications engineering at the Technical Highschool (RWTH) in Aachen and has been responsible for the Special Office for ISDN Applications in Berlin till 1991. Currently he is Assistant Director in the R&D-Division of Deutsche Telekom's headquarters focussing on the development of network-oriented products and services.

Christoph Mayser received his MSc degree in electrical engineering and information technologies from the Technical University Munich, Germany in 1992. He started working as a software engineer at Berner & Mattner Systemtechnik. Since early 1994 he has been in charge for the field of agent based communications. Now he focuses on General Magic technologies, espacially on Magic Cap.

Prof. Dr. Dr. h.c. mult. Peter Mertens is head of the research group of business information systems at the Bavarian Research Center for Knowledge-Based Systems

(FORWISS) and head of the research group of Computer Science B (Business Applications) at the FAU Erlangen-Nuremberg. He is chair of Business Administration, Information Systems I, of the Business Administration Faculty of the FAU Erlangen-Nuremberg. Mertens manages many projects in cooperation with enterprises of different types.

Prof. Dr. Norbert Mundorf is associate professor of communication studies and a faculty associate of the Research Institute for Telecommunications and Information Marketing at the University of Rhode Island. He received his Ph.D. from Indiana University in 1987. Dr. Mundorf was a visiting professor at the University of Mainz in 1994. His research interests include acceptance of new information technologies, factors influencing media use, and international telecommunications. He has published in a variety of journals.

Dr. Joachim Niemeier is executive director of the Multimedia Software GmbH Dresden, a subsidiary company of the German Telecom group, since May 1995. He has an academic education in business administration and holds an Ph.D. from the University of Stuttgart, Germany. He was head of a research group at the 'Fraunhofer-Institut für Arbeitswirtschaft und Organisation (IAO)' of Prof. Dr.-Ing. Bullinger. Before joining Multimedia Software GmbH Dresden he headed the department for corporate management at IAO.

Torsten Oppermann works in the interactive entertainment industry since 1986. Since 1992, he works at SEGA, Germany. Since March 1995 he has taken over the position of the marketing manager.

Peter Petersen, master of science in electronic engineering from Danish Technical University 1977. Carrier within Bang & Olufsen: Electrical Design Engineer, 1978. Technology Manager, Digital Signal Processing, 1983. General Manager, Research & Development Technology, 1988. Director of Technology, 1991. Member of EACEM Council (European Association of Consumer Electronic Manufacturers). Co-Chairman of Euro-Japanese Working Group on Multimedia Standardisation.

Dr. Dr. Heribert Popp is assistant head of the research group of business information systems at the Bavarian Research Center for Knowledge-Based Systems (FORWISS) in Erlangen since 1992. He has studied economics, maths, and chemistry in Regensburg.

Prof. Dr. Werner Rammert, professor of sociology, Freie Universität Berlin (Free University of Berlin), Germany; president of the section 'Science and Technology Studies'; co-editor of the yearbooks 'Technology and Society'; funded research projects: 'Product innovation in enterprises', 'Computer use in everyday life', 'The construction and implemen‌:tion of expert systems', 'The rise of high technologies'; recent books: 'Das Innovationsdilemma', 1988; 'Vom Umgang mit

Computern im Alltag' (with others), 1991; 'Technik aus soziologischer Perspektive', 1993; 'Soziologie und künstliche Intelligenz', 1995.

Felix van Rijn worked for several years on laboratory automation after his graduation as chemical engineer at the University of Amsterdam. Next he had a university research position in the field social implications of information technology. Since 1993 he is head of the department for informatics teaching at the Faculty of Education of Hogeschool van Amsterdam. He is founding chairperson of the IFIP Working Group 9.3 (Home-Oriented Informatics and Telematics).

Martin Römer received the MSc degree in electrical engineering from Technical University Munich, Germany, in 1988. Since 1989 he is working as a software engineer at Berner & Mattner Systemtechnik GmbH, specialising in object-oriented technologies. In 1994 he started to work in the field of agent-based communications, focusing on Telescript.

Manuela Rost-Hein, born in 1959, economist and PR-Consultant. Different apprenticeships at TV-stations and newspapers. Since 1988 working for IBM as project manager in the communications department (press, advertisement, external communications).

Dr. Gary Sager joined Silicon Graphics in August 1993 as director of engineering for interactive television systems. From 1984 to 1993, Mr. Sager was director of engineering for systems and networking at Sun Microsystems, Inc., where he managed the team that designed and developed the NFS as well as a number of features adopted into UNIX System 5 Release 4. Prior to joining Sun, Mr. Sager worked on science at the University of Waterloo. Mr. Sager has a Ph.D. in computer science from the University of Washington.

Prof. Dr. Claus Sattler received a diploma in informatics in 1973. He worked for 17 years in a research institute in Berlin in the field of computer networking. In 1991 he joined Eutelis Consult, Ratingen, Germany, where he today is a partner. His main topics are now private and public networks and value-added voice and multimedia services.

Luc Stakenborg started his career at PTT Telecom where he held several positions as innovation specialist, project manager and product manager in the VAN and VAS business unit (now Unisource). His experience includes the commercial and technological feasibility of on-line services and multimedia applications and projects, multimedia system and application design, interactive technologies such as VRS, videotex, CD-ROM, CD-i, Internet, ITV, and systems, network and service management. He completed studies in physics at University of Utrecht and computer science at University of Technology in Delft. He is senior-consultant and co-founder of CD-Matics.

Bruno Struif received his master degree in 1971 at the Technical University in Darmstadt. He is the head of the GMD smartcard research group, which belongs to the GMD Institute for Telecooperation Technology (the GMD is the German National Research Center for Computer Science). Mr. Struif works in the field of smartcard technology since 1982 and has special experience in the design of smartcard chip operating systems and high sophisticated smartcard applications. He is one of the German delegates in ISO/IEC JTC1/SC17/WG4 and the related task forces. On the national level he is convener of the DIN Working Group NI-17.4.

Stephan Thesmann gained selling experience as an active partner and sales manager of Res Oeconomica GmbH during his studies in business administrations. After graduation in 1991 he joined the research staff at the FORWISS research group business information systems. Thesmann already has completed his thesis about tools for electronic product catalogues.

Prof. Dr. Alladi Venkatesh is on the faculty of Graduate School of Management, and a Research Associate at CRITO (Center for Research on Information Technology in Organizations) at the University of California, Irvine. His broad research area is technology and social change and he specializes on the impact of information technologies on families/households. Recently, he completed a major study for the National Science Foundation looking at how American families are adapting to the presence of computers at home. Professor Venkatesh's scholarly publications on technology in the home have appeared in various journals. Professor Venkatesh is an editor of the forthcoming journal 'Consumption, Markets and Culture (CMC)'.

Rob de Vogel has been working for Philips since 1986 on groupware products, communication devices and electronic services within Philips Research, Xerox PA, Consumer Electronics and Philips Communication Systems. He is one of the founders of Philips Advanced Communication Enterprise (PACE), established in 1992 to exploit the Philips investment in General Magic. He is responsible for marketing and product planning.

Dr. Friedrich-Carl Wachs is heading the electronic media division of Heinrich Bauer Verlag, Hamburg, one of Europe's key publishing companies. He studied law and history and started his career at Bertelsmann's electronic subsidiary, Ufa Film und Fernseh GmbH.

Johann-Reinhardt Wachs is working in the planning department of Saatchi & Saatchi, Frankfurt. He mastered in art history in Berlin after studies in Paris, London and New York.

Dr. Bernd W. Wirtz is Management Consultant within the Strategic Services Group. Dr. Wirtz studied business administration at the universities of Cologne, London and Dortmund, and holds a Ph.D. in economics and a masters degree in business administration. Before he joined Andersen Consulting he worked as a lecturer at the university of Düsseldorf as well as an associate consultant for Kienbaum Management Consultants and Roland Berger & Partner, International Management Consultants. His primary professional and research areas are the convergence of industries and the strategic transformation of enterprises. He is author of the book 'Corporate strategies in the media market' and has published several articles on strategic and transformation management.

J. A. van Woerden studied electrical engineering and joined TNO-TPD (Institute of Applied Physics) in 1966. Presently he is manager of the group Hardware Systems of the Instrumentation Department of this Institute. His background is research in physical sensor systems, inspection with echo acoustics of the bottom, inspection of the overhead wires of the Dutch railway with optics, and the last ten years in the development of 'assistive devices' for handicapped persons, like the MANUS manipulator, and also in the field of integration technology for integrated systems of assistive devices, and information technology and applications for elderly and disabled people.

Georg Zimmermann belongs to the management of the software and information system house Berner & Mattner Systemtechnik in Munich and is there responsible for the business area traffic telematics. He received the MSc degree in mechanical engineering from Technical University Siegen, Germany, in 1987. Until 1992 he was employeed at Daimler-Benz Aerospace in Munich.

GPSR Compliance
The European Union's (EU) General Product Safety Regulation (GPSR) is a set
of rules that requires consumer products to be safe and our obligations to
ensure this.

If you have any concerns about our products, you can contact us on

ProductSafety@springernature.com

In case Publisher is established outside the EU, the EU authorized
representative is:

Springer Nature Customer Service Center GmbH
Europaplatz 3
69115 Heidelberg, Germany

www.ingramcontent.com/pod-product-compliance
Lightning Source LLC
LaVergne TN
LVHW012326060326
832902LV00011B/1745

9783790809077